FREQUENTLY CONSULTED ADVICE

USEFUL LISTS

THE
BORZOI HANDBOOK
FOR WRITERS

THE
BORZOI HANDBOOK
FOR WRITERS

THIRD EDITION

Frederick Crews
Professor of English
University of California at Berkeley

Sandra Schor
Late Professor of English
Queens College
The City University of New York

Michael Hennessy
Professor of English
Southwest Texas State University

McGraw-Hill, Inc.

New York   St. Louis   San Francisco   Auckland   Bogotá
Caracas   Lisbon   London   Madrid   Mexico   Milan
Montreal   New Delhi   Paris   San Juan
Singapore   Sydney   Tokyo   Toronto

This book was developed by STEVEN PENSINGER, Inc.

The Borzoi Handbook for Writers

1 2 3 4 5 6 7 8 9 0   KGP   KGP   9 0 9 8 7 6 5 4 3 2

ISBN 0-07-013638-6

This book was set in Century Schoolbook by Monotype
Composition Company.
The editors were Steve Pensinger and James R. Belser;
the production supervisor was Richard A. Ausburn.
The cover was designed by Larry Didona.
Arcata Graphics/Kingsport was printer and binder.

Library of Congress Cataloging-in-Publication Data

Crews, Frederick C.
    The Borzoi handbook for writers/Frederick Crews, Sandra Schor,
  Michael Hennessy.—3rd ed.
        p.   cm.
    Includes bibliographical references and index.
    ISBN 0-07-013638-6
    1. English language—Rhetoric—Handbooks, manuals, etc.
  2. English language—Grammar—1950- —Handbooks, manuals, etc.
  I. Schor, Sandra.   II. Hennessy, Michael.   III. Title.
  PE1408.C7145   1993
  808'.042—dc20   92-33521

ABOUT THE AUTHORS

Frederick Crews, Professor of English and chair of his department at the University of California, Berkeley, received the Ph.D. from Princeton University. In his career he has attained many honors, including a Guggenheim Fellowship, appointment as a Fulbright Lecturer in Italy, an essay award from the National Council on the Arts and Humanities, election to membership in the American Academy of Arts and Sciences, and, from his own university, recognition as a Distinguished Teacher and as Faculty Research Lecturer. His writings include the widely used *Random House Handbook* as well as highly regarded books on Henry James, E. M. Forster, and Nathaniel Hawthorne; the best-selling satire *The Pooh Perplex;* and three volumes of his own essays, *Out of My System, Skeptical Engagements,* and *The Critics Bear It Away: American Fiction and the Academy.* Professor Crews has published numerous articles in *Partisan Review, The New York Review of Books, Commentary, Tri-Quarterly, The American Scholar,* and other important journals. He has twice been Chair of Freshman Composition in the English Department at Berkeley.

Until her death in 1990, **Sandra Schor** was Associate Professor of English at Queens College (City University of New York), where she served as director of the writing program. Her essays and reviews on the theory of composition and the teaching of writing have appeared in *College English* and *College Composition and Communication* and in *The Writer's Mind, What Makes Writing Good, Audits of Meaning,* and *Linguistics, Stylistics, and the Teaching of Composition.* Her writings also include *The Random House Guide to Writing* (with Judith Summerfield) and a novel, *The Great Letter* E. Professor Schor received both a Mellon Fellowship and a grant from the Fund for the Improvement of Postsecondary Education for composition studies. In recognition of her contributions as a teacher of writing, the City University of New York named her a Master Teacher; for her academic writing, she received the Mina P. Shaughnessy Writing Award.

Michael Hennessy is Professor of English at Southwest Texas State University, where he directs the first-year writing program and teaches courses in beginning and advanced composition, modern literature, and the teaching of writing. He holds a Ph.D. in English literature from Marquette University and has taught at Memphis State University and John Carroll University. His publications include *The Random House Practice Book* and *The Borzoi Practice Book for Writers*. He is also the author of numerous articles and reviews on composition pedagogy and on the work of Shakespeare, W. H. Auden, and the contemporary British poet Charles Tomlinson. Professor Hennessy has served as chair of the Texas Association of Directors of Writing Programs and was recently awarded the Faculty Senate Award for Excellence in Teaching at Southwest Texas State University.

CONTENTS

VII   Conventions   369

VIII   Research Papers   441

IX   Applied Writing   555

PREFACE

In writing this third edition of *The Borzoi Handbook for Writers,* we have aimed once again to make the book a positive, comprehensive, and flexible guide to composition. Above all, the *Handbook* urges students to improve their work by stages, drafting and revising without allowing anxiety over correctness to interfere with the flow of ideas. At the same time, the book maintains its usefulness as a reference tool, a resource students can consult as needed for advice about the fine points of clear and effective expression.

While retaining its essential design and purpose, the *Handbook* includes improvements in every chapter: simplified explanations, fresh examples, and new boxes that summarize and graphically display key information. The sections on composing essays and writing research papers have been revised extensively to give full yet compact coverage of the entire writing process. Among the many significant changes in the book, several deserve special mention:

1. Much of the student writing is new, including full essays as well as shorter excerpts. The book now provides sample analytic and argumentative essays in both draft and final form as well as two complete student research papers illustrating MLA and APA style.

2. The opening chapter, "Arriving at a Topic," gives expanded advice about discovering ideas for an essay—a crucial but often neglected aspect of the writing process.

3. Chapter 2, now called "Developing a Thesis," includes more examples to show students the importance of building an essay around a limited, definite, and engaging idea.

4. The advice about organization, now in its own chapter (3), urges students to remain flexible as they plan their essays. The chapter includes additional sample outlines and a new section on using tree diagrams to organize.

5. Chapter 4, on drafting, brings together advice formerly scattered through three chapters. An expanded discussion of reasoning and logical fallacies is now grouped conveniently in two sections at the end of the chapter.

6. The chapter on revision (5), now entitled "Collaborating and Revising," gives new emphasis to peer editing. By studying a peer edited essay-in-progress, students learn that revision involves far more than tidying up minor errors.

7. Another new sample essay appears in "One Essay from Start to Finish," illustrating within a single chapter (6) the entire process of composition, from seeking a topic to making editorial revisions.

8. The chapters of stylistic advice on paragraphs, sentences, and words (7–16) contain new or expanded sections on, among other topics, paragraph continuity, idioms, levels of diction, and sentence variety.

9. A revised Chapter 37, now called "Conducting Research," outlines procedures for finding a research topic and gives more emphasis to on-line catalogs and CD databases. The chapter also contains new material on using field research and evaluating sources.

10. A new Chapter 38, "Writing from Sources," supplements earlier chapters on the writing process by focusing specifically on what students need to know as they draft and revise a research paper, including techniques for using quotation, summary, and paraphrase. The chapter also includes an expanded discussion about avoiding plagiarism.

11. The second edition's chapter on documentation is now two chapters: "Using MLA Documentation" (39) and "Using APA Documentation" (40). This arrangement means maximum clarity and ease of reference for students as they document their sources. Each chapter includes a sample student research paper.

12. Chapter 41, "Examination Answers and In-Class Essays," includes new student essays written for history and political science examinations.

13. Chapter 42, now called "Business Writing," includes new sections on writing business memos and designing cover sheets for facsimile transmissions.

14. Finally, a minor change in design improves the book's usefulness as a reference tool: Highlighted passages in examples are now shown in unmistakable boldface type.

Instructors should know that every new copy of the *Borzoi Handbook* comes shrink-wrapped with the third edition of *The Borzoi Practice Book for Writers,* an innovative workbook that goes beyond mere drill. the *Practice Book* offers exercises for individual instruction as well as material for group work and class discussion, including several student essays. As a package, the *Handbook* and *Practice Book* now provide a total of four sample research papers—two using MLA style and two APA style.

Along with the *Practice Book,* McGraw-Hill offers a full range of supplements to *Borzoi.* These include a new Instructor's Manual, *The Borzoi On-Line Handbook* (IBM and Macintosh versions), IBM and Macintosh diagnostic testing systems and practice programs, a Macintosh style-checking program (available for free duplication), the *EDIT!* IBM style checker, and an Answer Key for the *Practice Book.* *The Random House College Dictionary* is also available with the *Handbook* at a special discounted package price.

We remain grateful to many colleagues, students, and editors who helped shape earlier editions of this book, and we thank all those who showed us how this new edition could be improved. Student writers whose work is represented here include, among others, Jaime Baczkowski, Melanie Cain, Chad Campbell, Angela Day, Scott Diamond, Carol Dougherty, Craig Harris, Gary Hartman, John Higgins, Louise Hope, Chris Jenkins, Thomas Maggio, George McCoy, Alex Miller, Bryan Mills, Irene Patowski, Stephani Pont, Patricia Rodriguez, and Lovell White.

We owe special thanks to Steve Pensinger for his superb editorial guidance and to James Belser, Anita Kann, Rich Ausburn, and Laura Givner for skillfully turning a bulky manuscript into a finished book. And the following experts on composition offered advice that helped shape this edition in useful ways: Marlene S. Bosanko, Tacoma Community College; Wayne A. Buchman, Rose State College; Roger Christeck, Belleville Area College; Virgil Cook, Virginia Polytechnic Institute; Barbara Daniels, Camden County College; Gary L. Goodno, Community College of the Finger Lakes; M. Kip Hartvigsen, Ricks College; Mary-Lou Hinman, Plymouth State College; James L. Johnson, Eastern New Mexico University; William B. Lalicker, Murray State University; Anne Laskaya, University of Oregon; Susan Monroe

Nugent, Keene State College; Stuart D. Morton, Macomb Community College; Katherine R. Pluta, Bakersfield College; Joyce G. Smoot, Virginia Polytechnic Institute; Janet Streepey, Indiana University Southeast; and Jan Zlotnik Schmidt, State University of New York at New Paltz.

Helpful advice was also received from the following instructors: Craig F. Ash, Sophia B. Blaydes, Phyllis Brooks, Mary Burns, David J. Burt, Christopher L. Couch, Gerald Evans, Philip Greene, Duane A. Grimme, Andrew Halford, Morgan Y. Himelstein, Francis X. Jordan, David Kann, Shelby J. Kipplen, Martin Ley, Mary Meiser, Hazel Pierce, Ruth F. Redel, Donetta Suchon, Barbara Traister, Elaine D. Travenick, Margaret Whitt, Johnny Wink, and Richard Zbaracki. Finally, we wish to dedicate this edition to the memory of our friend Sandra Schor, coauthor of the first and second editions of the *Handbook*. In preparing this third edition, we have tried to stay mindful of her high standards.

Frederick Crews
Michael Hennessy

TO THE STUDENT WRITER

The Borzoi Handbook for Writers is at once a reference work, to be consulted as needed, and a guide to writing essays—a book of advice about finding a topic and maneuvering successfully through the whole process of composition, including the constructing of effective sentences and paragraphs. Chapters 1–16 in particular cover the principles of **rhetoric,** the art of arranging ideas and choosing language to achieve a particular effect. You can profitably read these chapters straight through. You may want to examine other chapters more selectively, either to resolve a point of usage or to refresh your memory about the best way to handle quotations, punctuation marks, and the like. If you will be asked to write a research paper, however, you should study Chapters 37 and 38 as a unit and consult Chapter 39 or 40 for advice about documenting your paper.

Any part of this book can be understood independently of the others, and you will find cross references to any unfamiliar terms. But you should also have a general sense of the *Handbook*'s features. Before going further, turn to the following pages:

1. The **inside front cover** contains a Checklist for Revision, a series of questions you can run through before submitting a paper; a guide to Frequently Consulted Advice; and a guide to Useful Lists found throughout the text.
2. The **Table of Contents** (pps. vii–xi) shows how the whole book is organized into parts and chapters.
3. The **inside back cover** provides a list of Symbols for Comment and Revision that your instructor may use in marking your papers. Note that problems such as a comma splice can be marked either by a symbol (*cs*) or by a section number (*18b*). Since section numbers accompany the symbols on the inside back cover, you can always find the relevant discussion by locating its *thumb index*—the colored box in the margin.
4. The **index** (p. 639) is your surest means of locating any point you need to look up.
5. The **Index of Usage** (p. 585) is a handy alphabetical list that

can help you resolve common problems of word choice—for example, *affect* versus *effect*.

6. The **Glossary of Terms** (p. 606) offers definitions of grammatical and rhetorical terms and indicates where you can find a fuller treatment of each term.

Once you grasp the various ways in which this book can be consulted, you should find it of lasting value to your writing in college and beyond.

THE
BORZOI HANDBOOK
FOR WRITERS

I
COMPOSING
ESSAYS

Composing Essays

*An **essay** is a relatively brief piece of nonfiction that tries to make a point in an interesting way. To explain:*

1. It is fairly brief. *Some classic essays occupy only a few paragraphs, and in a composition course you may be asked to keep your first essay to 500 words. But an essay generally falls between two and twenty typed pages, a length that allows for the development of an idea as a single, unbroken reading experience.*

2. It is nonfiction. *An essayist tries to tell the truth or to speculate about possible changes in the world we all recognize. If the essay contains a story or a description, we assume that the details are based on actual experience.*

3. It makes a point. *An essay characteristically expresses an attitude, explains an idea, or defends an opinion. Unlike a poem or a story, an essay directly addresses a specific topic, and its usual aim is to win sympathy or agreement for its main point, or **thesis.***

4. It is meant to be engaging. *An essay should arouse curiosity, convince the reader that its main idea is worth bothering about, and move toward a satisfying finish.*

Taken together, the chapters in Part I give an overview of the art of writing essays. Consulted separately, they can guide you through the various stages of the writing process—discovering a topic; forming a thesis; organizing and developing your ideas; and revising your prose to engage, inform, and persuade a reader.

1 Arriving at a Topic

1a Recognize the flexibility of the writing process.

Some students see "good writing" as a one-time challenge—a brass ring to be seized or, more probably, missed on their first and only try. In their view the world is divided into the lucky few who "can write" and the rest who cannot. But this division ignores an important fact: by and large, *writing is rewriting.* Even the most accomplished authors start with drafts that would be woefully inadequate except *as* drafts—that is, as part of an exploratory process that usually includes many setbacks and shifts in direction. To feel dissatisfied with a draft, then, is not a sign of deficient talent. A "good writer" is one who can turn such dissatisfaction to a positive end by pressing ahead with the work of revision, knowing that fine points of style can wait until an adequate structure of ideas is down on paper.

And how will you arrive at such ideas? Many students believe that sheer inspiration or luck must be the answer. But experienced writers know that good ideas, instead of dropping (or not dropping) from the sky, are built by placing one thought into relation with another. And one of the best ways to do that is by writing itself. In the very act of writing, you are forced to zero in on examples, connections, questions, hunches, and contradictions, any one of which may point you toward a central idea or alter the one you started with.

Thus finding that idea, or **thesis,** is not a fixed early stage of the writing process but a concern that is crucial at first and may become crucial again when you realize that a better idea has come into view. The sooner you arrive at a thesis, the better. But your choice is always tentative, always open to revision, until you have typed the final copy of your essay. At any point you may have to take more notes, argue against a point you favored in an early draft, or throw away whole pages that no longer support your improved thesis. Such "setbacks" are not setbacks at all; they are the usual way that writers develop ideas.

So, too, other parts of the writing process normally overlap. Although you cannot finish organizing until you have arrived at a tentative thesis, unexpected problems of organization may point the way to a better thesis. And as you write the first draft, you may discover that a new organization is taking shape, one that had escaped you during the planning stages. Indeed, even the revising of a single paragraph for internal unity may prompt a more fundamental change of direction.

Writing, then, is almost never a linear process; it typically doubles back on one phase when a later one opens new possibilities. Thus, though we will discuss composing as a logical sequence of steps, its actual order in any one instance defies summary. As the model on the opposite page suggests, you are free at nearly every point to move ahead or to reconsider a previous decision. Such rethinking is the way that writers normally shape, reshape, and polish their work.

1b   Recognize the differences between a subject area, a topic, and a thesis.

The key to writing a successful college essay is a strong, clear *thesis*— that is, a central idea that gives direction to the entire essay. You cannot get by with only a *subject area* or even a *topic*.

Subject Area

A **subject area** is a large category within which you hope to find your topic. Thus, if your instructor asks for an essay about open admission to college, about a personal experience, about technology and the quality of contemporary life, or about a short story by Eudora Welty, you have been assigned not a topic but a broad subject area, one you will have to narrow considerably before moving ahead.

Topic

The **topic** of an essay is the specific, narrowly focused issue or phe-

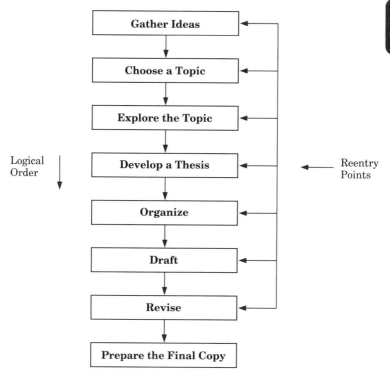

Logical
Order

Reentry
Points

nomenon that you intend to discuss. Thus, within the subject area "open admission to college," you might find several workable topics:

My debt to the policy of open admission

The effect of open admission on "older-than-average" students

Should open admission be used to promote social equality?

How have colleges changed their open admission programs in the 1990s?

The success (or failure) of open admission

Notice that these topics take up considerably more words than "open admission to college." Potential "topics" expressed in few words may be subject areas in disguise.

Thesis

A **thesis** (Chapter 2) is the central point that you intend to develop in your essay. A thesis is not simply a narrowed topic; rather, it is an assertion *about* a topic. And because it always states a point, a thesis lends itself to expression in one clear sentence.

Here is a chart showing the differences between a subject area, a topic, and a thesis. Notice that two possible theses are given for each topic.

SUBJECT AREA	TOPIC	THESIS
Open admission to college	The success of open admission	1. Open admission at my large urban university has fostered the development of an effective program in reading and writing for all first-year students.
		2. "Older-than-average" students admitted under an open-admission policy have had a healthy influence on the education of traditional college students.
A personal experience	My night in jail	1. After my night in jail, I will have more respect for prisoner's rights.
		2. My night in jail helped make me a safe driver.
Technology and the quality of contemporary life	VCRs: blessing or curse?	1. VCRs allow small-town Americans to see—and learn from—a variety of quality films once available only in big-city theaters.

SUBJECT AREA	TOPIC	THESIS
		2. Installing video vending machines on campus encourages the use of VCRs in the dorms and thus undermines the university's stated aim of "promoting a dormitory atmosphere conducive to study and reflection."
Eudora Welty's "A Worn Path"	Phoenix Jackson, Welty's central character	1. Although she is old and frail, Phoenix Jackson demonstrates the physical, mental, and moral courage typical of a traditional literary hero.
		2. In "A Worn Path," Welty illustrates the nature of selfless love through the words and actions of her central character, Phoenix Jackson.

1c Narrow your subject area.

If you have been given a subject area rather than a topic, you can work toward possible topics by dividing and subdividing the subject area. If, for example, your instructor has assigned an essay on the broad subject "The Contemporary Family," you can start by making a list of informal categories:

The Contemporary Family:

nuclear—parents and children

extended—grandparents, aunts, uncles, etc.

intact/separated

two-parent/single-parent

small/large

nontraditional—blended/adopted/substitute

Suppose that the last category on the list strikes you as the most promising. A further set of categories might bring you closer to a topic:

Substitute Families:

coworkers as "family"

friends as "family"

dormitory residents as "family"

temporary families—foster care/exchange students

Now study each item in your second list, and ask what issues or questions it raises. One of them should be a suitable topic. Thus, if you are looking at *coworkers as "family,"* you might pose these questions:

1. Do people who lack the emotional and moral support of a traditional family rely on coworkers for that support?

2. In what ways do relationships on the job (between supervisors and employees and among employees) mirror relationships within the family?

3. Does promoting a "sense of family" in the workplace lead to better working conditions? Or does it promote strife among employees?

Such questions give you a place to start; they articulate specific issues that can lead toward a promising thesis.

1d Consider your purpose.

In settling on a topic, you should keep in mind the intended **purpose** of your essay—that is, your goal or aim in writing it. Writers typically pursue a variety of purposes; they try to inform, persuade, speculate, entertain, or arouse emotions—sometimes within a single piece of writing. Traditionally, however, essays and parts of essays have been divided into four basic types according to their varying purposes.

TYPE OF WRITING	PURPOSE
Description	To create visual images for the reader
Narration	To tell the reader what happened
Analysis	To explain something for the reader
Argument	To win the reader's agreement

Note that the first two types of writing, **description** and **narration,** are presentational; they call scenes or episodes to the reader's mind. The third type, **analysis,** or explanation, characterizes most college writing; virtually every paper you write will require that you analyze or explain some idea, procedure, or phenomenon. And **argument** uses facts, descriptions, narrations, and/or explanations to support an opinion. An argument typically attempts to *refute* opposing positions (prove them wrong) while offering positive evidence to back up the writer's position.

Many college writing assignments specify a purpose, asking you, for instance, to *describe* a particular place, to *analyze* how something works, or to *argue* for or against a certain point of view. Often, however, instructors expect you to define your own purpose. Suppose, for example, you were asked to write about the bubonic plague, a disease that flourished in the Middle Ages and that remains dangerous today on a smaller scale. You might begin to narrow this broad subject area by considering various purposes:

To Describe: You might give your readers a detailed, physically vivid account of the symptoms: fever, boils, discoloration, chills, and so forth.

To Narrate: You might tell how the plague swept through Europe from 1348 to 1349.

To Analyze: You might explain how the plague bacillus is transmitted by rats and their fleas or how it differs from another bacterium.

To Argue: You might support as essential, or oppose as no longer necessary, public health regulations designed to prevent outbreaks of the plague.

Most college essays involve two or more purposes. In arguing for a local recycling program, for example, you will first have to analyze—or explain—how the program works. And in order to be persuasive, you may want to describe what the town's landfill will look like if the program is not adopted. Nevertheless, thinking about the *main* purpose of a given essay can help you define your topic and stay on track once you start writing.

For a sample analytic essay, see pages 68–70, 5f. For a sample argumentative essay, see pages 83–86, Chapter 6.

1e   Use notes to develop your thoughts.

As you develop your topic—and throughout the writing process—you should take notes, raising questions, commenting on earlier notes, jotting down new ideas, and reminding yourself of points for future consideration. Some writers use index cards for note taking, restricting themselves to one idea per card. Others prefer loose sheets of scratch paper, a yellow legal pad, or a bound notebook. Whatever your preference, develop the habit of working with pen in hand. As you think or read about a potential topic, use your notes to quote key passages, record facts and observations, launch a trial topic, express doubts, or develop a list of pros and cons.

Annotating a Text

When your essay is supposed to deal with an assigned text, your note taking should begin during your reading of the text. If you own the book, mark it up. If the book belongs to someone else, photocopy the relevant pages and mark them. Watch especially for details that bear on the topic you have in mind. Underline key passages, and write comments and questions in the margins. Whenever one part of the text helps you understand another part, make a marginal cross reference such as "see p. 43."

If you were asked, for example, to write an essay about Eudora Welty's story "A Worn Path," you might annotate her opening paragraph like this:

> It was December—a bright frozen day in the early morning. Far out in the country there was an old Negro woman with her head tied in a red rag, coming along a path through the pinewoods. Her name was Phoenix Jackson. She was very old and small and she walked slowly in the dark pine shadows, moving a little from side to side in her steps, with the balanced heaviness and lightness of a pendulum in a grandfather clock. She carried a thin, small cane made from an umbrella, and with this she kept tapping the frozen earth in front of her. This made a grave and persistent noise in the still air, that seemed meditative like the chirping of a solitary little bird.

figurative language

Dictionary says: mythological bird that dies and rises from its own ashes. Symbol of renewal/rebirth?

After marking an entire text this way, you can easily gather your miscellaneous impressions on note paper and begin dealing with *them* instead of with the whole text. With your notes in hand, you can later return to the text with pointed, specific questions in mind.

1f Draw ideas from your experience and reading.

Instructors sometimes assign essays of a certain structural type (comparison and contrast, for example) without specifying a subject area or topic. When you find yourself thus free to choose a topic, think about your own interests and knowledge. However limited your experience may be, it is nonetheless a rich and unique source of ideas. Have you had a job? Have you traveled or lived in another state, province, or country? Do you have a memorable friend or a favorite hobby? Are you enthusiastic about a current political idea or candidate? Does some campus policy make you angry? Did a recent film or magazine article catch your interest? If you can answer "yes" to even one of these questions, you have the raw material you need. Drawing ideas from firsthand experience will not guarantee an engaging essay, but one thing is certain: what doesn't interest you is not likely to interest a reader.

A particular source of interest may be your course work in composition or another discipline. Have you come across a significant problem in an assigned reading? Does a point you heard in a lecture connect with your own experience or knowledge? Do your class notes contain questions or observations that might lead to a thesis? Whenever you record some doubt or agreement, you may have in hand the beginnings of an essay.

Keeping a Journal

Your search for ideas will be easier if you keep a journal. Unlike a diary, which has little focus or direction, a journal is a disciplined record of your experiences or, more significantly, your thoughts and observations. Journal writing works best when it becomes a habit, a daily routine that lets you voice your opinions, plans, and ambitions or reflect on the world around you. Alternatively, a journal can trace your progress in learning a particular subject or skill—anything from music theory to child rearing. And sometimes you can turn your journal into a reading notebook, a collection of responses to the essays, poems, and stories you read in your college courses or on your own.

Whatever material it includes, a journal should be a place to experiment with language and test ideas you might not want to try in an essay or even in a conversation with a friend. Kept faithfully, a journal can make you a more fluent writer and give you a rich source of ideas for future writing assignments.

1g Try freewriting, brainstorming, or clustering.

Freewriting

Sometimes it helps to begin writing before you have a definite idea of what your topic will be. When you feel stymied, assign yourself a ten- or fifteen-minute stint of **freewriting.** The trick is to write nonstop without worrying about logic or grammar, letting each sentence carry you into the next. If you get stuck, repeat a word from your last sentence until a new thought appears. And even if one freewriting session seems to lead nowhere, a second one, started a few minutes later, may yield ideas that were not quite ready for expression the first time.

Freewriting can begin with a random word, thought, or image. Note how one student—starting with little more than his own frustration—moved toward a topic:

> Stuck—staring at a blank page with nothing to say, so I'll try some freewriting. Keep the pencil moving, keep the pencil gliding across the page—words words words words words. I can't stop till I fill up this page. The page looks like a sheet of ice and my pencil is an ice skater gliding across it. My hand guides the pencil and my brain guides my hand. I watch my hand. Blank page—words words words words. Watching my hand. Does the old saying "I know it like the back of my hand" make sense? Hands do tell a lot about a person. I always notice my dads hands—rough, worn, battered from working outside all day. My hands are smooth and soft except where I have a bump from holding this pencil. Our hands are a sign of how different our lives are. He grew up working on a farm and never went to college, I got to go away to college and probally wont ever have rough hands. I'm glad I'm free not to follow his path, but something *is* lost in the shift between the generations. I'm removed from the life I grew up in. Like a plant pulled out by the roots and moved to a diffrent spot. Maybe I could write about that—idea that important things (emotional security? traditions?) get lost when sons follow different paths from fathers. Does anything make up for what gets lost?

With its ungainly structures and misspellings, this passage obviously lacks the polish of finished prose, but in writing it, the student found a likely-looking topic.

Brainstorming

Freewriting teases forth ideas by tapping our natural tendency to link one sentence with another. **Brainstorming** works by the opposite principle—discontinuity. To brainstorm is to toss out suggestions without regard for their connections, letting assorted notions accumulate quickly on the page. Here is a sample from the student whose freewriting raised the issue of father-son relationships:

fathers/sons	prodigal son—or daughter
emotional bonds	double standard?
breaking away	—ok for sons to "sow wild oats"?
—leaving home	—daughters? different rules?
—independence	mothers/daughters—closer bonds?
—new identity/values	*Hamlet*—father/son theme
homecoming celebration!	Ophelia—daughter/father

You can brainstorm by yourself, listing random words and phrases as they occur to you, scribbling on a note pad. Or you can work in a group, either with friends or in the classroom, where the "note pad" is a shared chalkboard. The resulting list can move you toward a topic or help you modify one already in hand.

Clustering

A third strategy, **clustering,** combines the continuity of freewriting with the discontinuity of brainstorming. The idea is to write a word or phrase in the center of a sheet of paper, circle it, and then map out "clusters" of information triggered by the original concept. Because of its graphic orientation, clustering allows writers to make odd leaps between ideas and to see how those ideas mesh. The student exploring father-son relationships built this cluster (p. 15) around the word *independence,* which he first jotted down while brainstorming.

This exercise finally gave the student writer a topic: the inevitable risk—and loss—involved in achieving personal independence. The paper he eventually wrote drew on his earlier freewriting and brainstorming for two key examples—his sense of separation from his father and his memory of an emotional homecoming.

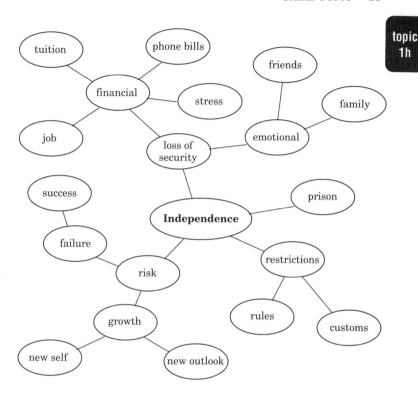

1h Explore your trial topic.

Once you have arrived at a topic rather than a subject area, you may feel the urge to start drafting your essay. It is best, however, to resist that urge until you have in mind a tentative thesis—a main point or assertion *about* your topic. And before devising a thesis, you should make sure your **trial topic** can pass five tests:

1. Is the trial topic sufficiently focused?

2. Is it complex enough for an essay of the assigned length?

3. Is it likely to sustain my interest?

4. Is it appropriate for my intended audience?

5. Do I have enough supporting material to work with?

If you can answer "yes" to all five questions, consider yourself lucky: you are ready to draft a thesis. More probably, you will need to explore your trial topic, using one or more of the following techniques.

Focused Freewriting or Brainstorming

If freewriting and brainstorming can lead to preliminary ideas for an essay, they can also help you explore a trial topic. The same rules apply (see pp. 13–14). The only difference is that now you begin with a definite focus and try to develop specific features of your trial topic. As before, the idea is to set aside worries about organization and correctness and to see what happens.

Reporters' Questions

Another simple yet surprisingly helpful way to explore your trial topic is to run through the standard list of questions used by newspaper reporters: *who? what? when? where? how? why?* The procedure works because it keeps returning you to the same material from fresh perspectives.

Suppose your trial topic were the merits of a proposed law that would encourage recycling of glass by requiring a five-cent returnable deposit on all bottles. Asking the six standard reporters' questions, you might come up with answers like these:

Who? Elected officials voting on the proposal; consumers; environmental groups; bottle manufacturers; lobbyists.

What? A proposed deposit on bottles; the amount of the deposit; competing proposals; similar laws in other places.

When? Final vote at the next session of the city council or legislature; law to take effect one month after passage.

Where? Only within this community or state; restaurants and bars; biggest effect in grocery stores.

How? Fix penalties for bottle sellers who violate the law; give the law wide publicity; warn first offenders before penalizing.

Why? Reduce waste and pollution; raise public awareness about conservation; cut prices through use of recycled glass.

Any of these brief notes could carry you beyond your first thoughts and lead to an adequately focused thesis. Given inflation, for example, will a five-cent deposit be large enough to ensure returns? Will there be special problems associated with putting the law into effect so soon? If the law applies only within a small geographic area, will consumers take their business elsewhere? Are the penalties for noncompliance too strict? Not strict enough?

Analytic Strategies

You can also explore a trial topic by applying classic analytic strategies: *definition, division, illustration, cause and effect, comparison and contrast, process analysis,* and *analogy.* These maneuvers are so basic that they will almost certainly stimulate new trains of thought.

Definition: How does a law differ from a regulation? A misdemeanor from a felony? What kinds of containers would be included or excluded?

Division: What are the separate provisions of the bill? What types of stores would be affected?

Illustration: Which communities and states have already established deposit laws? What reports of success or failure are available?

Cause and effect: What events and trends have made passage of the law likely or unlikely? What differences in consumers' behavior would the law bring about? Would littering be significantly curtailed? In the long run, would prices of bottled products go up or down?

Comparison and contrast: In what way does this law resemble others that have been enacted elsewhere? How does it differ from them? Do young people and older people hold different views of the law?

Process analysis: How will violations of the law come to public notice, arrive at a prosecutor's desk, and be subsequently handled? What flow of payments and reimbursements is expected between the consumer, the grocer, and the distributor?

**topic
1h**

Analogy: Is five cents too little to encourage real conservation—like expecting people to stay home just because gas goes up a penny a gallon? Is asking grocery stores to handle the empty bottles like asking banks to count millions of coins by hand—too labor-intensive and too costly?

2 Developing a Thesis

2a   Write out a one-sentence trial thesis.

Let us assume that, using one or more of the strategies described in the previous chapter, you have arrived at a **trial thesis,** or tentative idea for your essay. Instead of mulling that thesis over in your head, get it down on paper. Your first effort may be paltry, imprecise, or awkward, but at least you have something to work with—a single sentence you can reshape and refine until it says exactly what you want it to say. That sentence may or may not find its way into your essay. For now, its function is to let you make sure that you have *one* central idea—not zero, not two—and that your idea looks sufficiently challenging and defensible.

Here are several one-sentence trial theses based on topics explored in Chapter 1:

1. Recent television sitcoms create make-believe images of single-parent families, images that tell us little about the economic and emotional hardships faced by such families in the real world.

2. People who lack intimacy with family and friends often turn to coworkers for that intimacy and thus undermine the professional relationships needed for success on the job.

3. After one semester living on my own, I know that achieving personal independence will take a long time and will require painful adjustments in the way I see myself and my family.

4. Although it is no longer a major threat to public safety, bubonic plague still poses enough danger to warrant strict enforcement of health regulations designed to prevent outbreaks of the disease.

Note that each thesis focuses on *one* controlling point and states that point in a single sentence. Once you have a trial thesis on paper, you can revise it as you see fit, drawing on the advice of your instructor or a classmate to supplement your own evolving sense of what you want to say.

Thesis Question

If you have trouble formulating a trial thesis, try asking yourself a **thesis question**—that is, the central question you expect your essay to answer. Some writers find it easier to define a specific problem or issue after they have posed such a question. Suppose, for example, you were asked to develop an opinion on a proposed smoking ban in campus dormitories. After deciding to argue in favor of the ban, you still might be unsure about the best way to frame a trial thesis. A pointed question might help:

THESIS QUESTION:
Why is the ban on smoking in the best interest of dormitory residents?

ANSWER (TRIAL THESIS):
The ban will protect nonsmokers from the health hazards of passive smoke, will reduce the likelihood of fire in the dorms, and may help ease growing tension between smokers and nonsmokers in several campus dorms.

Note how the thesis question helps identify a key issue—the *benefits* to dormitory residents—and thus points the way to a one-sentence trial thesis.

TOPIC	THESIS QUESTION	TRIAL THESIS
Describe an admirable person.	Why do I admire Ms. Flores, my world history professor?	My world history professor, Ms. Flores, has an admirable ability to balance discipline and imagination in teaching her subject.
Recount a memorable experience.	Did I learn anything from my bungee-cord jump last summer?	Although I did it mainly for fun, my bungee-cord jump helped me appreciate the nature of trust and cooperation.
Analyze the structure of John Keats's poem "To Autumn."	How does the three-part structure of "To Autumn" contribute to the meaning of the poem?	The three-part structure of "To Autumn" allows Keats to show both the distinct phases of autumn and the season's continuity within the larger cycle of nature.

2b   Adapt your thesis to your purpose.

Once you have drafted a trial thesis, you should make sure it matches the intended purpose of your essay (p. 9, 1d). If you are responding to an assigned topic, be especially careful to see that your thesis meets the terms of the assignment. Watch for key words and phrases that indicate the aim your instructor has in mind. If the assignment asks you to *analyze, illustrate,* or *discuss* a particular topic, then your dominant purpose is analytic, and your main goal should be to explain—to make your reader understand your thesis. If, on the other hand, your instructor asks you to *argue, convince, evaluate, take a stand,* or *develop an opinion,* your overriding purpose is argumentative, and your thesis should be a debatable claim, one you will have to support in order to win the reader's sympathy.

Here are some typical analytic and argumentative trial theses about instituting a bottle deposit law (p. 16, 1h):

ANALYTIC THESES:
Explaining public interest in deposit laws: Concern about the environment and about the scarcity of raw materials has spawned widespread interest in bottle deposit laws.

Explaining a link between voter age and support for deposit laws: The passage or failure of bottle deposit laws in a given state or locality correlates directly with the proportion of voters under age thirty.

ARGUMENTATIVE THESES:
Arguing for the law: The minor inconvenience of paying a deposit and having to return empty bottles is far outweighed by the benefits that all citizens would receive from a well-drafted deposit law.

Arguing against the law: A bottle deposit law not only would hurt small-business owners by adding to their expenses but also would lead to more, not less, pollution because of the increased trucking it would require.

Implied Thesis

An analytic or argumentative essay almost always demands a strong, explicit thesis, usually stated prominently near the beginning of the essay. Occasionally, though, you might be asked to write an essay—usually a description or a narration (p. 9, 1d)—that calls for an **implied thesis,** a central point or impression that is nowhere stated in a single sentence but is nevertheless clearly implied by the details of the essay. Implied theses are especially useful in narratives, where the writer may want to let the story suggest a point. Stating that point might rob an otherwise moving essay of its subtlety and force. If you do decide to imply, rather than openly state, the point of your essay, check with your instructor first, and be aware that using an implied thesis can be tricky.

2c   Give your thesis definite content.

Proposing a substantial, challenging idea is the surest way to engage your reader's interest. While you need not say something profound or strikingly original in every essay you write, you should at least aim for a thesis that makes a definite point, one you can support with conviction. Avoid an unassertive **weaseling thesis** that makes a limp, indecisive statement.

DON'T:
x A deposit law is very controversial.

x Although some people support a deposit law, others do not.

x A deposit law has many different aspects that should be examined.

Compare these vacant assertions with the "deposit law" theses above, which do say something definite about the topic.

To make sure you have a substantial idea, ask yourself whether your classmates would willingly read an essay based on your thesis. Would your main point secure their interest? Would it challenge them to think? Would it tell them something new or give them a fresh perspective on a familiar topic? If not, rework your thesis until it says something decisive and lively. Be especially wary of a sentence that states the obvious or merely announces a topic.

OVERLY OBVIOUS THESIS:
x Farming methods are different from country to country.

IMPROVED THESIS:
• Chinese farmers use their land and raise their crops in ways that might surprise North American farmers.

"THESIS" ANNOUNCING A TOPIC:

x In this essay I will discuss the effects of depression on first-year college students.

IMPROVED THESIS:

• When first-year college students are depressed by their inability to meet unfamiliar academic and social demands, their depression makes it even harder for them to satisfy those demands.

2d Limit the scope of your thesis.

A thesis that quickly proves unworkable may suffer from too broad a scope. Remember that you have only a short essay in which to develop your idea. Instead of discarding a thesis that seems to lead nowhere, try recasting it in narrower terms, replacing vague general concepts with more specific ones.

TOPIC	THESIS TOO BROAD	THESIS IMPROVED
The popularity of garage sales	x Garage sales reflect the times we live in.	• Garage sales circulate goods during periods of high inflation and high unemployment.
A "star wars" missile defense system	x We should not invest in a "star wars" missile defense system.	• Given the decreased Soviet military threat and the high cost of high-tech weaponry, we should suspend development of a "star wars" missile defense system.
Persuasive techniques in Martin Luther King's "Letter from Birmingham Jail"	x King uses many techniques to convince us that passive resistance is a legitimate way to change unjust laws.	• King uses a skillful balance of logical and emotional appeals to convince us that passive resistance is a legitimate way to change unjust laws.

Note how in each case the improved thesis narrows the scope of the overly broad one. In the first example, "the times" are carefully defined. In the second, considerations of cost and a reduced military threat limit the claim. And in the third, King's persuasive techniques—logical and emotional appeals—are specified.

2e Try developing your trial thesis into a full thesis statement.

Let us suppose that your trial thesis is no longer on trial: it says something definite, and it has a limited scope. At this point you may be anxious to start writing, but before doing so, you should consider an extra step that may look unnecessary at first. Cast your thesis into a full **thesis statement**—a sentence that not only names your central idea but also announces the main points you intend to develop to support that idea. This statement will probably be long and cumbersome. Never mind: it will *not* appear in your essay. It is simply a private guide to help you control and organize your material.

Sometimes your unexpanded thesis will be complex enough to carry you into the work of organizing and drafting. We have already looked at several such theses, including this one: *A bottle deposit law not only would hurt small-business owners by adding to their expenses but also would lead to more, not less, pollution because of the increased trucking it would require.* This sentence suggests a rudimentary essay structure: one section about the ill effects of the deposit law on business owners and a second section arguing that the law would damage the environment. If your thesis gives as much direction as this one does, you may want to go directly to the next stage of planning.

More often than not, though, a thesis will be too simple in form to specify the major divisions of an essay. The remedy is to spell out some of the large considerations that led you to develop the thesis in the first place. You can add *main details, reasons,* and/or *objections* to form a full thesis statement.

Including Main Details

Suppose you have settled on this trial thesis: *Chinese farmers use their land and raise their crops in ways that might surprise North*

American farmers. If you need more guidance to get a handle on your material, you might recast this sentence, expanding it to include the *specific* ways in which Chinese and North American farming methods differ. And since you will eventually have to decide how to organize the main details within your essay, why not list them right now in the order you plan to discuss them, saving the strongest point for the emphatic final position?

- Chinese farming differs strikingly from American farming in its greater concern for using all available space, its handling of crop rotation, its reliance on natural fertilizers, and, above all, its emphasis on mass labor instead of advanced machinery.

Supplying Reasons

In some theses the main statement does not lend itself to the kind of expansion we have just considered. Yet you can always find more "parts" for your essay—and thus for your full thesis statement—by listing the reasons why you think the thesis deserves to be believed. Suppose, for example, you intend to maintain that *Students who come to a large urban university from small towns often enjoy a newfound sense of freedom.* A fair beginning. But can a whole paper grow from such a simple statement? It can if you ask yourself *why or in what ways* students enjoy the newfound sense of freedom. Note how the addition of three *because* clauses makes the thesis statement an organizational blueprint:

- Students who come to this large urban university from small towns often enjoy a newfound sense of freedom, because the university and the city expose them to a greater variety of people than they have met before, because they experience an enlarged sense of space when living in a major city, and because they can achieve an anonymity and impersonality that are hard to achieve in a small town.

If this ungainly sentence appeared in your essay, it would overwhelm the reader and give away too much information all at once. The first part of the sentence—before the *because* clauses—might well suffice to announce your central point. The added clauses serve you, not the reader; they set forth the points you will discuss one by one in your essay.

thesis
2e

Meeting Objections

If your thesis is controversial—and all argumentative theses and many analytic ones are—you should plan to deal with at least one major objection to it. Typically, you will handle that point through either **refutation** or **concession** (p. 53, 4l)—that is, either by showing that the objection is wrong or by granting its truth while showing that it does not overrule your thesis. Like supporting details or reasons, an objection can appear in your full thesis statement:

* Although some students who come to this university from small towns feel confined by its size and its urban setting, many others enjoy a newfound sense of freedom, because the university and the city. . . .

Again, suppose you intend to argue that the government should place severe restrictions on the use of animals in laboratory tests. To be convincing, you will have to address at least one strong point on the opposing side. Get that point into your full thesis statement, add your positive reasons, and you are ready to go:

* Although the government should continue to allow licensed research facilities to use animals for important medical research, it should sharply curtail animal testing for commercial, nonmedical purposes, because the testing is often unnecessary to assure product safety and because the limited amount of data gathered in the tests does not justify the suffering inflicted on laboratory animals.

A mouthful! But, again, a full thesis statement is only a road map, not an excerpt from your essay. You need not make it concise. It will serve its purpose if it allows you to move confidently to the next phase of planning.

3 Organizing

3a Be flexible in organizing your essay.

The principles of organization discussed in this chapter will serve
you best if you take them as a starting point rather than a rigid set
of rules. A full thesis statement and an outline can be useful for
planning a successful essay, but they should never become a strait-
jacket. Some writers work best when they are free to move beyond a
fixed pattern, and while you may do well to start with a definite
plan in mind, your evolving sense of problems, opportunities, and
paragraph-by-paragraph tactics should be your final guide.

Suppose, for instance, you intend to write a paragraph answering
a probable objection to your thesis but later find that one of your own
supporting points answers that objection. It would be wasteful to
treat the objection and the supporting evidence separately. Or, again,
you might plan to include a summary paragraph at the end of your
essay but then discover that a final striking sentence wraps up what
you want to say more effectively than a formal conclusion could (p.
136, 10 m). Be ready to modify your plan whenever a better alternative appears.

Even if you write a full and detailed outline for your essay, you
should regard it as a flexible guide, subject to adjustment as you
compose. And remember that outlining alone can never replace a
sound thesis. Some writers, equating an outline with "good organization," are tempted to go directly from a general topic to an outline:

DON'T:

x Topic: Computers on the College Campus
        I. Computers available in the library
       II. Word processing
     III. Laptop computers
     IV. Relaxing with computer games

Such an outline merely identifies assorted subtopics that the writer hopes to cover. It actually does the writer a disservice by giving a deceptive appearance of order and purpose. Be sure, then, that any structure you use is preceded by and derived from a sound thesis.

Good writers differ greatly in their preferred methods of organizing. If, like some, you find it difficult to work from a fixed pattern, you should nevertheless be prepared to construct an outline once you have finished a draft. There is no better way of spotting redundancies and inconsistencies that need fixing.

3b Find the most effective organization for your ideas.

One way to arrive at a sound essay structure is to put yourself in your reader's place. Beginning in ignorance, the reader wants to know certain things that fall into a natural order:

1. What is your topic?

2. What is your point about that topic?

3. What objections to your point deserve to be met?

4. What evidence can you give to make your point convincing?

As a diagram, then, a basic essay structure would look like this:

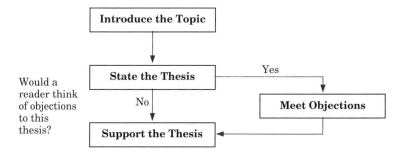

While various organizational patterns are possible for any given essay, most of them fall within the broad guidelines of this common

structure. The reader needs to know your topic before considering
your thesis, and your evidence will make little sense unless it comes
after the thesis it is designed to support. Even the optional part of
the sequence, the handling of objections, appears in a logical place.
When (as in an argumentative essay) it becomes important to address
objections, the handiest place to do so is right after the thesis has
been revealed—for that is where the objections are most likely to
occur to your reader and hence to threaten your credibility.

Using the Full Thesis Statement as a Guide

By following the simplified model just discussed, you can draw the
structure of a brief essay directly from your full thesis statement (p.
25, 2e).

1. The *topic,* the first element in the model, is the issue or subject
   matter addressed by the thesis.

2. The *thesis* is directly named in the full thesis statement.

3. If the thesis contains an *although* clause, at least one important
   objection has been isolated.

4. *Because* clauses in the thesis statement specify the final element of structure, the main points of *support* for your thesis.

3c For a brief essay, try a scratch outline.

If your essay is going to be brief and you simply need to plan for a
few paragraphs, you can probably make do with a **scratch outline**—
that is, an informal list of the main points you intend to develop.
Here is an example based on a thesis we saw earlier (p. 21, 2a):

Thesis: My world history professor, Ms. Flores, has an admirable ability
to balance discipline and imagination in teaching her subject.

¶1—Introduction: start with examples of teachers who don't achieve
balance; then pivot to Ms. Flores and thesis.

¶2—Explain "discipline" with examples from her History 102 class—
demanding, organized, no wasted time.

¶3—Explain "imagination," especially her use of "storytelling" in lectures and her use of journals (maybe 2 ¶s here).

¶4—Show how two traits—seemingly incompatible—are balanced in her teaching; use term project as main example; conclude here, but maybe add one additional ¶ to wrap up essay.

org
3d

And here is a second example, also based on a thesis we saw before:

Thesis: The three-part structure of "To Autumn" allows Keats to show both the distinct phases of autumn and the season's continuity within the larger cycle of nature.

—Briefly define Romantic nature poetry.

—Introduce "To Autumn" (three-part structure).

—1st stanza: late summer/fruitfulness/Sept.

—2d stanza: harvest time/Oct.

—3d stanza: end of season/onset of winter/Nov.

—Season's beauty softens the images of death.

—Death and cycle of nature; hints of renewal and return.

3d Use a formal outline to show main and subordinate points.

For longer and more complex essays you may want to use a **formal outline,** one that shows—through indention, numbering, and lettering—that some points are subordinate to others.

Suppose, for instance, you had decided to write a 1000-word argument opposing rent control of off-campus housing, and you were satisfied with the following thesis statement: *Although off-campus rent control is aimed at securing reasonable rents for students, it would actually produce four undesirable effects: establishment of an expensive, permanent rent-control bureaucracy; landlord neglect of rental property; a shortage of available units; and a freezing of cur-*

rently excessive rents. Knowing that your argument would be fairly complex, you might want to draw up a full outline:

  I. The problem is that students now face hardships in securing adequate housing.
     A. Students are currently subject to rent gouging.
     B. High rents force many students to live far from campus.

 II. The promise is that rent control will guarantee reasonable rents near campus.

III. Thesis: The reality is that the actual effects of rent control would be undesirable.
     A. An expensive, permanent rent-control bureaucracy would be established.
     B. Landlords would neglect rent-controlled property.
     C. The shortage of units would *worsen,* because:
        1. Owners would have no incentive to increase the number of rental units.
        2. Competition for rent-frozen units would be more intense.
     D. Currently excessive rents would be frozen, thus ruling out any possible reduction.

Notice that this outline establishes three degrees of importance among ideas. The Roman numerals running down the left margin point to the underlying structure of the essay, a movement from problem to promise to reality. At the next level, indented capital letters introduce ideas that contribute to the three main categories. Note, for example, how the four parallel points under Part III (A, B, C, and D) give reasons to support the thesis. One of these points, C, is supported in turn by two narrower points (1 and 2). Three degrees of subordination thus display the whole logic of the essay.

Sentence versus Topic Outline

The example just given is a *sentence outline,* using complete sentences to state every planned idea. A sentence outline is the safest kind because its complete statements ensure that you will be making assertions, not just touching on subjects, in every part of your essay.

But if you have a thorough grasp of your key points, you may want to use the simpler *topic outline,* replacing sentences with concise phrases:

I. The problem
   A. Rent gouging
   B. Students forced to live far from campus (etc.)

The form you choose for an outline is hardly an earthshaking matter; just be sure the outline gives you enough direction, and avoid making your categories more intricate and hairsplitting than your essay itself will be.

For a sample topic outline, see page 501, 39c.

Keeping Outline Categories in Logical Relation

If you do use subordination in an outline, make sure that each heading or subheading has at least one mate—no *I* without *II,* no *A* without *B.* Each item in the outline is part of a larger unit, and it is illogical to divide something into just one part. If you have a lonesome *A* in a draft outline, work it into the larger category.

ILLOGICAL:
x I. Problems
      A. Excessive noise
   II. Cost factors
      A. Overruns

BETTER:
• I. Problem of excessive noise
   II. Cost overruns

In addition, you should always check a draft outline to make sure that all the subheadings under a given heading logically contribute to it.

3e Try organizing with a tree diagram.

For maximum flexibility in organizing your essay, use a **tree diagram** to arrange ideas graphically on the page. Put your main idea

**org
3e**

at the top, with your subpoints branching downward toward the bottom. Like a cluster (p. 15, 1g), a tree diagram has a strong visual orientation; it lets you *see* how the parts of your essay relate to one another. And tree diagrams have another advantage: they let your organization "grow," even as you draft your essay. You can add details to one branch of the tree whenever they occur to you, and you can prune away part or all of a branch that no longer seems worth developing.

Asked to write about a favorite pastime, sport, or hobby, one first-year student used a tree diagram to organize an essay about stamp collecting. Her initial plan called for three main points—the three pleasures of stamp collecting—but as her diagram grew, the right branch withered and the middle one flourished. The student ended by writing about *two* pleasures of philately, and she devoted most of her space to discussing the pleasure of learning.

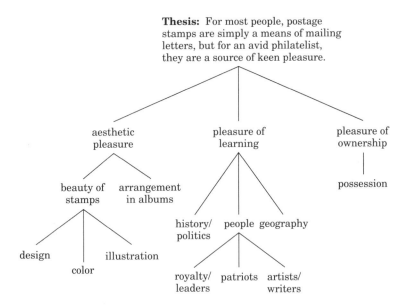

Thesis: For most people, postage stamps are simply a means of mailing letters, but for an avid philatelist, they are a source of keen pleasure.

4 Drafting

4a Mix improvising with planning in writing your first draft.

> **IF YOU HAVE TROUBLE STARTING A DRAFT ...**
>
> - avoid staring at a blank page: use focused freewriting to break the ice (p. 16, 1h)
> - skip your opening paragraph and start with a later one
> - scan your notes for an idea or image that prompts you to write
> - work quickly without pausing over fine points
> - explain your ideas to a friend or classmate before you start the draft

Even after much preparation, you may feel some resistance to committing your first draft to paper. If the opening paragraph (pp. 123–133, 10a–h) looms as an especially big obstacle, try skipping it and starting with a later one. If your outline leads to a dead end, abandon it temporarily and pursue a new, more fruitful line of thought. And if you start to lose momentum in the middle of a sentence, shift into a private shorthand to keep yourself from getting bogged down in fine points of expression. Do not be afraid to include too much, to leave blank spaces, or to make errors of usage and punctuation. What matters now is that you move ahead, knowing that everything you write is open to later revision (see Chapter 5).

As you finish one sentence and struggle to begin the next one, you may find new possibilities coming into view. Some of your best ideas—perhaps even a radically improved thesis—can be sparked by this friction between the written sentence and the not-yet-written one. So long as you anticipate the need to reconsider and reorganize after your first draft is complete, the tug-of-war between plans and inspirations should result in a subtler, more engaging essay than you originally expected to write.

ADDRESSING THE READER

4b Consider your audience.

As you draft an essay, you should pay special attention to audience expectation. Experienced professional writers face down the blank page by working with a strong sense of audience, using structures and patterns of thought that they know will be familiar to their readers. How do they know? Simply by reading the magazines or journals to which they submit their work. Every field of knowledge—medicine, psychology, forestry, and so on—has its specialized vocabulary, its typical way of introducing and concluding a report or article, even its characteristic tone. You, too, when you write for a specialized audience, will find that many composing choices "come naturally" because you are already a member of the community formed by your prospective readers.

When you write for a general audience—and that, by and large, is the role your composition instructor and your classmates expect to play—you cannot take so much for granted. If you are treating, say, bicycle repair or particle physics or the popular music of the 1960s, you need to ask yourself how much background information the general reader is likely to need. And since you are writing for a stranger rather than an interested specialist, you must take greater pains to interest your audience in what you have to say. Furthermore, you cannot presume that the general reader agrees with your politics, your religion, or your tastes. Insofar as possible, you will have to appeal to facts and judgments that are widely held to be plausible.

Nevertheless, you and your general reader have a good deal in common. You both value straightforward, honest writing in which shrewd ideas are backed by evidence. And you both appreciate freshness of language and point of view. In drafting—and later in revising—you want to give the reader the same kind of substance and craft you yourself would expect from another essayist.

Classmates as Audience

Understandably, some students find their inspiration leaking away when they contemplate their instructor as a stand-in for the general reader. But you have to write with *somebody* in mind or you will find yourself paralyzed by indecision. Why not try casting your classmates in the role of audience?

This is not to say that you should begin writing in chummy slang. It is more a question of trying to please and convince readers who are much like yourself. Your classmates share your world in important ways, and you can usually trust their good sense. If the student sitting next to you would choke on some contrived generalization, leave it out. If you suspect that the class as a whole would say *Make that clearer* or *Find a better example,* do so. Your instructor will be delighted with any essay that would impress most of your classmates.

draft
4c

4c   Choose between a personal and an impersonal voice.

Voice refers to the "self" projected by a given piece of writing. The relevant question to ask is not "What am I really like?" but "What voice is appropriate for my purpose and audience?" In drafting some essays, you will want to maintain a formal, impersonal air; for others, you will want readers to feel much closer to you as an individual.

Consider the following deliberately impersonal paragraph.

IMPERSONAL VOICE:

Asked to compare the benefits of academic jobs with jobs in government or business, over 90% of humanities graduate students cited greater flexibility in the use of time. Two-thirds or more mentioned freedom to do as one wished, opportunities to experiment with differing life-styles, and ability to flout social conventions. On the down side, one-quarter to two-fifths expressed suspicion that a teaching job would carry less social prestige and less job security. They were divided almost evenly on whether teaching would involve less leisure or more. The chief drawback to the academic career identified by the majority was relatively lower earning power.

—ERNEST R. MAY and DOROTHY G. BLANEY,
Careers for Humanists

The authors of this passage want to show serious, well-informed readers that they are reliable transmitters of information. They do not refer even distantly to their own experiences, opinions, or feelings, nor do they ask their readers for anything beyond attention to the facts at hand. When your chief purpose is conveying information—as, for example, in a statistical summary or a laboratory report—you will want to adopt such an *impersonal voice,* letting "the facts speak for themselves."

The following student paragraph illustrates an opposite effect:

PERSONAL VOICE:

During my three semesters as a finance major, I managed to convince myself that a great-paying job would be ample reward for the dry and dreary work it took to earn a business degree. But last spring, right in the middle of a lecture on federal banking regulations, I realized that I could hide the truth no longer: I wanted to read poetry, write papers, and—yes—teach school. Rashly tossing aside my calculator and my "earning potential," I signed on as an English major. You may marvel at my folly, but as the daughter of two veteran teachers who love their work, I decided that I would gladly trade a little "earning potential" for the job I really wanted.

This writer, using a *personal voice,* draws freely on private experience and involves her readers by addressing them as individuals: *You may marvel at my folly.* The paragraph blends direct statement (*I signed on as an English major*) with playful exaggeration (*Rashly tossing aside my calculator*), suggesting the presence of an amiable personality behind the words.

In adopting a voice, you also establish the **tone** (p. 41, 4e), or quality of feeling, conveyed by your writing. An impersonal voice necessarily carries a dry, objective tone, while a personal voice can be somber or playful, earnest or droll, excited or deliberate, angry or tolerant. Compare the friendly tone of the "finance major" passage, for example, with the tone of the following lines by Martin Luther King, Jr., responding to eight Alabama clergymen who had urged him to proceed cautiously in seeking racial justice. Both voices are personal, but King's tone is noble and angry:

We know through painful experience that freedom is never voluntarily given by the oppressor; it must be demanded by the oppressed. Frankly,

I have yet to engage in a direct-action campaign that was "well timed" in the view of those who have not suffered unduly from the disease of segregation. For years now I have heard the word "Wait!" It rings in the ear of every Negro with piercing familiarity. This "Wait" has almost always meant "Never." We must come to see, with one of our distinguished jurists, that "justice too long delayed is justice denied."

—Martin Luther King, Jr., *Why We Can't Wait*

This is the voice of a writer who knows he cannot bank on much agreement from his immediate readers—the timid clergymen who had urged him to go slow. Instead of swallowing his feelings, King defiantly stands on personal authority: *For years now I have heard the word "Wait!"* He and other blacks *know through painful experience* how freedom is won, and they have a personal basis for asserting that *"Wait" has almost always meant "Never."*

Choice of Governing Pronoun

Notice that the **governing pronoun** you choose for your essay helps to establish a consistent voice. If you call yourself *I,* you are guaranteeing at least a degree of personal emphasis. Even greater intimacy is implied if, like the "finance major" writer (p. 38), you presume to call your reader *you.* That pronoun can quickly wear out its welcome, however; a reader resents being told exactly what to think and feel. If, like King, you occasionally shift from the personal *I* to the community *we,* you can imply a sense of shared values between yourself and all fair-minded readers. And if you want a strictly formal, impersonal point of view, you should refer to yourself rarely, if at all—and then only as a member of the indefinite "editorial" *we,* as in *We shall see below. . . .*

4d Generally prefer a forthright stance.

Most essays and nearly all college papers are meant to be taken "straight." Readers sense that the writer is adopting a *forthright stance*—addressing them in a sincere, trustworthy manner. Note this student example:

FORTHRIGHT STANCE:
When this University switched from quarters to semesters, my first reaction was dismay over my shortened summer. The last spring quarter ended in mid-June; the first fall semester began in August. Was this what the new order would be like—a general speedup? It took me a while to realize that my lost vacation was not a permanent feature of the semester system but a one-time inconvenience. Now that I have survived nearly two whole semesters, I am ready to admit that there is much to be said for the changed calendar. As for vacations, those five weeks of freedom around Christmas have turned my vanished summer into a trivial, faded memory.

Using middle diction (p. 180, 14d) and maintaining an earnest manner, this writer carefully lays out her reasons for having had first one reaction and then another to the semester system. Her straightforward, measured language gives us no cause to doubt the sincerity of what she says.

Using Irony

Once in a while, instead of taking the usual forthright stance, you may want to strike an *ironic stance,* writing something in a way that expresses a different or even opposite meaning. In using **irony,** as in the following student paragraph, you let the reader know that your words are *not* to be taken "straight."

IRONIC STANCE:
Eating the catered meals they serve on airplanes is always a memorable experience. In the first place, you have to admit it is exciting to open that little carton of salad oil and find a stream of Thousand Island dressing rocketing onto your blouse. Then, too, where else would you be able to dig into a *perfectly* rectangular chicken? And let's not forget the soggy, lukewarm mushrooms which are accused by the menu of having "smothered" the geometrical bird. They look and taste exactly like the ear jacks that are forever falling off your rented headset. Come to think of it, what *do* they do with those jacks when the flight is over?

When the writer says that eating a catered meal is *always a memorable experience,* we know at once that she means the opposite: such

draft
4e

meals are rarely, if ever, "memorable." Nor, we gather, is it really "exciting" to stain one's blouse with salad dressing. The writer's witty exaggerations amuse us and reveal at least as much about her mildly cynical attitude toward life as they do about airline food.

A whole essay taking the stance of the "airline food" passage would quickly become tiresome. But used subtly and selectively, irony can be a splendid way to persuade—and entertain—readers. Even an ironic sentence or two in an otherwise straightforward essay can give sharp expression to a key point. A student's assertion, for example, that *the financial aid office on campus was a bit late in issuing loan payments* ironically understated a three-month delay that nearly forced him to quit school. Or note how writer Peter De Vries uses an ironic discrepancy between two brief sentences to comment wryly on his craft: *I love being a writer. What I can't stand is the paperwork.*

Whether you use irony in a sentence, a paragraph, or a whole essay, remember that it can fall flat if it becomes too heavy-handed. Be especially wary of **sarcasm**—abusive ridicule that rarely serves a useful purpose in a college essay. If you plan to submit an entire essay that adopts an ironic stance, check with your instructor first.

4e Aim for a measured tone.

One of the surest ways to earn your reader's trust is to maintain a measured, consistent **tone,** or quality of feeling, throughout your essay. Some tones are clearly inappropriate in essay prose. If your writing sounds hostile, contemptuous, or bombastic, for example, readers will be hard-pressed to take it seriously. They will be more inclined to hear you out if you speak with composure and control.

This does not mean your writing should sound flat and impassive; strong emotions do have a place in analytic and argumentative essays. But there is rarely a good reason for drowning your reader in a flood of uncontrolled emotion. Compare, for instance, the following paragraphs:

AVOID:

x Animals raised on fur farms suffer horribly brutal treatment! They are viciously kept in cramped cages and ruthlessly deprived of decent living conditions. The COLD-BLOODED farmers who perpetuate these inhumane conditions for millions of animals don't give a damn about anything but their obscene profits! They make a living by exploiting animals and feeding off the whims of a bunch of overfed rich people who have nothing better to do than throw away their spare millions on mink coats. The next time you wear a fur or see one of your friends wearing one, just think about the fascist system that produced it!

BETTER:

- If you have been convinced your fur is "OK" because the animals were raised on a farm, think again. "Fur farm" is a euphemism for a nightmarish place that is home for about six million "ranched" animals in this country. Animals live in small wire cages that offer no place to burrow or nestle, where food is dumped on the top and animal droppings fall through the bottom. The mortality rate runs as high as 20%; infections spread rapidly because of close confinement.
  —RUE MCCLANAHAN, "Don't Support Cruelty"

Both paragraphs make an emotional appeal, but the first one veers wildly out of control. The inflammatory language (*horribly, ruthlessly, obscene, fascist*), the sarcasm (*bunch of overfed rich people*), the emphatic capitalization, and the repeated exclamation points say more about the writer's emotional state than they do about the issue at hand. The paragraph ends by trying to intimidate the reader, a tactic guaranteed to lose sympathy.

The second paragraph shows at least as much conviction as the first. But while McClanahan is clearly angered by fur farming, she manages to turn her anger to constructive uses, offering two precise statistics to support her point and giving the reader a clearheaded description of the animals' living conditions. Two of her words—*nightmarish* and *dumped*—verge on excess but are balanced by otherwise temperate language.

SUPPORTING A THESIS

Your readers want to know that your thesis rests on sound **evidence**—supporting examples, facts, reasons, and testimony. As you draft an essay, you should back up not only its central idea but also any opinion or generalization that departs from what readers are already likely to accept.

draft
4f

TO SUPPORT YOUR THESIS ...

- use examples to flesh out general points (4f)
- use "facts and figures" to bolster your case (4g)
- quote from a printed text or a person's speech (4h)
- cite reliable authorities to strengthen your position (4i)
- use reasoning to draw a conclusion (4j)
- watch for logical fallacies that undermine your case (4k)
- be fair to opposing points of view (4l)

4f Use examples to back up general points.

The heart of analysis and argument consists of supporting general points with specific examples. As the writer of the following paragraph understood, readers expect a broad assertion to be fleshed out with specific instances:

> Among cultures of the West, the number of nonsexual uses of the kiss is staggering. The simple kiss has served any or all of several purposes: greeting and farewell, affection, religious or ceremonial symbolism, deference to a person of higher status. (People also kiss icons, dice, and other objects, of course, in prayer, for luck, or as part of a ritual.) Kisses make the hurt go away, bless sacred vestments, seal a bargain. In story and legend a kiss has started wars and ended them, and awakened Sleeping Beauty and put Brunnhilde to sleep.
>
> —LEONORE TIEFER, "The Kiss"

Drawing on her own observation and reading, Tiefer supplies the kind of concrete detail that convinces readers and holds their interest. (See page 189, 15a, for further advice about making your writing concrete.)

Even when your ideas are not controversial, you need to back them up with examples and details. The success of a descriptive essay—for example, showing that your ninety-year-old grandfather is a colorful, vibrant man—would depend almost entirely on vivid supporting details. And note how the writer of the following passage uses one striking example to substantiate a purely subjective impression about her home state:

> Friendliness is a tradition. Strangers passing on the road wave hello. A common sight is two pickups stopped side by side far out on a range, on a dirt track winding through the sage. The drivers will share a cigarette, uncap their Thermos bottles, and pass a battered cup, steaming with coffee, between windows. These meetings summon up the details of several generations, because, in Wyoming, private histories are largely public knowledge.
> —GRETEL EHRLICH, *The Solace of Open Spaces*

A humorous or whimsical thesis stands in just as much need of illustration as a serious one:

> What is the good side to Thanksgiving, you ask. There is always a good side to everything. Not to Thanksgiving. There is only a bad side and then a worse side. For instance, Grandmother's best linen tablecloth is the bad side: the fact that it is produced each year, in the manner of a red flag being produced before a bull, and then is always spilled upon by whichever child is doing the poorest at school that term and so is in need of greatest reassurance. Thus: "Oh, my God, *Veronica,* you just spilled grape juice [or plum wine or tar] on Grandmother's best linen tablecloth!" But now comes worse. For at this point Cousin Bill, the one who lost all Cousin Edwina's money on a car dealership three years ago and has apparently been drinking steadily since Halloween, bizarrely chooses to say: "Seems to me those old glasses are always falling over."
> —MICHAEL J. ARLEN, "Ode to Thanksgiving"

4g Cite "facts and figures" from trustworthy sources.

When most people think of evidence, they call to mind "facts and figures"—reliable, well-established information and numerical data. Though useful evidence goes well beyond such items, they can have a compelling effect on a reader. Suppose, for example, you wanted to show that class size on your campus was increasing dramatically.

While anecdotal evidence from faculty and students about over-crowded classrooms would carry considerable weight, you could settle the issue promptly by citing registration statistics.

draft 4h

To see how facts and figures can add weight to a claim, study the following paragraph:

> We are the world's most air-conditioned society. Ninety percent of our new cars have air conditioners, as do two thirds of all homes (new and old). Even in 1960, we had "decided that it's part of the American standard of living, something we're entitled to," as Secretary of Commerce Frederick Mueller put it. This was well before air conditioning became universal. In 1960, only 12 percent of households had it. For cars, the figure hovered around 5 percent. The only Americans now without air conditioning are the very, very poor and people—mostly in the North—who don't want it.
>
> —ROBERT J. SAMUELSON, "The Chilling of America"

Samuelson could have supported his point with vivid details—air-conditioned cars moving commuters to and from their air-conditioned office buildings, for example. But in this instance, statistics help him make his point quickly and efficiently. Although an essay based solely on such evidence would lack flavor and variety, strategically placed facts and figures can do much to win a reader's confidence.

4h Use quotations sparingly and pointedly.

Whenever you want to make a point by telling a story—whether a full-length narrative (p. 9, 1d) or a brief anecdote within an essay—you can use quoted speech to give readers a sense of being right on the scene. Notice, for example, how the dialogue in this passage helps give a vivid, economical picture of the author's racist boss:

> I also worked at a land developer's association. The building industry was planning a banquet for contractors, real estate dealers, and real estate editors. "Did you know the restaurant you chose for the banquet is being picketed by CORE and the NAACP?" I squeaked.
>
> "Of course I know." The boss laughed. "That's why I chose it."
>
> "I refuse to type these invitations," I whispered, voice unreliable.

He leaned back in his leather chair, his bossy stomach opulent. He picked up his calendar and slowly circled a date. "You will be paid up to here," he said. "We'll mail you the check."

—MAXINE HONG KINGSTON, *The Woman Warrior*

Quotation also lends credibility to any claim you make about the language of a text—a claim, for instance, that Hemingway's sentences are more complex and varied than most people suppose or that Alice Walker's essays are rich in metaphor. Such assertions ought to be backed by quoted evidence from the text. If a quotation alone does not make your point, follow it with a passage of analysis. Note how, in this paragraph about John Keats's poem "To Autumn," a student writer mixes quotation with commentary:

In the third stanza of the poem, the presence of death becomes more obvious, but even here that presence is softened by images of beauty and serenity. At sunset, "clouds bloom the soft-dying day, / And touch the stubble-plain with rosy hue." Thus images of life and vitality ("bloom," "rosy") exist side by side with images of death (the "dying day" and the harvested wheat field, now reduced to "stubble"). Likewise, gnats "sing," but they do so in a "wailful choir," their life cycle near its end. The small insects are "borne aloft" or sink "as the light wind lives or dies." Here again, Keats subtly joins images of life and death. Even the word "borne" may suggest the meaning of its homonym "born."

Observe, finally, how quotation can neatly wrap up an essay's central point. Malcolm Cowley concludes his discussion of the pleasures and griefs of being eighty years old with this paragraph:

"Eighty years old!" the great Catholic poet Paul Claudel wrote in his journal. "No eyes left, no ears, no teeth, no legs, no wind! And when all is said and done, how astonishingly well one does without them!"

—MALCOLM COWLEY, *The View from 80*

For information on the mechanics of quotation, see Chapter 29. And for advice about using quotations in a research paper, see page 472, 38b. Note also that whenever you include a quotation, you should take care to acknowledge your source (p. 477, 38c).

4i   Cite authorities who share your point.

In theory, the least impressive evidence ought to be the citing of authority; after all, authorities are often proved to have been wrong. In practice, however, we all wisely respect the judgment of people who are better placed than we are for understanding a given issue or technical field. Thus, if a committee of distinguished scientists declares that a proposed weapons system lies beyond the reach of existing technology, we have to be impressed—even if we may harbor some doubts about those scientists' unstated political motives. An opponent of placing warning labels on alcoholic beverages could score a telling point by mentioning that the prestigious American Council on Alcoholism *disapproves* of such labeling. Such citation of authority does not by itself win an argument, but it can leave your reader favorably disposed toward your more substantial evidence.

4j   Use reasoning to reach well-founded conclusions.

Whenever you support a thesis, you give reasons why the reader ought to believe your point. By **reasoning,** however, we mean something narrower: basing a logical conclusion on a set of established facts or premises.

In its most common form, reasoning consists of **induction,** or drawing a general principle from a number of specific instances. If, for example, you observed that your roommate ate ice cream for dessert twelve nights in a row, you could reasonably state, "My roommate is fond of ice cream." Likewise, if you examined a substantial number of poems by Emily Dickinson and noted that each one contained extremely short lines, you could logically conclude that such lines are typical of Dickinson's work. The more instances you can accumulate (of ice cream consumption or short lines), the more nearly certain you can be that your conclusion is sound.

Unlike induction, **deduction** applies general principles to a specific instance. When fully spelled out, deductive reasoning takes the form of a **syllogism**—a set of two premises, or propositions, that lead to a conclusion:

draft
4j

Major Premise:	All students living in Retama Hall are enrolled in the Honors Program.
Minor Premise:	Shelley Rios lives in Retama Hall.
Conclusion:	Shelley Rios is enrolled in the Honors Program.

Induction and deduction rarely function as neatly as the above examples suggest. To get some sense of how reasoning works in practice, consider a familiar example: Thomas Jefferson's Declaration of Independence. While this document is built on a number of subtle deductive and inductive steps, we can see its overall structure in this syllogism:

Major Premise:	People have the right to sever ties with any government that denies them the rights to life, liberty, and the pursuit of happiness.
Minor Premise:	Under the rule of King George III, the British government has denied American colonists these rights.
Conclusion:	American colonists therefore have the right to sever ties with the British government.

Jefferson asks that we accept his major premise as "self-evident." His minor premise, however, is based on a detailed list of inductive observations: King George's "repeated injuries and usurpations" of the American colonists. Jefferson thus merges both types of reasoning—induction and deduction—in building a case for independence.

Needless to say, Jefferson's argument itself is richer and more compelling than an x-ray of his logic. Like Jefferson, you can credit your audience with a commonsense grasp of sound reasoning: you need not move stiffly from premise to conclusion. Nor should you "prove" widely held premises or give a dozen examples when one will do. Simply, you should appeal to the reader's good judgment, basing conclusions on the best available evidence.

4k Watch for faulty reasoning.

The principles of sound reasoning are violated by logical **fallacies,** shortcuts in thinking that undermine your credibility as a writer. While the fallacies may seem technical, they are actually just a convenient way to classify commonsense advice about faulty reasoning. You should be especially alert for such reasoning when you revise an essay. But even before that—as you write the first draft—you should try to avoid logical shortcuts. Doing so can help you forestall major repairs at a later stage of the writing process.

Faulty Generalization

When you base a broad assertion on too little evidence, you make a **faulty generalization.**

AVOID:
x Any child whose parents get divorced suffers major psychological damage.
x The decay of our society has been accelerating every year.

Encyclopedias of support could not establish the plausibility of such sweeping statements. The problem stems not just from insufficient evidence but from broad, ill-defined terms like *major psychological damage* and *decay of our society.* And note the all-inclusive terms *any* and *every.* Whenever you make a claim, watch for these and other telltale words that often signal faulty generalization: *all, always, everyone, never, no, none,* and *only.*

Faulty generalization also occurs when you use a stereotype, assuming, without sufficient evidence, that all members of a group share a certain trait or opinion: x *When faced with a major career decision, women react more emotionally than men do* or x *The Wild-West mentality of Texans makes them wary of gun control legislation.* (For advice on avoiding sexist and racist language, see page 184, 14f.)

**draft
4k**

Oversimplification

Be suspicious when someone makes a simple assertion about a complex issue. A point worth debating almost always involves subtleties that get lost through **oversimplification.**

> AVOID:
> x A state lottery is nothing but a hidden tax on the poor.

A more reasonable assertion would acknowledge the complexity of the issue:

> BETTER:
> • A state lottery would draw a high proportion of its revenue from the poor and would provide only a small and unreliable source of funding for government programs.

Begging the Question

You are **begging the question** when you treat a key point that is in dispute as if it were already established. Suppose, for example, you were arguing for the repeal of motorcycle helmet laws. If you expected readers to take your position seriously, you would have to address the social effects of repealing the laws. If, instead, you assumed that social effects were not in dispute, you would "beg" an important part of the question.

> DON'T:
> x Since helmet laws are designed solely to protect motorcyclists from their own bad judgment, the laws should be repealed. People over eighteen should be allowed to decide for themselves whether they want to wear helmets.

While this argument may seem plausible at first glance, it makes a sweeping assumption that is, in fact, open to debate: *helmet laws are designed solely to protect motorcyclists.* A careful reader would question that assumption: *What about the families of motorcyclists? What about those who pay taxes and insurance premiums for medical care?* To face the issue squarely and convincingly, the writer would

have to address the possible social effects of repealing helmet laws—
perhaps through concession or refutation (p. 53, 41).

Non Sequitur

A **non sequitur** (Latin for "it does not follow") implies a logical connection between two statements when no such connection is evident.

> **ILLOGICAL:**
> x Last year, twenty percent of the students who completed their
> first year at Western State College transferred to other institu-
> tions. The college should initiate a program of small discussion
> courses for first-year students.

Since there is no apparent link between transfer rates and establishing a program of small discussion courses, the second assertion "does
not follow" from the first. If a logical connection *does* exist, the writer
needs to spell it out.

> **LOGICAL:**
> • Last year, twenty percent of the students who completed their
> first year at Western State College transferred to other institu-
> tions. A survey shows that most of these students left because
> they were deeply dissatisfied with large, impersonal lecture
> courses. To address this problem, the college should initiate a
> program of small discussion courses for all first-year students.

Post Hoc Reasoning

When two events follow each other in close sequence, the first does not
necessarily cause the second. Writers who forget this commonsense
principle sometimes lapse into ***post hoc* reasoning** (named for the
Latin *post hoc, ergo propter hoc,* meaning "after this, therefore because of this").

> **DON'T:**
> x Our old oak tree started dying less than two months after the
> house painters spilled a gallon of turpentine under it. I plan to
> sue the painting contractor.

draft
4k

Turpentine *may* have killed the tree, but old age or oak wilt may also be the culprit. The writer implies that A (the spill) caused B (the death), but sequence in time is not enough to establish a causal relationship. The painters are innocent until proven guilty.

Either-Or Reasoning

America: Love It or Leave It, a popular slogan from the 1960s, is a classic case of **either-or reasoning**—that is, pretending that only two alternatives exist when, in fact, others are possible. If you find yourself telling readers to make a simple choice about a complex issue, consider a change in tactics.

DON'T:

x We must build more nuclear power plants or put ourselves totally at the mercy of foreign oil suppliers.

This sentence tries to bully readers into making a clear-cut choice: either build nuclear power plants or rely solely on foreign oil. But a thoughtful reader would ask *What about domestic oil supplies? What about other sources of energy?*

Ad Hominem Reasoning

Still another logical shortcut is criticizing the person who favors a position rather than the position itself. In its crudest form, reasoning **ad hominem** (Latin "to the man") is little more than mudslinging: x *Senator Bardo's son once served time in jail, so how can we trust her to be tough on crime?* Judgments about the senator's stance on crime should rest, of course, on her public record, not on troubles within her family.

Sometimes writers try to discredit ideas by linking them to a particular group, arguing, in effect, "to the group," not to the issue.

DON'T:

x By now we should all recognize the dangers of national health insurance schemes advocated by liberals and socialists.

x The benefits of a higher minimum wage are obvious to everyone except greedy big-business owners who stand to lose by it.

Only a reader strongly predisposed to the writer's viewpoint would take these assertions seriously. General readers expect a more balanced approach.

draft
4l

DO:
- To judge from the British example, national health insurance might impose an intolerable burden on the economy.
- While a higher minimum wage would temporarily lower the profits of some businesses, in the long run it would improve living conditions for many impoverished working people.

Bandwagon Appeal

A **bandwagon appeal** tries to excite our herd instinct: *Join the crowd! Be on the cutting edge!* As advertisers know, such appeals are remarkably effective in selling everything from blue jeans to luxury cars. But in "selling" ideas, you should assume that readers want solid evidence.

DON'T:
x In our democracy, a majority of the population strongly supports capital punishment, so why should we take seriously those who question its morality or legality?

If you dismiss a position because it does not square with the majority view, you ask readers, in effect, to agree with you because other people do. Bandwagon appeals ask readers *not* to think for themselves.

4l   Handle objections through concession and refutation.

For some essays, positive evidence alone will adequately support your thesis. But if your central claim is controversial, you should consider likely objections and respond to them. Not doing so is a gamble. Your readers may not notice, but if they do, your whole argument can fall flat. A wiser course is to grant, or make a **concession** of, minor points that count against your case and to disprove, or make a **refutation** of, points that lack merit.

When you decide to concede an objection, you should do so early and then move quickly to restore your own positive point of view. Observe how the author of this passage grants his opponents a good deal of ground before staking out his own:

> The proponents of drug legalization are right to say that some things will get better. Organized crime will be driven out of the drug business, and there will be a sharp drop in the amount of money (currently about $10 billion per year) that society spends to enforce the drug laws. There will be some reduction in the cost in theft and injury (now about $20 billion) by addicts to get the money to buy prohibited drugs. Internationally, Latin American governments presumably will stop being menaced by drug cartels and will peaceably export cocaine as they now do coffee.
>
> However, this is virtually the limit of the social benefits to be derived from legalization, and they are far outweighed by the costs. . . .
>   —MORTON M. KONDRACKE, "Don't Legalize Drugs"

When you decide to refute a major objection, make sure to state it fairly instead of sneering at it. Let your readers know that you are willing to consider the merits of an opposing position *before* you explain its faults. Notice, for example, how Morton Kondracke, in another passage from the essay just cited, calmly summarizes a point against his case before refuting it:

> Legalizers also argue that the government could tax legal drug sales and use the money to pay for anti-drug education programs and treatment centers. But total taxes collected right now from alcohol sales at the local, state, and federal levels come to only $13.1 billion per year—which is a pittance compared with the damage done to society as a result of alcohol abuse. The same would have to be true for drugs—and any tax that resulted in an official drug price that was higher than the street price would open the way once again for black markets and organized crime.

5 Collaborating and Revising

Many students are willing enough to revise their work but are held back by two misconceptions. First, they suppose that revision begins only when an essay is nearly ready to be turned in; and second, they think that revision involves only a tidying up of word choice, spelling, punctuation, and usage. But experienced writers revise their prose even as they first produce it—adding, deleting, replacing, and rearranging material at every opportunity (p. 3, 1a). They always assume that a draft can be improved. And they stand ready to make conceptual and organizational changes as well as editorial ones.

5a Learn to give constructive advice as a peer editor.

Increasingly, composition instructors have been asking students to collaborate as **peer editors** of one another's writing. Working in pairs or in small groups, students take turns reading drafts and making suggestions for revision. Although collaboration has only recently become standard practice in the college classroom, conscientious writers—students and professionals alike—have always known how important it is to solicit opinions about their work. Precisely because they stand outside your thoughts and feelings, your classmates may spot problems that you have overlooked.

As a peer editor, you should offer encouragement as well as criticism. Try to find something praiseworthy in your classmate's draft, and mention that feature before offering any criticism. For example: *Your main idea is clear and interesting* or *Your two paragraphs about Halloween customs are full of vivid details.* When you do criticize, stress possibilities for further development or clarification. Try something like *Does this paragraph contradict your third paragraph?* or *I've lost track of your main idea. Should you reempha-size it here?* Questions can be especially helpful because they sound polite and unthreatening and because they pass the initiative for revision back to the writer.

When offering advice, you want to highlight large issues—the writer's thesis, organization, evidence, and tone. And while you may also point out errors of usage, punctuation, and spelling, you should avoid leaving the impression that you were simply waiting to pounce on such errors. To make sure you cover major categories and maintain a sense of proportion, use a standard set of questions to critique a classmate's work. Something as simple as this brief list can guide your first efforts at collaboration.

BASIC QUESTIONS FOR PEER EDITORS

1. Does the writer state a clear, definite thesis and stay with it throughout the essay?
2. Is the essay organized effectively? What improvements do you recommend?
3. What points need further—or less—development?
4. Are the opening and closing paragraphs effective? How could they be improved?
5. Do you see any errors of usage, punctuation, or spelling that need attention? Mark examples on the draft.

As you gain skill in responding to your classmates' work, you may want to use a more detailed Peer Editing Worksheet like the one on pp. 59–60. And when revising your own work, you should apply an even fuller set of criteria (see the Checklist for Revision on the inside front cover).

5b Note the features of a peer-edited essay.

To see how a peer editor works, study the following draft, which Patricia Rodriguez wrote in her first-semester composition course. She and her classmates had just finished several assigned readings about language and personal identity. They were then asked to write a 500-word essay explaining how some aspect of their spoken language helped define who they are. A completed Peer Editing Worksheet follows Rodriguez's draft.

coll/
rev
5b

Tex-Mex

context
?

I grew up in the Valley speaking both English and Spanish. Most of my friends were brought up in nearly

cs the same way, therefore we all pretty much speak and understand two languages. Out of this situation came a new language we call Tex-Mex.

Tex-Mex is often the result of a speaker starting off a sentence in one language (English or Spanish), and ending it in another. It is also spoken when a

agr person substitute an occasional English word for a

cs Spanish word, sometimes the opposite occurs. Someone will start a sentence or conversation in English and

more
ples finish it in Spanish. For example, I usuly say, "I

sp want some agua," the Spanish "agua" meaning water.

Tex-Mex is also produced out of necessity or laziness. If one can't remember a certain word in Spanish, he/she will often substitute the English equivalent and add new syllables. The result is a new Spanish word. This is how "watchamos," meaning "we watch," came to be. The same can be done with Spanish words.

more
examples

Tex-Mex is simple enough for anyone who knows both languages. The language is especially easy for

choppy

teenagers to use. They are the founders of the
language. My friends and I became the largest
perpetrators of the language. We used it all the time. *right word*
It was easy for us. It fit our needs. It was the
perfect language, or so we thought. The elders of our
predominantly Mexican families soon let us know how
badly we had "tainted" two otherwise beautiful
languages. According to them, we had made a mockery
out of both languages. Tex-Mex is just not accepted or
understood by people over fourty. *sp*

In the Valley Tex-Mex is spoken so frequently that
no one seems to realize anything different, but to
someone who only speaks either English or Spanish, a
person who speaks Tex-Mex is speaking a foreign
language. All-English or all-Spanish speakers can only
understand bits and pieces of a Tex-Mex speaker's

give example?

conversation. Tex-Mex speakers have to continually
stop and explain what they have just said. As a fluent
Tex-Mex speaker, I can tell you that this is a very
annoying process to go through.

Tex-Mex is confusing to some, but it gives the
Valley a unique touch. The Valley is a product of two
different cultures. It is fitting that such a special
place should have it's own representational language. *its*
Tex-Mex is the blending of two to make one.

Peer Editing Worksheet

Writer's name *Patricia Rodriguez*

Title of paper *Tex-Mex*

Peer editor *Matthew Makusky*

1. After an initial reading, what is your main impression of the draft? What strikes you as its strongest and weakest features?

   Patty—Interesting topic! I learned something new in reading the draft, but I wish you had given more examples to support and explain your ideas. Also, you need to edit for grammar, spelling, etc.—Matt

2. Is the thesis (a) clearly and prominently stated, (b) adequately limited, and (c) interesting enough to merit development? Suggest improvements.

   The idea in your last ¶ about Tex-Mex blending two cultures looks like your main (and best) point. Should you move it up to the intro. ¶? Then could you revise the other ¶s slightly to link them to that point?

3. Is the essay well organized? What could the writer do to improve the arrangement of ideas and examples?

   Looks OK. I like the way you describe Tex-Mex in ¶s 2–3 before you show how it affects life in the Valley.

4. Are the writer's points adequately developed? Where would you like to see more evidence or explanation?

   Should you give more examples of Tex-Mex in ¶s 2, 3, & 5?

5. Is the tone consistently appropriate to the writer's purpose? If not, explain.

   No problems overall, but your opening sentences sound flat. Can you liven them up?

6. Does the essay begin effectively by engaging your interest and setting a clear direction for the paper? Is the title appropriate? Suggest improvements.

   Intro. and title are OK, but they could do more to reveal your main point. Should you give more background about the Valley for readers who haven't been there?

7. Is each paragraph in the body of the essay well organized, unified, and coherent? Suggest improvements.

   Since ¶s 2 and 3 cover the same topic, maybe you should combine them. Also, you might give ¶4 a stronger focus by highlighting the "generation gap" idea.

8. Does the essay end effectively by giving an appropriate sense of completion? Suggest improvements.

   Looks good, but if you move the "culture" point to the first ¶, you will have to revise the conclusion.

9. Check the style of the writing. Are the sentences clear and varied? Are there adequate transitions within and between paragraphs? Are words chosen effectively? Mark suggested improvements on the draft.

   Watch for choppiness. You might combine the short sentences and/or add transitions within ¶4.

10. Do you notice errors in usage, punctuation, mechanics, or spelling? Mark examples on the draft.

    I spotted two comma splices and a s-v agreement problem. Lab or handbook can help. Also, check your final version for spelling errors.

5c   Welcome suggestions for improving your draft.

Professional writers know that the difference between effective and dreary prose is usually not sheer talent but a writer's willingness to accept criticism. To be sure, you cannot always count on your peer editor to supply the kind of detailed advice Patricia Rodriguez got from hers (5b). Ultimately, *you* must decide which advice to take and which to disregard. But if your peer editor lets you down, you should keep showing your draft to others until you get an objective judgment. A roommate, a writing lab tutor, or your instructor may be willing to help. Sometimes it takes no more than one key suggestion to spark a new line of thought or prompt a major structural improvement.

Let your peer editor know that you want no punches pulled. Without reassurance on this point, some peer editors—especially if they happen to be your friends—will waffle or, worse, give general praise when you want specific criticism. If your peer editor is not equipped with a list of questions (p. 56) or a Peer Editing Worksheet (p. 59), supply one yourself. You may find some of your editor's suggestions painful, but if they help you clarify your thesis or trim the fat from your prose, you will end by being grateful.

To see how Patricia Rodriguez used the advice of her peer editor, read the next three sections (5d–f). The final version of her essay appears on page 68, 5f.

5d Make large-scale revisions.

In reviewing your first draft, you and your peer editor may find major gaps in logic, contradictory ideas, poorly developed paragraphs, even a badly flawed thesis. You should be prepared, then, to make major conceptual and organizational changes once you have a draft in hand. *Revision* means to "see again," and you should be willing to do just that. If you decide that the central idea of your essay is one you no longer believe, abandon it and move in a new direction. If you realize that you lack the evidence to support a key point, "see again" whether you can muster that evidence, either through further reading or by exploring your topic in greater depth (p. 16, 1h). And if your essay strikes you or your peer editor as disorganized, rewrite and rearrange until you fix the problem. Fortunately, you will not have to make such drastic changes in all your drafts, but accomplished writers always stand ready to revise in fundamental ways.

CONSIDER MAKING THESE FUNDAMENTAL CHANGES

- Recast your thesis to highlight the point and purpose of your essay (Chapter 2).
- Reorganize your essay (Chapter 3).
- Reconsider your voice, stance, and tone (Chapter 4, 4c–e).
- Rethink your evidence—adding, deleting, or altering supporting material (Chapter 4, 4f–l).

CONSIDER MAKING THESE FUNDAMENTAL CHANGES

- Reshape paragraphs that lack unity and continuity (Chapter 7).
- Redevelop poorly organized, skimpy, or rambling paragraphs (Chapters 8 and 9).
- Refine your opening and closing paragraphs (Chapter 10).

After considering the advice of her peer editor, Patricia Rodriguez decided to make a number of fundamental changes in her "Tex-Mex" essay (p. 57). She wanted, first of all, to improve her opening paragraph, giving additional background information and making her tone more lively. Next, she planned to sharpen her focus by moving the key idea in her final paragraph closer to the beginning. And finally, she hoped to improve the development of her essay by adding more detail, especially to the second and third paragraphs.

Instead of trying to accomplish all her goals at once, Rodriguez worked in cycles, attending to one problem at a time. Here, for example, is a second draft of her opening paragraph, in which she tried to supply more detail and enliven her tone (her original introduction appears on page 57).

SECOND DRAFT:

Growing up in the Rio Grande Valley of Texas, I was
exposed to my share of languages. The first language I
learned was Spanish. My two grandmother's raised me,
and they only spoke Spanish, so naturally I learned
Spanish first. As I grew older, I learned English. In
everyday activities I now use English more than
Spanish, but Spanish is still a part of my vocabulary.
Most of my friends were brought up in nearly the same
way, therefore we all pretty much speak and understand
two languages. Out of this situation came a new

```
language we call Tex-Mex.  Generally, it is the mixing

of English and Spanish in a person's vocabulary and

conversation.
```

Next, Rodriguez turned attention to her thesis. She wanted to highlight the main point of her essay in the opening paragraph, letting readers know that her purpose went well beyond merely describing Tex-Mex. Here is the third draft of her introduction. Note how she not only emphasizes her thesis but also makes a number of less obvious improvements in sentence structure and wording.

THIRD DRAFT:

```
Growing up in the Rio Grande Valley of Texas, I was

exposed to two languages--English and Spanish.  Since

my Spanish-speaking grandmothers raised me, I

naturally learned Spanish first.  As I grew older, I

learned to speak English.  Today I use English more

than Spanish, but Spanish is still a fundamental part

of my vocabulary.  Most of my friends were brought up

in nearly the same way, and so we all speak and

understand two languages.  Out of these two languages

comes a third one called Tex-Mex--the mixing of English

and Spanish in a person's vocabulary and conversation.

While some adults disapprove of teenagers speaking Tex-

Mex, I believe that this language is a fitting

reflection of that part of Texas which is known for its

unique blending of Hispanic and Anglo culture.
```

Yet another version of this opening—with a number of stylistic improvements—appears in Rodriguez's finished essay (p. 68). Her final copy also shows other instances of large-scale revision, including improved paragraph development. Compare, for example, the second and third paragraphs in her first draft (p. 57) with the more detailed second paragraph in the final essay (p. 68).

For another example of large-scale revision, see Chapter 6, pages 78–86.

5e   Make editorial revisions.

Though editorial revision—improvements in sentences, word choice, and conventions—is rarely the most important kind, it does cover the greatest number of problems. You will find, too, that editorial changes often overlap with more fundamental ones. Improving the unity and continuity of a paragraph, for example, may involve revising sentences for better subordination. And achieving a consistent tone throughout your essay may require several minor changes in word choice. In every case, effective editorial revision means putting the reader's convenience ahead of yours, making sure that details of expression support the fundamental ideas you want to express.

FEATURE	REVISE FOR	HELPS READER TO
sentences (Chapters 11–13)	clarity, subordination, emphasis, variety	follow ideas, tell which ideas are major, remain engaged
words (Chapters 14–16)	appropriateness, economy, liveliness	get clear and vivid information, participate imaginatively
usage, punctuation, conventions (Chapters 17–36)	conformity with standard written practice	concentrate on substance of essay
citation form (Chapters 39–40)	accuracy, fullness, consistency	have access to sources with a minimum of distraction

For an idea of how instructors and peer editors typically draw attention to editorial problems and how students then revise, consider the following paragraph from Patricia Rodriguez's "Tex-Mex" essay. The marginal **symbols for comment and revision** (see the inside back cover) point to particular errors and stylistic flaws within the paragraph.

**coll/
rev
5e**

FIRST DRAFT:

[Tex-Mex is often the result of a speaker starting off] a *wdy*

sentence in one language (English or Spanish), and *p*

ref ending it in another. It is also spoken when a <u>person</u>

agr substitute an occasional English word for a Spanish

cs word, sometimes the opposite occurs. [Someone will *red*

start a sentence or conversation in English and finish

it in Spanish.] For example, I <u>usuly</u> say, "I want some *sp*

agua," the Spanish "agua" meaning water.

In the actual revision of her essay, Rodriguez addressed most of the indicated editorial problems by rethinking this entire paragraph. But had she chosen to repair the problems one by one, the diagnoses and likely remedies would have been as follows:

SYMBOL	PROBLEM	REVISION
wdy (15b–d)	wordy expression	Tex-Mex speakers often start . . . and end in. . . .
p (25–30)	punctuation error	[delete unnecessary comma]
ref (22i–m)	faulty pronoun reference	Tex-Mex . . .
agr (19c–n)	faulty agreement of subject and verb	. . . person substitutes . . .
cs (18b)	comma splice	. . . word. Sometimes . . .

SYMBOL	PROBLEM	REVISION
red (15b)	redundant (repeats information in the first sentence)	[delete whole sentence]
sp (33)	misspelled word	. . . usually . . .

In practice, editorial revision is rarely as tidy as the above chart suggests, but if Rodriguez had incorporated the recommended editorial changes as given, her revised paragraph would have looked like this:

REVISION (HAND-EDITED):   *Speakers often start*

Tex-Mex ~~is often the result of a speaker starting off~~ a sentence in one language (English or Spanish) /and end~~ing it~~ in another.   ~~It~~ is also spoken when a person substitute *s* an occasional English word for a Spanish word /. *S*ometimes the opposite occurs.   ~~Someone will start a sentence or conversation in English and finish it in Spanish.~~   For example, I ~~usuly~~ *usually* say, "I want some agua," the Spanish "agua" meaning water.

REVISION (TYPED COPY):

Tex-Mex speakers often start a sentence in one language (English or Spanish) and end in another.   Tex-Mex is also spoken when a person substitutes as occasional English word for a Spanish word.   Sometimes the opposite occurs.   For example, I usually say, "I want some agua," the Spanish "agua" meaning water.

Note how the editorial changes shorten the paragraph and highlight its real problem, skimpiness (p. 108, 8d). In her final version (p. 63), Rodriguez addresses that problem by fleshing out the description of Tex-Mex. For further examples of editorial revision, compare Rodriguez's entire draft (p. 57) with her finished essay (p. 68), and study the changes in the sample essay on pages 83–86, Chapter 6.

coll/
rev
5f

5f Make your title definite.

You need not worry about a title until you have completed at least one draft. In fact, the only title that matters is the one you give the final version of your essay. An early title—like Patricia Rodriguez's "Tex-Mex"—will probably be no more than a general indication of your subject matter.

Once you have a definite idea of your essay's point, try to find a title that expresses it. Thus, if you are asked to write about revision, do not settle for "Revision" or "Revising a College Essay"; such tone-less titles suggest that you have no thesis at all. Instead, try something like "The Agony of Revision," "Revision as Discovery," or "Is an Essay Ever Really Finished?" Each of these versions tells the reader that you have found something definite to say.

That impression will be especially strong if you can make your title vivid by using a figure of speech (see Chapter 16), a telling expression, or a relevant quotation to anticipate your thesis. One common device is to combine such a phrase with a more straightforwardly informative subtitle:

- Dying to Be Thin: The Lure of High-Risk Fad Diets
- "Zero at the Bone": Metaphors of Coldness in Emily Dickinson's Poetry

As the final step in revising her "Tex-Mex" essay, Patricia Rodriguez looked for a title that would forecast her point about the Hispanic-Anglo culture of the Rio Grande Valley. She considered "Tex-Mex: Language of the Valley" but settled, finally, on the more informative "Tex-Mex: Two Cultures, One Language."

Here is the final version of her essay:

Tex-Mex: Two Cultures, One Language

Growing up in the Rio Grande Valley of Texas, I was exposed to two languages--English and Spanish. Since my Spanish-speaking grandmothers raised me, I naturally learned Spanish first. English came later, after I moved into the public world beyond my immediate family. Today I use English more than Spanish, but Spanish is still a basic part of who I am. In high school, most of my friends were also bilingual. Out of our two languages came a third one we call Tex-Mex--the mixing of English and Spanish in a person's vocabulary and conversation. While some adults disapprove of teenagers speaking Tex-Mex, I see this language as a fitting reflection of the Valley--a unique blend of Hispanic and Anglo cultures.

Tex-Mex speakers express themselves in several ways. They often start a sentence in one language and end in another: "Sacale punta al [sharpen the] pencil." Sometimes they blend Spanish and English in their conversation: "Donde estabas [where were you]? I wanted to talk with you about el gato [the cat]. I think está [he is] sick." If I'm with my friends and feel thirsty, I might say, "I want a glass of agua [water]," even though I know the English word. Sometimes, however, when I can't remember a certain word in Spanish, I will quickly substitute the English

equivalent and add new syllables. The result is a new
Spanish word like "el trucka [the truck]" or
"watchamos/huachamos [we watch]."

coll/
rev
5f

Although Valley residents of all ages speak Tex-
Mex, it often becomes a source of conflict between the
generations. The language is especially popular with
young Hispanics, who see it as a form of slang that is
fun and easy to use. Speaking Tex-Mex, for example,
helps me and my friends feel that we are part of a
select group. The elders in our predominantly Mexican-
American families see it differently. They tell us how
badly we taint two otherwise beautiful languages.
According to them, we make a mockery of both English
and Spanish, but their opinion has done little to
discourage young people in the Valley from speaking
Tex-Mex.

In fact, Valley residents speak Tex-Mex so
frequently that many people don't give it a second
thought. To someone who speaks only English or
Spanish, however, Tex-Mex can be a foreign language.
All-English or all-Spanish speakers only understand
bits and pieces of a Tex-Mex conversation and are
constantly asking what was just said. When talking
with my grandmother, for example, I often have to
"translate" Tex-Mex words that slip into my Spanish.
And sometimes I have to force myself to stay in one

language or the other when a non-Tex-Mex speaker takes part in the conversation.

Tex-Mex may confuse some, but I think it gives the Rio Grande Valley a unique flavor. The Valley is a product of two very different cultures. It is fitting that such a place should have a language that blends those cultures in a single voice.

5g   Test your draft against a checklist for revision.

Since you cannot always count on having a friendly critic available, and since even a peer editor will see only a preliminary version of your essay, you yourself will need to test your drafts against commonly held standards. A Peer Editing Worksheet (p. 59) can help you to begin seeing how those standards apply to an early draft, but eventually you will want more thorough guidance. For this purpose, consult the Checklist for Revision found on the inside front cover of this book. Running through its twenty-one questions should help you pinpoint remaining problems and locate the relevant discussions of them elsewhere in the book.

5h   Follow standard form in preparing your final copy.

No matter how many changes you make between drafts, the essay you eventually submit should look unscarred, or nearly so. It should also meet certain technical requirements of form. The following advice reflects general practice and should be followed whenever your instructor does not specify something different.

1. Type your essay if possible, using one side of standard (8$\frac{1}{2}$″ × 11″) unlined white paper of ordinary weight. If you must write longhand, choose paper with widely spaced lines or write on every other line. Type with an unfaded black ribbon, or write in dark ink. If you are using a dot-matrix computer

coll/
rev
5h

printer, check the print quality and insert a new ribbon if necessary. Remove the perforated sides of continuous-feed paper.

2. If you are submitting a title page, arrange it like the model on page 500, and repeat *the title only* on your first page of text, as on page 502.

3. If you are not submitting a title page, treat your first page like the model on page 83.

4. If you are asked to supply a thesis statement and/or an outline, put them on a separate page, as on page 501.

5. Allow at least one-inch margins on all four sides of each page of your main text. Your right margins need not be even. In a handwritten essay, be sure to leave as much space as in a typewritten one.

6. If you have a separate title page, leave it unnumbered; begin numbering on the next page, placing your last name and un-punctuated Arabic numerals (1, 2, 3) in the upper right corners of the pages (follow the sample on pages 502–524). If you do not have a title page, number *all* pages in this manner (see the model on pages 83–86).

7. Double-space your whole essay, including any reference list, endnotes, or bibliography (p. 533, 39d). Single-space any foot-notes. Unless your instructor tells you otherwise, double-space indented quotations (p. 354, 29h).

8. Indent the first line of each paragraph by five type-spaces; that is, press the space bar five times and then begin typing. In a handwritten essay, indent by about an inch. Do not skip extra lines between paragraphs. When a quoted passage is long enough to require indention (see p. 354, 29h), generally indent it by ten spaces—fewer if a quoted poem uses very long lines.

9. Retype any pages on which you have had to make more than a few last-minute changes. Otherwise, type those changes or write them clearly in ink, using the following conventions:

coll/
rev
5h

a. Remove unwanted letters with a diagonal slash:

indigestio/n

b. Remove unwanted words by running a line through them:

~~nasty~~ slur

c. Replace a letter by putting the new letter above your slash:

compo/ition
    ^s

d. Replace words by putting the new word above your canceled one:

               writer
please every ~~reader~~

e. Add words or letters by putting a caret (∧) at the point of insertion and placing the extra words or letters above it:

      notable
Another feature of this device
      ∧

f. Separate words or letters by placing a vertical line between them:

steel and|iron

g. Close up separated letters with a curved line connecting them from above:

hic⌢cup

h. Transpose (reverse) letters or words with a curved enclosing line:

Alpce. Carroll Lewis

i. Indicate a paragraph break by inserting the paragraph symbol before the first word of the new paragraph:

depends on development. ¶Transitions, too, have a

certain importance.

j. Run two paragraphs together by connecting them with an arrow and writing no¶ in the margin:

She has found a way of turning "nothing" time into

 pleasure or learning.⟩
↳Isn't that better than having some trivial
chitchat on the sidewalk?

10. Carefully proofread your final copy, looking especially for typing errors. Check all quotations against your notes or, better, against the printed passages.

11. Make sure you have assembled your pages in order. Fasten them with a paper clip unless your instructor specifies another method.

12. Keep a photocopy of your essay until you get the graded original back, and keep the original at least until the course is over. These steps will protect you should your instructor mislay an essay or misrecord a grade.

For the forming and spacing of punctuation marks, see Chapter 30. For citation form, see Chapter 39 (MLA style) or Chapter 40 (APA style).

6 One Essay from Start to Finish

Sarah Altschul, a student in a first-year composition course, found herself with a week and a half to complete the following assignment:

> In our reading and class discussion, we have considered how traditions reveal the attitudes of a group or a society. Write a 500-word essay about a particular tradition in the United States (a holiday custom, a political ritual, an educational practice, etc.). You may analyze the tradition or develop an opinion about it. In either case, you should suggest what the tradition reveals about American attitudes.

Sarah began searching for a topic by reviewing her class notes. She was struck initially by two possibilities: eating habits and sports traditions. Knowing that either of these subject areas (p. 4, 1b) would have to be narrowed drastically, she did some brainstorming (p. 14, 1g) about American sports traditions:

> "Big" traditions
> —Super Bowl, World Series
> —rowdy behavior, parties, betting
> Professional wrestling / boxing
> —organized violence?
> —like gladiators?
> Little League
> —pressure from coaches / parents
> —girls softball division = second-class status
> —how does the L.L. tradition affect kids?

—what does it say about attitudes toward competition / toward girls vs.
    boys?
TV football
    —holiday tradition?
    —great tradition—women cook dinner / men watch game!
Do sports traditions stress individual over group?
    —see article on U.S. vs. Japanese customs or one about swimming in
        Brazil vs. USA
High school sports "rituals"—marching band, cheerleaders, dance teams, etc.

While some of the ideas on her list struck Sarah as usable, none of
them sparked her interest. In looking through a stack of old magazines in her dorm lounge the next day, however, she came across
something that did: an article about a recent beauty pageant. A year
earlier, a classmate at her high school had won a local pageant, and
she remembered being surprised by the publicity and excitement
surrounding the victory. Pageants were a well-established American
tradition, and they seemed to reveal a great deal about American
attitudes—especially attitudes toward women. To pursue this line of
thought, Sarah jotted down some preliminary notes (p. 10, 1e):

—Pageants are superficial and trivial—they value women only for their
    looks.
—Talent & interview sections are token efforts—all that counts is
    pretty face and good figure.
—Must be big $ in pageants or TV wouldn't be covering them.
—Pageants seem old-fashioned and outdated, not in touch with reality of
    women today, but they are still very popular (prime-time TV coverage).
—Do pageants exploit women? Maybe a topic here? But no one is forced to
    participate. Don't want to argue that pageants should be "banned."
—Maybe develop opinion that they exploit and demean women—sex objects /
    swim-suit / evening gown competition, etc.

Since she had a strong opinion about beauty pageants, Sarah decided to make her main purpose argumentative (p. 9, 1d). She knew she could support her opinion with firsthand evidence—she had seen pageants on television and was personally acquainted with a winning contestant. To explore her ideas further, she used focused brainstorming (p. 16, 1h):

Opinion: Pageants demean / exploit women.

—Profit motive—someone getting rich off the contests? TV networks? contest organizers?
—Image of docile, well-mannered woman, the ideal "lady"—but whose ideal?
—Posing and parading on stage for (mostly male) judges.
—"Talent" competition—baton twirling / tap dancing.
—Emphasis on physical beauty—perfect doll-like figure.
—Superficial "interviews" on stage with celebrity host.
—Passive, polite, <u>constantly</u> smiling contestants.
—Women like clones / robots / cardboard cutouts.

Reading through her notes, Sarah decided that her main point should be not the exploitation of women who, after all, voluntarily participate in beauty pageants but, rather, the way pageants create harmful stereotypes of women. With that idea in mind, she wrote a trial thesis (p. 19, 2a):

Beauty pageants have a negative effect on society in general because they create demeaning stereotypes of women as mere sex objects.

To get an outside opinion on this thesis, Sarah consulted her roommate, who said that the phrase "negative effect on society in general" seemed vague and exaggerated. The roommate also wondered if pageants actually "create" stereotypes. With these comments in mind, Sarah redrafted her thesis several times and finally produced this version:

> *Beauty pageants perpetuate outdated stereotypes about women, suggesting that the "ideal" woman is passive, superficial, and valuable only for her physical beauty.*

Although Sarah was not completely satisfied with her thesis, she decided to move forward, knowing that she could modify her idea, if necessary, after getting advice from a peer editor. Before starting her draft, she wrote this scratch outline (p. 30, 3c):

> 1. *Intro ¶ —state thesis.*
> 2. *Typical pageant emphasizes superficial aspects of women—looks, not brains (despite talent and interview competitions).*
> 3. *Glamour and glitter of pageant promote idea that the winner is "our ideal"—the all-American woman.*
> 4. *But the "ideal" is far from the reality of women's lives—a stereotype that doesn't fit the variety of roles open to women today.*
> 5. *This stereotype reflects an underlying attitude toward women still popular in USA.*
> 6. *Conclusion—we should be more critical, more aware of what pageants tell us about our attitudes / values.*

Sarah wrote her first draft in one sitting (p. 35, 4a), pausing only to consult her outline and notes and to reread what she had already written. Here is the typed copy that she took to class the next day and got back with marginal comments from her peer editor, Cheryl McCabe:

Choppy

Do Beauty Pageants Demean Women?

Beauty pageants today seem to be as popular as
ever. It is interesting to consider what they reveal
about the attitudes of our society. Many people
believe they are a relic of the past. Most women today
no longer see their ideal model as "Miss America." I
agree. Beauty pageants perpetuate outdated stereotypes
about women, suggesting that the "ideal" woman is
passive, superficial, and valuable only for her
physical beauty.

good

A typical national beauty pageant emphasizes superficial aspects of women--looks, not brains. True,
there are talent contests and two-minute "interviews" *comma*
but these are not the real focus of pageants. Women
pose on stage waving and smiling. There is always a
swimsuit competition and an evening gown competition.
Both of these events stress the contestants looks. *apos*
Their figures and the way they look in expensive designer gowns are what really decide the winner.

You may wonder what all the fuss is about. But I
believe that these pageants promote a horrible stereo- *seems*
type of women. [The role model they offer is one of a *exaggerate*
woman who has succeeded because of her looks and figure *wordy*
alone. And the contestants today are even screened and
grilled to make sure they have nothing abnormal or im-

moral in their past lives. We want our all-American
"ideal" to look great <u>and</u> have a "perfect" background.

But this "ideal" is a far cry from the reality of
women's lives; it places women in an artificial, outdated role. Today's women have gained an equal place
with men on the job, in politics, and in <u>other aspects</u> *such as?.*
<u>of life</u>. The stereotype of the glamorous beauty queen
was never in touch with reality, but today it seems
more unrealistic than ever. There is nothing wrong
sp with <u>haveing</u> heroes and models, but [beauty pageants offer us clones, not real women.] *good*

Does the beauty queen image of women reflect <u>under-</u>
<u>lying attitudes</u> still popular in the USA? Yes, if the
popularity of beauty competitions is an indication.
The pageants are shown on prime-time TV and the winners
are featured on talk shows and interviewed by the me-
cs dia, therefore it appears that many Americans do take
beauty contests seriously.
It doesn't explain what the attitudes are.

I'm not sure who the main audience is for beauty
pageants, but whoever watches these horrible spectacals *exagg.*
should think more about what they tell us about our un- *sp*
derlying attitudes towards women.

And here is the completed Peer Editing Worksheet that Sarah got back from Cheryl:

Writer's name *Sarah Altschul*

Title of paper *Do Beauty Pageants Demean Women?*

Peer editor *Cheryl McCabe*

1. Does the writer state a clear, definite thesis and stay with it throughout the essay?

   Sarah—The thesis comes through loud and clear. You're entitled to your totally negative view of pageants, but since some readers may disagree, watch out for language ("horrible," etc.) that prejudges the issue. To be fair-minded, you might want to acknowledge other viewpoints through concession or refutation. See p. 53 of BHW.

2. Is the essay organized effectively? What improvements do you recommend?

   Looks OK. Good transitions btwn. paragraphs. But maybe you could combine 2d and 3d ¶s. They develop a single point.

3. What points need further—or less—development?

   Should you give more balanced evidence? Some women do enter pageants to win scholarships so they can pay for college. There's also more emph. today on talent / brains. Does 5th ¶ need more examples / explanation? It doesn't really discuss the "underlying attitudes" mentioned in the opening sentence.

4. Are the opening and closing paragraphs effective? How could they be improved?

   The two opening sentences are sort of dull. Conclusion is also weak— seems tacked on. Chapter 10 of BHW might help.

5. Do you see any errors in usage, punctuation, or spelling that need attention? Mark examples on the draft.

   I marked a few errors. Once you finish another draft, you may want to revise line by line for clear sentences. Overall a good start.—Cheryl

Sarah was unpleasantly surprised by the claim that her argument was too one-sided, but a rereading of the draft convinced her that Cheryl was right. Discussing her ideas with Cheryl and another classmate helped Sarah revise her essay in fundamental ways. Here, for instance, is her modified thesis statement:

> *Although the organizers of beauty pageants have modified the contests in response to changing attitudes towards women, the pageants continue to reinforce outdated stereotypes, suggesting that the "ideal" woman is conventional, submissive, and valuable mainly for her physical beauty.*

And here is a new paragraph she drafted to acknowledge likely opposition to her main point (p. 53, 4l):

DRAFT:

```
It is true that beauty contests have changed in the
last few years.  This may be due to criticism and
declining popularity.  There is more emphasis on scol-
arships, and many women enter to get money to go to
school.  On one TV pageant there were contestants who
were in graduate school.  Which goes against the image
of the "brainless beauty."  In judging pageants, the
emphasis is now on the contestants speaking skills.
Heavy emphasis is put on long behind the scenes
interviews with judges, not the short ones shown on TV.
```

Sarah felt that this paragraph would give her argument some balance without undercutting her thesis. Before adding the paragraph to her essay, she made several editorial changes (p. 64, 5e):

one
essay
6

REVISED:

It is true that beauty contests have changed in the ~~past~~ last few years, *giving more attention to brains* ~~This may be due to criticism and~~ *and talent. Pageants now offer more* ~~declining popularity. There is more emphasis on~~ scholarships, and many women enter to get money to go to school. On one TV pageant, *several* ~~there were~~ contestants <u>who</u> were ~~in~~ graduate *students — definitely not* ~~school. Which goes against the image~~ ~~of the~~ "brainless beaut*ies*." *Change is also obvious* ~~In judging pageants, the~~ *in the* ~~emphasis is now on the~~ contestants' speaking skills. *Much of the competition is now based on detailed* ~~Heavy emphasis is put on long behind the scenes~~ interviews with judges, not *on the televised swimsuit* ~~the short ones shown on TV.~~ *and evening gown competitions*.

The final copy of Sarah's essay begins on the next page. Notice these revisions:

1. a new title and an improved opening paragraph

2. the added "concession" paragraph (see draft versions above), with further editorial changes

3. new examples in the third paragraph

4. deletion of the paragraph beginning "You may wonder . . ." (see p. 78)

5. redeveloped fourth and fifth paragraphs

6. a new closing paragraph

7. extensive editorial changes throughout, making sentences clearer and more varied

Note that in preparing the final copy of her essay, Sarah used margins and other conventions recommended by the Modern Language Association (MLA). She double–spaced throughout and placed her last name and a page number in the upper right corner of each page, including the first. For a sample title page following MLA conventions, see p. 500.

↑
|
1″
↓

↑
1/2″
↓
Altschul 1

Sarah Altschul

English 1310.09

Mr. Parigi

2 December 1992

The Beauty Queen: Our Ideal?

As the newly crowned Miss America waves at a
television audience of millions, the pageant's theme
song announces, "There she is . . . your ideal." But
is she our "ideal"? For some Americans, the beauty
pageant is a relic of the past, a reminder of
traditional attitudes toward women that still influence
our thinking more than we like to admit. Despite
recent changes in emphasis, beauty pageants continue to
perpetuate outdated stereotypes, suggesting that the
"ideal" woman is conventional, submissive, and valuable
mainly for her physical beauty.

It is true that beauty pageants have changed in
the past few years, giving more attention to brains and
talent. Even local pageants now offer attractive
scholarships, and many women compete in order to help
pay college expenses. In one recently televised
pageant, several contestants were graduate students--

↑
1″
↓

Altschul 2

definitely not "brainless beauties." Change is also obvious in the greater emphasis on contestants' ideas and speaking skills. Much of the competition is now based on detailed offstage interviews with the judges, not on the televised swimsuit and evening gown competitions.

But despite these changes, a nationally broadcast beauty pageant still gives a superficial image of women. Contestants pose on stage, waving and smiling. They participate in song and dance routines that emphasize their physical skills and beauty. They parade before the judges wearing swimsuits--and high heels. And they voice safe, conventional opinions in two-minute interviews with a "celebrity host." At least for the television audience, most of the competition centers on the contestants' superficial appearance. We get the impression that women care most about physical beauty, glamorous clothes, and elaborate hairdos.

This impression, however, is not in touch with the lives of most women today. The illusion of the glamorous beauty queen gave way long ago to a greater realism about women's roles. My own sister, for example, is so busy with her family and career that she has little time to think about how glamorous she might be. And most of my female friends wear tennis shoes more often than they wear high heels--not to mention high heels and swimsuits! There is certainly nothing wrong with having heroes and models, or with an occasional fantasy, but beauty pageants offer us caricatures, not real women.

Does the beauty-queen image reveal an underlying attitude toward women that is still prevalent today? Maybe so. After all, pageants remain enormously popular with television viewers. And contest winners routinely appear on talk shows and in glossy magazines. Whether consciously or not, many of us still may buy into the idea that the "perfect" woman is one who succeeds by being beautiful, glamorous, and conventional. And that belief has a darker side: independent, original, unconventional women lack "femininity."

While beauty pageants are not likely to fade into the past anytime soon, we should at least take a

Altschul 4

critical look at this popular tradition. If a
society's traditions reveal its fundamental values and
attitudes, maybe beauty pageants tell us that we still
too often want women to be sex objects or goddesses
instead of real people.

II
PARAGRAPHS

Paragraphs

Although each sentence conveys meaning, an essay is not a sequence of sentences but the development of one central point through a series of steps. Those steps are, or ought to be, paragraphs. And just as paragraphs work together to develop a thesis, the sentences within an effective paragraph support and extend one another to develop a single idea. In key respects, then, you can think of a paragraph as a mini-essay. Like a full essay, a typical paragraph

1. *presents a main idea that is usually, but not always, stated near the beginning;*

2. *supports or illustrates that idea;*

3. *arranges ideas and supporting material in an orderly pattern; and*

4. *uses logical associations and transitions to link one idea to the next.*

In one sense, nothing could be easier than to form paragraphs; you simply indent the first word of a sentence by five spaces. But those indentions must match real divisions in thought if you are to keep your reader's attention. All readers sense that a new paragraph signals a shift: a new subject, a new idea, a change in emphasis, a new speaker, a different time or place, or a change in the level of generality. By observing such natural breaks and by signaling in one paragraph how it logically follows from the preceding one, you can turn the paragraph into a powerful means of communication.

7 Paragraph Unity and Continuity

PARAGRAPH UNITY

7a Highlight your leading idea.

As a rule, every effective paragraph has a **leading idea** to which all other ideas in the paragraph are logically related. A reader should be able to tell, in any paragraph, which is the **main sentence** (often called *topic sentence*)—the sentence containing that one central point to be developed or otherwise supported in the rest of the paragraph.

It is true that some paragraphs contain no single sentence that stands out as the controlling one. Descriptions, narrations, and reports that present data or run through steps of an experimental procedure often include paragraphs in which the main sentence is implied: *This is the way it was* or *These are the procedures that were followed.* But in college essays and term papers that call for analysis and argument (p. 9, 1d), you should try to give each paragraph not only a leading idea but an easily identified main sentence as well.

We will see (Chapter 8) that a main sentence can occur anywhere in a paragraph if the other sentences are properly subordinate to it. More often than not, however, a main sentence comes at or near the beginning:

> **There is nothing fundamentally playful about boxing, nothing that seems to belong to daylight, to pleasure.** At its moments of greatest intensity it seems to contain so complete and so powerful an image of life—life's beauty, vulnerability, despair, incalculable and often reckless courage—that boxing *is* life, and hardly a mere game. During a superior boxing match we are deeply moved by the body's communion with itself by way of another's flesh. The body's dialogue

with its shadow-self—or Death. Baseball, football, basketball—these quintessentially American pastimes are recognizably sports because they involve play: They are games. One *plays* football; one doesn't *play* boxing.

—JOYCE CAROL OATES, *On Boxing*

¶ un
7b

The heart of this paragraph is its opening sentence, which reveals the leading idea: there is nothing playful about boxing. Everything that follows contributes to that idea, remaining within its organizing control.

7b   Keep to your point.

A paragraph can include negative as well as positive considerations, but it should never "change its mind," canceling one point with a flatly contrary one.

DO:

- A. The seepage of dioxin into a community's water supply always terrifies everyone once it has been discovered. Citizens naturally expect the Environmental Protection Agency and the guilty industry to remove the source of risk as soon as possible. Unfortunately, however, this chemical is so incredibly toxic in small doses that decades may pass before the threat to public health is truly over.

DON'T:

x B. The seepage of dioxin into a community's water supply always terrifies everyone once it has been discovered. Citizens naturally expect the Environmental Protection Agency and the guilty industry to remove the source of risk as soon as possible. Yet many people react to the crisis quite calmly, refusing to worry about cancer, birth defects, and other proven results of contact with dioxin.

Each of these paragraphs ends with a sentence that "goes against" the preceding two sentences. In paragraph A, however, there is no contradiction; the writer simply turns from one aspect of the dioxin problem (citizens' demand for a speedy solution) to a more serious aspect (long-term toxicity). But in paragraph B the writer says two *incompatible* things: that everyone is alarmed and that some people are not alarmed. The writer of paragraph B could eliminate the contradiction by rewriting the opening sentence:

- The seepage of dioxin into a community's water supply provokes mixed reactions once it has been discovered. Citizens naturally expect the Environmental Protection Agency and the guilty industry to remove the source of risk as soon as possible. Yet many people react to the crisis quite calmly, refusing to worry about cancer, birth defects, and other proven results of contact with dioxin.

¶ un
7c

A paragraph that shows strong internal continuity (7d–h), hooking each new sentence into the one before it, can cover a good deal of ground without appearing disunified. Every sentence, however, should bear some relation to the leading idea—either introducing it, stating it, elaborating it, asking a question about it, supporting it, raising a doubt about it, or otherwise reflecting on it. A sentence that does none of those things is a **digression**—a deviation. Just one digression within a submitted paragraph may be enough to sabotage its effectiveness.

Suppose, for example, paragraph A on dioxin contained this sentence: *The Environmental Protection Agency, like the Federal Communications Commission, is an independent body.* Even though that statement deals with the EPA, which does figure in the paragraph, it has no bearing on the paragraph's leading idea: that dioxin can remain hazardous for decades. Thus the statement amounts to a digression. Unless the writer decided to shift to a different leading idea, the digression would have to be eliminated in a later draft.

7c Give your leading idea the last word.

If it is sometimes useful to include statements that limit the scope of a paragraph's leading idea or that raise objections to it (pp. 104–106, 8b), you should never *end* a paragraph with such a statement. Final positions are naturally emphatic. If your last sentence takes away from the main idea, you will sound indecisive or uncomfortable, and the paragraph will lack emphasis.

¶ con
7d

INDECISIVE:

x A. One reason for the recent popularity of Hollywood autobiographies must surely be the decline of serious fiction about important, glamorous people. We know that readers crave intimacy with the great, and we also know that modern novelists have ignored that craving. What people no longer get from fiction, they now seek in true confessions from Tinseltown. Of course, other factors must be at work as well; literary fads are never produced by single causes.

FIRM:

● B. One reason for the recent popularity of Hollywood autobiographies must surely be the decline of serious fiction about important, glamorous people. Of course, other factors must be at work as well; literary fads are never produced by single causes. But we do know that readers crave intimacy with the great, and we also know that modern novelists have ignored that craving. What people no longer get from fiction, they now seek in true confessions from Tinseltown.

Notice that these paragraphs say the same thing but leave the reader with different impressions. Paragraph A trails off, as if the writer were having second thoughts about the leading idea. Paragraph B gets its "negative" sentence about *other factors* into a safely unemphatic position and then ends strongly, reinforcing the idea that was stated in the opening sentence. The confident treatment of an objection makes the paragraph supple rather than self-defeating.

PARAGRAPH CONTINUITY

7d   Use one sentence to respond to the previous one.

To maintain **continuity,** or linkage between sentences or whole paragraphs, you need to write each new sentence with the previous one in mind. You want your reader to feel that one statement has grown naturally out of its predecessor—an effect that comes from picking up some element in that earlier sentence and taking it further.

If, for example, the most recent sentence in your draft reads *The economic heart of America has been shifting toward the Sunbelt,* you could maintain continuity in any of the following ways:

ASK A QUESTION:

¶ con
7d

- The economic heart of America has been shifting toward the Sunbelt. But how much longer will this trend continue? [Note that the next sentence would probably *answer* the question.]

ILLUSTRATE YOUR POINT:

- The economic heart of America has been shifting toward the Sunbelt. The recent history of Buffalo, New York, is a case in point. [Here the second sentence invites further support—one or more sentences explaining why Buffalo "is a case in point."]

LIMIT YOUR POINT:

- The economic heart of America has been shifting toward the Sunbelt. It may be, however, that the country has another kind of heart—one that is not so easily moved. [Again, the second sentence invites support; we want to know what kind of "heart" the writer has in mind.]

BROADEN YOUR SCOPE:

- The economic heart of America has been shifting toward the Sunbelt. If so, it can only be a matter of time before the moral or spiritual heart of the country is similarly displaced. [The second sentence considers the implications of the first one, broadening the scope of the discussion and striking a reflective note.]

CHANGE DIRECTION:

- The economic heart of America has been shifting toward the Sunbelt. Without forgetting that trend, let us now consider less obvious but possibly more important developments. [In turning explicitly away from the first sentence, the second one provides a transition to a new line of thought.]

7e Include transitions.

Though you may sometimes want to delay stating your paragraph's leading idea (pp. 104–107, 8b–c), you should never put your reader to the trouble of puzzling out hidden connections. You can let the reader see at a glance that a certain train of thought is being started, developed, challenged, or completed by using **transitions**—words or phrases that tell the reader exactly how a statement relates to the one before it.

¶ con
7e

TO SHOW	USE ONE OF THESE WORDS OR PHRASES
● addition	again, also, and, further, furthermore, in addition, moreover, too
● likeness	in the same way, likewise, similarly
● example	for example, for instance, in one case, that is
● consequence	accordingly, as a result, consequently, hence, then, therefore, thus
● insistence	in fact, indeed, of course, no, yes
● sequence	first, second, finally
● restatement	in other words, in simpler terms, that is, to put it differently
● recapitulation	all in all, altogether, finally, in conclusion, to summarize
● contrast	but, however, nevertheless, on the contrary, on the other hand, yet
● concession	granted, it is true, of course, to be sure
● time/place	above, afterward, at the same time, below, earlier, elsewhere, farther on, formerly, here, hitherto, later, simultaneously, so far, subsequently, there, this time, until now

Notice how the careful use of transitions (boldfaced) helps bring out the logical connections in this student paragraph:

Mardi Gras revelers engage in all sorts of irrational behavior, hiding their identities behind colorful masks, eating and drinking to excess, and dancing wildly in the streets. **But** nothing seems more bizarre to me than the free-for-all that takes place during Mardi Gras parades. Revelers go to ridiculous extremes, **for example,** to catch the beads, drinking cups, and doubloons tossed from passing floats. Many people actually haul a ladder, bucket, or long stick downtown for catching these worthless "throws." **Indeed,** some people are so desperate for the trinkets that they risk injury to get them. **In one case,** I saw a man fall from a ladder while reaching for a string of plastic beads. **Later,** I saw the same reveler crash through a group of children, lunging for a throw.

¶ con
7f

7f   Include signal words.

Besides using explicit transitions (7e) to show logical connections within a paragraph, you can also gain continuity through **signal words** indicating that something already treated is still under discussion:

PRONOUNS:
- Ordinary people know little about the causes of inflation. What **they** do know is that **they** must earn more every year to buy the same goods and services.

DEMONSTRATIVE ADJECTIVES:
- Mark Twain died in 1910. Since **that** date American literature has never been so dominated by one writer's voice.

REPEATED WORDS:
- We should conserve fossil fuels on behalf of our descendants as well as ourselves. **Our descendants** will curse us if we leave them without abundant sources of light and heat.

RELATED WORDS:
- Diane gave her money and her sympathy to Frank. Unfortunately, she never saw the **cash** again.

IMPLIED REPETITIONS:
- Some fifty Germans were trapped in the embassy when the

revolution broke out. **Six more** managed to scramble into the last helicopter that was permitted to land on the roof.

Note how a student writer uses signal words (boldfaced) to link the sentences in this paragraph:

¶ con
7f

> Many men, on the other hand, think nothing of spending several hours on Saturday watching a TV football game. **They** enjoy the adrenaline rush **they** feel during a **game** and imagine **themselves** playing heroically alongside the professionals. **This vicarious experience** becomes so real that some **men** actually shout at the television screen, jump up off the couch, and move their bodies in imitation of the ball carrier weaving his way down the field. For such **men,** watching a weekend **football game** makes perfect sense.

Three repeated words—*men, football,* and *game*—help knit this paragraph together. But notice how the student writer also uses pronouns (*they, themselves*), a demonstrative adjective (*This*), and an implied repetition (*vicarious experience*) to promote continuity.

Sometimes a single key word, repeated several times within a paragraph, can make for effective continuity. Look again at the "boxing" paragraph (p. 89), which is held together in part by a pointed repetition of the key word *boxing.* Or note how the repetition of *legs* links the sentences in this paragraph:

> For a cow or horse, cat or dog, **legs** are used almost exclusively as a means of transportation. Among the insects, however, **legs** have innumerable other uses. Often they are whole tool kits. The rear **legs** of the bumblebee and the honeybee contain spine-ringed depressions— baskets for carrying pollen home from the fields. The fore**legs** of the mole cricket and the seventeen-year cicada nymph are enlarged into digging shovels. The swimming **legs** of the diving beetles are fringed with hairs to increase their effectiveness as oars.
> —Edwin Way Teale, *The Strange Lives of Familiar Insects*

Observe, finally, that a particular device rarely works alone in achieving paragraph continuity. While a repeated word does much of the work in the above paragraph, for example, an explicit transition (*however*) and a personal pronoun (*they*) also contribute. More subtly, the last three sentences contain words (*baskets, shovels,* and *oars*) that link them to the word *tool* in the third sentence.

7g Keep related sentences together.

¶ con
7g

You can serve continuity by keeping together related sentences that all bear the same general relation to the paragraph's leading idea. To simplify, let us reduce all such relations to *support* and *limitation* (qualification). Sentences that support the leading idea by restating it, illustrating it, offering evidence for its truth, or expanding upon it belong in an uninterrupted sequence. So do all sentences that limit the leading idea by showing what it does *not* cover or by casting doubt on it.

Continuity is especially threatened when a paragraph contains two isolated sets of limiting sentences. To see why, examine the following draft paragraph:

limitation	x Not many people would want to endure the lonely hours, the aches and pains, and the probable injuries awaiting anyone who trains seriously for a marathon.
main sentence	The pride, however, that comes from finishing one's first marathon makes all the struggle seem worth-
limitation	while. But is it really worthwhile? What does running twenty-six miles in glorified underwear have to do with real life? But for veteran marathoners, long-distance
support	racing *is* real life, while all other claims on their time are distractions or nuisances.

Here the main sentence establishes a pro-marathon direction. But that direction is opposed twice in the course of the paragraph; the main sentence is hemmed in by qualifications, and the reader is bounced back and forth between "pro" and "con" points. Compare:

limitation	• Not many people would want to endure the lonely hours, the aches and pains, and the probable injuries awaiting anyone who trains seriously for a marathon. Is all the effort worthwhile? More than once, no doubt, exhausted beginners must ask themselves what run- ning twenty-six miles in glorified underwear has

main
sentence { to do with real life. Yet the pride that comes from finishing one's first marathon makes all the struggle seem worthwhile. And for veteran marathoners, long-

support { distance running *is* real life, while all other claims on their time are distractions or nuisances.

¶ con
7h

Now the paragraph's shuffling between pros and cons has been re-placed by *one* definitive pivot on the word *Yet*. One such turn per paragraph is the maximum you should allow yourself. To observe that principle, make sure that your limiting and supporting sentences remain within their own portions of the paragraph—with the limiting sentences first to keep them from "having the last word."

For further discussion of the kind of paragraph that pivots to its leading idea, see pages 104–106, 8b.

7h   Achieve continuity through varied and repeated sentence structure.

A further means of making the sentences of a paragraph flow together is to give them some variety of structure. In particular, avoid an unbroken string of choppy sentences, each consisting of one statement unmarked by pauses (see p. 164, 13f).

Within certain limits, however, you can show continuity by *re-peating* a sentence pattern. Those limits are that (a) only parts of paragraphs, not whole paragraphs, usually lend themselves comfort-ably to such effects, and (b) the sentences so linked must be parallel in meaning. When you want to make their association emphatic, you can give them the same form.

Notice, for example, how the writer of the following paragraph uses two identical structures (here boldfaced) to underscore social and political changes that have made American history books less predictable than they used to be:

But now the texts have changed, and with them the country that Ameri-can children are growing up into. **The society that was once uniform is now** a patchwork of rich and poor, old and young, men and women, blacks, whites, Hispanics, and Indians. **The system that ran so smoothly** by means of the Constitution under the guidance of benevolent conductor Presidents **is now** a rattletrap affair. The past is no highway to the present; it is a collection of issues and events that do not fit together and that lead in no single direction.

> —FRANCES FITZGERALD, *America Revised: History Schoolbooks in the Twentieth Century*

¶ con
7i

Again, note how an even more conspicuous use of repetition helps hold this paragraph together:

An elephant is a bawling baby squeezed under its mother's belly as a dozen older relatives surround the pair, facing out in defense against an approaching lion. **An elephant is** a frisky adolescent ripping up hundred-year-old trees and flinging them about. **An elephant is** 20,000 pounds sliding down a muddy bank, splashing into a river, and totally submerging itself until a fleshy snorkel breaks the waves for air. **And an elephant is** a lonely wanderer, happening upon the bones of a long-dead elephant and stopping for half an hour to trace the bleached forms gently with its trunk.

> —BOYCE RENSBERGER, "In Elephant Country"

The repeated sentence structure (boldfaced for emphasis) draws attention forcefully to the various stages of the elephant's life span. Used occasionally, such repetition can be striking; overused, it can become tedious. As a general rule, you should aim for a more subtle effect, using *varied* sentence structure to carry readers smoothly from one sentence to the next.

7i Provide transitions between paragraphs.

Just as linked sentences help to establish the internal continuity of a paragraph, so linked paragraphs help to establish the continuity of a whole essay. Of course, your paragraphs must actually *be* logically connected, not just appear so. But once again you can bring out the connections through conjunctions like *but* or *yet* and through sentence adverbs and transitional phrases like *thus, however, in fact,* and *on the contrary.* And the linkage is surest of all in a paragraph whose first sentence refers directly to a point made near the end of the preceding paragraph: *The problems, however, . . . ; Nevertheless, that argument can be answered;* and so forth.

   Note, for instance, how, in the student essay on pp. 83–86, two of the paragraphs explicitly "answer" a preceding one:

¶ con
7i

> **Change** is also obvious in the greater emphasis on contestants' ideas and speaking skills. . . .
>   **But** despite these **changes.** . . .
>
> We get the **impression** that women care most about physical beauty, glamorous clothes, and elaborate hairdos.
>   **This impression, however,** is not. . . .

Enumeration

One rather formal but occasionally helpful way of linking paragraphs is to enumerate points that have been forecast at the end of the earlier paragraph. If you assert, for example, that there are three reasons for favoring a certain proposal or four factors that must be borne in mind, you can begin the paragraphs that follow with *First, . . . , Second, . . . ,* and so on.

Transitional Paragraphs

From time to time, you may want to devote an entire paragraph to announcing a major shift of direction. When you do so, keep that paragraph brief—usually no more than a sentence or two—and make sure that it smoothes, rather than impedes, the overall progress of your essay.

> But how can such violations of human rights be swept under the rug? Unfortunately, as we will see, the method is simple and practically foolproof.

This brief paragraph tells us quickly where the essay has been (discussing a cover-up of human rights violations) and where it is going (explaining how that cover-up works). Transitional paragraphs are used most often in long essays as a way to introduce a **paragraph block** (p. 471, 38a)—a closely related group of paragraphs that covers a major point within the essay.

8 Paragraph Development

Most of the advice you may have seen about constructing paragraphs deals with just one kind of development, which we will call *direct* (8a). Direct paragraphs are indeed the most common type. Capable writers, however, also feel at home with other ways of putting a paragraph together. For simplicity's sake we will recognize three patterns—the *direct,* the *pivoting,* and the *suspended* paragraph. They illustrate classic ways of combining the types of sentences most frequently found in paragraphs:

1. a **main sentence,** which carries the paragraph's leading idea;

2. a **limiting sentence,** which "goes against" the leading idea by raising a negative consideration either before or after that idea has been stated; and

3. a **supporting sentence,** which backs or illustrates the leading idea.

8a Use the direct pattern.

In a **direct paragraph,** the most usual pattern, you place the main sentence at or near the beginning, before you have mentioned any limiting (negative or qualifying) considerations. The "boxing" paragraph (p. 89), the second "Hollywood" paragraph (p. 92), the "Mardi Gras" paragraph (p. 94), the "football" paragraph (p. 96), and this present paragraph all exhibit the direct pattern.

The following example is typical:

> **In the nineteenth century, most of the great gunfighters of the American West were notorious for their florid good manners,**

¶ dev
8a

being all too aware that if they let things get out of hand, they
would have to draw and shoot. Good manners helped those men
survive, since even the best gunfighter could win only so many gunfights
before his luck ran out. They were not "big-talking men"; they were
soft-spoken and courteous. It was said of "Wild Bill" Hickok that the
moment he stopped smiling at you, you were dead, and John Wesley
Hardin always did his best to persuade people who wanted to start a
fight with him to have a drink on him instead and then go on home.

—MICHAEL KORDA, *Success*

Here the main sentence (boldfaced) announces the point: gunfighters'
good manners helped them avoid having to "draw and shoot." The
rest of the paragraph consists of supporting or explanatory sentences
that develop the point. The result is a clear, straightforward unfolding
of an idea. We arrive at the end of the paragraph with the leading
idea firmly in mind and with two specific instances—Hickok and
Hardin—to give that idea substance.

Again, note how the opening sentence of this paragraph controls
everything that follows:

In Athens, women had no more political or legal rights than
slaves; throughout their lives they were subject to the absolute
authority of their male next of kin. They received no formal education, were condemned to spend most of their time in the women's quarters of their home, and were subject to arranged marriages. A wife
seldom dined with her husband—and never if he had guests—and on
the rare occasion that she went out of doors, was invariably chaperoned;
it was illegal for her to take with her more than three articles of clothing
or an obol's worth of food and drink (in today's terms, a sandwich and
a glass of milk); and if she went out after dark she had to go in a
carriage with a lighted lantern.

—REAY TANNAHILL, *Sex in History*

Note that a direct paragraph, just like an essay whose thesis is
stated near the outset, can comfortably include *limiting* considerations—those that "go against" the leading idea. In the following student paragraph, for example, the writer can afford to offer a "con"
remark, which is placed strategically between the main sentence and
two final sentences of support for that statement:

main sentence { The "greenhouse effect," whereby the temperature of the atmosphere rises with the increased burning of hydrocarbons, may have devastating consequences for our planet within one or two decades.

limiting sentence { Similar scares, it is true, have come and gone without leaving any lasting mark. Yet there is an

supporting sentences { important difference this time. We know a good deal more about the greenhouse effect and its likely results than we knew, say, about invasions from outer space or mutations from atomic bomb tests. The greenhouse effect is already under way, and there are very slender grounds for thinking it will be reversed or even slowed without a more sudden cataclysm such as all-out nuclear war.

¶ dev
8a

Direct paragraphs, then, can follow two models, one including and one omitting limiting sentences:

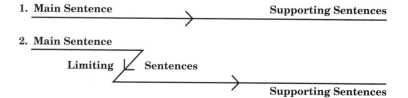

1. **Main Sentence** ⟶ **Supporting Sentences**

2. **Main Sentence**
   Limiting ⟋ **Sentences**
   ⟶ **Supporting Sentences**

Main Sentence Delayed

The main sentence in a direct paragraph need not be the first one; it must simply precede any limiting sentences. Note, for example, how the following student paragraph puts the main sentence second, after an introductory sentence that prepares for a shift of emphasis:

introductory sentence { But the statistics do not tell the whole story. If we set

main sentence { aside the government reports and take the trouble to interview farm workers one by one, we find an astounding degree of confidence in the future. The workers are

supporting sentences ⎰ already thinking a generation ahead. Even if they have little expectation of improving their own lives, most of them are convinced that their children will begin to participate meaningfully in the American dream.

¶ dev 8b

8b Use the pivoting pattern.

A **pivoting paragraph** not only delays the main sentence but begins by "going against it" with one or more limiting sentences. Characteristically, the pivoting paragraph then turns sharply ("pivots") toward the main sentence, usually announcing that shift of emphasis with a conspicuous transition word such as *but, yet,* or *however.* The leading idea, once announced, then dominates the rest of the paragraph. The opening paragraph of this chapter (p. 101) typifies the pattern. Its third sentence, containing the pivoting word *however,* reverses the paragraph's direction while stating the leading idea, which is then illustrated in the remaining sentences.

Notice how the following student paragraph pivots neatly on the word *But* and then develops its leading idea:

limiting sentence ⎰ When we think of Gandhi fasting, plastering mud poultices on his belly, and testing his vow of continence by sharing a bed with his grand-niece, we can easily regard him as a fanatic who happened to be politically

pivot to the main sentence ⎰ lucky. **But** the links between his private fads and his political methods turn out to be quite logical. Gandhi's

supporting sentences ⎰ pursuit of personal rigors helped him to achieve a rare degree of discipline, and that discipline allowed him to approach political crises with extraordinary courage. The example of his self-control, furthermore, was contagious; it is doubtful that a more worldly man could have led millions of his countrymen to adopt the tactic of nonviolent resistance.

Similarly, the classic transition word *however* shows us that the third sentence of this next paragraph is making a reversal of emphasis:

Health experts always seem to be telling Americans what *not* to eat. Cholesterol, salt and sugar are but a few of the dietary no-no's that threaten to make dinnertime about as pleasurable as an hour of push-ups. In a report last week on the role of nutrition in cancer, **however,** a blue-ribbon committee of the National Academy of Sciences offered a carrot—as well as oranges, tomatoes and cantaloupes—along with the usual admonitory stick. While some foods appear to promote cancer and should be avoided, said the panel, other comestibles may actually help ward off the disease.

> —MATT CLARK and MARY HAGER, "A Green Pepper a Day"

¶ dev
8b

The further you venture from the direct pattern, the more important it is to guide your reader with transition words such as *but* or *however*. You can also make your pivot, if you prefer, by means of a whole sentence such as *That is no longer the case.* The next sentence can then state your leading idea. You can even pivot in the very last sentence, as this writer does to give her opening paragraph a powerful sense of irony and drama:

The Shining Path threw a square dance any mother could love. The hall was freshly painted, decorated with balloons filled with confetti and colored-paper snowflakes. As Javier and I walked in, young people were eating plates of chicken and rice or square dancing in Andean folk style as men in ponchos played guitars and flutes. We had picked our way through the rubble in the unlit streets outside, filled with broken glass and fermenting garbage; few places are as menacing as a Lima barrio at night. But inside was all light and laughter, good clean fun— **except that the band's lyrics were a hymn to the People's War, and among the young dancers were people who attached bombs to dogs and slit policemen's throats.**

> —TINA ROSENBERG, "Guerilla Tourism"

A scheme of the pivoting paragraph would look like this:

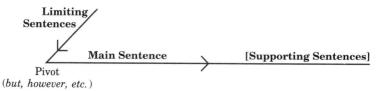

The brackets around "Supporting Sentences" indicate that some pivoting paragraphs—like the one just cited—end with a main sentence. More commonly, though, the main sentence is supported by one or more following sentences, as in the second "marathon training" paragraph (p. 97), the "insect" paragraph (p. 96), and the "Gandhi" and "nutrition" paragraphs examined above.

¶ dev
8c

8c Use the suspended pattern.

The final pattern that repays practice is the **suspended paragraph**—that is, a paragraph building to a climax or conclusion by some means other than a sharp reversal of direction. In a suspended paragraph the main sentence always comes at or near the end. Instead of taking a sharp turn, like the pivoting paragraph, the suspended paragraph moves from discussion or exemplification to leading idea, maintaining the reader's sentence-by-sentence interest until it arrives at a statement that brings things together at last:

Discussion ⟶ **Main Sentence**

Here are two examples:

discussion

On the morning of August 7, 1987, a battery of emergency X-rays was run in the diagnostic unit of Executive Health Examiners in Manhattan. Five men nervously waited outside the twenty-first-floor radiology room while technicians inside went through their paces. When the film was processed, the pictures were snapped onto a light box for study. The X-rays were negative. Everyone breathed a collective sigh of relief.

main
sentence

New York Mets third baseman Howard Johnson's bat was indeed a solid piece of wood.

—DAN GUTMAN, "The Physics of Foul Play"

discussion {

The hunting and eating of mammoths, those now-extinct elephantlike creatures pushed southward by the advancing glaciers of the Ice Age, date back only about 300,000 years. And even then, meat was not the central item in the diet. Plants were. Dairy products did not become a significant part of the diet until the domestication of cattle, about 10,000 years ago. Eggs, too, were a rare luxury, obtained only by robbing birds' nests before fowl were domesticated. **In short, if the human**

main sentence {

species had had to depend on large supplies of animal protein for its survival, it would have died out two million years ago.

—JANE BRODY, *Jane Brody's Good Food Book*

Looking back on the "discussion" sentences in these paragraphs, we could regard them as providing support for the leading idea. But we cannot perceive a sentence as "supporting" if we have not yet been told what it supports. By withholding that information until the end, the suspended paragraph establishes itself as the most dramatic pattern as well as the hardest to manage.

Once you feel at ease with the suspended paragraph, you will find it especially useful as a means of introducing or concluding an essay (Chapter 10). An opening paragraph that ends with its main sentence—a sentence revealing either your topic or your thesis—can gradually awaken the reader's interest and eagerness to move ahead. And a suspended final paragraph allows you to finish your essay with a "punch line"—an excellent tactic if you have saved a strong point for the end.

8d   Keep to a manageable paragraph length.

There is no single "right" size for all paragraphs. In newspaper reporting, where the purpose is to communicate information with a minimum of analysis, paragraphs consist of one, two, or three sentences at the most. Paragraphs of dialogue also tend to be short; most writers indent for every change of speaker. So, too, scientific and technical journals favor relatively brief paragraphs that present facts and figures with little development. And essayists vary considerably among themselves, both in their general preference for short or long paragraphs and in the paragraph sizes they use in a given essay.

¶ dev
8d

Even so, you can often tell at a glance whether the paragraphs in your essay fall within an acceptable range. If you hardly ever write paragraphs of more than three brief sentences, you are erring on the side of skimpiness. Readers will suspect that your writing lacks substance and detail. And if your typical paragraph occupies nearly all of a typewritten, double-spaced page, you are being long-winded, making your reader work too hard to retain the connection between one leading idea and the next. The goal is to show careful sentence-by-sentence thought within a paragraph without allowing the main sentence to lose its prominence.

Fleshing Out a Skimpy Paragraph

If you tend to write brief, stark paragraphs without much development, reread the main sentence of one of your draft paragraphs and ask yourself what else the reader might want to know about its implications. Do any of its terms need explaining? Where does it lead? What questions or objections does it call to mind? The new statements thus generated can become supporting or limiting sentences (p. 101) that will flesh out the skeleton of your draft paragraph.

Suppose, for example, your draft paragraph looks like this:

SKIMPY DRAFT PARAGRAPH:
Acid rain has been destroying the forests of Canada. Although it blows northward from the United States, no one is sure that American factories are the only guilty ones. The damage is extensive, and it may take a court case to find out who is liable.

To gather material for a more developed paragraph, ask yourself what else your reader might profit from knowing:

What questions might be asked about acid rain? What is it? Is the damage irreversible? Can it be prevented?

*What objections might be raised to the charge that American facto-
ries are responsible for destroying the forests of Canada?* Are there
other causes? Are American factory emissions mixed with those
from Canada itself?

Where does the issue of acid rain lead? For example, to questions
of legal liability for "pollution at a distance"?

**¶ dev
8d**

Your revised paragraph might look like this:

ADEQUATELY DEVELOPED PARAGRAPH:
American factories, we are told, have been discharging atmospheric
wastes that drift northward and fall on Canada as acid rain, destroying
valuable forests. We cannot yet tell for certain how extensive the damage is, whether it is irreversible, and whether the pollution could be
effectively stopped at its source. Indeed, we cannot be sure that American factories are the only guilty ones. Yet there is little reason to doubt
that those factories are the primary source of acid rain and that the
damage being caused is very considerable. If so, a landmark case of
liability for "pollution at a distance" would seem to be in the offing.

Exception: The Emphatic Brief Paragraph

If you establish a norm of paragraphs containing three or more sentences, you can gain a powerful effect by including a rare paragraph
consisting of a single sentence or even an intentional sentence fragment (p. 220, 17e). In an essay about his alcoholic father, for example,
one writer charged such a paragraph with emotional implication:

Three years ago, my recovering alcoholic father called me into my
mother's kitchen to apologize for all the pain he inflicted on me for so
many years. "One of the things I've learned through Alcoholics Anonymous is that you have to admit that you've hurt people and have to let
them know how sorry you are," he explained to me. "Son, I'm sorry for
anything I may have done to harm you." He then shook my hand.
   "*May* have done" was the part I liked.
                              —JOSEPH M. QUEENAN, "Too Late to Say, 'I'm Sorry'"

Here a choked sarcasm, confined to just eight bitter words, conveys the writer's feeling that old wounds cannot be healed with a mere apology and handshake. The one-sentence paragraph is rendered even more effective by being sandwiched between more ample and reasoned paragraphs.

**¶ dev
8d**

Focusing a Rambling Paragraph

If your draft contains a rambling paragraph—one that goes on and on without a strong sense of purpose—seek out its main sentence. If you cannot find it, decide what you want your leading idea to be. As soon as you are sure you have a leading idea, check to see that every sentence has some bearing on it. In some cases your long paragraph will split neatly into two new ones, but you should never indent for a fresh paragraph without verifying that both units are internally complete.

Many draft paragraphs begin purposefully but start to drift as the writer gets absorbed in details.

RAMBLING DRAFT PARAGRAPH:

limiting
sentence

1. If a person feels guilty about something, the obvious thing to do is to get that guilt out in the open. 2. But

main
sentence

many people take a different approach, one that only makes matters worse: they try to stifle their bad feelings by means of depressants or stimulants such as alcohol, Methedrine, or marijuana. 3. A friend of mine

supporting
sentences

felt guilty about getting low grades. 4. Her solution was to stay high nearly all the time. 5. But of course that made her get even lower grades and it thus redoubled her guilt, so she had even more bad feelings to hide in smoke. 6. I tried to talk to her about her problems, but she was already too depressed to allow anyone to get through to her. 7. Finally, she left school. 8. I lost touch with her, and I never did learn whether she straightened herself out. 9. I think that people like her deserve a lot of pity, because if she hadn't been so sensitive in the first place, she wouldn't have had the guilt feelings that sent her into a tailspin. 10. People who just don't care are sometimes better off.

This begins as a competent pivoting paragraph, contrasting two approaches to the problem of handling guilty feelings and providing an example of the second, self-defeating, approach. The momentum, however, begins to drag as the writer shifts attention to herself in sentence 6, and the paragraph falls apart completely at sentence 9, which escapes the control of the main sentence, number 2. Revising for economy and relevance, the writer decided to do without the sentences about herself and her compassionate attitude.

¶ dev
8d

ADEQUATELY FOCUSED PARAGRAPH:

limiting sentence

main sentence

supporting sentences

If a person feels guilty about something, the obvious thing to do is to get that guilt out in the open. But may people take a different approach—one that only makes matters worse. They try to stifle their bad feelings with stimulants or depressants such as alcohol, Methedrine, or marijuana. A friend of mine, for example, feeling guilty about her low grades, tried to stay high nearly all the time. The result was that she got even worse grades, felt guiltier still, smoked even more dope, and eventually dropped out of school. Her supposed remedy had become a major part of her problem.

9 Paragraph Functions

In Chapter 8 we considered the *direction* of paragraph development: forward from an opening main sentence in a **direct paragraph,** taking one tack and then an opposite one in a **pivoting paragraph,** and leading to a conclusion in a **suspended paragraph** (pp. 101–107, 8a–c). If you gain control of these three patterns, you can adapt your paragraph structure for nearly any purpose you want to achieve in an essay.

Another, more traditional, way of mastering paragraphs is to familiarize yourself with typical functions that they serve, trying your hand at each type. With a minimum of general discussion, we here offer and comment on sample paragraphs illustrating nine common functions. With or without your instructor's guidance, you can sharpen your sense of paragraph structure by studying and emulating the following examples.

9a Create a vivid description.

It was an unattractive low-rent building in the Winter Hill section of Somerville. A strange exterior of deteriorating shingles, tarpaper, peeling clapboard, and weathered plywood gave the house a haunted look. When my young daughter and I moved in, the outer doors were never locked and the back hall was filled with old chairs and underbrush. In our apartment the ceilings were peeling, wallpaper buckled off the walls, and a mouse lived behind the stove. There were code violations too numerous to count. But light streamed in through the windows. It warmed the rooms, created brilliant patterns on the floor, made our houseplants thrive. When the sun was out it was easy to understand why this had once been the most beautiful house in the neighborhood.

—BEVERLY BELFER, "Stealing the Light"

Good descriptions are supposed to provide concrete details, and this one comes up with them—*deteriorating shingles, tarpaper, peeling clapboard,* and so on. But details alone cannot guarantee a strong effect. You should also try to orchestrate your reader's responses in a purposeful, coherent way. Note how Belfer's paragraph progresses from the "bad news" to the "good news"—from unattractiveness to beauty, from a depressing scene to an exhilarating one.

¶
funct
9b

> His voice was quiet, his movements slow and cautious. He stood in front of the desk, not behind the podium, dressed neatly in a pair of blue slacks, a slightly rumpled white shirt, and a gray knit tie. His shoes, newly polished, looked old, the heels worn smooth and the toes heavily creased. He was tall, but he slumped slightly, which made him look older than he probably was. His hair lay in thin wisps across the top of his head. What brought everything together was his beard: large, unruly, and flaming red. It took possession of the face, animating his whole figure and transfixing the class as he started to lecture.

Again, notice how an accumulation of concrete details helps us see what the student writer saw. Those details culminate in a striking final image—the lecturer's impressive red beard. By saving this key detail till the end, the writer leaves us with a strong, memorable impression of her subject.

9b Recount an event.

> One of my earliest memories, from about four, is of my older brother and younger sister experimenting with matches. "They shouldn't be doing that," I thought. Sure enough, the kitchen curtain caught fire. There was smoke, flames; my mother came home in the nick of time and doused the fire with pots of water. When it was over she demanded, "What happened?" My brother and sister pointed fingers at each other. "I didn't do anything," I kept telling her. Finally she said, "I know, cookie, I know you didn't." The question years later is, *Why* didn't I do anything? Why was I such a goody-goody? Was I good because I chose to be or because I was too timid, too programmed, to do otherwise?
> —PHILIP LOPATE, "Tests of Weakness: Samson and Delilah"

The story of the fire that he didn't cause has become important to this writer's sense of his early identity. Rather than head at once into a discussion of his "goody-goody" years, he engages us in an efficiently told narrative and *then,* when he knows he has caught our interest, raises the general question he has had in mind from the outset.

¶
funct
9c

> Bees are filled with astonishments, confounding anyone who studies them, producing volumes of anecdotes. A lady of our acquaintance visited her sister, who raised honeybees in northern California. They left their car on a side road, suited up in protective gear, and walked across the fields to have a look at the hives. For reasons unknown, the bees were in a furious mood that afternoon, attacking in platoons, settling on them from all sides. Let us walk away slowly, advised the beekeeper sister, they'll give it up sooner or later. They walked until bee-free, then circled the fields and went back to the car, and found the bees there, waiting for them.
>
> —LEWIS THOMAS, "Clever Animals"

A brief anecdote like the one in this paragraph can go a long way toward fleshing out a generalization. Thomas starts with a *general* point—that bees astonish and confound those who study them—and then makes that point credible by recounting a *particular* event. His story ends with a punch line, a small surprise that confirms his opening assertion: . . . *and found the bees there, waiting for them.*

9c   Illustrate a point with details.

> Like all great works, *The Canterbury Tales* speaks differently to us at different ages. Rereading the tales after twenty years, I found some aspects less meaningful—for example, the hot astrology tips—and others much more so. This time, it occurred to me that the Merchant's diatribes against women from Eve on down might refer to me. This time, perhaps because I have children, the tale of patient Griselda—whose husband tests her by making her think that her children are dead and then threatens to divorce her and marry their daughter—revealed itself in all its true horror, and I was greatly relieved by Chaucer's caveat, at the end, warning husbands and wives against trying such ordeals by psychotorture on their own.
>
> —FRANCINE PROSE, "Naughty, Bawdy, and Wise—
> A Valentine for Chaucer"

Note how all the reflections in this paragraph give substance, and therefore interest, to the writer's opening statement that Chaucer's book *speaks differently to us at different ages.*

> Living things are endowed with a strange and marvelous ability to handle their life activities with a clocklike precision. Potatoes sprout in the bin in February. That is the time for which their built-in chemical alarm is set; December will not do. Lilacs have an appointed time for blooming; no coddling of the plants in a heated greenhouse will change the time. The wild asters by the roadside bloom when the lengthening nights of autumn approach; they seem to wait for these days. Such examples can be extended almost endlessly. Running through them is the general conclusion: each organism has its own built-in timing system.
>
> —KEITH G. IRWIN, *The 365 Days: The Story of Our Calendar*

¶
funct
9d

Here again an opening generalization sets the stage for a paragraph that is rich in detail. In this case, however, the writer uses the details to support a scientific principle rather than a subjective judgment about a literary work. Note how the final sentence concisely restates the assertion made in the first one, neatly framing the specifics between two general statements.

9d Support a point with reasons.

> Not only is putting the most difficult skill in the game, it's by far the most important. If par for a course is 72 strokes, 36 of those strokes are allotted for putts. Thus a round is evenly divided between putting and all the other skills combined that are needed to move a ball from tee to green. Further, from the standpoint of scoring, sinking a putt is always worth more than hitting a perfect drive or lofting a lovely iron. Every time you sink a putt you save a stroke; for all the brilliance of a drive or an approach, what you earn is a leg up on your next shot, which won't necessarily be worth a thing on the scorecard. Another way of saying this is that putting is important because it comes last. "You can recover from a bad shot," notes Chi Chi Rodriguez, the former P.G.A. player who dominated the senior tour last year. "But you can't recover from a bad putt."
>
> —PETER DE JONGE, "When the Putting Goes Bad"

This paragraph begins with an assertion that could provoke disagreement. Consequently, the writer follows it with observations that all go to show the correctness of that first idea. Notice how, after presenting his reasons for regarding a putt as the most important golf stroke, he clinches the point with an apt quotation from someone whose authority cannot be doubted.

¶
funct
9e

> The university administration tells us that a new dormitory with sealed windows and a powerful air circulation system will be energy efficient and will keep allergens and pollutants outside. This argument, however, overlooks three important reasons for including operable windows in the new building. First, such windows will allow residents to let fresh air into the dormitory during power outages and malfunctions in the air-conditioning system. Second, even when they are closed, operable windows allow a small amount of outside air to leak into the building, reducing the chance that indoor pollutants will accumulate in rooms if the circulation system works inefficiently. Such pollutants—caused by chemicals used in building materials—are a widely recognized health hazard in many sealed high-rise buildings. Finally, the ability to open windows will give residents a psychological sense of having some control over their environment; rather than breathing filtered air every day, students will be able to open a window occasionally to smell the spring flowers or the rain-washed air.

In this pivoting paragraph (p. 104, 8b), a student writer first summarizes the case against operable windows and then gives three reasons to support her opinion that such windows make sense. Notice how she enumerates her key points (*First . . . , Second . . . , Finally . . .*) as a way of guiding readers smoothly through the paragraph.

9e Draw a comparison or contrast.

> As one would expect, the formative years of Jefferson and Lincoln represent a study in contrasts, for the two men began life at opposite ends of the social and economic spectrum. There are, however, some intriguing parallels. Both men suffered the devastating loss of a parent at an early age. Jefferson's father, an able and active man to whom his son was deeply devoted, died when his son was fourteen, and Thomas was left to the care of his mother. His adolescent misogyny and his subsequent

glacial silence on the subject of his mother strongly suggest that their relationship was strained. Conversely, Lincoln suffered the loss of his mother at the age of nine, and while he adored his father's second wife, he seems to have grown increasingly unable to regard his father with affection or perhaps even respect. Both Jefferson and Lincoln had the painful misfortune to experience in their youth the death of a favorite sister. And both were marked for distinction early by being elected to their respective legislatures at the age of twenty-five.

—DOUGLAS L. WILSON, "What Jefferson and Lincoln Read"

¶
funct
9e

After making an initial point of contrast about Jefferson's and Lincoln's "formative years," the writer develops three points of similarity: the loss of a parent at an early age, the death of a favorite sister, and election to public office at the age of twenty-five. Note how Wilson uses the word *however* to "pivot" to his leading idea and how he achieves paragraph continuity through repeated sentence structure (p. 98, 7h): *Both men suffered . . . , Both Jefferson and Lincoln had . . . , And both were marked. . . .*

Quilts are generally made for either of two reasons—for warmth or for decoration. Those intended for the practical purpose of keeping warm are formed from old scraps of clothing, whatever is available at the time. The quilter sews these scraps together with small, single—and often irregular—stitches that will endure many winters and generations. Such quilts are pieced together for pure necessity. Decorative quilts, on the other hand, are mainly wall hangings made from carefully selected fabrics with just the right texture and color. The pattern of an ornamental quilt is usually an elaborate design, sketched and pieced out in advance. The decorative quilter takes great care to make neatly uniform, aesthetically pleasing stitches. To me, both practical and decorative quilts are works of art, but a quilt made for warmth has a human dimension that a purely decorative one can never have.

This student paragraph functions like a miniature essay. The writer announces her subject in the opening sentence; develops a contrast in the middle sentences, discussing first one type of quilt and then the other; and draws a conclusion about the two types of quilts in the final sentence. Notice how the transitional expression *on the other hand* links the two halves of the discussion.

9f   Analyze causes or effects.

In recent decades the reported death rate from cancer has been rising dramatically. How alarmed should we be by this statistical change? One cause of the mounting curve is probably the simple fact that we are more conscious of cancer now than we used to be, and less ashamed to mention the feared disease. Another cause may be the fact that more and more people are dying in hospitals and undergoing autopsies: in earlier times the comparable deaths at home from cancer might have been attributed to "old age." But factors like these take us only so far. Eventually we have to admit that cancer has been gaining on us in an absolute sense. If so, the real causes must be environmental: the continued increase in smoking, the use of dangerous pesticides and food additives, and increased pollution from automobiles and industry. Some of those causes must be more responsible than others, but until we know more than we do, we had better give urgent attention to all of them.

This student writer, asking herself why the death statistics for cancer have kept going up, avoids the trap of simply offering a routine list of causes. Instead, she has sorted possible causes into insignificant and fundamental ones. Observe how she places the least important factors first, leaving the substantial ones for the naturally stronger late position.

For those who have become dependent on cigarettes, the first few days of withdrawal are likely to bring about a number of physiological and psychological reactions. Among them may be decreases in heart rate and blood pressure, decreases in the excretion of some of the hormones which affect the nervous system, occasional headaches, and gastrointestinal discomfort. For some people, a weight gain may take place; it is uncertain whether this is caused by increased appetite or a changed metabolism or both. Behavioral and mood changes may also occur, usually peaking within a few days after quitting. Common symptoms are irritability, aggressiveness, and difficulty in sleeping.

—U.S. DEPARTMENT OF HEALTH AND HUMAN SERVICES,
Why People Smoke Cigarettes

Here the focus is on effects rather than causes. The paragraph begins by naming a "cause"—giving up cigarettes. The ensuing discussion divides the effects of withdrawal into two categories, physiological and psychological, a distinction that gives the paragraph its basic structure.

9g   Clarify the meaning of a key term or concept.

> We often hear today that police should be concentrating on violent offenses instead of wasting so much time, effort, and taxpayers' money on so-called victimless crime. This seems like a fine idea; nobody, after all, would want an officer to make a possession-of-marijuana arrest while a rape or murder was occurring across the street. But what exactly *is* a "victimless" crime? Are there no victims when pimps, prostitutes, and drug pushers take over the streets of a residential neighborhood, confining the fearful citizens to their homes at night? I too am against the prosecution of truly victimless "crimes"; I don't regard them as crimes at all. But let's be clear about our terms. For me, *victimless* means that the act in question produces *neither direct nor indirect* victims. If this meaning of the term is understood, the whole issue of victimless crime loses its air of simplicity and righteousness.

This student writer puts a definition to work in behalf of her argument for a crackdown on prostitution and drug dealing. Note how this tactic differs from the pathetic "dictionary opener" (p. 131, 10g)— the uncalled-for definition whose only function is to get the flow of words running. In the paragraph above, the writer prepares us with careful reasoning for her crucial definition of victimless crime, first showing us why a definition is necessary at all: without it, only a superficial and distorted view of the problem would be possible.

> I was taught all the ceremonies of *respeto*—the proper greetings for delivering messages to the neighbors; to press myself against the walls to allow adults to pass me on the narrow sidewalks; to speak only when addressed and not to put my spoon into adult conversation; never to show that I was bored with the questions adults asked me when we were visiting; never under any circumstances to ask for anything to eat; to enter the house with my cap in my hand; to answer instantly when called; to address everyone as *señor* or *señora*; and to talk quietly in conversation. Breaches of these rules of *respeto* fell somewhere between a sin and a crime. Not to know them thoroughly and to observe

them unfailingly showed more than anything else that you were *muy mal educado*. In my mother's book, to be well instructed was to know how to read, write, and count; to be well educated was to show deference to persons older than yourself. The older they were, the more *respeto* they were entitled to.

—ERNESTO GALARZA, *Barrio Boy*

¶
funct
9h

Using details from his own experience, this writer develops a definition of *respeto*, showing how deeply the notion of respect governed his childhood attitude toward adults. This type of definition can be useful whenever you want to show that, in your own experience, a particular term has important emotional connotations that go far beyond its customary meaning.

9h Show the steps or parts that make up a whole.

I begin my compost heap with a layer of twigs and small dead branches. These allow excess moisture to drain from the heap during heavy rains. Next, I alternate layers of different kinds of vegetation. This type of "sandwiching" is necessary to ensure that the heap decomposes properly. One layer must contain "carbonaceous" materials (mainly autumn leaves, straw, and dried hay), the other "nitrogenous" materials (mainly grass clippings and spent garden plants). Between layers, I usually toss a light covering of soil. Vegetable peelings and trimmings from the kitchen also go onto the pile as they are available, as do egg shells and coffee grounds. Every few weeks I turn the layers with a pitch fork to keep the pile from matting down. In dry weather, I sprinkle the material with a garden hose to speed decomposition.

The student gardener who wrote this paragraph manages to set forth the steps in a process without sounding overly mechanical. Although his subject matter and tone are strictly business, the variety of sentence structure and the use of a first-person governing pronoun (p. 37, 4c) help prevent monotony.

What should you look for when shopping for a ten-speed bike? It is easy to get confused by glossy advertisements saying that you can't do without the latest molybdenum frame and cantilever brakes. But you can bring some sense into the matter if you keep in mind that all ten-speed bikes are designed primarily either for *touring* or for *racing*. Which activity do you prefer? The answer will tell you whether to go for a stiff frame or a more comfortable one; whether you want tight steering or a capacity for no-hands cruising on the highway; whether you should be more interested in quickness of shifting or in having a low enough bottom gear for hauling luggage up a mountain road.

¶
funct
9i

By dividing a subject into parts, you can quickly bring order out of apparent confusion. In this student paragraph, for example, the act of division—separating all ten-speed bikes into touring and racing cycles—leads to a series of further distinctions, each of which can be developed in a subsequent paragraph.

9i Develop an analogy.

Reading poetry is not a completely passive pleasure, as is sitting in the sun or watching television. It is more like the pleasure you get from playing tennis or listening to music. There is a difference between what you feel the first time you play tennis and the fiftieth time. Or between the first time you go to a concert and later on, when you know more about the music and are used to concerts. Poetry is like that. The more you know about it and the more you read it, the more at ease you'll feel with it, the better you'll get at reading it, and the more you'll like it.
—KENNETH KOCH AND KATE FARRELL, *Sleeping on the Wing*

When you use an **analogy,** you ask your reader to apply principles from one situation to another one that needs explanation. In this paragraph, Koch and Farrell explain the pleasure of reading poetry by using the more readily apprehended pleasures of playing tennis and attending a concert.

Taking courses in the English Department is like going to an amusement park. It's possible to play it safe, selecting a professor who offers about as much challenge as the merry-go-round. You mount the horse, the professor turns on the motor, and you move in a circle, taking a mildly pleasant ride three times a week. You enjoy the experience, but it's not particularly invigorating or memorable. Then there are the professors whose courses are more like roller coasters. Every class is a series of dips and loops. New ideas come flying at you around every curve. Occasionally—on exam days—you feel like you're hanging upside down in mid air, moving toward the ground at eighty-five miles an hour. You don't soon forget the ride.

¶ funct 9i

Here a student writer uses an analogy to make an amusing distinction between two types of English courses. The easily imagined experiences of alternately riding a merry-go-round and a roller coaster help us understand—in a colorful and striking way—the writer's academic experience.

10 Opening and Closing Paragraphs

OPENING PARAGRAPHS

A good introduction typically does three things. It catches your reader's interest; it establishes your voice and stance (pp. 37–41, 4c–d); and—usually but not always—it reveals your thesis. Only rarely does a shrewd writer begin by blurting out a thesis and immediately defending it. An effective introduction *moves toward* disclosure of a central idea, inviting the reader to come along.

But if your mind goes blank when you try to write an opening paragraph, delay the opener until you have drafted subsequent paragraphs. Some writers routinely compose in that order, and nearly all writers return to adjust and polish their introduction to suit the rest of the essay.

10a Establish a context for your topic or thesis.

The most common function of an opening paragraph is to put the topic into a setting of some kind. Typically, the writer begins by sketching a context that leads to a statement of the thesis. Some longer essays devote more than one paragraph to this work, but most brief essays do the job in a single paragraph, as in the following student example:

> When professional baseball scouts search for prospective pitchers, they invariably watch for two characteristics in the throwing styles of the young men: a fast ball with good speed and movement and a curve ball that breaks sharply. These two pitches are the backbone of any successful pitcher's repertoire. And although they may look the same to the

occasional baseball viewer, a fast ball and a curve ball differ vastly in the way they are thrown and in the way the baseball moves on its way to the catcher. **It is the difference between these two pitches that makes them effective weapons against even the most formidable batting order.**

¶
open
10a

Or again:

We live with it and by it every day—almost every hour—yet many Americans know all too little about just what it is, how we came to have it, what it really does for us and how few people in other lands have it. The Bill of Rights was not adopted until nearly three years after the Constitution, and at the time some people doubted that it was really needed. No American would suggest doing away with it today, for it guarantees the freedoms we take for granted—freedom of religion, speech, the press and the right of assembly, as well as of other basic liberties. **But it is more than a set of working guarantees for the rights of Americans; it is an inspiring example of human freedom for the rest of the world.**

—WARREN E. BURGER, "What It Means to Us"

Note how the last sentence in each paragraph (boldfaced) grows out of the context that precedes it. Instead of baldly announcing a thesis, each writer leads us gradually to a concise statement of a central idea.

The Funnel Opener

One way of establishing a context is to write a **funnel opener,** a paragraph that begins on a general level and then narrows your focus to the topic:

Only a few politicians have taken a craftsman's pride in self-expression, and fewer still—Caesar, Lord Clarendon, Winston Churchill, De Gaulle—have been equally successful in politics and authorship. Of these, Churchill may be the most interesting, for he was not only among the most voluminous of writers, but also commented freely on the art of writing. He was, in fact, a writer becoming a politician.

—MANFRED WEIDHORN, "Blood, Toil, Tears, and 8,000,000 Words: Churchill Writing"

By the end of this paragraph we know that the topic will be Churchill's writing, but we arrive at that knowledge by sliding down the funnel:

those politicians who took pride in self-expression

those who were equally successful
in politics and authorship

the most interesting
of these: Churchill

Churchill
as writer

¶
open
10a

It is not necessary, however, to descend through several levels of generality before revealing your topic. You can get the funnel effect simply by starting with an appropriately broad perspective and then narrowing your focus just once. Notice, for example, how the following paragraph moves directly from a subject area—the function of the immune system—to the essay's real topic, autoimmune *disorders:*

**more
general
level**

It is generally assumed that the main job of the immune system is to distinguish between what is "self" and what is "not self." Once the distinction has been made, "self" is preserved and "not self" is destroyed. At the most general level, of course, this is true, and human beings remain alive and healthy only because it is so. Recently it has become clear, however, that at a finer level of detail the distinction between self and other is not absolute. One of the paths to this insight has been provided by the autoimmune disorders, in which the immune system attacks normal, healthy tissue. Autoimmune disease, which may be crippling or fatal, can strike any tissue or organ. Its victims are often in the prime of life, and for unknown reasons they are more frequently women than men.

**level
of the
thesis**

—IRUN R. COHEN,
"The Self, the World and Autoimmunity"

10b Pose a question and answer it.

If you find that your draft opener sounds vague, windy, and spiritless, try revising to begin with a blunt question—not any question, but one that leads directly or indirectly to your thesis. Jolted to attention, your reader will realize at once that you have something definite to say. Note this student example:

> **What does lunacy have to do with the moon?** In the past, popular belief had it that the fluctuating phases of the moon dramatically influenced the mental and emotional well-being of people. This belief, rooted in Roman mythology, supposed that the moon goddess, Luna, was responsible for tormenting mortals with madness. Although this notion has largely passed into history, superstition lingers. I still hear tales told by hospital personnel that suggest a connection between the number of psychiatric patients seen in an emergency room and the appearance of the full moon. And many people assume that frivolous or illicit behavior—wild parties and vandalism, for instance—occurs more fre quently when the moon is full.

It is not necessary, of course, to pose your question in the very first sentence. In the following paragraph, the writer *ends* with two questions that set up the subsequent discussion:

> When my grandfather was a boy he saw the wild-haired magician escape from a riveted boiler. He would remember that image as long as he lived, and how Harry Houdini, the rabbi's son, defeated the German Imperial Police at the beginning of the twentieth century. Hearing those tales and others even more incredible, sixty years after the magician's death we cannot help but wonder: **What did the historical Houdini *really* do? And how on earth did he do it?**
> —DANIEL MARK EPSTEIN, "The Case of Harry Houdini"

And here, finally, is a two-paragraph opening that ends with a question:

> I belong to that classification of people known as wives. I am A Wife. And, not altogether incidentally, I am a mother.
>
> Not too long ago a male friend of mine appeared on the scene fresh from a recent divorce. He had one child, who is, of course, with his ex-

wife. He is looking for another wife. As I thought about him while I was ironing one evening, it suddenly occurred to me that I, too, would like to have a wife. **Why do I want a wife?**

—JUDY SYFERS, "I Want a Wife"

10c   Try a baited opener.

A **baited opener** is an introductory passage of one paragraph or more that not only saves its main idea for last (pp. 106–107, 8c) but also teases the reader by withholding a clear sense of the essay's topic. We are drawn ahead in the hope of getting our bearings.

> At the funeral, the priest read from Ecclesiastes: "One generation cometh and another passeth away, but the land abideth forever." He stopped short of the words, "The sun also rises." Three men sat in the front pew, listening. Each had come into this old Idaho valley on a light plane, fixing on his own mortality. Afterward these three sons, who now had children of their own, received the news that their father had disinherited them.
>
> The stone the family picked was flat to the ground and wide, as if to accommodate the special bulk beneath it. You can see this stone, between two 30-foot-high pines, in the town cemetery just north of Ketchum, and there is also a rough-made white wooden cross at the head of its smooth gray marble. There is only the name, "Ernest Miller Hemingway," and his dates, 1899–1961, cut carefully in.
>
> Fathers and sons. It is a conflict that haunts literature—but life far more. And what is it like when your father is a kind of totem for the 20th century, an icon for maleness and grace under pressure, when he owns a terrifying unconscious and, not least, is gnawed on as you grow up, secretly and not so secretly, in ever larger bites, by fame and his own demons, until that Sunday morning in July when he blows away his entire cranial vault with a double-barreled 12-gauge Boss shotgun he had once shot pigeons with?
>
> —PAUL HENDRICKSON, "Papa's Boys"

Readers who know their Hemingway can already guess whose funeral is being described in the first of these paragraphs. Only in the third paragraph, however, does the writer remove all doubt as to his topic: not Hemingway but his surviving, troubled sons.

Again, notice how firmly "hooked" we are by the following two-paragraph opening of a brief essay:

> Natasha Crowe, a close acquaintance of mine, recently received an unsolicited invitation from Joanne Black, senior vice president of the American Express Co.'s Card Division. "Quite frankly," the letter began, "the American Express Card is not for everyone. And not everyone who applies for Card membership is approved." Tasha (as she is affectionately called) ignored the letter. A few weeks later she received a follow-up offer from a different vice president, Scott P. Marks Jr. "Quite frankly," Mr. Marks reminded her, "not everyone is invited to apply for the American Express Card. And rarer still are those who receive a personal invitation the second time."
>
> Despite the honor, Tasha has continued to disregard this and similar invitations she has lately been receiving. For one thing, she has no job. Her savings are minimal. Her credit history is essentially a vacuum and therefore her credit rating, I'd imagine, is lousy. She doesn't even speak English. She's my cat, and I love her.
>
> —STEVEN J. MARCUS, "How to Court a Cat"

For another example of a baited opener, look ahead to pages 129–130, 10e.

10d   Begin on an opposite tack.

One useful way of getting started is to move in a direction *opposite* to the one you eventually plan to take. The strategy is especially well suited for an argumentative essay, in which you can start by acknowledging a widely held opinion or assumption before challenging it. The trick is to think about how your thesis *differs from* some pattern and then start with that pattern. Thus you are approaching your main idea by isolating its boundaries, showing its uniqueness:

> Back in the 1970s I thought I could make my 14-month-old baby safe from drowning: I signed him up for swimming instruction. Virginia Hunt Newman's book *Teaching an Infant to Swim* had appeared not long before, and infant "waterproofing" programs were springing up at

YMCAs and aquatic organizations everywhere. It was all the rage, with photos in national magazines of tiny "waterbabies" bubbling and bobbing in backyard pools. I was swept along in the movement: we were saving the nation's toddlers from the perils in their own backyards.

During that time, however, the statistics on childhood drowning accidents didn't decline; they went up. And now most swimming experts admit that this buoyant national experiment failed: swimming lessons in infancy do not make for waterproof toddlers. In fact, the popular waterproofing programs may actually have led to even more tragedies by giving youngsters and their parents a false sense of security.

> —DIANE DIVOKY, "Waterproofing Your Baby:
> Too Good to Be True"

¶
open
10e

This writer could have begun by declaring flatly that "waterproofing" doesn't work. Instead, she devotes her opening paragraph to the contrary possibility and then turns toward her thesis in the second paragraph. Her "opposite tack" opener provides historical background and a sense of dramatic reversal and control. Note that such a two-paragraph introduction serves the same purpose as a single **pivoting paragraph** (pp. 104–106, 8b).

10e Begin with a story.

Look back to the "Hemingway" passage on page 127. Would you find it possible to stop reading the writer's essay after those three paragraphs? Everyone loves a story, and one of the best ways to introduce an essay—even if your main purpose is not a narrative one—is to recount an intriguing incident. Here, for example, is the first paragraph of an essay-review about a seemingly undramatic topic, dictionaries and other books about language:

In 1897 James Murray, the first editor of *The Oxford English Dictionary,* paid a courtesy visit to one of the most prolific of his "voluntary readers"—the army of retired curates, amateur philologists, widows, and other people with time on their hands who supplied the dictionary with the hundreds of thousands of quotations needed to illustrate the history of words. The reader was a Dr. W. C. Minor, who gave his address as Crowthorne in Berkshire. When Murray arrived, he was driven from the station to an imposing brick building that seemed too large to be a house. In fact, he discovered, it was not a house; it was the Broadmoor Criminal Lunatic Asylum. Dr. Minor was an inmate.

—Louis Menand, "Talk Talk"

¶
open
10f

The reader, needless to say, will eagerly plunge ahead to learn more. But like all storytellers, this writer is not simply "baiting" us; he has a larger point to make. As he says in his next sentence, "The story has piquancy not only because it suggests the ad hoc conditions in which the world's most famous dictionary was produced, but because the enterprise itself had something of a lunatic quality."

10f   Try speaking directly to the reader.

One of the hardest things about drafting an opening paragraph is the sense that you do not really know your reader. One simple remedy is to imagine the reader standing right before you, awaiting your instruction to think of a scene or issue. In effect, you *command* the reader to share your responses—as, for example, in this beginning to an essay about motorcycle touring:

> The road glides beneath you. The sky flows over you. The wind rushes past, bringing new sounds and smells. Uninsulated, you touch the world as you press through it unencumbered by a cage. Beneath you, the machine hums and throbs, almost alive. It blends with you, telling you of the road surface and responding to your every movement.
>
> —Art Friedman, "Uninsulated, Unencumbered"

Again, study this opening to an essay about dinosaurs who, it has been found, were able to survive winters near the North and South Poles. Since the very existence of dinosaur fossils in those localities is just now coming to light, the writer begins by demanding that we get over a misconception:

> Picture a dinosaur in your mind. Then take a look at the surrounding landscape. What do you see?
>   The images that come to mind are probably reminiscent of horror movies with either "lagoon" or "swamp" in the title. Clouds of fog blan-

ket the still surface of some tropical waterway. Overhead, some mushy growth, the consistency of cooked spinach, hangs off lush, drooping leaves.

Snow just doesn't seem to fit into the picture.

—RICHARD MONASTERSKY, "Dinosaurs in the Dark"

¶ open 10g

Observe that one or two very brief, pointed paragraphs, like the first and third ones here, can sometimes make for an energetic beginning.

10g Avoid the deadly opener.

An experienced reader can usually tell after two or three sentences whether the writer commands the topic and will be able to make it engaging. Never reach for one of these classic sleeping pills:

1. The solemn platitude:

   x Conservation is a very important topic now that everyone is so concerned about the environment.

   Ask yourself if *you* would continue reading an essay that began with such a colorless sentence.

2. The needless dictionary definition:

   x According to Webster, to lie is "to make an untrue statement with intent to deceive." This definition applies to many things said by the main character in "On Tour with Max."

   Ask yourself if the reader is actually in the dark about the meaning of *lying*. Definition can be a useful way of developing an idea (p. 119, 9g), but a pointless dictionary definition will do little to advance your case or engage your reader.

3. Restatement of the assignment, usually with an unenthusiastic declaration of enthusiasm:

   x It is very interesting to study editorials to see whether they contain "loaded" language.

   If you are actually interested in the topic, *show* enthusiasm with a thoughtful, pointed opening sentence (10h).

¶
open
10h

4. A bald statement of the thesis:

   x In this essay I will prove that fast-food restaurants are taking the pleasure out of eating.

   But you are also taking the pleasure out of reading. You want to *approach* your thesis (p. 123, 10a), not drop it on the reader's foot like a bowling ball that has slipped out of your grasp.

5. The "little me" apology:

   x After just eighteen years on this earth, I doubt that I have acquired enough experience to say very much about the purpose of a college education.

   Will this whet your reader's appetite for the points that follow?

10h Sharpen your opening sentence.

If your first paragraph is the most important one, its first sentence is your most important sentence as well. When that sentence betrays boredom or confusion, you reduce your chances of gaining the reader's sympathy. If your first sentence is crisp and tight and energetic, its momentum can carry you through the next few sentences at least. This is why some people take pains to make that first sentence *epigrammatic*—pointed and memorable. Thus one writer begins a review of a book about Jewish immigrants by declaring:

> The first generation tries to retain as much as possible, the second to forget, the third to remember.
>
> —THEODORE SOLOTAROFF,
> review of *World of Our Fathers,* by Irving Howe

Another wittily begins an essay on divorce:

> There was a time when a woman customarily had a baby after one year
> of marriage; now she has a book after one year of divorce.
> —SONYA O'SULLIVAN, "Single Life in a Double Bed"

And a student writer advocating gun control begins:

> Thousands of people in this country could make an overwhelming case
> for the banning of handguns, except for one inconvenient fact: they
> aren't so much *in* the country as *under* it, abruptly sent to their graves
> with no chance to protest or dissuade. Arguing with a gun nut may be
> futile, but have you ever tried arguing with a gun?

¶ open 10i

CLOSING PARAGRAPHS

10i Save a clinching statement for your closing paragraph.

Remember that the final position within any structure—sentence,
paragraph, or whole essay—is naturally emphatic. To take advantage
of that fact, delay writing your conclusion until you have found material that bears reemphasizing or expanding. Look especially for a
striking quotation or story that might drive your point home. Thus,
for example, an essay about the revival of interest in roller coasters
ends with this paragraph:

> For the legion of admirers who queue up to ride, however, getting
> terrified is what coasters are all about. "It's the ultimate daring adven-
> ture that pushes the edge of our own bravery," explains Randy Geisler,
> president of the American Coaster Enthusiasts, which has tripled its
> membership to 3,200 in five years. The sentiment was echoed by Greg
> Blum, 15, of Dallas as he bounded off the Texas Giant recently. **"That
> was almost too much to stomach," he cried. "Let me on again."**
> —RICHARD WOODBURY, "Eeeeeyyooowiiii!!!!"

A striking image, whether figurative (p. 199, 16a) or drawn directly from observation, can also be an effective closer. Here, for

instance, is how one writer ends an essay on the bustling entrepreneurial colony of Hong Kong, which is looking ahead uneasily to its scheduled incorporation into China:

> ¶ close 10k

> As I prepare my own departure, I often think of an image that captures the melancholy of this slowly breaking city. **It is a scene I saw on the television news, almost surreal in its violent intensity, the scene of a great bulldozer crushing a mountain of fake gold watches, all made in Hong Kong, until there was nothing left but dust.**
> —IAN BURUMA, "The Last Days of Hong Kong"

10j Try recalling your opening paragraph in your closing one.

Look for ways of making your concluding paragraph show some evident, preferably dramatic, relation to your introductory one. If you already have a sound first paragraph and are groping for a last one, reread that opener and see whether it contains some hint that you can now develop more amply. Here, for instance, is the concluding paragraph of the essay (quoted on p. 104) that began by asking whether Mahatma Gandhi was nothing more than a fanatic:

> Gandhi's arguments reveal an underlying shrewdness. Far from betraying the dogmas of a fanatic, they are at once moral and cunningly practical. His genius, it seems, consisted in an unparalleled knack for doing right—and, what isn't quite the same, for doing the right thing. It is hard to come up with another figure in history who so brilliantly combined an instinct for politics with the marks of what we call, for lack of a better name, holiness.

Note how the writer has put his opening question into storage until it can be answered decisively, with a pleasing finality, in his closing lines.

10k Try looking beyond your thesis in a closing paragraph.

Just as you can lead to your thesis by beginning on a more general plane (p. 124, 10a), so you can end by looking beyond that thesis, which has now been firmly established. Thus, in a paper defending the thesis that unilateral disarmament is a dangerous and unwise policy, a student writer concluded as follows:

> There is no reason to expect, then, that the world would be safer if we laid down our arms. On the contrary, we could do nothing more foolhardy. **We must look to other means of ensuring our security and that of the nations we have agreed to protect.**

¶
close
10l

The sentence we have emphasized "escapes" the thesis, posing a relevant goal for future investigation. But note that it does so without embarking on a new topic; it provokes thought by looking further in the direction already taken.

10l Avoid the deadly conclusion.

Readers want to feel, at the end of a piece of writing, that it has truly finished and not just stopped like some toy soldier that needs rewinding. Further, they like to anticipate the end through a revealing change in tone or intensity or generality of reference. If you end by sounding bored or distracted or untrustworthy or even hesitant, you are encouraging your reader to discount everything you have worked so hard to establish.

Though you may not always come up with a punchy conclusion, you can avoid certain lame devices that would undermine your reader's confidence. Check your draft endings against these cautions:

1. Do not merely repeat your thesis.

2. Though you can look beyond your thesis (10k), do not embark on a completely new topic.

3. Do not pretend to have proven more than you have.

4. Do not apologize or bring your thesis into doubt. If you find anything that requires an apology, fix it!

5. Avoid starting your final paragraph with a formulaic phrase like *In conclusion*. Find a fresher way to signal completion.

10m   If your essay is brief, feel free to omit a formal conclusion.

¶
close
10m

A short essay may make its point thoroughly within five hundred words; your readers will be insulted or bored by a heavy-handed reminder of the points they have just finished reading. Sometimes a brief concluding paragraph—consisting of no more than one or two sentences—can effectively end a short essay. But you can also save one of your strong supporting points for the last paragraph, counting on an emphatic final sentence to give a feeling of completion.

III
SENTENCES

Sentences

Strong sentences have much in common with strong paragraphs and whole essays, including a clear idea, emphatic placement of that idea, and subordination of other elements. You can think of a fully developed sentence as a skeletal paragraph containing major and minor elements that ought to be easy for a reader to spot:

	ESSAY		**PARAGRAPH**		**SENTENCE**
MAJOR	Thesis	=	Leading Idea	=	Independent Clause
MINOR	Supporting Paragraphs		Supporting Sentences		Free Elements

On each level—essay, paragraph, sentence—your chief purpose in revising should be to highlight the major element and to see that it is adequately backed by minor elements that are clearly subordinate to it.

The chapters in Part III assume that you can already recognize the parts of sentences—subjects and verbs, for example, or independent and subordinate clauses—and put together grammatically coherent statements of your own. If you feel uncertain about basic sentence structure, you may want to begin by reviewing several chapters in Part V. But since you have already succeeded in getting countless sentences onto paper, we start our discussion not with the blank page but with draft sentences that a student writer might want to improve. Our keynote will be revising to make your meaning easier to grasp and your sentences more fluent and varied.

11 Sentence Clarity

11a Put your meaning into grammatically important words.

When you think of revising a draft sentence, start by looking for its main idea—the point that *ought* to be conveyed by a clear, concise **independent clause** (p. 213, 17c). If, instead, you see that the point goes on and on or is trapped in a subordinate part of the sentence, you are ready to make your most essential improvement. Move your idea into an independent clause, making sure that the grammatically strongest parts of that clause convey important information.

The strongest parts of a clause are generally a *subject* and a *verb*, possibly linked to either a *direct object* or a *complement* (p. 210, 17a):

-         S   V
  The **committee exists.**

-         S   V
  The **committee meets** on Tuesdays.

-         S   V   D OBJ
  The **committee is drafting** a **report.**

-         S   V   C
  The **committee is** an official **body.**

-         S   V   C
  The **committee seems prepared.**

Consider the "correct" but unimpressive sentence that follows.

DON'T:

        S   V
x The **departure** of the airplane **is thought** to be dependent on the weather.

Here the essential grammatical elements are a subject and verb, *The departure . . . is thought.* This is scanty information; we must root around elsewhere in the sentence to learn what is being said *about* the departure. The idea is that bad weather—here tucked into a prepositional phrase, *on the weather*—may delay the airplane's departure. Once we recognize that point, we can get *weather* into the subject position and replace the wishy-washy construction *is thought to be dependent on* with a verb that transmits action to an object.

DO:

**clear
sent
11a**

        S   V   D OBJ

• Bad **weather may ground** the **airplane.**

Notice that we now have three grammatically strong elements—a subject, a verb, and a direct object—that do carry significant meaning.

DON'T:

      S   V

x The **thing** Fitzgerald says **is** that the human race is lacking what is needed to keep from being deceived.

Notice how little information is conveyed by this subject and verb: *The thing is.* To find the writer's meaning, we must disentangle embedded subordinate clauses, an infinitive, and a prepositional phrase, each of which adds a little more strain to our memory.

DO:

                                        S   V

• According to Fitzgerald, **human beings** necessarily **deceive**

   D OBJ
themselves.

Now the subject and verb do convey information. The key grammatical elements, subject–verb–direct object, bear the chief burden of meaning: *Human beings deceive themselves.* And as a result of this realignment, the sentence core now takes up just a few words instead of nineteen. Notice, too, how setting off the introductory phrase at the beginning of the sentence helps highlight the central statement.

Avoiding Clusters of Prepositional Phrases

Prepositions—*to, with, toward,* and so forth—are essential function words that combine with nouns and pronouns to form prepositional phrases such as *to the contrary, with gusto,* and *toward nightfall.* Though they are rarely emphatic, isolated prepositional phrases constitute no threat to efficient sentence structure. Closely bunched, however, they sometimes make for an annoyingly clogged, stop-and-start effect. Consider, for example, the following unrevised student sentences:

clear
sent
11b

> When health science was **in its stages of development before the modern age,** the publicity received **in the press by this branch of science** was negligible. Accordingly, the public was unaware **of the significance of balanced nutrition for the maintenance of good health.**

These sentences contain no errors, but their clusters of (boldfaced) prepositional phrases try the reader's patience. Compare the student's revision:

> Many years ago, when health science was still largely undeveloped, the public heard little about this branch of science. Accordingly, the connection between balanced nutrition and good health remained generally unknown.

The improvement here is subtle, but if you learn to spot your own clusters of prepositional phrases and revise wherever they sound awkward, you will automatically be curing several of the other faults covered in this chapter.

11b   Control a sprawling sentence.

Check your drafts for formless sentences that do not distinguish primary from subordinate elements:

DON'T:

x It was what she recalled from her childhood about the begonia gardens that were cultivated in Pascagoula that drew Barbara to return to the coast every summer.

A sentence like this strains our patience, demanding that we hold all its elements in mind until the point eventually becomes clear. The solution, as we will see more fully in the next chapter, lies in shortening the independent clause and setting apart minor elements.

clear sent 11c

DO:

x Every summer, drawn by childhood memories of the Pascagoula begonia gardens, Barbara returned to the coast.

Note how, through a separating out of significant elements, the sentence becomes more dramatic and easier to grasp. Its core, instead of being twenty-seven words jostling together in a mass, is a readily understood five-word statement: *Barbara returned to the coast.*

DON'T:

x To think that an answer that would be satisfactory had taken so long to arrive was something that put him into a state of deep resentment.

DO:

• He deeply resented the long wait for a satisfactory answer.

Note that every sprawling sentence will also show a poor alignment of meaning and grammatically important words (11a).

11c Limit your use of the verb *to be.*

You can make your writing more vivid by cutting down on the colorless, actionless verb *to be* (*is, was, are, were, has been, would be,* etc.) and substituting action verbs.

"CORRECT" BUT ACTIONLESS:

x It **is** clear that Deanna **is** in need of practice before the concert. The last time she played her violin **was** three weeks ago, and she **is** familiar with only the first movement of the Mozart symphony on the program.

STRONGER:

- Clearly, Deanna **needs** to practice before the concert. She **hasn't touched** her violin in three weeks, and she **knows** only the first movement of the Mozart symphony on the program.

  The revised version trims away needless words—notably several plodding prepositional phrases (*in need, of practice, with only the first movement*)—and conveys meaning with three strong verbs: *need, touch,* and *know.*

clear
sent
11d

"CORRECT" BUT ACTIONLESS:

x One source of tension in Dickinson's poetry **is** the fact that her shyness **is** in conflict with a tendency **to be** stagey.

STRONGER:

- In Dickinson's poetry, tension **arises** when shyness **conflicts** with staginess.

You need not worry about eliminating every last instance of *to be;* that would be pointless and impossible. Forms of *to be* are often justified, as in this very sentence and the previous one. But you can combat weakness and woodenness in your drafts by circling each use of that verb and seeing where you could replace it with a more vivid expression.

11d Convey action through a verb, not an abstract noun.

VERBS	ABSTRACT NOUNS
intend	intention
permit	permission
employ	employment
move	movement
insist	insistence
persist	persistence

As the first example in 11c shows, a sentence whose central statement is unclear typically expresses action through an abstract noun (p. 189, 15a) instead of a verb: *Deanna is in need of practice* instead of *Deanna needs to practice.* When you put the action in a strong verb, your sentence gains vigor and economy:

"ACTION" THROUGH AN ABSTRACT NOUN:
x Roger takes **enjoyment** in sunbathing.

**clear
sent
11e**

ACTION THROUGH A VERB:
• Roger **enjoys** sunbathing.

Note the relative vitality of the "stronger" examples below.

"CORRECT" BUT COLORLESS:
x Many college students make financial **arrangements** that enable them to experience **relaxation** on the beach during spring break.

STRONGER:
• Many college students **arrange** their finances so that they can **relax** on the beach during spring break.

"CORRECT" BUT COLORLESS:
x Miles has an **expectation** of seeing his daughters over Christmas.

STRONGER:
• Miles **expects** to see his daughters over Christmas.

11e   In most contexts, prefer the active voice.

In addition to choosing verbs that show action (11d), you can make your sentences more distinct by generally putting your verbs into the active rather than the passive voice: not *was done* but *did,* not *is carried* but *carries.* (For further illustration of the active and passive voices, see pp. 377–380, 31c–d.)

Passive verbs typically saddle you with three problems. First, they make the sentence a little longer, risking an effect of wordiness. Second, since they can never take direct objects, their energy isn't conveyed to another element in the sentence. And third, they oblige the performer of the deed to go unnamed or to be named only in a postponed and grammatically minor element. All three features go to make up a wan and evasive effect.

DON'T:

x **It is believed** by the candidate that a ceiling **must be placed** on the budget by Congress.

clear
sent
11e

DO:

• The candidate **believes** that Congress **must place** a ceiling on the budget.

DON'T:

x Their motives **were applauded** by us, but their wisdom **was doubted.**

DO:

• We **applauded** their motives but **doubted** their wisdom.

In scientific writing, which often stresses impersonal, repeatable procedures rather than the individuals who carried them out, passive verb are common. You can also use them in an essay whenever you want to emphasize the person or thing acted upon. Suppose, for example, you are narrating the aftermath of an accident. Both of the following sentences would be correct, but you might have good reason to prefer the second, passive one.

ACTIVE VERB:

• Then three hospital attendants and the ambulance driver **rushed** Leonard into the operating room.

PASSIVE VERB:

• Then Leonard **was rushed** into the operating room.

Although the second sentence is less vivid, it keeps the focus where you may want it to be, on the injured man.

Passive verbs, then, are not automatically "wrong." As you revise your prose, look at each passive form and ask yourself whether you have a good justification for keeping it.

11f Use formulas like *it is* and *there are* only for special emphasis.

clear
sent
11f

If one of your sentences begins with a subject-deferring expression such as *it is* or *there are,* take a close look at the subject (*it is the* <u>*weather;*</u> *there was a* <u>*princess*</u>). That "announced" word stands out emphatically in its unusual position. If you have a special reason for highlighting it, your delaying formula may be justified:

- It is the weather that causes her arthritis to act up.
- There was a princess whose hair reached the ground.

  In the first of these sentences, *weather* is isolated as the cause of the arthritis; in the second, the writer succeeds in getting an intended "fairy tale" effect.

More often than not, however, delaying formulas show up in first-draft prose simply because the writer is postponing commitment to a clearly stated idea. The price of delay is that, without any gain in emphasis, essential information is pushed further back into subordinate parts of the sentence (see p. 139, 11a). Frequently the result is an awkward and indistinct statement.

DON'T:

x **There is** no reason to suspect that **there is** much difference between what she wrote in her last years and what she felt when **it was** not so easy for her to be candid in her thirties.

DO:

- Her statements in her last years probably express ideas she already held, but had to censor, in her thirties.

  Note how much more easily you can take in the revised sentence; you do not have to hold your breath until you can discover what the statement is about. The complete grammatical subject, *Her statements in her last years,* immediately gives us our bearings.

11g   Avoid an unnecessary *that* or *what* clause.

Look at the last "don't" example above in 11f. The sentence *There is no reason to suspect . . .* lacks clarity partly because of its *that* and *what* clauses, which tax the reader's patience. Such clauses can, it is true, serve a good purpose—for example, arousing curiosity about information placed later in the sentence:

> • **What he needed** above all, after eight hours of steady questioning, was simply a chance to close his eyes.

In much first-draft prose, however, *that* and *what* clauses serve only to nudge the intended statement along in little jerks.

DON'T:

x During the Cold War, the realities of nuclear terror were such **that** countries **that** possessed equal power found, when they opposed each other, **that** the weapons **that** carried the most force were precisely the weapons **that** they could not use.

DO:

• During the Cold War, equal adversaries were equally powerless to use their strongest weapons.

> Here forty words have been compressed into fourteen, and a slack, cud-chewing sentence has become tight and balanced (*equal adversaries were equally powerless*). And notice how the grammatical core of the sentence has been given something definite to convey: not *realities were such* but *adversaries were powerless*. Strong, message-bearing elements of thought have been moved into subject-verb-complement positions, where they normally belong.

clear
sent
11g

12 Subordination

The first thing to do with any draft sentence—even an adequate-looking one—is to see whether you can clarify its key idea (Chapter 11). In doing so, you will often find yourself using **subordination**—that is, giving secondary grammatical emphasis to certain parts of the sentence. As a rule, the act of subordinating brings out the primary importance of the elements that remain unsubordinated. We will see some interesting exceptions, however; on occasion a subordinated element, shrewdly placed, can pack a curious wallop (pp. 155–156).

Our discussion emphasizes the usefulness of *free subordination* (12c–d), which typically gets set off by commas. Once you can manage free subordination effectively, you have in hand one of the most fruitful of all revision strategies.

12a Subordinate to highlight the key idea of your sentence.

When one of your thoughts in a sentence is less important than another, you should put it into a subordinate structure. Thus, if your draft sentence says *The government collects billions of dollars in taxes, and it must meet many obligations,* you should recognize that by using *and* you have given equal weight to two independent remarks. Are they of equal importance in your own mind? If you decided that you really meant to stress the collecting of money, you would want to turn the statement about meeting obligations into a subordinate element:

- **Because it has many obligations to meet,** the government collects billions of dollars in taxes.

But if you wanted to stress the meeting of obligations, you would subordinate the remark about collecting money:

- **By collecting billions of dollars in taxes,** the government is able to meet its obligations.

When you make an element subordinate, it will usually fit into one of the following (left-column) categories. Note how subordinating words like *because, where,* and *although* (p. 214, 17c) not only spare us the trouble of locating the main idea but also specify the relation between that idea and the subordinate element.

	WITHOUT SUBORDINATION	WITH SUBORDINATION
Time	The earthquake struck, and then everyone panicked.	Everyone panicked **when the earthquake struck.**
Place	William Penn founded a city of brotherly love. He chose the juncture of the Delaware and Schuylkill rivers.	**Where the Schuylkill River joins the Delaware,** William Penn founded a city of brotherly love.
Cause	She was terrified of large groups, and debating was not for her.	**Because she was terrified of large groups,** she decided against being a debater.
Concession	He claimed to despise Vermont. He went there every summer.	**Although he claimed to despise Vermont,** he went there every summer.
Condition	She probably won't be able to afford a water bed. The marked retail prices are just too high.	**Unless she can get a discount,** she probably won't be able to afford a water bed.
Exception	The grass is dangerously dry this year. Of course, I am not referring to watered lawns.	**Except for watered lawns,** the grass is dangerously dry this year.
Purpose	The Raiders stayed in Los Angeles. Their deal to return to Oakland fell through.	**Since their deal to return to Oakland fell through,** the Raiders stayed in Los Angeles.

sub 12a

	WITHOUT SUBORDINATION	WITH SUBORDINATION
Description	The late Edward Steichen showed his reverence for life in arranging the famous exhibit "The Family of Man," and he was a pioneer photographer himself.	The late Edward Steichen, **himself a pioneer photographer,** showed his reverence for life in arranging the famous exhibit "The Family of Man."

**sub
12b**

12b Avoid such vague subordinators as *in terms of* and *being as.*

Sometimes you can make a sentence more distinct not by adding subordination but by sharpening a vague subordinate element or eliminating it altogether. In rereading your drafts, watch especially for formulas like *in terms of, with regard to,* and *being as.* Such expressions are inherently woolly; they fail to specify exactly *how* the subordinated element relates to the primary one.

DON'T:

x **In terms of swimming,** she was unbeatable.

> Here a rather pompous subordinate element hints at a cloudy connection between swimming and being unbeatable. The connection can be stated more straightforwardly.

DO:

● **As a swimmer** she was unbeatable.

or

● She was an unbeatable swimmer.

DON'T:

x He felt sympathetic **with regard to their position.**

DO:

- He sympathized with their position.

DON'T:

x **Being as it was noon,** everyone took a lunch break.

DO:

- Everyone took a lunch break at noon.

Other potentially vague subordinators include *with, as, as to, in the area of, in connection with, in the framework of, along the lines of, pertaining to,* and *as far as.*

**sub
12c**

DON'T:

x **With all that he says about the English,** I believe he has misrepresented them.

DO:

- I believe he has altogether misrepresented the English.

DON'T:

x **As far as finals,** I hope to take all of them in the first two days of exam week.

> To be correct in usage the writer would have to say *As far as finals are concerned, . . .* But unless there is some special reason for singling out *finals,* a more concise statement would be preferable.

DO:

- I hope to take all of my finals in the first two days of exam week.

12c   Gain clarity through free subordination.

Note that, in the right-hand column of the chart on pp. 149–150, all but one of the boldfaced elements are set apart from the main statements by commas. They are **free elements** in the sense of standing alone. By contrast, the sentence *Everyone panicked when the earth-*

quake struck contains a **bound element**—that is, it is tied together with the main statement. Here are some further contrasts:

**sub
12c**

BOUND:	**FREE:**
The Germany **that he remembered with horror** had greatly changed.	Germany, **which he remembered with horror,** had greatly changed.
Germany was now inclined toward neutralism **instead of being fiercely militaristic.**	**Instead of being fiercely militaristic,** Germany was now inclined toward neutralism.
Hitler had vanished from the scene **along with everything he stood for.**	**Along with everything he stood for,** Hitler had vanished from the scene.

In general, bound elements are **restrictive,** or defining, and thus they should not be set off by commas (see p. 264, 20m). Free elements, being **nonrestrictive,** or nondefining, should be set apart. But since any phrase or subordinate clause at the beginning of a sentence can be followed by a comma (p. 261, 20i–j), a restrictive element that comes first can be free—that is, followed by a comma:

> RESTR AND FREE
> • **In September or October,** heating bills begin to rise.

The distinction between free and bound elements is a valuable one for mastering an efficient style. When one of your draft sentences is clumsily phrased, you can often attack the problem by looking for bound elements and then setting them free.

WITH BOUND SUBORDINATION:

x The censorship **that is not directly exercised by a sponsor when a program is being produced** is often exercised by the producers themselves.

WITH FREE SUBORDINATION:

• **Even when a sponsor does not directly censor a program,** the producers often censor it themselves.

Note the importance of the comma after *program,* leaving the reader in no doubt about where the main statement begins. Observe, too, that the revised sentence replaces passive with active verbs (pp. 144–146, 11e). Use of the passive voice almost always results in the addition of bound prepositional phrases (*by a sponsor, by the producers*).

Here are two further examples.

sub 12d

WITH BOUND SUBORDINATION:
x Any time an accident **that involves a spill of toxic wastes** occurs is a time **that causes alarm to everyone who lives in the area around the spill.**

WITH FREE SUBORDINATION:
• **Whenever a spill of toxic wastes occurs,** everyone in the surrounding area has cause for alarm.

WITH BOUND SUBORDINATION:
x The town **where Jaime grew up** had become a place **that he hardly recognized when he returned there for a visit.**

WITH FREE SUBORDINATION:
• **When he returned to his hometown for a visit,** Jaime hardly recognized the place.

Observe, in each case, how free subordination not only highlights the key idea but also makes the sentence less wordy.

12d Follow sentence logic in placing a subordinate element.

One important feature of free subordinate elements is that they can be moved without significant loss of meaning. How can you tell where a free element would be most effective? Consider these guidelines:

1. If the free element explains your main statement or puts a

condition on it, you should consider placing the free element *first:*

- **Unless Hiroko comes up with a new explanation,** we will have to believe her old one.
- **Although Amy finished the test on time,** she missed many of the answers.
- **Because he becomes nervous whenever he isn't listening to music,** Frank wears headphones while he works.

**sub
12d**

In first-draft prose, main statements tend to come first, with limiting or explanatory elements dragging behind. If you move those elements into early positions, they show that you have the entire logic of the sentence under control. And since last positions tend to be naturally emphatic, you can generally make a stronger effect by putting your main statement after your free subordinate element.

2. If your free element, instead of explaining the main statement or placing a condition on it, merely adds a further thought, you should place the free element *last:*

- Lisa's smile disguised her fierce competitiveness, **a trait revealed to very few of her early teammates.**
- Jeremy's life revolved around his older brother, **who never ceased making unreasonable demands.**

3. If your free element modifies a particular word or phrase, consider placing it *right after* that element:

- They gave Nathan, **a complete newcomer,** more information than he could possibly absorb.
- Cézanne's colors, **earthy as his native Provence,** are not adequately conveyed by reproductions.

Placing Sentence Adverbs and Transitional Phrases

A **sentence adverb** (p. 226, 18c) such as *however, nevertheless,* or *furthermore* constitutes a movable subordinate element in its own right. The placement of a sentence adverb is highly flexible, but different positions suggest different emphases. In general, a sentence adverb puts stress on the word that precedes it:

- I, **however,** refuse to comply. [I contrast myself with others.]
- I refuse, **however,** to comply. [My refusal is absolute.]

In the first and last positions of a sentence, where a sentence adverb cannot be set off on both sides by commas, it makes a less pointed effect:

- **However,** I refuse to comply. ⎱ No single element within the
- I refuse to comply, **however.** ⎰ main statement is highlighted.

sub
12d

The final position is the weakest—the one that gets least stress from the logical force of the sentence adverb. In some sentences, however, this may be just the effect you want.

The same principles of emphatic placement apply to **transitional phrases** like *in fact, on the contrary,* and *as a result,* which are really multiword sentence adverbs. Note how meaning as well as emphasis can sometimes be affected by different placement of the same transitional phrase:

- **In fact,** Marie was overjoyed. [Marie was not unhappy. No, indeed. . . .]
- Marie, **in fact,** was overjoyed. [Others were happy, but one person—singled out here—was more so.]

For fuller lists of sentence adverbs and transitional phrases, see pp. 226–227, 18c.

Emphatic Subordination

Once you are sure of your control over subordination, you can occasionally surprise your reader by saving a "bombshell" for a late, subordinate element:

There was nothing unusual in the visit **except that Thoreau fell utterly in love with her as soon as she arrived.**
—ROBERT D. RICHARDSON, JR., *Henry Thoreau: A Life of the Mind*

In one sense, this statement means what it starts out to say; nothing outwardly noteworthy happened during Ellen Sewell's visit to Concord, Massachusetts, in July 1839. But something privately momentous did happen: Henry Thoreau fell in love. The writer gains an effect of **irony** (p. 40, 4d), or incongruity between what is said and meant, by tucking that important news into an "afterthought" subordinate clause.

Free subordinate elements, "casually" appended to straightforward-looking sentences, are especially suited to ironic effects:

**sub
12d**

Perhaps the Las Vegas wedding industry achieved its peak operational efficiency between 9:00 P.M. and midnight of August 26, 1965, **an otherwise unremarkable Thursday which happened to be, by Presidential order, the last day on which anyone could improve his draft status merely by getting married.**

—JOAN DIDION, "Marrying Absurd"

This writer mocks the "peak operational efficiency" of the Las Vegas wedding industry by explaining it away in an "unremarkable" sequence of subordinate clauses and phrases. Her sentence is an exploding cigar, with the explosion timed to occur when we could least expect it.

We have previously advised you to "subordinate to highlight the key idea of your sentence" (12a). Here you see, however, that the rule can be twisted for purposes of irony or humor; you can put your key idea into the subordinate structure if you know exactly why you are doing so.

13 Sentence Emphasis and Variety

13a Use parallelism to show that elements belong together.

You can write more forceful sentences by making your main statements as clear as possible (Chapter 11) and by highlighting them through subordination (Chapter 12). In addition, you can revise to give the same grammatical structure to elements that are closely related in meaning. Such use of **parallelism** (Chapter 23) is emphatic because it makes logical relations immediately apparent to your reader. The idea is to have your grammar reinforce your meaning, not only through the choice of a main subject and verb but also through the aligning of key words, phrases, and clauses.

To appreciate the advantage that parallelism brings, compare two passages that convey the same information:

A. Animals think *of* things. They also think *at* things. Men think primarily *about* things. Words are symbols that may be combined in a thousand ways. They can also be varied in the same number of ways. This can be said of pictures as well. The same holds true for memory images.

B. Animals think, but they think *of* and *at* things; men think primarily *about* things. Words, pictures, and memory images are symbols that may be combined and varied in a thousand ways.

—SUSANNE K. LANGER, "The Lord of Creation"

157

Passage A, a classically choppy paragraph, takes seven sentences and fifty-one words to say what passage B says in two sentences and thirty-one words. In passage B, seven statements are condensed to four, with a corresponding gain in understanding. And the key to this concentration is parallelism—of paired clauses *Animals think, but they think* . . .), of conspicuously equal halves of a sentence marked by a semicolon, of nouns in a series (*Words, pictures, and memory images*), and of verb forms (*combined and varied*). Passage B inspires confidence in the writer's control; we feel that she could not have packed her sentences with so much parallel structure if she had not known exactly what she wanted to say.

**emph
13a**

Most instances of parallelism involve two items that are conspicuously equivalent in emphasis. The following table shows how such items can be made parallel, with or without conjunctions (joining words such as *and* and *or*).

PATTERN	EXAMPLE
x and *y*	She was tired of **waiting** and **worrying**.
x or *y*	If he had continued that life, he would have faced death **in the electric chair** or **at the hands of the mob**.
x, y	He strode away, **the money in his hand, a grin on his face**.
x: y	He had **what he wanted: enough cash to buy a new life**.
x; y	**He wanted security; she wanted good times**.

As you can see from these few examples, parallelism can involve units as small as single words (*waiting* and *worrying*) or as large as whole statements (*He wanted security* and *she wanted good times*).

For problems of usage and punctuation arising with parallelism, see pages 304–307, Chapter 23.

13b Use anticipatory patterns.

In the boxed sentences on page 158, each *y* element comes as a mild surprise; we discover that a parallel structure is in process only when we reach the second item. Other parallel formulas, however, anticipate the pairing of items by beginning with a "tip-off" word.

PATTERN	EXAMPLE
both *x* and *y*	**Both** guerrillas **and** loyalists pose a threat to the safety of reporters covering foreign revolutions.
either *x* or *y*	**Either** reporters should be recognized as neutrals or they should not be sent into combat zones.
neither *x* nor *y*	**Neither** the competition of networks **nor** the ambition of reporters justifies this recklessness.
whether *x* or *y*	Reporters must wonder, when they wake up each morning in a foreign city, **whether** they will be gunned down by the loyalists **or** kidnapped by the guerrillas.
more (less) *x* than *y*	It is **more** important, after all, to spare the lives of journalists **than** to get one more interview with the typical freedom fighter.
not *x* but *y*	It is **not** the greed of the networks, however, **but** the changed nature of warfare that most endangers the lives of reporters.

emph
13b

PATTERN	EXAMPLE

not only *x* but also *y*	Now reporters covering a guerrilla war find it
	
	             x
	 hard **not only** to distinguish "friendly" from
	
	 "unfriendly" elements **but also** to convince each
	
	       y
	 side that they are not working for the other one.

so *x* that *y*	x Such reporting has become **so** risky **that** few y knowledgeable journalists volunteer to undertake it.

emph 13b

Note how the first word of the anticipatory formula prepares us for the rest. As soon as we read *both* or *either* or *so,* we know what kind of logical pattern has begun; we are ready to grasp complex paired elements without losing our way. Anticipatory parallelism always means improved readability—provided, of course, that the grammar and punctuation of your sentence make the intended structure clear.

To see how anticipatory patterns can aid a reader, compare an imagined first-draft passage with the actual finished version:

A. He swore a lot. He would swear at absolutely anybody. For him it was just the natural thing to do. The people who worked for him probably thought he was angry at them all the time, but it wasn't necessarily true. A man like that could have been just making conversation without being angry at all, for all they knew.

B. He swore so often and so indiscriminately that his employees were sometimes not sure whether he was angry at them or merely making conversation.

            —NORA EPHRON, "Seagram's with Moxie"

Passage A uses more words to make more assertions, yet it never lets us see where it is headed. Nora Ephron's more economical passage B uses two anticipatory structures—*so x and so y that z* and *whether he was x or y*—to pull elements of thought into alignment without squandering whole sentences on them.

13c Make your series consistent and climactic.

One indispensable form of parallelism (13a) is the **series** of coordinated items, three or more elements in parallel sequence. A series tells your reader that the items it contains each bear the same logical relation to some other part of the sentence:

emph
13c

- **Small classes, an innovative curriculum, and a first-rate faculty** draw students to the university's honors program.

The boldfaced elements name three factors that contribute to a particular effect: *x, y, and z draw students. . . .* The series makes possible a condensed, immediately clear statement that might otherwise have occupied as many as three rambling sentences.

To see how a series can promote efficiency, compare the following passages:

A. At one moment, chunky, muscle-bound Sylvester Stallone looks repulsive. At other moments he looks noble. And sometimes Stallone looks both repulsive and noble at the same time.

B. Chunky, muscle-bound Sylvester Stallone looks **repulsive one moment, noble the next, and sometimes both at once.**
—PAULINE KAEL, *When the Lights Go Down*

The imagined draft version (A) contains twenty-seven words and a good deal of needless repetition. Kael's actual sentence (B) packs the same information into a memorable, tightly constructed sixteen-word sentence.

Although the parts of a series must be alike in form, they may have different degrees of importance or impact. Since the final position is by far the most emphatic one, that is where the climactic item should go:

- He was prepared to risk everything—**his comfort, his livelihood, even his life.**

If you try to put *his life* into either of the other positions in the series, you will see how vital a climactic order is.

As the example above shows, you do not always have to put *and* or *or* before the last member of a series. Omitting the conjunction can give the series an air of urgency or importance:

- A moment's **distraction, hesitation, impatience** can spell doom for an aerialist.

° emph 13d

For problems of usage and punctuation arising with series, see page 303, 23i, and pages 305–306, 23k–l.

13d   Use balance for special emphasis.

When a sentence uses emphatic repetition to achieve parallelism (13a), it shows **balance.** A balanced sentence usually does two things: (1) it repeats a grammatical pattern, and (2) it repeats certain words so as to highlight key differences. Thus the two halves of *He wanted security; she wanted good times* use the same subject-verb-object pattern and the same verb, *wanted,* in order to contrast *he* with *she* and *security* with *good times.*

You can see the ingredients of balance in the following **aphorisms,** or memorable sentences expressing very general assertions:

- What is **written without effort** is in general **read without pleasure.** (Samuel Johnson)
- We must indeed **all hang together,** or, most assuredly, we will **all hang separately.** (Benjamin Franklin)
- Democracy substitutes **election by the incompetent many** for **appointment by the corrupt few.** (George Bernard Shaw)

Notice in each instance how the writer has used identical sentence functions to make us confront essential differences: *written / read, effort / pleasure, together / separately, election / appointment, incompetent / corrupt, many / few.*

The art of creating balance consists in noticing elements of sameness and contrast in a draft sentence and then rearranging your grammar so that those elements play identical grammatical roles.

DRAFT SENTENCE:

- Love of country is a virtue, but I think that it is more important today to love the human species as a whole.

BALANCED VERSION:

- Love of country is a virtue, but love of the human species has become a necessity.

The first sentence is adequately formed, but it still reads like an idea-in-the-making, the transcript of a thought process. The second, radically concise, sentence uses balance to convey authority and finality.

**emph
13e**

13e Take advantage of the emphatic final position in a sentence.

If you want to make an expression dramatic and memorable, try putting it at the end of a sentence. With a proper buildup, the final position is naturally punchy. Notice, for example, how each of the following sentences saves a vivid, forceful statement for the end:

Like Mem, a character in *The Third Life of Grange Copeland,* **my mother adorned with flowers whatever shabby house we were forced to live in.**

And I remember people coming to my mother's yard to be given cuttings from her flowers; I hear again the praise showered on her because **whatever rocky soil she landed on, she turned into a garden.**

Guided by my heritage of a love of beauty and a respect for strength— in search of my mother's garden, **I found my own.**
                    —ALICE WALKER, *In Search of Our Mothers' Gardens*

The same effect is even more striking in this passage, with its one-word punch line:

No wonder the TV industry is finally wooing black audiences. They've come to embody its favorite color, which is, of course, **green.**
                    —HARRY F. WATERS, "TV's New Racial Hue"

Whenever, in your own drafts, you find a sentence that seems to trail off weakly, see if its most important element is tucked away somewhere in the middle. Consider this student example and its revision:

UNREVISED SENTENCE:

x Tom Wolfe establishes a stamp of authority as a writer who can describe "the right stuff" because he uses a technical vocabulary that a pilot would know.

var
13f

Notice how two bound subordinate elements (p. 152, 12c)—*because he uses a technical vocabulary* and *that a pilot would know*—come at the end, reducing the energy of the sentence. In the revision, the key idea comes last, after a free subordinate element that leaves us ready for an emphatic statement.

REVISED SENTENCE:

• Because he has mastered the technical vocabulary of aviation, Tom Wolfe convincingly describes "the right stuff."

VARIETY

13f Combine choppy sentences.

Bear in mind that your prose will be read not in isolated sentences but in whole paragraphs. You, too, should read your drafts that way, checking to see that the sentences within each paragraph sound comfortable in one another's company. If they seem abrupt and awkward, the problem may be a discontinuity of thought. Yet your sentences can be related in thought and still feel unrelated because they are too alike in structure. Watch especially for **choppiness**—a monotonous string of brief, plain statements containing few if any internal pauses. What you want instead is movement between relatively plain sentences and sentences that do contain pauses.

You can break up monotony just by adding one punctuated modifier—a *however* or a *furthermore*—to a sentence in a choppy sequence: *The storm, however, was not expected to end the drought.* But you can also look for ways to combine two or more choppy sentences into one. Ask yourself what the logical relation between those sentences is, and then turn one statement into a punctuated modifier of the other.

CHOPPY:

x The president serves a four-year term. He must seek reelection when it is over.

**var
13f**

COMBINED:

• After serving a four-year term, the president must seek re-election.

The first sentence in the choppy sequence has been turned into a **free element** (p. 151, 12c), duly set off by punctuation.

CHOPPY:

x Some experts favor a six-year term of office. They say that reelection causes too many pressures. Long-term problems get neglected. These problems are both domestic and foreign.

COMBINED:

• Some experts, maintaining that both domestic and foreign problems get neglected in the rush for reelection, favor a six-year term of office.

Here four abrupt, disjointed sentences, each as unemphatic as the next, have been transformed into one sentence that sorts out major and minor elements and gets its key point into the emphatic final position (see 13e).

CHOPPY:

x Some knowledgeable observers do think that the present arrangement is superior. One of them is the noted historian Arthur Schlesinger, Jr. He argues that a president must be accountable to the people. It is the core of our democracy. Schlesinger says that a four-year term answers this need.

COMBINED:

- Some knowledgeable observers, among them the noted historian Arthur Schlesinger, Jr., believe that the present arrangement is superior. In Schlesinger's opinion, a four-year term answers our fundamental democratic need to keep the president accountable to the people.

To appreciate the gain in economy and variety that comes with eliminating choppiness, compare these student paragraphs.

var 13f

DRAFT:

x Doctors and business people often carry "pagers." These electronic devices help them stay in contact with their offices. Pagers are small boxes. The user can easily clip them onto a belt. They can also be kept in a purse. Most people who have pagers rent them. The fees range from ten to thirty dollars per month. This is a small price for doctors and business people to pay for instant communication with their offices.

REVISED:

x **Doctors and business people often carry "pagers,"** small electronic devices that help them stay in contact with their offices. **These small boxes,** which clip easily onto a belt or fit conveniently in a purse, **rent for ten to thirty dollars a month**—a small price to pay for instant communication with the office.

The seventy-four-word draft uses no free subordination (p. 151, 12c) to highlight main ideas; each sentence is a separate, isolated statement. The revision, by contrast, conveys essentially the same information in fifty-three words, building everything around two independent clauses (boldfaced). The draft passage strains our patience, asking *us* to pluck essential information out of a string of choppy Dick-and-Jane sentences. In revising, the student writer takes control, directing our attention through varied and emphatic sentence structure.

13g Gain contrast through varied sentence length.

If a string of short, choppy sentences (13f) can drain variety from your prose, a single short sentence, strategically placed, can have the opposite effect. Notice, for example, how the boldfaced nine-word sentence below highlights the writer's point and varies the pace of her writing:

> I live in gratitude to my parents for initiating me—and as early as I begged for it, without keeping me waiting—into knowledge of the word, into reading and spelling, by way of the alphabet. They taught it to me at home in time for me to begin to read before starting school. I believe the alphabet is no longer considered an essential piece of equipment for traveling through life. **In my day it was the keystone to knowledge.** You learned the alphabet as you learned to count to ten, as you learned "Now I lay me" and the Lord's Prayer and your father's and mother's name and address and telephone, all in case you were lost.
>
> —EUDORA WELTY, *One Writer's Beginnings*

var
13g

Welty starts and ends this paragraph with sentences that are nearly forty words long. Maintaining sentences of that length over the course of the paragraph would have made a heavy, sluggish effect. If, like Welty, you vary sentence length—hers are thirty-six, eighteen, seventeen, nine, and thirty-eight words long—you can subtly modulate the forward movement of your prose.

A short sentence can be especially useful in making a pithy restatement of the discussion that precedes it:

> The original purpose of taste is survival: to know with a single sip or lick whether a food is edible or toxic, nourishing or deadly, out of the enormous range of sensations the world offers. In the natural world bitter means poison, and sweet, fuel. Even one-celled animals move slithering away from the bitter alkaloids; our own love of coffee is a learned response, requiring careful testing and a certain reward. It is the dilemma of the omnivore, as Paul Rozin says, to seek new sources of food at the risk of sudden death—or at least discomfort. The hunter-gatherer peruses every tree, every bush, bug, animal, seed, every root, flower, bone, shell, and fluid, and wonders if it might make a dinner. **Taste is his guardian angel, his guide.**
>
> —SALLIE TISDALE, *Lot's Wife: Salt and the Human Condition*

And remember, too, that an occasional sentence drastically longer than the norm can have a powerful effect. An extended cumulative sentence (p. 170, 13k) or a suspended sentence (p. 171, 13l) is an especially useful way to supply a catalog of details that might otherwise occupy a whole series of shorter sentences.

13h   Try an occasional question or exclamation.

var

13i

Usually a paragraph develops as a succession of statements, or **declarative sentences.** But to show strong feeling, to pinpoint an issue, to challenge your reader, or simply to enliven a string of sentences, you can make use of a strategically placed question or exclamation:

- **What are we to make of such turmoil over the narrow, arid Gaza Strip?** A full answer would take us back to the era of the Roman emperors.
- And this is all the information released so far. **Does anyone doubt that the Congressman has something to hide?**
- **A million tons of TNT!** The power of this bomb was beyond anyone's imagination.
- Once the grizzlies were deprived of garbage, their population declined steeply. **So much for the "back to nature" school of bear management!**

Note, in the second of these examples, that the writer asks the question without expecting an answer, for the question "answers itself." Such a **rhetorical question** can work well for you in driving home an emphatic point. Since rhetorical questions have a coercive air, however, you should use them sparingly. And the same holds true for exclamations; see page 324, 25j.

13i   Try an occasional interruption.

To give special emphasis to one statement or piece of information, try turning it into an interruption of your sentence:

- The street Jerry lived on—**it was more like an alley than a street**—was so neighborly that he scarcely ever felt alone.

- The hot, moist summer air of Florida—**people call it an instant steambath**—makes an air conditioner a necessity in every home and office.
- A woman of strong opinions—**her last movie grossed $50 million, and she calls it a turkey**—she is not exactly a press agent's dream come true.

As you can gather, dashes are the normal means of punctuating an emphatic interruption.

var
13j

The "False Start"

In a variation on the interruptive pattern, you can begin your sentence with a lengthy element—for example, a series (p. 161, 13c)—and follow it with a dash announcing that the grammatical core of the sentence is about to begin:

- **Going to hairdresser school, marrying the steady boyfriend, having the baby, getting the divorce**—everything in her life seemed to follow some dreary script.

Such a sentence takes the reader off guard by making a **"false start."** We assume at first that the opening element will be the grammatical subject, but we readjust our focus when we see that the true subject will come after the dash. (The first element is actually in apposition to the subject; see page 268, 20n.)

13j Try reversing normal word order.

Readers normally expect subjects to come before verbs, but for that very reason you can gain emphasis by occasionally reversing that order. The subject becomes more prominent as a result of such **inverted syntax:**

- In the beginning was the **Word.**
- Most important of all, for the would-be-tourist, is a **passport** that has not expired.

Similarly, any other sentence element that has been wrenched out of its normal position and placed first gets extra attention.

- **Never again** will she overlook the threat of an avalanche.
- **Not until then** had he understood how miserable he was.

Again:

- **About such a glaring scandal** nothing need be said.

   The subject and verb, *nothing* and *need,* are in the usual
   sequence, but the writer begins with a prepositional phrase
   that would normally come last.

13k   Practice the cumulative sentence.

A **cumulative sentence** is one whose main statement is followed
by one or more free subordinate elements (p. 151, 12c). It is called
cumulative because it "accumulates," or collects, modifying words,
phrases, or clauses at the end. The following sentences, encountered
earlier, are typical:

- Lisa's smile disguised her fierce competitiveness, **a trait revealed to very few of her early teammates.**
- He was prepared to risk everything—**his comfort, his livelihood, even his life.**
- Jeremy's life revolved around his older brother, **who never
  ceased making unreasonable demands.**

   The beauty of the cumulative pattern is that it offers refinement
without much risk of confusing the reader. Since the basic structure
of the sentence is complete before the end-modifiers (boldfaced above)
begin, your reader has a secure grasp of your idea, which you can
then elaborate, illustrate, explain, or reflect on.

   Since much of our speech follows the cumulative model of state-
ment-plus-adjustment, a cumulative sentence can have a pleasantly
conversational effect, as if one afterthought had brought the next to
mind. Notice, for example, how three sentences in this passage end
with free subordinate elements (boldfaced):

   There is a place called "the farm" where I lived once, **in a time that
   was very lonely.** Fortunately I was unconscious of my loneliness then,
   and felt it only deeply, **bewildered, in the half-bright way that a**

puppy feels pain. I loved the place, and still do. It was an ordinary farm, **a calf-raising, haymaking farm, and very beautiful.**

—ANNIE DILLARD, "A Field of Silence"

13l Practice the suspended sentence.

If you substantially delay starting or completing your main assertion, forcing the reader to wait for essential information, you have written a **suspended sentence** (often called a *periodic* sentence). The suspended sentence uses a tactic exactly opposite to that of the cumulative sentence (13k), adding details before, not after, the main statement. Through its use of delaying elements (boldfaced in the following examples), a suspended sentence can be an effective means of leading to a climax:

var
13l

- **His palms sweating, his hands shaking, his jaw clenched in anticipation of the worst,** Kevin stood before the judge.
- The states argued that they had indeed complied, **if compliance can mean making a good-faith effort and collecting all the required data,** with the federal guidelines.
- If you are still unused to the idea of gasohol, you will certainly not be ready to hear that some diesel engines will soon be running on **that most humble and ordinary of products, taken for granted by homemakers and never noticed by auto buffs,** vegetable oil.

Suspended sentences are especially appropriate when you have a reason for building tension. Notice, for example, how the boldfaced elements in this sentence first postpone the start of the main element, then delay its completion.

As I sat reading Derickson's chapter describing how miners died of black lung, how car painters died of fumes from some of the first autospraying machines, how felt-hat makers went slowly mad, how radium dial painters became palsied, I came to realize that we are, **just as our grandparents before us, in the midst of the latest technological/industrial maelstrom,** facing a new set of health-related issues little understood by our peers.

—JERRY BORRELL, "Is Your Computer Killing You?"

IV
WORDS

Words

To convey your ideas successfully, you need to know words well and to respect their often subtle differences from one another. Specifically, when revising your drafts you should make sure that your words

1. mean what you think they mean;

2. are appropriate to the occasion;

3. are concise;

4. are neither stale, roundabout, nor needlessly abstract; and

5. show control over figurative, or nonliteral, implications.

Chapters 14–16 discuss these requirements of **diction,** *or word choice. For an alphabetically arranged treatment of problem expressions, see the Index of Usage beginning on page 585.*

14 Appropriate Language

14a   Know how to use your college dictionary.

To improve your control of **denotation,** or the dictionary meaning of words, you should own a college dictionary such as *The Random House Webster's College Dictionary, Funk and Wagnalls Standard College Dictionary, Webster's New World Dictionary of the American Language, Webster's New Collegiate Dictionary,* or *The American Heritage Dictionary of the English Language.* These volumes are large enough to meet your daily needs without being too cumbersome to carry around. Once you learn from the prefatory guide to your dictionary how to interpret its abbreviations, symbols, and order of placing entries, you can find in it most—perhaps all—of the following kinds of information:

spelling	usage levels
parts of speech	syllable division
definitions	principles of usage
synonyms	abbreviations
antonyms	symbols
alternative forms	biographical and given names
pronunciation	places and population figures
capitalization	weights and measures
derivations	names and locations of colleges

To see what a college dictionary can and cannot do, look at *Random House*'s entry under *fabulous:*

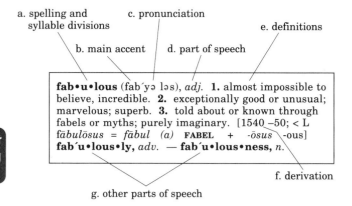

a. spelling and syllable divisions   c. pronunciation   e. definitions
b. main accent   d. part of speech

fab•u•lous (fab´yə ləs), *adj.* **1.** almost impossible to believe, incredible. **2.** exceptionally good or unusual; marvelous; superb. **3.** told about or known through fabels or myths; purely imaginary. [1540 –50; < L *fābulōsus = fābul (a)* **FABEL** + *-ōsus* -ous] **fab´u•lous•ly,** *adv.* — **fab´u•lous•ness,** *n.*

f. derivation

g. other parts of speech

The entry shows, in the following order:

a. how the word is spelled and the points where syllable divisions occur (*fab•u•lous*);

Comment: The lowercase *f* shows that *fabulous* is not normally capitalized.

If this word could be spelled correctly in different ways, the less common form would appear in a separate entry with a cross reference to the more common form; thus the entry for *reenforce* merely sends you to *reinforce.* In your writing, use the spelling that appears with the full definition.

Syllable division is not completely uniform from one dictionary to another, but you cannot go wrong by following your dictionary's practice. (You can also spare yourself trouble by not breaking up words at all; a little unevenness in right-hand margins is normal.)

b. where the main accent falls (*fab'*);

Comment: If the word had another strongly stressed syllable, like *hand* in *beforehand,* you would find it marked with a secondary accent: *bi•for' hand'.*

c. how the word is pronounced;

Comment: The pronunciation key at the bottom of every pair of pages reveals, among other things, that ə = *a* as in *alone.* (One dictionary's key will differ from another's.)

d. the part of speech (*adj.* for *adjective*);

Comment: Some words, like *can* and *wait,* occupy more than one part of speech, depending on the context. Definitions are grouped according to those parts of speech. Transitive verbs (those that take an object—p. 209, 17a) are usually listed separately from intransitive verbs (those that take no object). Thus *Random House* gives all the intransitive senses of *wait* (*v.i.*), as in *Wait for me,* before the transitive senses (*v.t.*), as in *Wait your turn!*

appr lang 14a

e. three definitions of *fabulous;*

Comment: No dictionary lists definitions in the order of their acceptability. *Random House* begins with the most common part of speech occupied by a given word and, within each part of speech, offers the most frequently encountered meaning first. To make sure you understand your dictionary's system, read its prefatory material.

f. information about the history of *fabulous,* including the date it first appeared in English and its derivation from the Latin word *fabulosus;*

Comment: The history, or *etymology,* of a word is given only if its component parts are not obviously familiar—as they are, for example, in *freeze-dry* and *nearsighted.* Many symbols are used in stating etymologies; look for their explanation in the prefatory material of your dictionary.

g. an adverb and a noun stemming from the main word;

Comment: Fabulously and *fabulousness* are "run-on entries," words formed by adding a suffix (p. 404, 33f) to the main entry.

So much for *fabulous.* But other sample entries would reveal still further kinds of information:

1. *inflected forms.* Some entries show unusual inflected forms—that is, changes in spelling expressing different syntactic functions. You will find unusual plurals (*louse, lice*); unusual principal parts of verbs (*run, ran, run*—see p. 372, 31b); pronoun forms (*I, my, mine,* etc.); comparative and superlative degrees of adjectives (*good, better, best*—see p. 251, 20a).

2. *restrictive labels.* The entry will show how a word's use may be limited to a region (*Southern U.S., Austral., Chiefly Brit.*); to an earlier time or a kind of occasion (*Archaic, Obs., Poetic*); to a subject (*Bot., Anat., Law*); and, most important for the writer, to a level of usage for words not clearly within standard American English (*Nonstandard, Informal, Slang*).

3. *usage study.* Beyond its usage levels, your dictionary may offer especially valuable discussions of usage problems surrounding certain controversial words or meanings, such as *ain't, different from/than,* or *hardly* with negative forms:

> —**Usage.** HARDLY, BARELY, SCARCELY all have a negative connotation, and the use of any of them with a supplementary negative (*I can't hardly remember*) is considered nonstandard except when done for humorous effect. See also DOUBLE NEGATIVE.

appr
lang
14b

14b   Keep a vocabulary list.

Many student writers rely on a *thesaurus,* or dictionary of synonyms and antonyms, to learn new words and to jog their memory of words already known. A thesaurus can be especially handy if it is included in the word processing program you happen to be using with a computer. You should realize, however, that the synonyms found in a thesaurus are only approximate. To use the thesaurus shrewdly in composing a given sentence, you must already be familiar with the term you select.

The best way to build vocabulary, with or without a thesaurus, is to notice how words are being used by published authors and to keep a record of your growing knowledge. Specifically:

1. Keep a section of your notebook for listing and defining words that you didn't previously know, words whose meanings you misunderstood, and words you understand and admire but haven't yet had occasion to use in your writing.

2. Begin your list by going over the Index of Usage on pages 585–605, making an entry for each expression whose indicated meaning is new to you. Note especially those terms that get easily confused (*affect* versus *effect, imply* versus *infer,* etc.).

3. Add to your notebook continually as you keep reading and receiving comments on your written work.

4. Every time you make an entry, quickly scan the previous entries to see if you have learned them yet. Check off any terms that you now consider part of your working vocabulary.

appr
lang
14c

14c Learn common idioms.

An **idiom** is a fixed expression whose meaning cannot be deduced from its elements—for example, *put up with*. No amount of grammar study or knowledge of the separate meanings of *put, up,* and *with* will yield the right meaning; this idiom, like all others, must be grasped as a unit. For students trying to learn a new language, idioms are especially bothersome, but even accomplished native speakers sometimes stumble over idioms as they write.

Most of the mischief caused by idioms centers on **prepositions**—words like *at, down, up, in, out, by, of,* and *with*.

DON'T:

x Pat is annoyed **at** his partner.

x Kim will abide **with** the rules.

DO:

• Pat is annoyed **with** [or **by**] his partner.

• Kim will abide **by** the rules.

How can you choose the right preposition to go with a given expression? First, consult a dictionary, looking up the word that comes immediately before the preposition. Second, study the common idioms given below and add any unfamiliar ones to your ongoing vocabulary list (14b).

FAULTY "IDIOM"	CORRECT IDIOM
agree to (an opinion)	agree **with** (an opinion)
comply to	comply **with**
contend against (an opponent)	contend **with** (an opponent)
die with (a disease)	die **of/from** (a disease)
equal with	equal **to**
frightened of	frightened **by**
impatient at (a person)	impatient **with** (a person)
inferior than	inferior **to**
preferable than	preferable **to**
prior than	prior **to**
superior than	superior **to**

appr
lang
14d

14d Use middle diction in most contexts.

SLANG	MIDDLE DICTION	FORMAL DICTION
mug	face	countenance
duds	clothes	apparel
big-mouthed	talkative	loquacious
kicks	pleasure	gratification
rip off	steal	expropriate
specs	glasses	spectacles

Different situations call for different levels of diction (word choice), from the slang that may be appropriate in a letter to a friend, to the formal language expected in a legal document, to the technical terms demanded by a scientific report. But whenever you are writing outside such special contexts, you should aim for *middle diction*—language that is neither too casual to convey serious concern nor too stiff to express feeling.

The best way to recognize levels of diction is to be an observant reader of different kinds of prose and a close listener to conversations. But if you have studied Latin or a "Latinate" modern language such as Spanish, French, or Italian, you have a head start toward spotting formal English diction. All the words in the right column above are both formal and Latinate.

As you revise your essays, watch especially for the inconsistent mixing of slang and formal language within a single piece of writing. Notice, for example, how levels of diction clash awkwardly in this draft student paragraph about a character from Kate Chopin's novel *The Awakening*.

appr lang 14d

DRAFT:

Edna Pontellier discovers that her marriage is a **flop.** Dimly **cognizant** of her own sensual and intellectual nature, she tries to **get it together** as a person, seeking an independent life in which she defies social convention. Her happiness, however, is fleeting. Realizing that she is **stuck** with few alternatives, Edna chooses suicide rather than facing the conventional life from which she cannot **extricate** herself.

And here is the paragraph after the student writer replaced the formal and slang terms with middle diction.

REVISION:

Edna Pontellier discovers that her marriage is a failure. Dimly aware of her own sensual and intellectual nature, she tries to form a new self, seeking an independent life in which she defies social norms. Her happiness, however, is fleeting. Realizing that she has few alternatives, Edna chooses suicide rather than facing the conventional life from which she cannot escape.

Fad Words

As you revise your essays for appropriate diction, be especially wary of **fad words,** terms that gain widespread but momentary popularity in everyday speech. Such diction annoys many readers; by being conservative in your choice of words, you can avoid arousing an automatically negative response to your ideas.

Many fad words have a common feature: they belong to one part of speech but are wrenched into service as another. Sometimes a suffix (p. 404, 33f) such as *-wise* or *-type* is tacked on to turn a noun into an adjective or adverb.

DON'T:

x **Gaswise,** the car is economical.

x **Preferencewise,** she is looking for a **commuter-type** car.

DO:

- The car gets good mileage.
- She wants a car suitable for commuting.

appr
lang
14d

More often, one part of speech simply takes over another.

DON'T:

x It was a **fun** party.

x She **authored** the book last year.

x We **gifted** the newlyweds with a toaster.

x Mark is a **together** person.

DO:

- The party was **fun.**
- She **wrote** the book last year.
- We **gave** the newlyweds a toaster.
- Mark is a **confident, competent** person.

The use of nouns as adjectives deserves special mention in an age of spreading bureaucracy. Standard English allows many such **attributive nouns,** as they are called, as in *mountain time, night vision, cheese omelet,* and *recreation director.* But officials have a way of jamming them together in a confusing heap. A frugal governor, for example, once proposed what he called a *community work experience program demonstration project.* This row of nouns was meant to describe, or perhaps to conceal, a policy of getting welfare mothers to pick up highway litter without receiving any wages. You would do well to avoid such strings of attributive nouns.

14e Control connotations.

The prime requirement for controlling meaning is to know the *denotations,* or dictionary definitions, of the words you use. (See 14a–b.) But words also have important **connotations**—further suggestions or associations derived from the contexts in which the words have been habitually used. By and large, you will not find connotations in your dictionary; you have to pick them up from meeting the same words repeatedly in reading and conversation. Of course, you cannot expect to learn all the overtones of every English word. But as a writer you can ask yourself whether the words you have allowed into your first drafts are suited to the occasion. When you are unsure, think of related words until you find one that conveys appropriate associations.

appr
lang
14e

Take, for example, the words *aroma* and *fragrance.* Both have roughly the same denotation—a pleasant odor—but their connotations differ significantly. While a dictionary might give you some advice, you would probably have to rely on your own grasp of language to choose the right word for a given context.

AVOID:

x That herbal shampoo gives Nancy's hair a wonderful **aroma.**

x Al's freshly baked bread has a marvelous **fragrance.**

BETTER:

• That herbal shampoo gives Nancy's hair a wonderful **fragrance.**

• Al's freshly baked bread has a marvelous **aroma.**

As these examples suggest, *fragrance* generally applies to the odor of perfumes, flowers, and clean hair. *Aroma* is usually reserved for food. Such distinctions are subtle, but choosing just the right word can sometimes make the difference between a barely adequate sentence and an effective one.

Consider two further examples, *complex* versus *complicated* and *workers* versus *employees.* Although the members of each pair are close in denotation, their connotations differ. Suppose you wanted to characterize an overelaborate instruction manual. Would you call it *complex* or *complicated?* We hope you would choose *complicated,* which can imply not just intricacy but more intricacy than is called for. And if you were criticizing harsh factory conditions, you would want to write about mistreated *workers,* not mistreated *employees.* These words denote the same people, yet *employees* characterizes them from a corporate point of view, whereas *workers* calls to mind laborers whose interests and loyalties may be quite different from those of the company.

Note that there is such a thing as getting connotations too lopsidedly in favor of your own position on an issue. Suppose, for example, you were writing an essay arguing that resident assistants in your dormitory had overstepped their authority in enforcing university policies. If you called the assistants *bullies* or *thugs* throughout your essay, you would certainly be making your feelings clear, but you would also be prejudging the issue, forcing readers to respond emotionally with you or against you. In revising your essays, tone down any inflammatory language that seems to convey ready-made conclusions.

appr lang 14f

14f Avoid racist and sexist language.

Since you are writing to convince, not to insult, nothing can be gained from using offensive terms. Racial slurs like *nigger, honky,* and *wop,* demeaning stereotypes like *pushy Jew* and *dumb Swede,* and sexually biased phrases such as *lady driver, female logic,* and *typical male brutality* make any fair-minded reader turn against the writer.

The problem of sexism in language deserves special discussion because it goes beyond any conscious wish to show prejudice. In recent decades people have been increasingly aware that long-accepted conventions of word choice imply that women are inferior or are destined for restricted roles. To keep sexist language out of your writing, then, it is not enough to avoid overtly insulting terms; you must watch for subtler signs of condescension as well.

Remember, for example, that *woman,* not *lady, girl,* or *gal,* is the verbal equivalent of *man.* And if you call William Shakespeare *Shakespeare,* why should you call Emily Dickinson *Miss Dickinson* or, worse, *Emily?* Such names imply that a woman who writes poems is not really a poet but a "poetess," a "lady poet," or even a "spinster poet." Write about *Dickinson's poetry,* thus giving it the same standing you would the work of any other author. Similarly, use *sculptor* and *lawyer* for both sexes, avoiding such designations as *sculptress* and *lady lawyer.* And do without *coed,* which suggests that the higher education of women is an afterthought to the real (male) thing. Make your language reflect the fact that, in North America at any rate, men and women are now considered equally eligible for nearly every role.

Tact is necessary, however, in deciding how far to go in changing traditional expressions. *Steward* and *stewardess* gave way long ago to *flight attendant,* while the distinction between *actor* and *actress* still holds. When in doubt, choose the sex-neutral term: not *mankind* but *humanity,* not *man-made* but *artificial.*

appr lang 14f

-Person

Try to find nonsexist alternatives to awkward *-person* suffixes, which sound ugly to many readers of both sexes.

SEXIST	NONSEXIST BUT AWKWARD	PREFERABLE
chairman	chairperson	chair, head
Congressman	Congressperson	Representative
mailman	mailperson	letter carrier
policeman	policeperson	police officer
weatherman	weatherperson	meteorologist

The Pronoun Dilemma

Perhaps the sorest of all issues in contemporary usage is that of the so-called **common gender.** Which pronouns should you use when discussing an indefinite person, a "one"? Traditionally, that indefinite person has been "male": *he, his, him,* as in *A taxpayer must check his return carefully.* For the centuries in which this practice went unchallenged, the masculine pronouns in such sentences were understood to designate not actual men but people of either sex. Today, however, many readers find these words an offensive reminder of second-class citizenship for women. Remedies that have been proposed include using the phrase *he or she* (or *she or he*) for the common gender, treating singular common words as plural (*A taxpayer must check their return*), combining masculine and feminine pronouns in forms like *s/he,* and using *she* in one sentence and *he* in the next.

Unfortunately, all of these solutions carry serious drawbacks. Continual repetition of *he or she* is cumbersome and monotonous; most readers would regard *A taxpayer must check their return* as a blunder (p. 283, 22a), not a blow for liberation; pronunciation of *s/he* is uncertain; and the use of *she* and *he* in alternation, though increasingly common, risks confusing the reader by implying that two indefinite persons, a female and a male, are involved.

To avoid such awkwardness, follow these six guidelines:

1. Avoid using *she* for roles that have been "traditionally female" but are actually mixed: secretary, schoolteacher, laundry worker, and so forth. Female pronouns in such contexts imply an offensive prejudgment about "women's place." Use plural forms to avoid bias.

   DON'T:
   x A kindergarten teacher has **her** hands full every day.

   DO:
   • Kindergarten teachers have **their** hands full every day.

2. Use an occasional *he or she* or *she or he* to indicate an indefinite person:

   • When a driver is stopped for a traffic violation, **he or she** would do well to remain polite.

      But be sparing with this formula; it can quickly become annoying.

appr
lang
14f

3. Try, throughout an essay, using *she* consistently as the "common gender" pronoun. Your reader will become quickly adjusted to the change, especially if you yourself are female.

4. If your uses of the common gender are few and widely spaced, try alternating the masculine and feminine forms.

5. Avoid the singular whenever your meaning is not affected.

   DON'T:
   x A taxpayer must check **his** return.

   DO:
   • Taxpayers must check **their** returns.

6. Omit the pronoun altogether whenever you can do so without awkwardness.

   ACCEPTABLE:
   • Everyone needs **his or her** vacation.

   BETTER:
   • Everyone needs **a** vacation.

appr
lang
14g

14g Avoid jargon.

Jargon is specialized language that appears in a nonspecialized context, thus giving a technical flavor to statements that would be better expressed in everyday words. When you are writing a paper in, say, economics, anthropology, or psychology, you can and should use terms that are meaningful within the field: *cash flow, kinship structure, paranoid,* and so forth. But those same terms become jargon when used out of context.

   DON'T:
   x I have had a poor **cash flow** lately.
   x Her **kinship structure** extends from coast to coast.
   x Roland was really **paranoid** about the boss's intentions.

DO:

- I have been short of **cash** lately.
- Her **family** is scattered from coast to coast.
- Roland was **suspicious** of the boss's intentions.

Most jargon today comes from popular academic disciplines such as sociology and psychology, from government bureaucracy, and from the world of computers. Here is some of the more commonly seen jargon, accompanied by everyday equivalents that would usually be preferable.

**appr
lang
14g**

JARGON	ORDINARY TERM
access (verb)	enter, make use of
behaviors	acts, deeds, conduct
correlation	resemblance, association
cost-effective	economical
counterproductive	harmful, obstructive
ego	vanity, pride
facilitate	help, make possible
feedback	response, reaction
finalize	complete, finish
input	response, contribution
interface (verb)	meet, share information with
maximize	make the most of
obsession	strong interest
parameters	borders
prioritize	prefer, rank
sociological	social
syndrome	pattern
trauma	shock
user-friendly	uncomplicated

You can put jargon to good comic or ironic use, but when you find it appearing uninvited in your drafts, revise.

15 Efficient Language

15a Be concrete.

Concrete words name observable things or properties like *classroom* and *smoky.* Words of the opposite sort, like *education* and *pollution,* are called **abstract;** they address the mind without calling the senses into play. Of course, there are gradations between the extremes: a *university* is more concrete than *education* but less so than *classroom,* a distinct physical place. The more concrete the term, the more vivid it will be to the reader.

Whenever you want to describe something or tell a story, you can hardly go wrong by using concrete language. Notice the sensory appeal of this student paragraph:

> Early September extends the glory of August. We still feel a bond with summer as we step over into the fall: the **smell of freshly cut grass,** the **thick green** of the landscape, the occasional **smoldering** days. We can **saunter down the street,** carefree and aimless, imagining **crystal blue lakes just over the horizon, county fairs** out there somewhere, and **barbecues** and **lawn chairs.** We can **stub a patch of dirt** and **watch the hot dust rise.** And while the neighborhood **honks** and **yells,** we can **watch lawn sprinklers slowly mist the warm air.**

No one would accuse this student writer of being too abstract; he packs his sentences with concrete diction, making readers see, hear, smell, and feel a late summer day. This passage also shows that an imagined experience can be rendered as concretely as an actual one.

Even in essays of analysis and argument (p. 9, 1d), where the thesis is necessarily abstract, concrete language will help you provide supporting details and retain your reader's interest. Here, for example, are two versions of a student paragraph. In drafting the first one, the writer relies almost entirely on abstract language.

DRAFT:

x In some early learning environments, educators are still hesitant to provide information relating to currently available illicit chemical substances, partly because they regard such information as having the potential to lead to later substance abuse. Studies have indicated, however, that when individuals are made aware at an early age of the dangers of available substances, those individuals tend toward greater caution in their future exploration of dangerous chemicals. Since the home environment is usually inadequate for providing early education regarding substance abuse, it is important that students be made aware of the harmful impact of chemical dependence through educational programs at the elementary school level.

effic
lang
15a

REVISION:

● Some administrators still hesitate to inform grade school students about the dangers of illegal drugs like marijuana and crack. They believe that giving such information to very young children can arouse their curiosity and lead them to try drugs at an early age. They imagine otherwise naive eight-year-olds smoking marijuana as they walk home from school. But studies show that when grade school children learn about dangerous drugs, the opposite effect occurs: they tend to avoid early drug use and regard playground pushers with caution, even fear. Since parents are usually ill-prepared to give their children specific information about illegal drugs, schools must do so—even if that means teachers discussing crack with third graders.

The revision addresses several problems besides abstract language, including overuse of the passive voice (p. 144, 11e). But the addition of concrete language goes a long way toward making the writer's ideas more vivid and understandable. Instead of *currently available illicit chemical substances* we get *dangers of illegal drugs like marijuana and crack.* And abstract concepts give way to images that we can actually see: *eight-year-olds smoking marijuana as they walk home from school* and *teachers discussing crack with third graders.* Notice, however, that these images are called forth to back up an abstract idea. The writer has not tried to eliminate *all* abstraction; rather, she has selectively shifted toward concreteness, allowing us to see the human stakes at issue.

15b Be concise.

Your reader's attention will depend in large part on the ratio between information and language in your prose. *Wordiness,* or the use of more words than are necessary to convey a point, is one of the most common and easily corrected flaws of style. The fewer words you can use without harm to your meaning, the better.

WORDY	CONCISE
among all the problems that exist today	among all current problems
an investment in the form of stocks and bonds	an investment in stocks and bonds
at this point in time	now
during the course of	during
for the purpose of getting rich	to get rich
for the simple reason that	because
in a very real sense	truly
in spite of the fact that	although
in the not too distant future	soon
in view of the fact that	since
it serves no particular purpose	it serves no purpose
majoring in the field of astronomy	majoring in astronomy
my personal preference	my preference
on the part of	by
proceeded to walk	walked
rarely ever	rarely
seldom ever	seldom
the present incumbent	the incumbent
to the effect that	that

effic
lang
15b

Avoiding Redundancy

A **redundancy** is an expression that conveys the same meaning more than once—for example, *circle around,* which says "go around

around." The difference between writing *She circled the globe* and
x *She circled around the globe* is that in the second version the word
around delivers no new information and thus strains the reader's
patience.

Examine your drafts to see if they contain redundancies, and be
uncompromising in pruning them. The following examples are typical.

effic
lang
15b

REDUNDANT	CONCISE
adequate enough	adequate
advance planning	planning
both together	both
but yet	but
contributing factor	factor
deliberate lie	lie
equally as far	as far
exact same symptoms	same symptoms
few in number	few
final outcome	outcome
free gift	gift
join together	join
large in size	large
past experience	experience
past history	history
refer back	refer
set of twins	twins
share in common	share
shuttle back and forth	shuttle
two different reasons	two reasons

Avoiding Circumlocution

All redundancies fall into the broader category of **circumlocutions**—
that is, roundabout forms of expression. But some circumlocutions,
instead of saying the same thing twice, take several words to say
almost nothing. Formulas like *in a manner of speaking* or *to make a*

long story short, for example, are simply ways of making a short story long. Watch especially for cumbersome verb phrases like *give rise to, make contact with,* and *render inoperative;* prefer *arouse, meet, destroy.* And if you mean *because,* do not reach for *due to the fact that.* When five words do the work of one, all five are anemic.

CIRCUMLOCUTION	CONCISE EXPRESSION
He was of a kindly nature.	He was kind.
It was of an unusual character.	It was unusual.
My father and I have differences about dating.	My father and I differ about dating.
I finally made contact with my supervisor.	I finally met my supervisor.
In this modern world of ours today, everyone has his or her own opinion regarding gun control.	Today everyone has an opinion about gun control.
The copy that is pink in color is for yourself.	Keep the pink copy.
She suspected that she would be in an unemployment type of situation when the overflow of customers owing to the Christmas shopping season was no longer in effect.	She suspected she would be laid off after the Christmas rush.

**effic
lang
15c**

15c Avoid exaggerated language.

In telling stories or expressing opinions, most of us veer toward exaggerated language. Our trip to the beach was *perfect, fantastic,* and *wonderful.* The election of a politician we oppose will have *horrible, awful,* or *terrible* consequences. We also tend to pepper our conversation with **intensifiers**—"fortifying" words like *absolutely, basically, certainly, definitely, just, positively, quite, really, simply, so, too,* and *very*—without pausing to worry about their meaning. Our listeners know how to allow for such exaggeration. Most written prose, how-ever, aims at a more measured tone. Look through your drafts for exaggerated diction, and see how much you can eliminate without loss of meaning. Doing so will make your writing more concise and your tone more assured.

AVOID:

x I **definitely** cannot support the **terrible** decision—made this week by our **incredibly** tightfisted city council—to close Lucio Park. The **very** idea of closing such a **constantly** used park is **truly** insensitive to the citizens and former council members who worked **extremely** hard to open it three years ago.

effic
lang
15d

x Dickinson's poems are **so fantastic.** They are a **wonderful** example of how a **truly great** poet, using **just** a few **perfect** words, can have an **absolutely astonishing** effect on the reader.

BETTER:

• I cannot support the decision—made this week by our tightfisted city council—to close Lucio Park. The idea of closing such a widely used park is insensitive to the citizens and former council members who worked hard to open it three years ago.

• Dickinson's poems show how a skillful poet, using a few well-chosen words, can have a powerful effect on the reader.

15d Put your statements in positive form.

Negative ideas are just as legitimate as positive ones; you may have to point out that something did not happen or that an argument leaves you unconvinced. But the negative modifiers *no* and *not* some-times make for wordiness and a slight loss of readability. If you write *We are not in agreement,* you are asking your reader to go through two steps, first to conceive of agreement and then to negate it. But if you simply write *We disagree,* you have saved three words and simpli-fied the mental operation. The gain is small, but good writing results from a sum of small gains.

Of course, you need not develop a phobia against every use of *no* or *not*. Observe, however, that negatively worded sentences tend to be slightly less emphatic than positive ones. Compare:

NEGATIVE	POSITIVE
She did not do well on the test.	She did poorly on the test.
He was not convicted.	He was acquitted.
They do not see anything.	They see nothing.
It was not an insignificant amount.	It was a significant amount.

15e   Avoid euphemisms.

A **euphemism** is a squeamishly "nice" expression standing in the place of a more direct one. Some words that began as euphemisms, such as *senior citizen* and *realtor,* have passed into common usage, but you should try to avoid terms that still sound like ways of covering up a meaning instead of conveying it.

Euphemisms often conceal a devious political or commercial motive. Thus, a military commander will describe *personnel adversely impacted by friendly fire* instead of *soldiers killed and wounded by gunfire from their own side*. A business enterprise will advertise *pre-owned automobiles* instead of *used cars*. And a funeral director will urge us to buy a *pre-need policy,* not *burial insurance*.

ORDINARY TERM	EUPHEMISM
airsickness	motion discomfort
cemetery	memory garden
clerk	sales associate
concentration camp	relocation center
demotion	reassignment
die	pass away
drug addiction	chemical dependency

ORDINARY TERM	EUPHEMISM
invasion	deployment of forces
kill	neutralize
lie (noun)	inoperative statement
lie (verb)	misspeak
pornography	adult entertainment
poverty	economic distress
tax increase	revenue enhancement

15f Avoid clichés.

A **cliché** is a trite, worn-out expression such as *throw money around* or *jump for joy.* Many clichés are **dead metaphors** (p. 204, 16b)—that is, figures of speech that no longer sound figurative. When someone writes *off the wall* or *bottom line,* no reader actually imagines a wall or a line. We have heard such expressions so often that they no longer conjure up the vivid mental pictures they once did. Such formulaic language thus robs your prose of freshness, making it dull and predictable. As soon as we register the first part of a cliché, the rest of it leaps to mind like an advertising jingle:

bolt from the . . . blue

lines of . . . communication

the foreseeable . . . future

nutty as a . . . fruitcake

slept like a . . . log

Three lists of clichés follow. List A includes examples of obvious clichés, which you can spot fairly easily as you revise. List B includes less obvious clichés, pairs of seemingly inseparable adjectives and nouns that drain vigor from your writing. List C contains pat expressions that say little in a wordy, predictable manner.

A: OBVIOUS CLICHÉS	
blind as a bat	playing with fire
bull in a china shop	quiet as a mouse
busy as a bee	rule with an iron fist
carve a niche for oneself	sly as a fox
happy as a lark	smart as a whip
live like a king	top of the heap
make a beeline for	tough as nails
old as the hills	white as a ghost

B: "INSEPARABLE" PAIRS	
cold sweat	meaningful dialogue
crushing blow	nuclear holocaust
dire consequences	painfully aware
flawless complexion	splitting headache
foregone conclusion	vast majority
harsh reality	vicious circle
high hopes	vital role

C: PAT EXPRESSIONS	
after all is said and done	in today's society
as luck would have it	it goes without saying
at this point in time	it stands to reason
far be it from me	once and for all
in a very real sense	slowly but surely
in the final analysis	the powers that be
in this day and age	time and time again

effic
lang
15g

15g   Watch for distracting sound patterns.

Knowing that repeated sounds draw attention, you can sometimes use them deliberately, as Mark Twain did in referring to

- the **calm confidence** of a **Christian** with four aces, or as Thomas Paine did in writing

- These are the **times** that **try** men's souls.

And a repeated sound often gives energy to a title:

- **"Why I Write"** (George Orwell)
- *Pride and Prejudice* (Jane Austen)
- **"Singing** the **Spring Break Blues"** (student writer)

In these examples the "poetic" quality goes along with the effort to make a concisely emphatic statement.

Unless you are after some such effect, however, beware of making your reader conscious of rhymes (*the side of the hide*) or alliteration (*pursuing particular purposes*) or repeated syllables (*apart from the apartment*). These bits of accidental "poetry" will draw your readers' attention away from rather than toward your ideas. You may want to read your draft aloud, attending to its sound patterns and not its sense, in order to see if you have lapsed into jingling.

Abstract Latinate words—the ones that usually end in *-al, -ity, -ation,* or *-otion*—are especially apt to make a repetitive sound pattern. It is worth the pains to rewrite, for example, if you find bunched words like *functional, essential, occupational,* and *institutional* or *equality, opportunity, parity,* and *mobility.*

effic
lang
15g

16 Figurative Language

16a **Be alert to figures of speech and their uses.**

Compare these two sentences:

LITERAL:
- This novel is dull and unappealing.

FIGURATIVE:
- This novel has all the zest of a bowl of cold oatmeal.

The first statement is **literal** because it makes its point without asking us to call a picture, or **image,** to mind. The second statement is **figurative** (also called *metaphorical*); it asks for an effort of imagination on our part. The writer wants us to see the point in different terms—specifically, to compare a novel to a bowl of cold oatmeal. Though exaggerated, the comparison is apt; it states an opinion about the novel in a surprising and memorable way. Whenever your language makes such a nonliteral appeal, you are using what is known as a *figure of speech.*

Why should you bother incorporating figures of speech into your writing? The answer is that such language, when thoughtfully managed, seasons your prose the way salt and pepper season an otherwise flat meal. A shrewdly placed figure of speech can bring wit, economy, and color to your prose. Notice the striking differences between the following literal and figurative passages.

LITERAL:
Elsa moved quickly and erratically around the bookshop. She went from one title to another, stopping to glance for a moment at each one.

199

FIGURATIVE:

Elsa darted around the bookshop like a hummingbird in a flower garden.

LITERAL:

Chicago used to have great vitality in its downtown area, but now the city has deteriorated. Much of its life has been transferred to the suburbs, occupying a larger area but lacking that optimism and concentration for which the original Chicago was known.

FIGURATIVE:

Chicago's rising star is now a worn-out supernova, which has exploded all over suburbia.

—Thomas Geoghegan, "Chicago, Pride of the Rustbelt"

**fig
lang
16a**

LITERAL:

In New England in autumn, the leaves on the trees are dying. Another common feature of that season is that the Red Sox have failed to fulfill people's expectation that they would win their league championship.

FIGURATIVE:

Dying leaves and dead Red Sox—that's the New England autumn.

—Russell Baker, "New England Gray"

LITERAL:

I am not consciously aware of grammatical rules as I write. Rather, I compose sentences that sound right to me.

FIGURATIVE:

Grammar is a piano I play by ear.

—Joan Didion, "Why I Write"

In each figurative expression above, we feel ourselves to be as far from the groping of first-draft prose as we can get. The writer has reduced a complex thought not only to relatively few words but also to a mental picture that lingers in our minds, giving pleasure and information at the same time.

Again, note how the boldfaced figurative expressions in the following passages bring our imagination into play:

> Her sketches are **as delicate and intricate as the design on a butterfly's wing.**

> Seeing Tina Turner onstage is **like watching a demented child who stamps her feet, twirls in circles, and bops around bow-legged as though she's wearing a diaper.**
>
> —MICK LASALLE, "She's Her Own Best Imitator"

> This generation thinks—and this is its thought of thoughts—that nothing faithful, vulnerable, fragile can be durable or have any true power. **Death waits for these things as a cement floor waits for a dropping light bulb. The brittle shell of glass loses its tiny vacuum with a burst, and that is that.**
>
> —SAUL BELLOW, *Herzog*

fig
lang
16b

16b Aim for unstrained similes and metaphors.

Two closely related figures of speech allow you to draw imaginative likenesses. A **simile,** by including the word *like* or *as,* explicitly acknowledges that a comparison is being made.

SIMILE:

- **Like** a patio rotisserie, George's mind always keeps turning at the same slow rate, no matter what is impaled on it.

    George's mind is explicitly compared to a rotisserie.

A **metaphor** omits *like* or *as.*

METAPHOR:

- George's hedgeclipper mind gives a suburban sameness to everything it touches.

    George's mind is compared to hedgeclippers, but without either of the explicit terms of comparison, *like* or *as.*

In theory a metaphor is a more radical figure of speech than a simile, for it asserts an identity, not just a likeness, between two things (George's mind "is" a gardening tool). But in practice one kind of figure can be as striking as the other. What counts is not the choice between simile and metaphor but the suitability of the **image** to your intended meaning. The two images about George, for example, call to mind not only his conformism but also his specifically suburban background (the carefully tended hedge, the patio rotisserie).

Simile and metaphor predominate among the figures of speech you have already studied in this chapter:

fig
lang
16b

SIMILE	METAPHOR
• Elsa darted around the bookshop **like** a hummingbird in a flower garden.	• This novel has all the zest of a bowl of cold oatmeal.
• Her sketches are **as** delicate and intricate **as** the design on a butterfly's wing.	• Grammar is a piano I play by ear.
• Seeing Tina Turner onstage is **like** watching a demented child who stamps her feet, twirls in circles, and bops around bow-legged **as though** she's wearing a diaper.	• Chicago's rising star is now a worn-out supernova, which has exploded all over suburbia.
	• Dying leaves and dead Red Sox—that's the New England autumn.

When a simile or metaphor succeeds, it usually seems natural, not forced. Even though the writer's image may startle and delight us, we can see at once the aptness of the intended comparison. In the just-cited "Tina Turner" sentence, for example, the image of a demented, childlike, diaper-wearing singer comes as a surprise, but anyone who has seen Turner perform knows immediately that the writer is on target.

Likewise, when you use a figure of speech in your own prose, you should make sure that its tone is appropriate for the effect you intend to achieve. If you want to suggest fragility and delicacy, find an image that conveys those qualities—a hummingbird or a butterfly. If, on the other hand, you want to make your readers smile or laugh, find an image that will strike them as slightly off-kilter or overdone—a diaper-wearing rock star or a bowl of cold oatmeal.

Besides making sure that your figurative language is apt, you should see that each image is carried through in a consistent way. By doing so, you will avoid a **mixed metaphor**—the clashing of one image with a neighboring one.

MIXED METAPHOR:

x A tiger in the jungle of politics, he was a cream puff around the house.

The reader's mind strains unsuccessfully to grasp how a *tiger* is meaningfully related to a *cream puff*—that is, how a wild animal can be changed into a dessert.

fig lang 16b

EFFECTIVE METAPHOR:

• A tiger in the jungle of politics, he was a pussycat around the house.

—CLIFTON DANIEL, "Presidents I Have Known"

The images of *tiger* and *pussycat* are closely related, and the writer (characterizing his father-in-law, Harry Truman) fully controls the different implications of the two terms.

Again, note how the following sentence jumbles several figures of speech.

MIXED METAPHOR:

The second major incident that stepped on the Reagan parade in 1981, and nearly derailed it, was another self-inflicted wound.

—HENDRICK SMITH, *The Power Game*

Instead of rain falling on the parade, we have an incident (a foot?) stepping on it. Then the parade almost gets derailed (like a train?) just before we find out that what stepped on it was, in fact, a self-inflicted wound! Instead of drawing attention to the writer's point, the clashing metaphors distract from it.

Perhaps you feel that you can avoid mixed metaphors by shunning figurative language altogether. But insofar as you do, your prose will be flat and colorless. Besides, it is not really possible to be completely unfigurative. Many ordinary terms, and most clichés (p. 196, 15f), are **dead metaphors**—that is, they contain the faint implication of an image that we are not supposed to notice as such (the *leg* of a table, a *blade* of grass). Sometimes you can accidentally resuscitate a dead metaphor by putting it in the wrong context: x *On the first day that June worked on the construction crew, Steve fell for her like a ton of bricks.* And when you use clichés in close succession, they can mischievously come back to life as mixed metaphors:

> x **Climbing to the heights** of oratory, the candidate **tackled** the issue.
>
> x Either we **get a handle** on these problems or we are all **going down the drain.**
>
> x You can't **sit on your hands** if a recession is developing, because **you don't know where the bottom is.**

fig
lang
16c

Figurative language, then, can be tricky. When you intend an abstract meaning, you have to make sure that your dead metaphors stay good and dead. But when you do wish to be figurative, see whether your image is vivid, fresh, and consistent. Literal statement may be safe, but a striking figure carried through consistently can unify and intensify your sentences.

16c Practice the extended figure of speech.

If you have hit upon a suitable image to convey your meaning, you can sometimes add a sentence or two, or even a whole paragraph, that will draw further implications from it. Such an **extended figure of speech** is very much like an **analogy** (p. 121, 9i). The difference is that whereas an analogy typically compares two literal objects or situations by extracting a rule from one and applying it to the other, an extended figure elaborates a metaphorical comparison.

One such extended figure of speech is the "light bulb" passage on page 201. Here, from a student writer, is another:

> For me, the idea of going on for an advanced degree is like that of rowing across the ocean. Perhaps I could do it and perhaps I couldn't. But what, I wonder, is waiting for me on the other side, and isn't there

some faster and safer way of getting there? Until I know the answers to these questions, I intend to keep my feet planted on familiar soil.

This writer begins with a simile (*the idea of going on for an advanced degree is like that of rowing across the ocean*) and then extends it through three more sentences, making sure that the rest of her language remains compatible with that initial image.

To be effective, an extended figure must be apt. That is, the chosen image ought to seem natural and unstrained, drawing appropriate comparisons without laboring over them. Here are two samples that manage to be witty without sounding forced. The first is from a student essay about revision.

> The first draft of my paper needed emergency surgery. I took scalpel in hand and made a long incision in the middle of page five. I removed a diseased paragraph or two and restitched some badly injured sentences. Three hours later I was ready to close the incision. The patient had survived and would be on her feet—pale and wobbly—for class tomorrow morning.

fig lang 16d

> I am a kind of human snail, locked in and condemned by my own nature. The ancients believed that the moist track left by the snail as it crept was the snail's own essence, depleting its body little by little; the farther the snail toiled, the smaller it became, until it finally rubbed itself out. That is how perfectionists are. Say to us Excellence, and we will show you how we use up our substance and wear ourselves away, while making scarcely any progress at all. The fact that I am an exacting perfectionist in a narrow strait only, and nowhere else, is hardly to the point, since nothing matters to me so much as a comely and muscular sentence. It is my narrow strait, this snail's road: the track of the sentence I am writing now; and when I have eked out the wet substance, ink or blood, that is its mark, I will begin the next sentence.
>
> —CYNTHIA OZICK, "On Excellence"

16d Experiment with understatement and hyperbole.

Language that conspicuously minimizes an extreme state of affairs can also be regarded as figurative, even if it doesn't draw a comparison. Thus imaginative effects are at work in the following examples of **understatement:**

- A dozen novels, three exams, and a thirty-page term paper— **the course should be a snap.**
- You get **a little sweaty** out there fighting a forest fire.
- To be born with a cocaine addiction is **not necessarily the most advantageous way to enter the world.**

Similarly, you can get a figurative effect through **hyperbole,** or overstatement:

- **I'd rather have a root canal** than take another one of Professor Ronan's quizzes.
- They won't do a thing about smokestack pollution **until the view from their penthouses is a solid wall of soot.**
- The moths on the Puerto Vallarta coast **were as big as B-52s, and the cockroaches looked like Winnebagos.**

fig
lang
16d

As you can see, understatement and hyperbole produce an effect of **irony** (p. 40, 4d), or the conveying of something quite different from what one's words seem to say. Like other successfully handled figures of speech, these devices tell the reader that the writer has been confident enough to play with language while still maintaining rhetorical control. The effect would be ruined, of course, if it were carried through an entire serious essay.

V
USAGE

Usage

Whatever you have to say in your writing, you will want to say it within the rules of standard written English—*the "good English" that readers generally expect to find in papers, reports, articles, and books. Fortunately, you already follow most of those rules without having to think about them. In fact, if you did think about them while composing, you would have trouble concentrating on your ideas. The time to worry about correctness is after you have finished at least one draft. Then you can begin making certain that your points will come across without such distractions as incomplete sentences, spelling errors, and subjects and verbs that are incorrectly related.*

Problems with standard written English are usually divided into those of usage *and those of* punctuation—*that is, between rules for the choice and order of words (usage) and rules for the insertion of marks to bring out a sentence's meaning (punctuation). But usage and punctuation work together toward the same end of making sentences coherent, or fitting together in an easily understood way. Certain classic "usage" problems, such as the sentence fragment and the run-on sentence, are punctuation problems as well. Therefore, though we review the punctuation marks and their functions separately (Chapters 25–30), we also deal with punctuation in the present set of chapters. For example, if you are having trouble with modifiers or parallel constructions, you will find those topics treated as whole units, without artificial postponement of the relevant comma rules.*

17 Complete Sentences

COMPLETE SENTENCES	SENTENCE FRAGMENTS
● One-lane country roads unnerve the best drivers.	x Which unnerve the best drivers.
● The zookeeper feeds the penguins at noon.	x The zookeeper feeding the penguins at noon.

Since a sentence is the basic unit of written discourse, you must be able to recognize complete and incomplete sentences in your drafts. A sentence begins with a capital letter and ends with a period, question mark, or exclamation point. Unfortunately, **sentence fragments** show those very features. You need to know, then, that a grammatically complete sentence normally requires a **verb** and its **subject** within an **independent clause**.

17a   Recognize a verb.

A **verb** is a word that tells the state of its subject or an action that the subject performs. (If the verb consists of more than one word, as in *was starting* or *would have been accomplished,* it is called a *verb phrase.*) Every verb functions in one of three ways:

1. A **transitive verb** transmits the action of the subject to a **direct object:**

       S   V   D OBJ
  ● The **doctor solved** the **problem.**

       S   V   D OBJ
  ● The **technician took** an **x-ray.**

2. An **intransitive verb** in itself expresses the whole action:

       S   V
- The **patient recovered.**

       S   V
- **Dr. McGill lectures** often.

or

3. A **linking verb** connects the subject to a **complement,** an element that helps to identify or describe the subject:

       S   V   C
- Her **training has been scientific.**

    S V   C
- **She is** a recognized **professional.**

The verb plus all the words belonging with it make up the **predicate.**

Verb Position

In normal word order for statements, the subject comes before its verb:

       S   V
- The **highway committee is meeting.**

       S   V
- The **law will remain** on the books.

But in some questions the verb comes before the subject:

      V   S
- **Are you** sure?

And in most questions the verb has two parts that surround the subject:

       V
- **Is he driving** the Honda tonight?
     S

      V
- **Do you know** where she left the car?
     S

Change of Verb Form

Verbs show **inflection,** or changes of form, to indicate **tense,** or time.

PRESENT TENSE	PAST TENSE	FUTURE TENSE
They **iron** their jeans.	They **ironed** their jeans.	They **will iron** their jeans.
He **fights** hard.	He **fought** hard.	He **will fight** hard.

Verb versus Verbal

VERB (In complete sentence)	VERBAL (In fragment)
V • We **will break** our record.	VERBAL x **To break** our record.
V • Eve **was laughing** out loud.	VERBAL x **Laughing** out loud.
⌐— V —⌐ • **Are** they **winning** the championship.	VERBAL x **Winning** the championship.

frag
17a

Certain words resemble verbs and can even change their form to show different times. Yet these **verbals**—namely, **infinitives, participles,** and **gerunds**—function like nouns or modifiers instead of like verbs. Thus they do *not* supply a key element for sentence completeness.

Compare the complete sentences with the fragments in the box above. Note how you can tell that the three verbals in the right column are not functioning as verbs:

1. One kind of verbal, an infinitive, often follows *to* (*to break*). A true verb in a sentence stands without *to*.

2. A verbal ending in *-ing* is one word. When a true verb ends in *-ing,* it always follows a word or words that count as part of the verb (*was laughing, have been winning*).

You can write complete sentences that include verbals, but only by supplying true subject-verb combinations.

- $\overbrace{\text{To break our record}}^{\text{S}}$ **will be** difficult

- $\overbrace{\text{Laughing out loud,}}^{\text{MOD}}$ **Eve ran** a victory lap.

- $\overbrace{\text{Winning the championship}}^{\text{S}}$ **is** not easy.

17b   Recognize a subject.

- $\overset{\text{S}}{\text{My}}$ **uncle** prefers a big car.

A **subject** is the person, thing, or idea about which something is said or asked. Locating a subject therefore involves locating its accompanying verb.

   Most subjects are **nouns**—words like *uncle, philosophy,* and *Eve.* Some subjects are pronouns, such as *she* or *they* or *someone.* Others are noun phrases like *a very fine day.* And still others, which we will call **nounlike elements,** are groups of words that function together as single nouns: *to run fast, winning the championship,* and so forth. Thus you cannot spot a subject simply by its form. Find the verb, and then ask who or what performs the action of that verb or is in the state expressed by it:

- That law $\overset{\text{V}}{\textbf{affects}}$ all drivers.

   What affects all drivers? *That law* is the subject.

- $\overset{\text{V}}{\textbf{Does}}$ anyone **speak** Japanese?

   Does who speak Japanese? The subject is *anyone.*

- Whatever you see $\overset{\text{V}}{\textbf{is}}$ for sale.

   What is for sale? *Whatever you see.* That whole clause is the subject.

Implied Subject

- [You] Watch out!

You cannot write a grammatically complete sentence without a verb, but in commands, the subject *you* typically disappears. Since that subject is implied, however, the sentence is not regarded as a fragment.

17c Distinguish an independent clause from a subordinate one.

INDEPENDENT CLAUSE	SUBORDINATE CLAUSE
S PRED **Mike sells chickens.**	S PRED Although **Mike sells chickens,** ...
S PRED The **poster was badly printed.**	S PRED When the **poster was badly printed,** ...
S PRED **Dogs were running wild.**	S PRED Because **dogs were running wild,** ...

frag
17c

A **clause** is a cluster of words containing a subject-predicate combination (pp. 209–212, 17a). To avoid sentence fragments, you must be able to tell the difference between two fundamental kinds of clauses. An *independent clause* is a grammatically complete statement, question, or exclamation. It is capable of standing alone as a sentence. A *subordinate clause* (sometimes called a *dependent clause*) cannot stand alone, because it is typically introduced by a word that relates it to another part of the same sentence. Subordinate clauses serve important functions, but by themselves they are sentence fragments.

A subordinate clause is usually introduced by either

1. a *subordinating conjunction,* a word like *although, as, because,* or *when,* which subordinates (makes dependent) the following subject and predicate,

or

2. a *relative pronoun,* a word like *who, which,* or *that,* which begins a relative clause.

A **relative clause** is a subordinate clause that functions like an adjective by relating its statement to an earlier, or *antecedent,* part of the sentence.

ANT   REL CLAUSE
- **Roy, who owns the farm next door,** is very proud of his new heifer.

ANT   REL CLAUSE
- You'd think he owned the **cow that jumped over the moon.**

Sometimes you will find that an independent clause, like many subordinate ones, follows a conjunction. But that word will always be one of the seven *coordinating conjunctions.* If you keep those seven words distinct in your mind from subordinating conjunctions and relative pronouns, you will have a head start toward distinguishing between independent and subordinate clauses.

frag
17c

COORDINATING CONJUNCTIONS (May precede independent clauses)			
and	for	or	yet
but	nor	so	

SUBORDINATING CONJUNCTIONS (Begin some subordinate clauses)			
after	because	than	whenever
although	before	that	where
as	if	though	wherever
as if	in order that	till	while
as long as	provided (that)	unless	why
as soon as	since	until	
as though	so (that)	when	

RELATIVE PRONOUNS (Begin relative subordinate clauses)			
who	whom	which	that

Remember, then, that each of your sentences will normally contain at least one independent clause—a construction which, like *Mike sells chickens,* contains a subject and predicate but is not introduced by a subordinating conjunction or relative pronoun:

IND CLAUSE
- Acting on a hunch, **I removed the book from the shelf.**

IND CLAUSE
- As I opened the book, **twenty-dollar bills fluttered to the carpet.**

IND CLAUSE   IND CLAUSE
- **I stared intently,** and **my palms began to sweat.**

IND CLAUSE
- Although I am tempted to keep it, **this money will have to be turned over to the police.**

frag
17d

17d   Repair an unacceptable sentence fragment.

A **sentence fragment** is a word or set of words beginning with a capital letter and punctuated as a sentence but lacking an independent clause (17c). Typically, a fragment is either a subordinate clause (17c) or a **phrase**—a cluster of words lacking a subject-predicate combination:

SUBORDINATE CLAUSE AS FRAGMENT:
x Because milk and eggs are still a bargain.

x Unless winning at chess is important to you.

x Which makes my uncle nervous.

PHRASE AS FRAGMENT:
x Such as milk and eggs.

x Winning at chess.

x My uncle being nervous.

Most unacceptable fragments are really detached parts of the preceding sentence that the writer has mistakenly set off with a period. The handiest way to correct most fragments is to rejoin them to that earlier sentence:

UNACCEPTABLE FRAGMENTS (Boldfaced)	COMPLETE SENTENCES
Local agencies will become overcrowded and ineffective. x **Unless the number of mental health services is increased.**	• Unless the number of mental health services is increased, local agencies will become overcrowded and ineffective.
Alex and Dolores played tennis in the park. x **Instead of at school.**	• Alex and Dolores played tennis in the park instead of at school.
They stood back and watched the crows. x **Wheeling and cawing over the splattered melon.**	• They stood back and watched the crows wheeling and cawing over the splattered melon.
When they had rested, they continued up a path. x **A winding path that led to the top.**	• When they had rested, they continued up a winding path that led to the top.

frag 17d

Again, the boldfaced parts of the following passage are unacceptable fragments.

CONTAINING FRAGMENTS:

On Thursday we reported the numbers of our missing traveler's checks. **Which were lost during our arrival in New Orleans that morning.** We sat down outside the American Express office and watched other tourists. **Who were sunning themselves on the levee.** We were feeling low because we thought we had missed our chance to hear some Dixieland jazz. We were overjoyed, though, when a group of musicians ambled by and set up their instruments. **Right there on the levee.** We spent the rest of the afternoon listening to their music. **The best open-air jazz concert in town.**

REVISED:

On Thursday we reported the numbers of our missing traveler's checks, which we had lost during our arrival in New Orleans that morning. We sat down outside the American Express office and watched other tourists sunning themselves on the levee. We were feeling low because we thought we had missed our chance to hear some Dixieland jazz. We were overjoyed, though, when a group of musicians ambled by and set up their instruments right there on the levee. We spent the rest of the afternoon listening to their music—the best open-air jazz concert in town.

How to Spot a Fragment

You can recognize many fragments by the words that introduce them—subordinating terms such as *although, because, especially, even, except, for example, including, instead of, so that, such as, that, which, who,* and *when.* Of course, many acceptable sentences also start with such words but are complete because they include a full independent clause (p. 213, 17c). When you see a draft "sentence" beginning with one of those words, just check to be sure that an independent clause is also present.

frag
17d

DRAFT (Fragments boldfaced):

I always helped my brother. **Especially with his car.** I assisted him in many chores. **Such as washing the car and vacuuming the interior.** He let me do whatever I wanted. **Except start the engine.** Now I drive my own car. **Which is a 1983 Chevy.** I am thinking of possible jobs to help pay the cost of upkeep. **Including driving a cab. Because maintaining a car these days can be expensive.**

REVISED:

I always helped my brother, especially with his car. I assisted him in many chores, such as washing the car and vacuuming the interior. He let me do whatever I wanted except start the engine. Now I drive my own car, a 1983 Chevy. I am thinking of possible jobs, including driving a cab, to help pay the cost of upkeep. Maintaining a car these days can be expensive.

Learn to recognize the following five types of fragments.

1. A subordinate clause (p. 213, 17c) posing as a whole sentence.

DRAFT:

Living in the city is more dangerous than ever. **Especially if you are wearing a gold chain.** During the past several weeks gold snatchers have been on a crime spree. **Although the police have tried to track down the thieves.** Nobody with a chain is safe. **Because the victims range from drivers stalled in traffic jams to students in gym classes.**

REVISED:

Living in the city is more dangerous than ever, especially if you are wearing a gold chain. Although the police have tried to track down the thieves, during the past several weeks gold snatchers have been on a crime spree. Nobody with a chain is safe; the victims range from drivers stalled in traffic jams to students in gym classes.

2. A verbal (p. 211, 17a) or a phrase (p. 215, 17d) unaccompanied by an independent clause.

frag
17d

DRAFT:

Before the start of the race, the drivers sat in their cars. **Revving up their engines.** They all had the same dream. **To see that checkered flag waving when they crossed the finish line.**

REVISED:

Before the start of the race, the drivers sat in their cars, revving up their engines. They all had the same dream: to see that checkered flag waving when they crossed the finish line.

3. An appositive (p. 268, 20n) standing alone.

DRAFT:

I love to read about the Roaring Twenties. **A decade that had its own personality.** People did their best to blot out the horrors of the recent past. **The Great War, the worldwide flu epidemic, the ominous revolution in Russia.**

REVISED:

I love to read about the Roaring Twenties, a decade that had its own personality. People did their best to blot out the horrors of the recent past—the Great War, the worldwide flu epidemic, the ominous revolution in Russia.

4. A disconnected second verb governed by a subject in the sentence before.

DRAFT:
The speech for my film course took a long time to prepare. **And then turned out poorly.** I needed a live audience. **But didn't have one for the test.**

REVISED:
The speech for my film course took a long time to prepare and then turned out poorly. I needed a live audience but didn't have one for the test.

5. A "sentence" lacking a verb in an independent clause.

DRAFT:
If there are no more malpractice suits, the hospital to win its license renewal. But no one can be sure. **Patients these days being very quick to go to court.**

REVISED:
If there are no more malpractice suits, the hospital will win its license renewal. But no one can be sure. Patients these days are very quick to go to court.

frag
17d

Sentence Beginning with a Coordinating Conjunction

As the last "revised" example indicates, there is nothing wrong with using a coordinating conjunction (p. 214, 17c) to begin a sentence: *But no one can be sure.* If you do so, however, make sure the sentence has its own subject and verb. Be aware also that such sentences usually make for an informal or conversational effect:

- I said farewell to my friends in high school. **And in September I began a completely new life.**

17e   Note the uses of the intentional sentence fragment.

Some composition instructors advise against any use of fragments in submitted work. They feel, understandably, that students should eliminate habitual mistakes before trying flourishes of style. But you should know that practiced writers do resort to an occasional **intentional fragment** when they want to reply to a question in the previous sentence or make a point concisely and emphatically.

ACCEPTABLE:

- He sets him up with jabs, he works to the body, he corners him on the ropes. INTENTIONAL FRAG **Then the finish, a left hook to the jaw that brings him down.**

- Many secretaries were outraged by the shift to a later working day. INTENTIONAL FRAG **But not quite all of them.**

- Truman Capote has made lying an art. INTENTIONAL FRAG **A *minor* art.**

    —GORE VIDAL, quoted in Jon Winokur's *Writers on Writing*

frag
17e

You will see from reading published authors that intentional fragments often have a certain "shock value." Whereas an unacceptable fragment looks like a missing part of a neighboring sentence, an intentional fragment is a condensed means of lending punch to the previous sentence or, in some instances, the following one. For example:

Newspapers. Telephone books. Soiled diapers. Medicine vials encasing brightly colored pills. Brittle ossuaries of chicken bones and T-bones. Sticky green mountains of yard waste. Half-empty cans of paint and turpentine and motor oil and herbicide. Broken furniture and forsaken toys. Americans produce a lot of garbage, some of it very toxic, and our garbage is not always disposed of in a sensible way.

—WILLIAM J. RATHJE, "Rubbish!"

18 Joining Independent Clauses

18a Note the two common ways of joining independent clauses.

An **independent clause** is a grammatically complete statement, question, or exclamation—one that could stand alone as a full sentence, whether or not it actually does stand alone (p. 213, 17c).

INDEPENDENT CLAUSES:
- I need a nap. [statement]
- May I take a nap? [question]
- Let me sleep! [exclamation]

Comma and Coordinating Conjunction

There are two usual ways of joining independent clauses within a single sentence. The first way is to put a comma after the first independent clause and to follow the comma with a coordinating conjunction—that is, one of the following seven connectives: *and, but, for, nor, or, so, yet.*

                COORD
  IND CLAUSE   **CONJ**   **IND CLAUSE**

- I am not prepared, **and** I dread seeing the questions.

                      COORD
     IND CLAUSE   **CONJ**   **IND CLAUSE**

- Many students took the course, **but** few kept up with the work.

            COORD
  IND CLAUSE   **CONJ**   **IND CLAUSE**

- Am I going crazy, **or** do I just need a good night's sleep?

Semicolon

Alternatively, you can join independent clauses with a semicolon alone if they are closely related in meaning and spirit or show a striking, pointed contrast:

> IND CLAUSE   IND CLAUSE
- I am not prepared; I dread seeing the questions.

> IND CLAUSE   IND CLAUSE
- Many students took the course; few kept up with the work.

When using a semicolon, test to see if what comes before it could make a complete sentence and if what comes after it could also make a complete sentence. If either test fails, your draft sentence is faulty.

DON'T:

x She said she was sorry I was leaving; especially because it would not be easy to find a replacement.

> *Especially because it would not be easy to find a replacement* could not stand as a complete sentence.

cs/fs 18a

DO:

- She said she was sorry I was leaving; it would not be easy, she said, to find a replacement.

DON'T:

x My wife thought I should have apologized since I was the one who had left the directions at home.

> The *since . . .* clause could not stand as a complete sentence.

DO:

- My wife thought I should have apologized; after all, I was the one who had left the directions at home.

In some cases you will find it easier simply to eliminate the semicolon or replace it with a comma.

DON'T:

x Jerry ate dinner every night; while watching the six o'clock news.

DO:

• Jerry ate dinner every night while watching the six o'clock news.

DON'T:

x His usual fare was a TV dinner; which he heated in the micro-wave oven.

DO:

• His usual fare was a TV dinner, which he heated in the micro-wave oven.

18b Repair a comma splice or a fused sentence.

COMMA SPLICES	PROPERLY PUNCTUATED SENTENCES
x I asked her many questions she had no answers.	• I asked her many questions, **but** she had no answers.
x James Joyce published *Finnegans Wake* in 1939 he died in 1941.	• James Joyce published *Finnegans Wake* in 1939; he died in 1941.

cs/fs
18b

FUSED SENTENCES	PROPERLY PUNCTUATED SENTENCES
x Smoke filled the room everyone started coughing.	• Smoke filled the room, **and** everyone started coughing.
x I was shocked to see Bill he had lost nearly fifty pounds.	• I was shocked to see Bill; he had lost nearly fifty pounds.

If you remember how to join independent clauses, you will be able to recognize comma splices and fused sentences—that is, sentences in which independent clauses are joined without proper punctuation. You can repair comma splices and fused sentences in several ways, but if you decide to keep two independent clauses in your sentence, remember the rules for joining them correctly (18a).

COMMA AND COORDINATING CONJUNCTION:
- I asked her many questions, **but** she had no answers.

SEMICOLON:
- I was shocked to see Bill; he had lost nearly fifty pounds.

Comma Splice

In a **comma splice,** two independent clauses are joined with only a comma. Such a construction may not seriously garble a writer's statement, but it does fail to show how the two clauses are related in meaning.

DON'T:

	FIRST IND CLAUSE	SECOND IND CLAUSE

x Lorca's poem is extremely complex, Dan decided to study it further.

	FIRST IND CLAUSE	SECOND IND CLAUSE

x Dan discussed the poem with Alice, he understood it better.

**cs/fs
18b**

How to Repair a Comma Splice

If you find a comma splice in your draft, you can repair it in several ways:

SEPARATE SENTENCES:
- Lorca's poem is extremely complex. Dan decided to study it further.

COMMA AND COORDINATING CONJUNCTION (p. 221, 18a):
- Lorca's poem is extremely complex, **so** Dan decided to study it further.

SEMICOLON (p. 222, 18a):
- Lorca's poem is extremely complex; Dan decided to study it further.

SUBORDINATE CLAUSE (p. 213, 17c):

- **After Dan discussed the poem with Alice,** he understood it better.

PHRASE (p. 215, 17d):

- Dan understood the poem better **after discussing it with Alice.**

Exception: Note that a tag such as *she thought* or *he said* can be joined to a quotation by a comma alone, even if the quotation is another independent clause.

$$\overbrace{\text{IND CLAUSE}} \qquad \overbrace{\text{IND CLAUSE}}$$

- "This stanza echoes the first one," Alice explained.

For further exceptions to the rule against committing comma splices, see page 229, 18d.

Fused Sentence

In a **fused sentence** (also called a *run-on sentence*), independent clauses are merged with no sign of their separateness—neither a comma nor a coordinating conjunction.

> cs/fs
> 18b

DON'T:

$$\overbrace{\text{IND CLAUSE}} \qquad \overbrace{\text{IND CLAUSE}}$$

x Some people can hide their nervousness I envy them.

$$\overbrace{\text{IND CLAUSE}} \qquad \overbrace{\text{IND CLAUSE}}$$

x Sometimes I have to speak before a group it makes me nervous.

How to Repair a Fused Sentence

Revise by choosing from the same options given above for correcting a comma splice.

SEPARATE SENTENCES:

- Some people can hide their nervousness. I envy them.

COMMA AND COORDINATING CONJUNCTION:

- Some people can hide their nervousness, **and** I envy them.

SEMICOLON:
- Some people can hide their nervousness; I envy them.

SUBORDINATE CLAUSE:
- I feel nervous **whenever I have to speak before a group.**

PHRASE:
- I feel nervous **speaking before a group.**

18c Watch especially for comma splices using connectors like *however, also,* and *then.*

COMMA SPLICES	PROPERLY PUNCTUATED SENTENCES
x We planted a garden, **however** nothing grew.	• We planted a garden; however, nothing grew.
x We used a plastic mulch, **also** we watered vigorously.	• We used a plastic mulch, and we also watered vigorously.
x We read a gardening book, **then** we asked our neighbor for advice.	• After reading a gardening book, we asked our neighbor for advice.

Review the following terms, which often cause writers to draft comma splices (p. 223, 18b):

SENTENCE ADVERBS		
again	hence	nonetheless
also	however	otherwise
besides	indeed	similarly
consequently	likewise	then
further	moreover	therefore
furthermore	nevertheless	thus (*etc.*)

TRANSITIONAL PHRASES		
after all	for example	in reality
as a result	in addition	in truth
at the same time	in fact	on the contrary
even so	in other words	on the other hand
		(*etc.*)

A **sentence adverb** (also called a *conjunctive adverb*) is a word that modifies a whole previous statement. Note how such a term differs from an ordinary adverb.

ORDINARY ADVERB:
- She applied for the job **again** in March.
- **Then** she made arrangements to have her furniture stored.

SENTENCE ADVERB:
- **Again,** there is still another reason to delay a decision.
- We see, **then,** that precautions are in order.

cs/fs
18c

An ordinary adverb modifies part of the statement in which it appears: she applied *again;* she stored her furniture *then.* But a sentence adverb modifies the whole statement by showing its logical relation to the preceding statement: after the already stated reason to delay, here (*again*) is another one; because of the preceding statement, we therefore (*then*) see that precautions are in order. A **transitional phrase** is a multiword expression that functions like a sentence adverb.

What makes these modifiers tricky is that they "feel like" conjunctions such as *and, but, although, so,* and *yet.* If you treat a sentence adverb or transitional phrase as if it were a conjunction, the result will be a comma splice. You can repair the problem in any of the ways previously discussed: making each independent clause (p. 221, 18a) a separate sentence, properly joining the two clauses, or changing the whole construction.

DON'T:

SENT ADV
x Rain washed out our seeds, **therefore,** we had to replant.

DO:

SENT ADV
• Rain washed out our seeds; **therefore,** we had to replant.

DON'T:

TRANS
PHRASE
x Our garden was a disappointment, **in fact** it was a disaster.

DO:

TRANS
PHRASE
• Our garden was a disappointment; **in fact,** it was a disaster.

If you are not sure whether a certain word is a sentence adverb, test to see whether it could be moved without loss of meaning. A conjunction must stay put, but a sentence adverb can always be moved to at least one other position:

cs/fs 18c

• We planted a garden; **however,** nothing grew.
• We planted a garden; nothing, **however,** grew.
• We planted a garden; nothing grew, **however.**

When you are sure of the difference between conjunctions and sentence adverbs, you will be able to avoid putting an unneeded comma after a conjunction.

DON'T:

CONJ
x He swam for the island, **but,** the current exhausted him.

DO:

CONJ
• He swam for the island, **but** the current exhausted him.

DON'T:

CONJ
x The threat is serious, **yet,** I think we have grounds for hope.

DO:

CONJ
* The threat is serious, **yet** I think we have grounds for hope.

Setting Off Sentence Adverbs and Transitional Phrases

Since these expressions modify a whole previous statement, they are usually set apart by punctuation on both sides. Do not allow a sentence adverb or transitional phrase to "leak" at one end or the other.

DON'T:

SENT ADV
x John, **however** was nowhere to be seen.

DO:

SENT ADV
* John, **however,** was nowhere to be seen.

DON'T:

TRANS
PHRASE
x Guatemala **in contrast,** has a troubled history.

DO:

TRANS
PHRASE
x Guatemala, **in contrast,** has a troubled history.

In some cases you can omit commas or other punctuation around a sentence adverb (*And thus it is clear that . . .*). But if you supply punctuation at one end, be sure to supply it at the other end as well.

cs/fs
18d

18d Recognize exceptional ways of joining independent clauses.

Optional Comma after Brief Independent Clause

If your first independent clause is brief, consider the comma optional:

* **I was late** and it was already growing dark.

  But a comma after *late* would also be correct. When in doubt, retain the comma.

Optional Conjunctions in Series of Independent Clauses

When you are presenting several brief, tightly related independent clauses in a series (p. 305, 23k), you can gain a dramatic effect by doing without a coordinating conjunction:

- He saw the train, he fell to the tracks, he covered his head with his arms.

  By omitting *and* before the last clause, the writer brings out the rapidity and urgency of the three actions. This is a rare case of an acceptable comma splice.

Reversal of Negative Emphasis

If a second independent clause reverses the negative emphasis of the first, consider joining them only with a comma:

- That summer Thoreau did not read books, he hoed beans.

  cs/fs
  18d

  The *not* clause leaves us anticipating a second clause that will say what Thoreau did do. The absence of a conjunction brings out the tight, necessary relation between the two statements.

Compare:

x Thoreau hoed beans all summer, he did not read books.

  Lacking a "reversal of negative emphasis," this sentence shows a classic *unacceptable* comma splice.

19 Joining Subjects and Verbs

SUBJECT-VERB COHERENCE

19a Repair a mixed construction.

DON'T:

x A hobby that gets out of hand, it becomes an obsession.

DO:

• A hobby that gets out of hand becomes an obsession.

If your subjects and verbs (pp. 209–212, 17a–b) are to work efficiently together, you cannot leave your reader wondering which part of a sentence is the subject. Do not start a sentence with one subject and then change your mind. In the "don't" example above, the reader begins by expecting that *hobby* will be the subject. After the comma, however, the writer serves up a new subject, *it,* leaving *hobby* grammatically stranded. The result is a **mixed construction,** whereby two elements in a sentence are competing to serve the same function.

DON'T:

x With a newspaper recycling program will save space in the city landfill.

> The sentence begins with a prepositional phrase (p. 625)— *With a newspaper recycling program*—that can only serve as a modifier (p. 250), not as the subject of the verb *will save.*

There are two ways of repairing the damage. The writer could omit the preposition *with,* leaving the subject *a newspaper recycling program.*

DO:

$$\overbrace{\text{A newspaper recycling program}}^{\text{S}} \quad \overbrace{\text{will save}}^{\text{V}}$$

• **A newspaper recycling program will save** space in the city landfill.

Or the writer could supply a new subject (*the city*), making the prepositional phrase a modifier.

DO:

$$\overbrace{\text{With a newspaper recycling program,}}^{\text{MOD}} \quad \overset{\text{S}}{\text{the city}} \quad \overset{\text{V}}{\text{will save}}$$

• With a newspaper recycling program, **the city will save** space in its landfill.

Here is another example of mixed construction in which a subordinate clause (p. 213, 17c) poses as the subject of the verb *kept*.

DON'T:

SUB CLAUSE

x **Because she drank two cups of coffee** kept Nancy awake all night.

To fix the sentence, the writer needs to make a logical match between subject and verb.

DO:

$$\overbrace{\text{Two cups of coffee}}^{\text{S}} \quad \overset{\text{V}}{\text{kept}}$$

• **Two cups of coffee kept** Nancy awake all night.

or

SUB CLAUSE

• Because she drank two cups of coffee, **Nancy was** up all night.

The problem of mixed construction actually extends beyond subjects and verbs. Consider the following sentence.

DON'T:

D OBJ?   D OBJ?

x They gave **it** to her for Christmas **what** she wanted most.

Here *it* and *what* are competing to be the direct object (p. 209,

s–v
coh
19a

17a) of the verb *gave*. The solution is to choose one or the other and make a consistent pattern.

DO:

• For Christmas they gave her what she wanted most.

If your prose contains mixed constructions, review the essential sentence elements: subject, verb, direct object, complement (pp. 209–212, 17a). And be aware that the first element in a sentence usually establishes a certain structure that you must follow. If you run into trouble, recast the sentence from the beginning.

19b Repair faulty predication.

Predication—saying something about a grammatical subject—is the essence of all statement. In first-draft prose, however, writers sometimes yoke a subject and a predicate (p. 210, 17a) that fail to make sense together. A mixed construction (19a), which typically prevents the reader from knowing which word is the intended subject, shows faulty predication in an extreme form. But predication can also go awry if the writer asks a subject to perform something it could not possibly do.

s–v
coh
19b

DON'T:

　　　　　S　　　　　　　　　　　　　V
x Lee's **ability** to pole-vault **performed** beautifully at yesterday's
track meet.　　　　　　　　　　　　　　　　PRED

A person or a thing can perform, but an *ability* cannot logically do so. The revised sentence must reflect that fact.

DO:

　　S　　V
• **Lee performed** beautifully in the pole vault at yesterday's
track meet　　　　　　　　　　　PRED

　　　　　　　　　　　　　　　　　　　S　　　　V
• At yesterday's track meet. **Lee pole-vaulted** beautifully.
　　　　　　　　　　　　　　　　　　　　PRED

         S   V

• Lee's **ability** to pole-vault beautifully **was** obvious at yesterday's track meet.
                                                 PRED

You can see that the problem in faulty predication often lies in treating an abstraction (p. 189, 15a) as if it were capable of performing an action. Once you have hit upon a subject like *ability* (or *inventiveness, symmetry, rationality, reluctance,* etc.), your predicate must reflect the fact that you are writing about an abstraction, not an agent.

SUBJECT-VERB AGREEMENT

19c Make a verb agree with its subject in person and number.

In grammar we refer to three **persons:**

**s–v
agr
19c**

	EXAMPLE	IDENTITY
First Person	I pull we pull	the speaker or writer the speakers or writers
Second Person	you pull	the person or persons addressed
Third Person	he, she, it pulls the mother spanks the signal changes	the person or thing spoken or written about
	they pull the mothers spank the signals change	the persons or things spoken or written about

We also refer to the *time* of a verb as its **tense**—present, past, future, and so forth.

In standard written English, the ending of a verb often shows the **number** of the subject—that is, whether the subject is *singular* (one item) or *plural* (more than one item). A singular subject requires a singular verb; a plural subject requires a plural verb.

```
       S    V
```
• The **river flows** south.

> Here the -*s* ending on the verb *flows* indicates that the verb
> is in the third person, is singular, and is in the present tense.

The grammatical correspondence of subjects and verbs is called
agreement. In *The river flows south* the verb *flows* is said to agree
with its singular, third-person subject *river.* Note that the singular
subject usually has no -*s* ending but that a singular, third-person
verb in the present tense does have an -*s* ending: *flows.* Compare:

```
        S    V
```
• The **rivers flow** south.

> The lack of an -*s* ending on the verb *flow* indicates that the
> verb is plural, in agreement with its plural subject *rivers.*
> Notice that the -*s* on *rivers* marks it as a plural noun.

Many native speakers of English use the same forms for both the
singular and plural of certain verbs in the present tense: *she don't,
they don't; he is, we is.* In standard written English, however, it is
important to observe the difference: *she does not, she doesn't, they do
not, they don't; he is, we are.*

s-v agr 19c

DON'T:

x They **is** having a party.

DO:

• They **are** having a party.

DON'T:

x He **don't** expect to rent a car.

DO:

• He **doesn't** expect to rent a car.

For further verb forms in various tenses, see pages 372–380,
31b–d.

19d Be sure you have found the true subject.

Sometimes you will have a good stylistic reason for putting your subject after its verb (*Chief among her virtues <u>was</u> her <u>honesty</u>*) or for separating the subject and verb with other language (*Her <u>honesty</u>, acquired from her strictly religious parents, <u>was</u> her chief virtue*). Be careful, though, that you don't lose track of the subject and mistakenly allow the verb to be governed by another word. Here are the constructions—allowable but potentially tricky—that call for particular attention.

Intervening Clause or Phrase

DON'T:

> S   INTERVENING CLAUSE
> x The **highway** that runs through these isolated mountain towns
> V
> **are** steep and narrow.

> The subject, *highway,* is so far from its verb that the writer has absentmindedly allowed that verb to be governed by the nearest preceding noun, *towns.*

DO:

> S   V
> • The **highway** . . . **is** steep and narrow.

Again:

DON'T:

> INTERVENING
> S   PHRASE   V
> x The **pleasures** of a motorcyclist **includes** repairing the bike.

DO:

> S   V
> • The **pleasures** . . . **include** repairing the bike.

Learn to locate the true subject by asking who or what performs the action of the verb or is in the state indicated by the verb. Test for singular or plural by these steps:

1. Locate the verb and its subject.

2. Put the phrase between them into imaginary parentheses:

   The pleasures (of a motorcyclist) $\frac{\text{include}}{\text{includes}}$. . . .

3. Then say aloud:

   "The pleasures include"

and

   "The pleasures includes."

The form of the verb that is correct without the element "in parentheses" is also correct with it. *The pleasures of a motorcyclist include. . . .*

A Phrase like <u>along with</u> or <u>in addition to</u>

DON'T:

    S   **ADDITIVE PHRASE**   V

x **Jill,** along with her two karate instructors, **are** highly disciplined.

DO:

• **Jill,** along with her two karate instructors, **is** highly disciplined.

An expression that begins with a term like *accompanied by, along with, as well as, in addition to, including,* or *together with* is called an **additive phrase.** Though it is typically set off by commas (p. 263, 20l), it can "feel like" part of the subject. If you write *Jill, along with her two karate instructors,* you certainly have more than one person in mind. But grammatically, additive phrases do *not* add anything to the subject. Disregard the additive phrase, just as you would any other intervening element. If the subject apart from the additive phrase is singular, make the verb singular as well.

s–v
agr
19d

DON'T:

          S   **ADDITIVE PHRASE**

x Practical **knowledge,** in addition to statistics and market theory,
    V
enter into the training of an economist.

DO:

- Practical **knowledge,** in addition to statistics and market theory, **enters** into the training of an economist.

Subject Following Verb

DON'T:

                            V   S

x Beside the blue waters **lie Claire,** waiting for Henry to bring the towels.

> To find the true subject, mentally rearrange the sentence into normal subject-verb word order: *Claire lies beside. . . .*

s–v agr 19d

DO:

- Beside the blue waters **lies** Claire, waiting for Henry to bring the towels.

Watch especially for agreement problems when the subject is delayed by an expression like *There is* or *Here comes.* By the time such a sentence is finished, its subject may be plural.

DON'T:

    V   S

x Here **comes a clown and three elephants.**

IMPROVED:

- Here **come** a clown and three elephants.

Or, since this example sounds strained:

PREFERABLE:

- Here **comes** a clown leading three elephants.

19e When the subject is a phrase or clause, make the verb singular.

PHRASE AS S

- **Having the numbers of several bail bondsmen is** useful in an emergency.

CLAUSE AS S

- **That none of his customers wanted to buy a matching**

  V

  fleet of Yugos was a disagreeable surprise for Roger.

A phrase or clause acting as a subject takes a singular verb, even if it contains plural items. Do not be misled by a plural word at the end of the phrase or clause. The two examples above are correct.

19f Usually treat a noun like *crowd* or *orchestra* as singular.

s–v
agr
19f

- The orchestra **is playing** better now that the conductor is sober.
- A strong, united faculty **is needed** to stand firm against the erosion of parking privileges.
- In Priscilla's opinion the middle class **is** altogether too middle-class.

A **collective noun** is one having a singular form but referring to a group of members: *administration, army, audience, class, crowd, orchestra, team,* and so forth. This conflict between form and meaning can lead to agreement problems. But in general you should think of a collective noun as singular and thus make the verb singular, too.

Once in a while, however, you may want to emphasize the individual members of the group. Then you should make the verb plural:

- The faculty **have** come to their assignments from all over the world.

When a sentence like this one sounds awkward, you may want to recast it using a more natural-sounding plural subject: *Faculty members have come. . . .*

19g If a subject contains two parts, usually treat it as plural.

- $\overbrace{\text{A teller and a guard}}^{\text{S}}$ $\overset{\text{V}}{\text{operate}}$ the drive-in window at the bank.

- $\overbrace{\text{A bouquet and a box of candy}}^{\text{S}}$ $\overset{\text{V}}{\text{are}}$ no substitute for a fair wage.

A **compound** subject, such as *a clown and three elephants,* is made up of more than one unit. In most instances, such a subject calls for a plural verb.

Note, in the second example above, that *substitute* is singular, even though the subject and verb are plural. Agreement does not extend to complements (p. 210, 17a)—words in the predicate that identify or modify the subject.

s–v
agr
19h

Exception: Both Parts Refer to the Same Thing or Person

Even when the parts of a compound subject are joined by *and,* common sense will sometimes tell you that only one thing or person is being discussed. Make the verb singular in such a case:

- My best friend and severest critic has moved to Atlanta.

  One person is both friend and critic. By changing the verb to *have* the writer would be saying that two people, not one, have moved to Atlanta. Both sentences could be correct, but their meanings would differ.

19h Avoid a clash of singular and plural subjects linked by *or* or *nor.*

Compound subjects (19g) joined by *or, either . . . or,* or *neither . . . nor* are called **disjunctive.** They ask the reader to choose between two or more parts. Consequently, the verb should agree with only one of those parts—the one nearest the verb.

DON'T:

$$\overbrace{\text{DISJUNCTIVE S}}$$ V

x **Either his children or his cat is** responsible for the dead goldfish.

BETTER:

NEAREST PART OF
DISJUNCTIVE S

• Either his children or **his cat is** responsible for the dead goldfish. V

> But such conflicts of number are awkward. Rewrite to avoid the problem.

PREFERABLE:

S V
• Either **his children are** responsible for the dead goldfish or

S V
his cat is.

or

S V
• **No one** but his children or his cat **could have killed** the goldfish.

Some disjunctive subjects "feel plural" even though each item within them is singular, for the writer is thinking about two or more things. But so long as the individual disjunctive items are singular, the verb must be singular, too.

DON'T:

$$\overbrace{\text{DISJUNCTIVE S}}$$ V

• **Neither WNCN nor WQXR carry** the country-western sing-off.

DO:

• Neither WNCN nor WQXR **carries** the country-western sing-off

---

19i If you have placed *each* or *every* before a compound subject, treat the subject as singular.

> ```
>                          s                              v
> ```
> • **Every linebacker and tackle in the league was pleased** with the settlement.

> ```
>                                             s
> ```
> • Before being put away for the summer, **each coat and sweater**
> ```
>   v
> ```
> **is** mothproofed.

Each or *every,* if it comes before the subject, guarantees that the subject will be singular even if it contains multiple parts.

Note, however, that when *each* comes *after* a subject, it has no effect on the number of the verb:

> ```
>   s      v
> ```
> • **They** each **have** their own reasons for protesting.

**s–v
agr
19j**

19j Observe the agreement rules for terms of quantity.

Numerical words (*majority, minority, number, plurality,* etc.) and plural terms of quantity (*three dollars, fifty years,* etc.) can take either a singular or a plural verb. If you have in mind the *totality* of items, make the verb singular:

> ```
>                   s        v
> ```
> • The Democratic **majority favors** the bill.

But if you mean the separate items that make up that totality, make the verb plural:

> ```
>        s                                       v
> ```
> • **The majority of Democrats** on the North Shore **are** opposed to building a bridge.

The Word Number

When the word *number* is preceded by *the,* it is always singular:

> ```
>        s                            v
> ```
> • The **number** of unhappy voters **is growing.**

But when *number* is preceded by *a,* you must look to see whether it refers to the total unit (singular) or to individual parts (plural).

TOTAL UNIT (SINGULAR):

S   V
* A **number** like ten billion **is** hard to comprehend.

INDIVIDUAL PARTS (PLURAL):

S   V
* **A number of voters have arrived** at their choice.

Note that although *of voters* looks like a modifier of the subject *number,* we read *a number of* as if it said *many.*

When your subject contains an actual number, decide once again whether you mean the total unit or the individual parts.

TOTAL UNIT (SINGULAR):

S   V
* **Twenty-six miles is** the length of the race.

INDIVIDUAL PARTS (PLURAL):

S   V
* **Twenty-six difficult miles lie** ahead of her.

S–V
agr
19k

19k   As a rule, use a singular verb with a subject like
everyone* or *nobody.

An *indefinite pronoun* leaves unspecified the person or thing it refers to.

INDEFINITE PRONOUNS					
all	anything	everybody	most	no one	some
another	both	everyone	much	nothing	somebody
any	each	everything	neither	one	someone
anybody	each one	few	nobody	others	something
anyone	either	many	none	several	such

Some of these words serve other functions, too; they are indefinite pronouns only when they stand alone without modifying another term.

ADJECTIVE:
- **All** leopards are fast.

INDEFINITE PRONOUN:
- **All** have spots.

Some indefinite pronouns, such as *another,* are obviously singular, and some others, such as *several,* are obviously plural. But there is also a borderline class: *each, each one, either, everybody, everyone, everything, neither, nobody, none, no one.* These terms have a singular form, yet they call to mind plural things or persons. According to convention, you should generally treat them as singular:

s   v

- **Everyone seems** to be late tonight.

s   v

- **Neither has brought** the music for the duet.

s–v agr 19k

Keep to a singular verb even when the indefinite pronoun is followed by a plural construction such as *of them:*

s   v

- **Neither** of them **has** the music for the duet.

s   v

- **Each** of those cordless phones **has** a touch-tone dial.

None

None is usually treated as singular:

s   v

- **None** of us **is** ready yet.

> But some writers recognize an option here. If you mean *all of us are not ready* rather than *not one of us is ready,* you can make the verb plural:

s   v

- **None of us are** ready yet.

Since some writers would consider this sentence mistaken, keep to the singular wherever it does not sound forced.

19l Note the special character of subjects like *politics and acoustics.*

Some nouns have an *-s* ending but usually take a singular verb: *economics, mathematics, news, physics,* and so forth:

- **Physics** has made enormous strides in this century.

Some nouns ending in *-s* can be singular in one meaning and plural in another. When they refer to a body of knowledge, they are singular.

AS BODY OF KNOWLEDGE:

-    S   V
  Politics is an important study for many historians.

-    S   V
  Acoustics requires an understanding of mathematics.

s–v
agr
19m

But when the same words are used in a more particular sense—not politics as a field but somebody's politics—they are considered plural.

IN PARTICULAR SENSE:

-             S   V
  Gloria's **politics are** left of center.

-       V   S
  How **are** the **acoustics** in the new auditorium?

19m In a *that* or *which* clause, make the verb agree with the antecedent.

Consider the following correctly formed sentence:

            REL CLAUSE
- The telephone bill **that is overdue** includes a charge for a twenty-minute call to Paris.

Here *that is overdue* is a **relative clause**—a subordinate clause (p. 213, 17c) that functions like an adjective. A relative clause usually begins with a word like *who, whom, whose, that,* or *which*. The relative clause modifies an **antecedent,** a noun or nounlike element in the previous clause. In this case the antecedent is *telephone bill.*

Relative clauses can make for tricky agreement problems. You will avoid trouble, however, if you remember that the verb in a relative clause agrees in number with its antecedent. Thus, in the example above, *is* agrees with the singular antecedent *telephone bill.* Again:

- There have been some complaints about **service** that **is** painfully slow.

   ANT   V

Note that you cannot automatically assume that the antecedent is the last term before the relative clause.

- There have been **complaints** about service that **were** entirely justified.

- The **oceans** of the world, which **have become** a dumping ground, may never be completely unpolluted again.

Ask yourself what the verb in the relative clause refers to:

What is painfully slow? Service.

What was entirely justified? Complaints.

What has become a dumping ground? Oceans.

Once you have an answer, a singular or plural term, you also have the right number for the verb in your relative clause.

Singular Complement in Relative Clause

Look at the following mistaken but typical sentence.

DON'T:

      PLURAL ANT   V   SING C

x **Math problems,** which **is** her **specialty,** cause her no concern.

s–v
agr
19m

A singular complement (p. 210, 17a) in a *who, which,* or *that* clause can trick you into making the verb in that clause singular when the antecedent is actually plural. Here the complement *specialty* has wrongly influenced the number of the verb *is.* That verb, like any other verb in a relative clause, must agree with its antecedent.

DO:

    PLURAL ANT   V
- **Math problems,** which **are** her specialty, cause her no concern.

One of those who

Consider the following sentences, both of which are correct:

               ANT   V
- Joe is one of those **chemists** who **feel** that science is an art.

           ANT   V
- Joe is the only **one** of those chemists who **feels** that science is an art.

The expression *one of those who* contains both a singular and a plural term—*one* and *those.* To avoid confusion, be careful to decide which of the two is the antecedent. In most cases it will be the plural *those* (or *those chemists,* etc.), but to be sure you must isolate the relative clause and ask yourself what it modifies.

s–v
agr
19n

19n Prefer a singular verb with the title of a work.

Titles of works are generally treated as singular even when they have a plural form, because only one work is being discussed:

        S   V
- Joyce's ***Dubliners*** **has earned** high praise from recent critics.

             S   V
- Larkin's ***Collected Poems*** **was** required reading in English 3370.

    The plural verb *were* would misleadingly refer to the individual poems rather than the whole book.

PUNCTUATION BETWEEN A SUBJECT AND VERB

19o Omit an unnecessary comma between a subject and its verb.

DON'T:

$$\overset{\text{S}}{} \qquad \overset{\text{V}}{}$$

x **Ishi** alone, **remained** to tell the story of his tribe.

DO:

- Ishi alone remained to tell the story of his tribe.

An element that comes between a subject and its verb may need to be set off by commas, as in the sentence *Teenage suicide, which has become common in recent years, is a matter of urgent public concern* (p. 263, 20l). But beware of inserting commas simply to draw a breath, for the demands of grammar and of easy breathing do not always match up. You want to show your reader that a subject is connected to its verb.

S–V agr 19p

DON'T:

$$\overset{\text{S}}{}$$

x **A pair of scissors, a pot of glue, and a stapler, are** still essential to a writer who does not use a word processor.

DO:

- A pair of scissors, a pot of glue, and a stapler are still essential to a writer who does not use a word processor.

19p Note where it is appropriate to insert punctuation between a subject and its verb.

Whenever you place an **interrupting element** (p. 263, 20l) between a subject and verb, you need to set that element apart by a pair of punctuation marks—usually commas:

INT EL
S ⏞⎯⎯⎯⎯⎯⎯⎯⎯⎯⎯⎯⎯⎯⎯⎯⎯⎯⎯⎯ V
- The pilot, **having failed to secure clearance to land,** circled the field as she pleaded desperately with the chief traffic controller.

INT EL
S ⏞⎯⎯⎯⎯⎯⎯⎯⎯⎯⎯⎯⎯⎯⎯⎯
- Tax simplification—**a major goal of this administration**—

V
remains a distant promise.

s–v
agr
19p

20 Modifiers

A **modifier** is an expression that limits or describes another element:

- **tall** messenger
- **the tall** messenger **with blond hair**
- **the tall** messenger **with blond hair who is locking his bicycle**
- **The tall** messenger **who is locking his bicycle** is **from Finland.**

A modifier can consist of a single word, a phrase, or a subordinate clause.

1. a single word:

   - The **tall** boy is from Finland.
   - A **new** star appeared in the **darkening** sky.
   - They did it **gladly.**
   - **That** proposal, **however,** was **soundly** defeated.

2. a **phrase,** or cluster of words lacking a subject-verb combination (p. 215, 17d):

   - The boy **with blond hair** is **from Finland.**
   - **At ten o'clock** she gave up hope.
   - **In view of the foul weather,** they remained **at home.**

3. a **subordinate clause,** or cluster of words that does contain a subject-verb combination but does not form an independent statement (p. 213, 17c):

- The tall messenger **who is locking his bicycle** is from Finland.
- The largest telephone company, **which once enjoyed a near monopoly on phone appliances,** is now being challenged in the open marketplace.

A single-word modifier is usually either an adjective or an adverb. An **adjective** modifies a noun, a pronoun, or some other element that functions as a noun. An **adverb** can modify not only a verb but also an adjective, another adverb, a preposition, an infinitive, a participle, a phrase, a clause, or a whole sentence.

All modifiers are subordinate, or grammatically dependent on another element. But there is nothing minor about the benefit that a careful and imaginative use of modifiers can bring to your style. Some modifiers lend vividness and precision to descriptions, stories, and ideas, while others establish logical relationships, allowing a sentence to convey more shadings of thought and complexity of structure.

mod 20a

DEGREES OF ADJECTIVES AND ADVERBS

20a   Learn how adjectives and adverbs are compared.

Comparing Adjectives

Most adjectives can be *compared,* or changed to show three **degrees** of coverage.

POSITIVE DEGREE	COMPARATIVE DEGREE	SUPERLATIVE DEGREE
wide	wider	widest
dry	drier	driest
lazy	lazier	laziest
relaxed	more relaxed	most relaxed
agreeable	more agreeable	most agreeable

POSITIVE DEGREE	COMPARATIVE DEGREE	SUPERLATIVE DEGREE
wide	less wide	least wide
dry	less dry	least dry
lazy	less lazy	least lazy
relaxed	less relaxed	least relaxed
agreeable	less agreeable	least agreeable

The base form of an adjective is in the *positive* degree: *thin.* The *comparative* degree puts the modified word beyond one or more items: *thinner* (than he is; than everybody). And the *superlative* degree unmistakably puts the modified word beyond all rivals within its group: *thinnest* (of all).

The comparative and superlative degrees of adjectives are formed in several ways.

mod 20a

1. For one-syllable adjectives: *wide, wider, widest* (but *less wide, least wide*).

2. For one- or two-syllable adjectives ending in *-y,* change the *-y* to *-i* and add *-er* and *-est: dry, drier, driest; lazy, lazier, laziest* (but *less lazy, least lazy*).

3. For all other adjectives of two or more syllables, put *more* or *most* (or *less* or *least*) before the positive form: *relaxed, more relaxed, most relaxed* (*less relaxed, least relaxed*).

4. For certain "irregular" adjectives, supply the forms shown in your dictionary. Here are some common examples.

POSITIVE DEGREE	COMPARATIVE DEGREE	SUPERLATIVE DEGREE
bad	worse	worst
good	better	best
far	farther, further	farthest, furthest
little	littler, less, lesser	littlest, least
many, some, much	more	most

Comparing Adverbs

Like adjectives, adverbs can be compared: *quickly, more quickly, most quickly; less quickly, least quickly.* Note that *-ly* adverbs—that is, nearly all adverbs—can be compared only by being preceded by words like *more* and *least.* But some one-syllable adverbs do change their form: *hard/harder/hardest, fast/faster/fastest,* and so forth.

20b Avoid constructions like *more funnier.*

DON'T	DO
x more funnier	● funnier
x least brightest	● least bright
x more quicklier	● more quickly

Be careful not to "double" the comparison of an adjective or adverb. A term like *funnier* already contains the meaning that is wrongly added by *more.*

**mod
20c**

CHOOSING AND PLACING MODIFIERS

20c Repair a dangling modifier.

DON'T:

        DANGL MOD
⎛‾‾‾‾‾‾‾‾‾‾‾‾‾‾‾‾‾‾‾‾‾‾‾⎞
x **Pinning one mugger to the ground,** the other escaped.

DO:

                MOD   MODIFIED
                                              TERM
⎛‾‾‾‾‾‾‾‾‾‾‾‾‾‾‾‾‾‾‾‾‾‾‾‾‾‾‾‾‾‾⎞
● **Pinning one mugger to the ground,** the **victim** helplessly watched the other escape.

When you use a modifier, it is not enough for you to know what thing or idea you are modifying; you must openly supply that modified term within your sentence. Otherwise, you have written a **dangling modifier**—one modifying nothing that the reader can point to. In the "don't" example above, the person doing the *pinning* is left out, and *the other* looks at first like the modified term. In the revised sentence, with its explicit mention of the *victim,* the uncertainty is resolved.

DON'T:

DANGL MOD

x **Once considered a culturally backward country,** Australian filmmakers have surprised the world's most demanding audiences.

> The writer, criticized for a dangling modifier, might protest, "Can't you see I was referring to Australia in the first phrase?" But since *Australia* is not in the sentence and since *Australian filmmakers* can hardly be called a *country,* the modifier does dangle.

**mod
20c**

DO:

MOD

• **Once considered a culturally backward country,**
**MODIFIED
TERM**
Australia has surprised the world's most demanding audiences with its excellent filmmakers.

DON'T:

DANGL MOD

x **To win in court,** an attorney's witnesses must convince the jury.

> Readers must do a double take to realize that it is the attorney, not the witnesses, who wants to win in court.

DO:

MOD   MODIFIED
                  TERM
• **To win in court, an attorney** must choose witnesses who can convince a jury.

DON'T:

      DANGL MOD

x **Fearing the worst,** it was decided to close Flowers Hall.

    Nobody is doing the fearing.

DO:

      MOD   MODIFIED
                                 TERM

● **Fearing the worst, the health department** decided. . . .

20d   Repair a misplaced modifier.

MISPLACED MODIFIER	REVISED
x **Driving to the basket unopposed,** it was an easy lay-up for Jordan.	● Driving to the basket unopposed, **Jordan** dropped in an easy lay-up.
x **Marinated in white wine and sprinkled with parsley,** Linda slid the halibut into the casserole.	● Linda slid the **halibut,** marinated in white wine and sprinkled with parsley, into the casserole.

**mod
20d**

Merely including a modifier and a modified term (20c) is not enough; you need to get them close together so that the reader will immediately grasp their connection. Otherwise, a nearby noun or nounlike element may be mistaken for the modified term. Thus, in the left column above, a mysterious *it* appears to be driving to the basket, and poor Linda gets *marinated* before the party has even begun. In the right-hand examples, note how the true modified terms, *Jordan* and *halibut,* are properly placed.

DON'T:

               MISPLACED MOD   MODIFIED
                                                 TERM?

x **Stolen out of the garage the night before, my grand-**

                 MODIFIED TERM?

mother spotted **my station wagon** on Jefferson Street.

At first glance, it appears that the grandmother, not the car, was stolen from the garage.

DO:

MOD   MODIFIED
                                              TERM

• **Stolen out of the garage the night before, my station wagon** was on Jefferson Street when my grandmother spotted it.

DON'T:

                                  MODIFIED
          MISPLACED MOD   TERM?

x **Towering across the African plain, it** seemed impossible to

MODIFIED TERM?
photograph **the giraffes.**

Here *it* is merely an anticipatory word, not a thing that could be towering across the plain. Unfortunately, readers are put to the trouble of reaching that conclusion for themselves after momentary confusion.

DO:

                MOD   MODIFIED
                                              TERM

• **Towering across the African plain, the giraffes** seemed impossible to photograph.

Squinting Modifier

You may find that in a draft sentence you have surrounded a modifier with two elements, either of which might be the modified term. Such a misplaced modifier is called **squinting** because it does not "look directly at" the real modified term.

DON'T:

                                                   SQ MOD

x How the mechanic silenced the transmission **completely** amazed me.

mod
20d

Did the mechanic do a complete job of silencing, or was the writer completely amazed?

DO:

MODIFIED
MOD   TERM
- How the mechanic **completely silenced** the transmission amazed me.

or

MODIFIED
MOD   TERM
- I was **completely amazed** by the way the mechanic silenced the transmission.

DON'T:

SQ MOD
x They were sure **by August** they would be freed.

Were they sure by August, or would they be freed by August?

DO:

MODIFIED
TERM   MOD
- They were **sure by August** that they would be freed.

mod
20e

or

MODIFIED
MOD   TERM
- They were sure that **by August** they **would be freed.**

Notice how the insertion of *that* either before or after the modifier clarifies the writer's meaning.

20e Repair a split infinitive if you can do so without awkwardness.

DON'T:

SPLIT INF
x It is important **to clearly see** the problem.

DO:

> INF   ADV
- It is important **to see** the problem **clearly.**

Some readers object to every **split infinitive,** a modifier placed between *to* and the base verb form: *to clearly see.* To avoid offending such readers, you would do well to eliminate split infinitives from your drafts.

But when you correct a split infinitive, beware of creating an awkward construction that announces in effect, "Here is the result of my struggle not to split an infinitive."

DON'T:

x It is important **clearly to see** the problem.

> The writer has avoided a split infinitive but has created a pretzel. The "split" version, *It is important to clearly see the problem,* would be preferable. But *It is important to see the problem clearly* would satisfy everyone.

**mod
20e**

Even readers who do not mind an inconspicuous, natural-sounding split infinitive are bothered by *lengthy* modifiers in the split-infinitive position.

DON'T:

> SPLIT INF
x We are going **to soberly and patiently analyze** the problem.

DO:

- We are going to analyze the problem soberly and patiently.

or

- We are going to make a sober and patient analysis of the problem.

20f Place a modifier like *only, just,* or *merely* where it will bring out your meaning.

An adverb or an ordinary adjective usually comes just before the term it modifies (*a beautiful moon; We hastily adjusted the telescope*). In contrast, a *predicate adjective* always follows the verb: *The moon was beautiful.* Writers rarely misplace such modifiers. But adverbs like *only, just,* and *merely* can be moved about rather freely. Their meaning, however, changes drastically from one position to another. Consider:

- **Only** I can understand your argument. [No one else can.]
- I can **only** understand your argument. [I cannot agree with it.]
- I can understand **only** your argument. [But not your motives; *or* The arguments of others mystify me.]
- She had **just** eaten the sandwich. [A moment ago.]
- She had eaten **just** the sandwich. [Not the rest of the food.]

You can see that it requires some thought to put "movable" adverbs exactly where they belong—namely, just before the terms they are meant to emphasize.

For the effective placement of whole modifying elements—that is, subordinate clauses and phrases—see page 153, 12d.

mod
20g

20g Do not hesitate to make use of an absolute phrase.

ABS PHRASE

- He rose from the negotiating table, **his stooped shoulders a sign of discouragement.**

Fear of dangling and misplaced modifiers (20c–d) leads some readers to shun the **absolute phrase,** a group of words that acts as a modifier to a whole statement. But a well-managed absolute phrase can be an effective resource. It allows you, for example, to craft a graceful **cumulative sentence** (p. 170, 13k)—one that sharpens or elaborates an initial main statement.

A classic absolute phrase differs from a dangling modifier by

containing its own "subject," such as *his stooped shoulders* in the
example above. Again:

> "SUBJECT"
> * <u>**All struggle** over</u>, the troops laid down their arms.
>
ABS PHRASE

> "SUBJECT"
> * The quarterback called three plays in one huddle, <u>**the clock**</u>
>   <u>**having stopped after the incomplete pass.**</u>
>
ABS PHRASE

Some other absolute phrases do look exactly like dangling modifiers, but they are accepted as **idioms**—that is, as fixed expressions
that everyone considers normal:

> ABS PHRASE
> * **Generally speaking,** the economy is sluggish.

> ABS PHRASE
> * **To summarize,** most of your encrgy is still untapped.

mod
20h

20h   Avoid a double negative.

DON'T:

x She **didn't** say **nothing.**

DO:

* She **didn't** say **anything.**

or

* She said **nothing.**

In written English the modifier *not* does all the work of denial that
a negative statement needs. A **double negative,** though common in
some people's speech, is considered a mistake rather than an especially strong negation.

PUNCTUATING MODIFIERS

20i Place a comma after an initial modifier that is more than a few words long.

SUB CLAUSE
- **When they learned that the Metroliner had been derailed,** they spent the night at the Y.

PHRASE
- **Instead of having the chocolate mousse,** Walter ordered an apple for desert.

If a modifying element preceding your main clause is itself a clause, as in the first example above, you should automatically follow it with a comma. A comma is also appropriate after an opening phrase (p. 215, 17d), as in the second example.

20j If your sentence begins with a brief phrase, consider a following comma optional.

mod
20j

If a modifying phrase (p. 215, 17d) preceding your main clause is no more than a few words long, you can choose whether to close it off with a comma. A comma indicates a pause, and it marks a more formal separation between the modifier and the main clause. Follow your sense of what the occasion calls for.

WITH COMMA: MORE FORMAL	WITHOUT COMMA: LESS FORMAL
Until this week, I had kept up with my assignments.	**Until this week** I had kept up with my assignments.
For a beginner, she did remarkably well.	**For a beginner** she did remarkably well.

Note, however, that some brief modifying elements must be set off in order to prevent misreading:

mod
20k

DON'T:

x **Soon after** Kelly left home and joined the Navy.

The two-word modifying phrase (*Soon after*) appears momentarily to be part of a longer modifier. A comma ends the confusion.

DO:

• **Soon after,** Kelly left home and joined the Navy.

When in doubt, include the comma; it is always an available option.

20k Use commas to set off a term like *however* or *on the other hand*.

       SENT ADV
• Lori **however,** finds the microwave oven too complicated to use.
       TRANS PHRASE
• **On the contrary** nothing could be simpler.

Look back to pages 226–227, 18c, for lists of *sentence adverbs* and *transitional phrases*. Such modifiers, instead of narrowing the meaning of one element in a statement, show a relationship between the whole statement and the one before it. To bring out this function, be sure your sentence adverbs and transitional phrases are "stopped" at both ends, either by two commas, by a semicolon and a comma, or by a comma and the beginning or end of the sentence:

       SENT ADV
• A circus, **furthermore,** lifts everyone's spirits.

              SENT ADV
• Laughter is good for the soul; **moreover,** it reduces bodily tension.

TRANS PHRASE
• **In reality,** she intends to stay where she is.

              TRANS PHRASE
• The deficit has continued to grow, **as a matter of fact.**

Exception: Some Brief Sentence Adverbs

Certain brief sentence adverbs such as *thus* and *hence* are often seen without commas:

- We can **thus** discount the immediate threat of war.

- **Hence** there is no need to call up the reserves.

20l Set off an interrupting element at both ends.

- Our leading advocate of clean streets **you understand,** is the mayor.

  INT EL

- The city council, **however,** has no funds for a cleanup squad.

  INT EL

- You, **Frank,** will sweep the sidewalk at 7 A.M.

  INT EL

- The mayor's televised plea, **which is rebroadcast every evening on the 6 o'clock news,** reaches everyone in town.

  INT EL

**mod
20l**

In each instance above, the boldfaced words constitute an **interrupting element** (also known as a *parenthetical element*). An interrupting element can be a phrase, a clause, a sentence adverb like *however,* a transitional phrase like *in fact,* an appositive (20n), a name in direct address (*you, Frank*), or an inserted question or exclamation. Since an interrupting element comes between parts of the sentence that belong together in meaning, you must set it off by punctuation at both ends. Note the commas in all four examples above.

The main risk in punctuating an interrupting element is that you may forget to close it off before resuming the main sentence. The risk increases if the last words of the interrupting element happen to fit grammatically with the words that follow.

DON'T:
x The mayor's televised plea, which is rebroadcast every evening on the 6 o'clock news reaches everyone in town.

You can expect to come across such "unstopped" interrupting elements in your first drafts. When in doubt as to whether the element is truly an interruption, reread the sentence without it: *The mayor's televised plea reaches everyone in town.* Since that statement makes complete sense, you know that the omitted part *is* interruptive and must be set off at both ends.

Other Punctuation

Commas are the most usual but not the only means of setting off an interrupting element. Extreme breaks such as whole statements, questions, or exclamations are often better served by parentheses or dashes:

INT EL
- The sky in New Mexico **(have you ever been there?)** is the most dramatic I have seen.

INT EL
- Our recent weather—**what snowstorms we have had!**—makes me long to be back in California.

mod
20m

When you need to interrupt quoted material to insert words of your own, enclose your insertion in brackets (p. 362, 29r).

20m Learn how to punctuate restrictive and nonrestrictive modifying elements.

RESTRICTIVE	NONRESTRICTIVE
The coffee **that comes from Brazilian mountainsides** is best.	The best coffee, **which comes from Brazilian mountainsides,** is also the most expensive.
Jane is a woman **who started her own business.**	Jane, **who started her own business,** is an enterprising woman.
A green salad **dripping with blue cheese dressing** hardly qualifies as diet food.	Kevin's green salad, **dripping with blue cheese dressing,** came with a large slice of brown bread.

To punctuate modifying elements in every position except the opening one (20i), you must recognize a sometimes tricky distinction between two kinds of modifiers—restrictive and nonrestrictive.

RESTRICTIVE: NO COMMAS	**NONRESTRICTIVE: COMMAS REQUIRED**
defining	nondefining
identifying	nonidentifying
essential to establishing meaning	meaning already established

Restrictive Element

A **restrictive element** is essential to the identification of the term it modifies. It restricts or narrows down the scope of that term, identifying precisely *which* coffee, woman, or salad the writer has in mind. Study the two columns in the first box above, and you will see that only the left-hand sentences contain modifiers of this kind. In the right-hand sentences the coffee, woman, and salad under discussion do not need to be identified by restrictive modifiers; presumably the reader already knows which person or thing the writer intends.

mod
20m

Note also how the absence or use of commas marks the difference of function. A restrictive element can do its job of narrowing only if it is *not* isolated by commas.

DONT:

x Women, **who are over thirty-five,** tend to show reduced fertility.

The commas absurdly suggest that all women are over thirty-five.

DO:

RESTR EL
• Women **who are over thirty-five** tend to show reduced fertility.

With the commas gone, the restrictive element narrows the subject to what the writer had in mind all along, women over thirty-five.

DON'T:

x I admire singers, **who write and perform their own songs.**

The comma misleadingly suggests that all singers write and perform their own songs and that the writer therefore admires all singers.

DO:

RESTR EL
● I admire singers **who write and perform their own songs.**

Without a comma, the modifier restricts the admired singers to one particular kind—those who write and perform their own songs.

mod
20m

DON'T:

x The basketball, **that Aaron got for his birthday,** sat unused on his closet floor.

Here a restrictive element, used to identify which basketball the writer has in mind, is wrongly punctuated as if it were nonrestrictive.

DO:

RESTR EL
● The basketball **that Aaron got for his birthday** sat unused on his closet floor.

Nonrestrictive Element

A **nonrestrictive element** is not essential to the identification of the terms it modifies. Instead of narrowing that term, it adds some further information about it. To perform this task the nonrestrictive element must be set off by punctuation, usually commas.

DON'T:

x Bridget **who took up hiking last year** plans to backpack this summer in Mount Rainier National Park.

The absence of commas after *Bridget* and *year* implies that the boldfaced element gives us essential information about Bridget. But *who took up hiking last year* does not help us to identify ("restrict") Bridget; the reader already knows who it is who *plans to backpack*.

DO:

NONR EL

• Bridget, **who took up hiking last year**, plans to backpack this summer in Mount Rainier National Park.

DON'T:

x They snack on trail mix **which is a wholesome blend of nuts, seeds, raisins, and other dried fruit.**

The absence of a comma after *mix* implies that one particular kind of trail mix is being identified. By adding a comma the writer can make it clear that trail mix in general is being defined.

mod
20m

DO:

NONR EL

• They snack on trail mix, **which is a wholesome blend of nuts, seeds, raisins, and other dried fruit.**

DON'T:

x In October Todd dazzled his classmates **writing a research paper in less than a week.**

The boldfaced phrase appears to modify only the word closest to it: *classmates.* An added comma sets off the phrase, making it clear that Todd, not his classmates, accomplished a dazzling feat.

DO:

NONR EL
- In October Todd dazzled his classmates, **writing a research paper in less than a week.**

20n **In punctuating an expression like *Shakespeare's play Hamlet* or *Teresa, an old friend,* observe the restrictive/nonrestrictive rule.**

APP
- Teresa, **an old friend of mine,** has scarcely changed through the years.

APP
- What they saw, **a black bear approaching the baby's cradle,** riveted them with fear.

mod 20n

An **appositive** is a word or group of words that identifies or restates a neighboring noun, pronoun, or nounlike element. Most appositives, like those above, are set off by commas. Nevertheless, you should not automatically make that choice. Instead, ask whether the appositive narrows down ("restricts") the term it follows or merely restates that term. To see why some appositives should appear without commas, compare these sentences.

NONR APP
- Yuri saw his favorite Shakespearean play, ***Hamlet,*** in Moscow last week.

RESTR APP
- Shakespeare's play ***Hamlet*** is a favorite among Muscovites.

The commas in the first sentence tell us that the title *Hamlet* is added information—an appositive that renames Yuri's favorite Shakespearean play. If we remove the appositive, the sentence still conveys its essential point. The absence of commas in the second example shows that the appositive is restrictive, limiting the word *play;* deleting the appositive would remove essential information from the sentence.

20o Use commas in constructions like *a sunlit, windy day* but not in constructions like *a popular rock group*.

If a draft sentence contains two or more modifiers in a row, should you put commas between them? The answer depends on whether the modifiers all modify the same term. Usually they do; such modifiers are *coordinate,* or serving the same grammatical function. You should separate coordinate modifiers from each other by commas:

                                      MODIFIED
                            MOD   MOD   TERM

- I arrived at my new school on a **sunlit, windy day.**

    Since *sunlit* and *windy* both modify the same term, *day,* they are separated from each other by a comma.

But sometimes you will find that two or more modifiers in a row do not modify the same term:

                        MODIFIED
                MOD   TERM

- Nora wore a **starched cotton dress** on the first day of school.

    Here *cotton* modifies *dress,* but *starched* does not; it modifies *cotton dress*. A comma after *starched* would imply that *starched* and *cotton* both modify the same word.

Again, note the contrast between these two sentences, both of which are punctuated correctly:

                                      MODIFIED
           MOD   MOD   MOD   TERM

- Bridget made a **daring, compassionate, moving speech.**

                            MODIFIED
                MOD   TERM

- Mary played drums in a **popular rock group.**

The first sentence contains three coordinate modifiers separated by commas. In the second example, the modifiers are not coordinate (*popular* modifies *rock group*); adding a comma after *popular* would be a mistake.

    To test whether you are dealing with coordinate modifiers, try shifting the order of the words. Truly coordinate terms can be reversed without a change of meaning: *a sunlit, windy day; a windy, sunlit day.* Noncoordinate terms change their meaning (*a blue racing car; a racing blue car*) or become nonsensical (*a popular rock group; a rock popular group*).

20p Omit a comma between the final modifier and the modified term.

When a modifier comes just before the modified term, no punctuation should separate them. Thus, however many coordinate modifiers you supply, be sure to omit a comma after the final one:

FINAL MOD
- O'Keeffe produced an intense, starkly simple, **radiantly glow-**
MODIFIED
TERM
  ing painting of a flower.

  A comma after *glowing* would be mistaken. The whole set of coordinate modifiers—*intense, starkly simple, radiantly glowing*—already stands in proper relation to the modified term, *painting.*

For an exception to this rule, keep reading.

20q Consider enclosing a modifier in commas if it qualifies the modifier just before it.

PRECEDING MOD MOD
- It was an **inaccurate, perhaps even deceitful,** account of the meeting.

If one modifier serves in part to qualify or comment on the modifier preceding it, you can bring out that function by enclosing it in commas. The sentence above would still be considered acceptable if the second comma were omitted, but that comma shows that *perhaps even deceitful* is a "second thought" about the first modifier, *inaccurate.*

If you set off a "backward-looking" modifier at one end, be sure to supply a second comma at the other end.

mod
20q

DON'T:

x She told a fascinating, but not altogether believable story.

DO:

• She told a fascinating, but not altogether believable, story.

or

• She told a fascinating but not altogether believable story.

mod
20q

21 Noun and Pronoun Case

21a Recognize the case forms and their functions.

CASES:	SUBJECTIVE	OBJECTIVE	POSSESSIVE
Personal Pronouns	I you he she it we they	me you him her it us them	my, mine your, yours his her, hers its our, ours their, theirs
Who	who	whom	whose
Nouns	car cars Janice Russia	car cars Janice Russia	car's cars' Janice's Russia's

Nouns and pronouns change form to show certain grammatical relations to other words within a sentence. These forms are called **cases.** They show whether a term is a subject of discussion or performer of action (*subjective case*), a receiver of action or an object of a preposition (*objective case*), or a "possessor" of another term (*possessive case*).

Most personal pronouns (*I, she,* etc.) show changes of form for all three cases, and so does the relative pronoun *who.* Nouns, however, do not change for the objective case.

A change in form helps to show which sentence function a word is performing. For example:

SUBJECTIVE CASE
1. Subject of verb (p. 212, 17b):

- **He** went home
- **They** went home.
- The one **who** went home was disappointed.

2. Complement (p. 210, 17a):

- It was **she** who was guilty.
- The victims are **we** ourselves.

OBJECTIVE CASE
1. Direct object of verb (p. 209, 17a):

- They praised **him.**
- We fed the child **whom** the agency had entrusted to us.

2. Indirect object of verb (p. 619):

- They taught **him** a lesson.
- The fine cost **them** a pretty penny.

3. Object of preposition (p. 625):

- She explained the software to **us.**
- For **whom** did you work last year?

4. Subject of infinitive (p. 632):

- They wanted **her** to stay.
- She expected **them** to give her a raise.

case
21a

POSSESSIVE CASE

1. With nouns:

- **Our** hats were all squashed.
- **James's** case was the worst of all.
- The **Beatles'** music still keeps its freshness.
- **Whose** pen is this?

2. With gerunds (p. 211, 17a):

- **His** departing left us sad.
- **Their** training every day made them too tired for fun.
- **Jane's** humming drove everyone wild.

In general, case forms must match sentence functions: subjective case for subjects of clauses, objective case for the various kinds of objects, and possessive case for words that "possess" another term.

case 21c

21b Keep the subject of a clause in the subjective case.

DO:

- $\overset{\frown{\text{S}}}{\text{He and I}}$ were good friends.

DON'T:

x $\overset{\frown{\text{S}}}{\text{Him and me}}$ were good friends.

Standard usage requires that you avoid using objective-case pronouns for subjects of clauses.

See page 278, 21g, for a pronoun subject in a subordinate clause.

21c Watch out for constructions like *for you and I.*

The rule for pronoun objects of all kinds is simple: put them in the objective case.

DIRECT OBJECT OF VERB:

• Many differences separate **us.**

INDIRECT OBJECT OF VERB:

• She gave **me** cause for worry.

OBJECT OF PREPOSITION:

• Toward **whom** is your anger directed?

SUBJECT OF INFINITIVE:

• They asked **her** to serve a second term.

> Note that the "subject" of the infinitive appears in the objective case because it is at the same time the indirect object of the verb.

Choice of a correct objective form becomes harder when the object is **compound,** or made up of more than one term. Knowing that it is wrong to write *Him and me were good friends,* some writers "overcorrect" and put the subjective forms where they do not belong.

case 21c

DON'T:

```
                OBJS OF
        PREP   ⟋PREP⟍
```
x That will be a dilemma for **you** and **I.**

DO:

• That will be a dilemma for you and **me.**

When in doubt, test for case by disregarding one of the two objects. Since you would never write x *That will be a dilemma for I,* you know that both of the objects must be objective in case.

The danger of choosing the wrong case seems to increase still further when a noun and a pronoun are paired as objects.

DON'T:

```
            OBJS OF
   PREP    ⟋PREP⟍
```
x As for **Jack** and **I,** we will take the bus.

> Would you write *As for I?* No; therefore, keep to the objective case.

DO:

- As for Jack and **me,** we will take the bus.

21d Observe the grammatical distinction between *who* and *whom*.

In informal speech and writing, *whom* has become a rare form even where grammar strictly requires it. When the pronoun appears first in a clause, the subjective *who* automatically comes to mind.

COLLOQUIAL:

- **Who** did he marry?
- **Who** will you play against?

In standard written English, however, the question of *who* versus *whom* is still determined by grammatical function, not by speech habits. Note the reason for choosing *whom* in each of the following revisions:

D OBJ   V

- **Whom** did he marry?

    Whom is the direct object of the verb *did marry.*

OBJ OF
PREP   PREP

- **Whom** will you play against?

or

        OBJ OF
PREP   PREP

- Against **whom** will you play?

    Whom is the object of the preposition *against.*

For more on *who* versus *whom,* see page 278, 21g.

21e Avoid an awkward choice of pronoun case after *than* or *as*.

Many writers agonize over the case of a pronoun following *than* or *as*. Should one write *Alex is taller than I* or *Alex is taller than me?*

Technically, the answer is that both versions are correct. In the first instance *than* serves as a subordinating conjunction: *Alex is taller than I [am]*. In the second, *than* has become a preposition with the object *me*.

In other sentences, however, one choice is clearly incorrect. Consider:

- The cows chased Margaret farther than $\left\{\begin{array}{c} \text{I} \\ \text{me} \end{array}\right\}$.

Here *I* would indicate that Margaret was chased by both the cows and the writer: *The cows chased Margaret farther than I did.* Since that is surely not the intended meaning, the right choice is *me*.

When in doubt, consider your intended meaning and mentally supply any missing part of the clause:

- The cows chased Margaret farther than (they chased) me.

The added words will tell you which case to use for the pronoun.

Wherever both choices sound awkward, as in the "Alex" example above, look for an alternative construction:

               SUB CLAUSE
- Alex is taller **than I am.**

    By supplying the whole subordinate clause, you can avoid any hesitation between *I* and *me*.

case 21f

21f   Avoid constructions like *for we students.*

DON'T:

                   PRO   APP
x Inflation is a problem for **we** students.

DO:

- Inflation is a problem for **us** students.

When an appositive (p. 268, 20n) follows a pronoun, some writers automatically put the pronoun in the subjective case (*we*). As often as not, the result is a usage error. A wiser course is to test for the right pronoun case by leaving the appositive out of account. In the

example above, *for we* is obviously wrong; so, then, is *for we students.*
The rule is that a following appositive should have no influence on
the case of a pronoun.

21g Choose a pronoun's case by its function within its own clause.

One of the hardest choices of case involves a pronoun that seems to
have rival functions in two clauses.

DON'T:

x He will read his poems to **whomever** will listen.

> The writer has made *whomever* objective because it looks like
> the object of the preposition *to: to whomever.* But the real
> object of *to* is the whole subordinate clause that follows it.

DO:

- He will read his poems to $\underbrace{\overset{\text{S}}{\textbf{whoever}} \ \overset{\text{V}}{\textbf{will listen.}}}_{\text{SUB CLAUSE}}$

> The subject of the subordinate clause *whoever will listen* be-
> longs in the subjective case.

Whenever a subordinate clause is embedded within a larger
structure, you can settle problems of case by mentally eliminating
everything but the subordinate clause.

DON'T:

x Josh had no doubt about **whom** would drive the car.

> The test for case shows that *whom would drive the car* is
> ungrammatical. The object of *about* is the whole subordinate
> clause, which requires a subject in the subjective case.

**case
21g**

DO:

S   V
• Josh had no doubt about **who would drive the car.**

SUB CLAUSE

When a choice of pronoun case is difficult, the air of difficulty may remain even after you have chosen correctly. Your reader may be distracted by the same doubt that you have just resolved. It is therefore a good idea to dodge the whole problem.

DO:

• He will read his poems to **anyone** who will listen.

• Josh was sure that **he** would drive the car.

21h   Use the possessive case in most constructions like *Marie's coming to Boston is a rare event.*

case
21h

In the phrase *Marie's coming to Boston,* the word *coming* is a **gerund**—that is, a verbal (p. 211, 17a) that functions as a noun. Most gerunds, like this one, end in *-ing,* but there is also a two-word past form.

PRESENT GER
• There is less **swooning** in Hollywood movies than there used to be.

PAST GER
• **Having swum** across the lake made him generally less fearful.

A gerund can be preceded not only by a word like *a, the,* or *this* but also by a governing noun or pronoun known as the subject of the gerund: *Wilson's achieving unity, his having achieved unity.* (A gerund can also take an object; see page 585.) The name *subject* is misleading, for most subjects of gerunds, just like words that "possess" nouns, belong in the possessive case.

POSSESSION OF NOUN	POSSESSION OF GERUND
our departure	our departing
Marian's reliance	Marian's relying
Jules's loss	Jules's having lost

In general, then, put subjects of gerunds into the possessive case:

- **Esther's** commuting ended with her graduation.

Even if the subject of a gerund feels like an object, you should keep to the possessive form.

DON'T:

OBJ OF
PREP?

PREP

x Harold wondered why people laughed at **him** wearing that hat.

> Here the writer has made *him* objective because it "feels like" the object of the preposition *at*. In fact, the object of that preposition is the whole gerund phrase *his wearing that hat*.

case
21h

DO:

S OF
GER   GER   OBJ OF
GER

- Harold wondered why people laughed at **his** wearing that hat.

> Note how the possessive *his* directs a reader's attention to the next word, *wearing*. The activity, not the person, inspired laughter.

Exceptions

When the subject of a gerund is an abstract or inanimate noun—one like *physics* or *chaos*—it can appear in a nonpossessive form.

ACCEPTABLE:

S OF GER   GER

- We cannot ignore the danger of **catastrophe striking** again.

> But the possessive *catastrophe's* would also be acceptable here. Rather than choose, however, why not recast the sentence?

PREFERABLE:

- We cannot ignore the danger that catastrophe will strike again.

When a gerund's subject is separated from the gerund by other words, the gerund tends to change into a modifier (a participle). In such a sentence the possessive form is not used:

        D OBJ   **PART**
- They admired **him,** a Canadian, **enduring** the heat of Kenya.

> Without the intervening appositive (p. 268, 20n), *a Canadian,* we would recognize *enduring* as a gerund: *They admired his enduring. . . .* But in the sentence as it stands, *him* is a direct object modified by the whole phrase *enduring the heat of Kenya.*

21i   Feel free to use constructions like *a friend of Nancy's.*

The possessive case for nouns is usually indicated either by *-'s* or *-s'* (*student's, students'*) or by an *of* construction (*of the student, of the students*). But sometimes you can combine the two forms to avoid confusion. Compare:

case
21i

- Mike sighed over a snapshot of Jane.
- Mike sighed over a snapshot of Jane's.

Both sentences are grammatical, but their meanings differ. The first deals with a snapshot *of* Jane, the second with a snapshot taken or owned *by* Jane.

Some writers worry that a **double possessive** such as *a snapshot of Jane's* may be a usage error, just as a double negative (p. 260, 20h) is. But everyone freely uses the double possessive with pronouns: *a friend of hers, an idea of his,* and so forth. Feel free to use nouns in the same way: *a friend of Nancy's, an idea of Plato's.*

22 Pronoun Agreement and Reference

PRONOUN AGREEMENT	PRONOUN REFERENCE
Does the pronoun have the same gender, number, and person as its antecedent?	Can the reader see without difficulty which term is the pronoun's antecedent?
DON'T:	**DON'T:**
x Although the union struck the **plant, they** remained open. The antecedent *plant* and the pronoun referring to it must be made to agree in number.	x The strikers used violence against the management, **which** made a final reconciliation difficult. Does *which* refer to *violence* or to *management?*
DO:	**DO:**
• Although the union struck the plant, **it** remained open.	• It was the strikers' **violence that** made a final reconciliation with management so difficult.

Pronouns—words used in place of nouns—offer you relief from the monotony of needlessly repeating a term or name when your reader already knows what or whom you mean. But precisely because many pronouns are substitutes for other words, they raise a variety of usage problems, including subject-verb agreement (Chapter 19) and choice of the correct case (Chapter 21). Here we consider the two main kinds of relation between a pronoun and its **antecedent,** the term it refers to. First, a pronoun should show **agreement** with its antecedent in gender, number, and person. And second, the identification of the antecedent—that is, the pronoun's **reference** to it—should never be in doubt.

PRONOUN AGREEMENT

22a Make a pronoun agree with its antecedent in gender, number, and person.

GENDER	NUMBER	PERSON
masculine (*he*) feminine (*she*)	singular (*her, it,* etc.) plural (*they, theirs,* etc.)	first (*I, we, our,* etc.) second (*you, your, yours*) third (*he, she, it, they, their,* etc.)

If the antecedent of a pronoun is explicitly female, make the pronoun feminine: *Ellen . . . she; her; hers.* If the antecedent is plural, make the pronoun plural: *cats . . . they; them; their; theirs.* And if the antecedent is first person, the pronoun should be first person as well: *I . . . me; my; mine.* The following examples show standard practice:

pr agr
22a

> ANT   PRO
- **Philip** still has not tried **his** sailboard in rough weather.

    The antecedent and pronoun are both masculine, singular, and third person.

>   ANT   PRO
- Sooner or later, all **dancers** suffer injuries to **their** feet.

    The antecedent and pronoun are both plural and third person.

> ANT   PRO   ANT   PRO
- **We** should allow **our daughter** to decide on **her** own career.

    The first antecedent-pronoun set is plural and first person; the second set is singular, feminine, and third person.

All this looks straightforward enough, but points 22b–g below take up some potentially tricky applications of the rule.

22b Usually refer to a noun like *mob* or *jury* with a singular pronoun.

ANT   PRO
- The **mob** of angry demonstrators pushed **its** way into the mayor's office.

ANT   PRO
- At last the **jury** came forward with **its** verdict.

A term like *mob* or *jury* is called a **collective noun** (p. 239, 19f) because, though singular in form, it designates a group of members. In most instances, like those above, a collective noun as antecedent calls for a singular pronoun.

When you wish to emphasize the separate members of the group, however, make the pronoun plural:

ANT   PRO
- The television camera followed the **jury** as **they** scattered

PRO
    through the courtyard to **their** waiting cars.

**pr agr
22c**

22c If the antecedent contains parts linked by *and,* usually refer to it with a plural pronoun.

—————ANT———   PRO
- The **architect** and the **contractor** worked out **their** differences.

Two or more items in the antecedent generally call for a plural pronoun, as in the sentence above. But when both parts refer to the same thing or person, make the pronoun singular:

/ ANT———————   PRO
- My **son** and **chief antagonist** tries out **his** debating speeches on me.

    One person is both son and chief antagonist; hence the singular pronoun *his.*

22d Avoid a clash of singular and plural antecedents linked by *or* or *nor*.

The schoolbook rule is that if two parts of an antecedent differ in number, the pronoun must agree with the *nearest* part.

"CORRECT":

                              NEAREST PART
                              OF ANT   **PRO**
- Neither the coach nor the **players** will tell **their** story to the press.

                              NEAREST PART
                              OF ANT   **PRO**
- Neither the players nor the **coach** will tell **his** story to the press.

But this "rule" often produces a strained effect, as in the second example above. You would do better to recast any sentence containing a conflict of number in the antecedent. Either remove that conflict (*Neither the coaches nor the players will tell their story . . .*) or do without the pronoun:

pr agr
22e

PREFERABLE:

- Neither the coach nor the players will tell the story to the press.

22e If you have placed *each* or *every* before a noun, refer to it with a singular pronoun.

      ANT
- **Each lion** that was tranquilized had a tag attached to
  PRO
  its ear.

            ANT   **PRO**
- **Every pregnant woman** in this exercise class is in **her** third trimester.

Use a singular pronoun even if the term is compound (22c):

                              ANT
- **Every financial vice president and accountant** gave
  ⌒**PRO**⌒
  his or **her** budgetary projections for the coming year.

22f When in doubt, treat a pronoun like *everyone* or *nobody* as singular.

Review pages 243–246, 19k, which treat verb agreement with such indefinite pronouns as *each, everybody, neither,* and *none.* Those pronouns are singular in form but not necessarily in meaning. As antecedents, however, they generally require singular pronouns:

- ANT
  Everyone on the swimming team had remembered to bring
  PRO
  her goggles and nose clip.

-   ANT   PRO
  Tests on the two viruses show that **neither** has had **its** life span shortened by the new drug.

Keep to a singular pronoun even when the indefinite pronoun is followed by *of them:*

- **Each of them** has brought **her** accessories.
- **Neither of them** has had **its** life span shortened.

None, however, forms a partial exception to the rule. Although some writers insist that *none* is always singular (*None of them has surrendered his gun*), others construe *none* as plural when the intended meaning is *all:*

- **None** of them have memorized **their** automatic teller numbers.

**pr agr
22g**

22g Watch for tricky antecedents like *politics* and *acoustics.*

-     ANT   PRO   PRO
  Statistics is a fine discipline, but **it** has **its** pitfalls.

-     ANT   PRO
  His **statistics** were at **their** most impressive in the middle of the season.

Both of these sentences are correctly handled. In the first, *statistics* carries a plural -*s* ending but is rightly construed as a singular thing, the discipline of statistics. In the second example, the writer has in mind a collection of many numbers; hence the plural pronoun. Review p. 244, 19l, for a discussion of antecedents that take this form.

22h Avoid an abrupt pronoun shift.

Your choice of a noun or pronoun in one sentence or part of a sentence establishes a certain person and number; see page 283, 22a. When you refer again to the same individual(s) or thing(s), do not shift unexpectedly between persons and numbers—for example, from the singular *someone* to the plural *they,* from the third-person *students* or *they* to the second-person *you,* or from the third-person plural *people* to the second-person singular *you.* Keep to one person and number.

DON'T:

        THIRD   **SECOND**
        PERSON   **PERSON**
x A good song stays with **someone,** making **you** feel less alone.

> Having committed the sentence to a third-person pronoun, the writer jars us by switching to the second-person *you.*

pr ref 22i

DO:

        THIRD   **THIRD**
        PERSON   **PERSON**
• A good song stays with **people,** making **them** feel less alone.

Or, more informally:

         ╱ **SAME PRO** ╲
• A good song stays with **you,** making **you** feel less alone.

PRONOUN REFERENCE

22i Make sure you have included a pronoun's antecedent.

In informal conversation, pronouns often go without antecedents, since both parties know who or what is being discussed: *He wants me to phone home at least once a week.* In writing, however, you want your antecedents to be explicitly (openly) stated.

DON'T:

x **They** say we are in for another cold winter.

Who is *They?*

DO:

            ANT   PRO

• **The weather forecasters** have more bad news for us. **They** say we are in for another cold winter.

DON'T:

x **It** explains here that the access road will be closed for repairs.

If the previous sentence has no antecedent for *It,* revision is called for.

DO:

            ANT

• **This bulletin** tells us why the backpacking trip was postponed.

PRO

  It explains that the access road will be closed for repairs.

pr ref 22j

22j Eliminate competition for the role of antecedent.

If you allow a pronoun and its antecedent to stand too far apart, another element in your sentence may look like the real antecedent. This confusion is usually temporary, but you should avoid putting your reader to any unnecessary work.

DON'T:

                        ANT?   ANT? PRO

x Keats sat under a huge **tree** to write his **ode. It** was dense and kept him from the Hampstead mist.

The nearness of *ode* to *It* makes *ode* a likely candidate for antecedent, especially since an ode might be described as dense. With a little extra thought the reader can identify *tree* as the real antecedent—but a good revision can make that fact immediately clear.

DO:

                                                    ANT   PRO
- Keats wrote his ode while sitting under a huge **tree, which** was
  dense and kept him from the Hampstead mist.

or

                                                    ANT   PRO
- Keats wrote his ode while sitting under a huge **tree, whose**
  dense foliage kept him from the Hampstead mist.

DON'T:

              ANT?   ANT?
x Before I sold **cosmetics,** I used to walk by all the **clerks**

                                    PRO
  in the cosmetics department, amazed by **their** variety.

  What was various, the cosmetics or the clerks?

DO:

- Before I sold cosmetics, I used to walk by all the clerks in
  the cosmetics department, amazed by the variety of makeup on
  display.

**pr ref
22k**

22k Watch especially for a *which* with more than one possible antecedent.

When you find a clause beginning with the relative pronoun *which,*
check to see whether that word refers to a single preceding term or
to a whole statement. If the antecedent is a whole statement, you
risk unclarity.

DON'T:

x In the subfreezing weather we could not start the car, **which**
  interfered with our plans.

  Although a reader can see on a "double take" that the antecedent of *which* is not *car* but the whole preceding statement,
  writers should not put readers to such pains.

DO:

• The subfreezing weather interfered with our plans, especially when the car would not start.

or

• Since the car would not start in the subfreezing weather, we had to change our plans.

DON'T:

     ANT?   ANT   PRO

x We **skate** on the frozen **pond, which** I enjoy.

What is enjoyed, the activity or the pond?

DO:

• I enjoy skating on the frozen pond.

---

pr ref 22I

22I Guard against vagueness in using *this, that,* or *it.*

Vague This or That

Study the following unclear passage.

DON'T:

x The town board voted to eliminate school crossing guards, even though a serious accident had recently occurred at the corner of Jefferson and Truman. **This** brought the parents out in protest.

Does *This* refer to the elimination of the crossing guards, to the accident, or to the whole preceding statement?

When the word *this, that, these,* or *those* is used alone, without modifying another word, it is known as a *demonstrative pronoun.* Inexperienced writers sometimes use the singular forms *this* and *that* imprecisely, hoping to refer to a whole previous idea rather than to a specific antecedent. The problem is that nearby terms may also look like antecedents. While all writers use an occasional demonstrative pronoun, you should check each *this* or *that* to make sure its antecedent is clear. The remedy for vagueness is to make *this* or *that* modify another term or to rephrase the statement.

DO:

• The town board voted to eliminate school crossing guards, even though a serious accident had recently occurred at the corner

                   MOD   **MODIFIED TERM**

of Jefferson and Truman. **This dangerous economy** brought the parents out in protest.

> The writer has gone from *This* to *This dangerous economy,* turning a vague demonstrative pronoun (*this*) into a precise modifier—a **demonstrative adjective.**

DON'T:

x The cat shed great quantities of fur on the chair. **That** made Mary Ann extremely anxious.

> Though the antecedent of *that* (the whole previous sentence) is reasonably clear, the second sentence is not very informative. What was Mary Ann anxious about, the cat's health or the condition of the chair?

DO:

• The cat shed great quantities of fur on the chair. Mary Ann worried that when her mother saw the chair, the cat would be banished from the house.

or

• The cat shed great quantities of fur on the chair. The possibility that he was ill made Mary Ann extremely anxious.

Vague It

DON'T:

    INDEFINITE   **PERSONAL**

    INDICATOR   **PRO**

x Although **it** is a ten-minute walk to the bus, **it** comes frequently.

It can serve as both a personal pronoun (*It is mine*) and an indefinite indicator (*It is raining*), but your reader will be momentarily baffled if you combine those two uses within a sentence.

DO:

• Although it is a ten-minute walk to the bus stop, **buses** come frequently.

pr ref 22l

22m   Make sure the antecedent is a whole term, not part of one.

The antecedent of a pronoun should not be a modifier or a fragment of a larger term.

DON'T:

                              ANT?   PRO

x Alexander waited at the **train station** until **it** came.

> Here the word *train* is part of a larger noun, *train station.* The sentence contains no reference to a train, and thus *it* has no distinct antecedent. The pronoun "dangles" like a dangling modifier (p. 253, 20c).

DO:

                                       ANT   PRO

pr ref 22m

• Alexander waited at the station for the **train** until **it** came.

DON'T:

                   ANT?

x He was opposed to **gun control** because he thought the Con-

                                     PRO

stitution guaranteed every citizen the right to own **one.**

DO:

                             ANT

• He was opposed to the control of **guns** because the thought the

                                PRO

Constitution guaranteed all citizens the right to own **them.**

or

• He was opposed to gun control because he thought the Constitution guaranteed every citizen's right to own a gun.

23 Parallelism

When two or more parts of sentence are governed by a single grammatical device, they are said to be structurally parallel, or in **parallelism.**

PATTERN	EXAMPLE
either x or y	She uses either **crayons** or **chalk.**
neither x nor y	He neither **boxed** nor **wrestled.**
not only x but also y	Ed not only **sleeps with a teddy bear** but also **bathes with a rubber duck.**
more x than y	It is more blessed **to give** than **to receive.**
x and y	**A delicious dinner** and **a good movie** will help you relax.
x but not y	Eric thinks about **building his muscles** but not about **forming his mind.**
x is y	**A penny saved** is **a penny earned.** (Benjamin Franklin)
x, y, and z	Pat vowed to **love, honor,** and **cherish.**

Note from these examples that parallelism can include both *comparisons* (more x than y) and **series,** or the alignment of three or more elements (x, y, and z). In general, parallelism involves matching the grammar, punctuation, and logic of two or more elements in a sentence.

Chapter 13 explains how the matching of parallel elements can give your prose clarity, conciseness, and emphasis (see especially pp. 157–163, 13a–d). But under the pressure of writing a first draft, it is sometimes hard to keep parallel constructions in proper alignment. This chapter discusses typical problems of faulty parallelism that you should watch for as you revise.

FAULTY PARALLELISM	ADEQUATE PARALLELISM
x The studio was large, square, and had a sunny aspect.	● The studio was **large, square, and sunny.**
x Not only did the painter splash her canvases, but also the floor.	● The painter splashed **not only her canvases but also the floor.**
x She wanted to express not so much the form of her subjects, but rather the nature of paint itself.	● She wanted to express **not so much the form of her subjects as the nature of paint itself.**
x She was not an easy person to understand, and neither was her work.	● **Neither she nor her work** was easy to understand.
x She loved obscurity as much as, if not more, than publicity.	● She loved **obscurity as much as publicity.**
x She was neither a fraud nor was she a major pioneer.	● She was **neither a fraud nor a major pioneer.**

**// join
23a**

JOINING PARALLEL ELEMENTS

23a Use like elements within a parallel construction.

No matter how many terms you make parallel, the first of them establishes what kind of element the others must be. If the first term is a verb, the others must be verbs as well. Align a noun with other nouns or nounlike elements, a participle (p. 211, 17a) with other participles, a whole clause (p. 213, 17c) with other clauses, and so forth. (In the following examples, parallel elements are marked by *x*'s and *y*'s.)

DON'T:

x His black leather jacket was both **snug** and **looked wet**.
      (x: snug)   (y: looked wet)

  The parallel formula here is *both x and y.* The first term within it is the adjective *snug.* Thus the *y* term should also be an adjective. Instead, we find the unwelcome verb *looked*. Revise to get the two adjectives *snug* and *wet* into parallelism.

DO:

* His black leather jacket looked both $\overset{x}{\textbf{snug}}$ and $\overset{y}{\textbf{wet}}$.

DON'T:

x She enjoyed $\overset{x}{\textbf{riding her horse}}$ and $\overset{y}{\textbf{to race her motorcycle.}}$

The *x* element is a gerund phrase (p. 626), requiring the *y* element to be a gerund or gerund phrase as well. The infinitive phrase (p. 626) *to race her motorcycle* breaks the parallelism.

DO:

x She enjoyed $\overset{x}{\textbf{riding her horse}}$ and $\overset{y}{\textbf{racing her motorcycle.}}$

DON'T:

x She likes to $\overset{x}{\textbf{wear designer clothes,}}$ $\overset{y}{\textbf{listen to classical}}$

$\overset{z}{\textbf{music,}}$ and $\textbf{gourmet food is essential.}$

// join 23a

The series begins with the completion of an infinitive: *to wear*. At this point the writer can either keep repeating the *to* or supply further verb forms to be governed by the original *to*.

DO:

* She likes $\overset{x}{\textbf{to wear designer clothes,}}$ $\overset{y}{\textbf{to listen to classical}}$

$\overset{z}{\textbf{music,}}$ and $\textbf{to eat gourmet food.}$

or

* She likes to $\overset{x}{\textbf{wear designer clothes,}}$ $\overset{y}{\textbf{listen to classical music,}}$

and $\overset{z}{\textbf{eat gourmet food.}}$

Either version adequately corrects the earlier one, in which a whole clause, *gourmet food is essential,* was forced into parallelism with two infinitive constructions. A further option, one that keeps the emphasis of the original statement, is to end the parallelism early.

DO:

- She likes to **wear designer clothes** and **listen to classical music,** and she finds gourmet food essential.

Comparing Comparable Things

The problem of mismatched parallel elements arises most frequently in comparisons. The writer knows what is being compared with what, but the words on the page say something else.

DON'T:

x **The office in Boston** is busier than **Seattle.**

The sentence appears to compare an office with a city. The writer must add *the one in* to show that one office is being compared with another.

DO:

- **The office in Boston** is busier than **the one in Seattle.**

DON'T:

x **Solar heating for a large office building** is technically different from **a single-family home.**

The writer is trying to compare one kind of solar heating with another, but the sentence actually compares one kind of solar heating with a single-family home.

// join
23a

DO:

- **Solar heating for a large office building** is technically different from **that for a single-family home.**

23b Make the second half of a parallel construction as grammatically complete as the first.

When you are aligning two elements *x* and *y,* be careful not to omit parts of your *y* element that are necessary to make it match the parts of the *x* element. The problem tends to arise when the parallelism comes at the beginning of the sentence, especially if the formula being used is *not only x but also y.*

DON'T:

x Not only **did Gregor Mendel study the color of the peas,** but also **the shapes of the seeds.**

> Some good writers would find this sentence adequate; after all, its meaning is clear. But other writers would want to make a better match between *x* and *y*. Since the *x* element contains a subject (*Gregor Mendel*) and a verb (*did study*), the *y* element should follow suit.

// join 23b

IMPROVED:

- Not only **did Gregor Mendel study** the color of the peas, but he also **studied** the shapes of the seeds.

> But this revision is wordy. Such a construction can be made more concise by shifting the *not only* to a later position.

PREFERABLE:

- Gregor Mendel studied not only **the color of the peas** but also **the shapes of the seeds.**

23c Be sure to complete the expected parts of an anticipatory pattern.

Many parallel constructions are governed by **anticipatory patterns** (p. 159, 13b)—formulas that demand to be completed in a certain predictable way. If you begin the formula but then change or abandon it, your sentence falls out of parallelism.

Neither . . . nor

A *neither* demands a *nor,* not an *or.*

> DON'T:
>
> x Banging his fist on the table, he insisted that he had **neither** a drinking problem **or** a problem with his temper.
>
> Change *or* to *nor.*

// join
23c

More like x than y

Do not sabotage this formula by adding the word *rather.*

> DON'T:
>
> x He seemed **more like** a Marine sergeant **rather than** a social worker.
>
> Delete *rather.*

No sooner x than y

Here the common error is to change *than* to *when.*

> DON'T:
>
> x **No sooner** had I left **when** my typewriter was stolen.
>
> *When* must be changed to *than* if the anticipatory formula is to complete its work.

Not so much x as y

Be sure that the necessary *as* is not replaced by an unwelcome *but rather.*

> **DON'T:**
> x She was **not so much** selfish, **but rather** impulsive.
>
> **DO:**
> • She was **not so much** selfish **as** impulsive.

or

> • She was **not so much** selfish **as she was** impulsive.

Note the absence of a comma in the two satisfactory versions.

23d   Watch for faulty parallelism with *not . . . neither.*

> **DON'T:**
>
> x The Marquis de Sade was **not an agreeable man,** and **neither are his novels.**

// join
23e

> The complement (p. 210) *man* in the *x* element makes the sentence appear to say that the novels were not an agreeable man.
>
> **DO:**
>
> • The Marquis de Sade was **not agreeable,** and **neither are his novels.**

23e   Beware of a suspended verb or a suspended comparison.

Suspended Verb

Be alert to likely difficulties with a **suspended verb**—the use of two forms of the same delayed verb, governed by the same subject: *The* *project can, and in all likelihood will, succeed.* That sentence, though cumbersome, is grammatically correct. But quite often the delayed verb turns out to fit with only one of the two expressions preceding it.

DON'T:

x They **can,** and indeed **have been, making** progress on the case.

The way to check such sentences is to read them without the interruption: *They can making . . . ?* Once you spot a problem, decide whether you want to repair the construction or get rid of it. As a rule you will want to do without the double statement.

DO:

• They can make, and indeed have been making, progress on the case.

or, better:

// join
23e

• They have been making progress on the case.

Suspended Comparison

Like those with a suspended verb, parallel constructions involving a **suspended** (delayed) **comparison** sometimes end in a tangle.

DON'T:

x Wendy likes jazz **as much,** if not **more than, folk music.**

Check the sentence by reading it without the interruption. *Wendy likes jazz as much folk music?* Recognizing that this is ungrammatical, you can either repair or discard the suspended comparison.

DO:

• Wendy likes jazz as much as, if not more than, folk music.

or, better:

• Wendy likes jazz at least as much as she does folk music.

23f Repeat *that* to show that two clauses are parallel.

When you are trying to make whole clauses parallel, watch out for allowing the parallel effect to lapse after the first clause. The danger is greatest when the *x* element is a *that* clause.

DON'T:

$$\overbrace{}^{\text{x}} \qquad \overbrace{}^{\text{y}}$$

x Sue wrote **that she hated her job,** but **she was glad to be**

working.

> As worded, this sentence allows the *y* element to become a direct statement about how Sue felt. But the writer's intention was to reveal two things that Sue *wrote*. A second *that* brings out that meaning.

DO:

- Sue wrote **that** she hated her job but **that** she was glad to be working.

**// join
23g**

23g Do not use *and who* or *and which* unless *who* or *which* appears earlier in the sentence.

DON'T:

x She is a woman of action, **and who** cares about the public good.

DO:

- She is a woman **who** takes strong action **and who** cares about the public good.

  > Alternatively, you can rewrite the sentence: *She is a woman of action, and one who cares about the public good.*

DON'T:

x That is a questionable idea, **and which** has been opposed for many years.

DO:

- That is a questionable idea, **and one which** has been opposed for many years.

or

- That is a questionable idea which has been opposed for many years.

23h   Do not let an earlier term invade a parallel construction.

Remember that elements already in place before a parallelism begins should not be repeated *inside* it.

Either . . . or, neither . . . nor

// join
23h

A parallelism involving one of these formulas may be grammatically dependent on an immediately preceding word or sentence element (*he wants either sausage or bacon*). Be sure to keep the preceding expression from reappearing inside the parallel construction itself.

DON'T:
x They serve **as** either guidance counselors or **as** soccer coaches.

The way to check such sentences is to take note of where the parallelism is introduced—in this case, at the word *either*. Next, isolate the whole parallelism—*either guidance counselors or as soccer coaches*—and see if it repeats the word that came just before it. Yes, the second *as* must go.

DO:

- They serve as either guidance counselors or soccer coaches.

or

- They serve either as guidance counselors or as soccer coaches.

  Here *as* is repeated *within* the parallelism in order to make the x and y elements, *guidance counselors* and *soccer coaches*, fully parallel. Note how the two allowable versions differ from the faulty one:

as either x or as y	wrongly repeats an earlier element, *as*
either x or y	fully parallel
either as x or as y	fully parallel

Not only x *but also* y

This formula, useful when it works, can be easily misaligned. Once again, you must see where the parallelism begins and avoid repeating an earlier element.

DON'T:

x She remembered not only **her maps** but **she also remembered her tire repair kit.**

The first *remembered* comes just before the parallel construction and governs both of its parts. The second *remembered* thus breaks the parallel effect.

// join
23i

DO:

• She remembered not only **her maps** but also **her tire repair kit.**

Now x and y are parallel; they are the two things that were remembered. The sentence lines up like this:

She remembered
$\begin{cases} \textit{not only} \text{ her maps} \\ \textit{but also} \text{ her tire repair kit.} \end{cases}$
(not only x but also y)

23i Carry through with any repeated modifier in a series.

If you begin repeating any modifier within a series, be sure to keep doing so for all the remaining items.

DON'T:

x He can never find **his textbooks, his tapes, calculator,** and

homework.

> The modifier *his* in the *x* element commits the writer to using
> the word again in *y* and *z*. Note the options for revision.

DO:

- He can never find **his textbooks, his tapes, his calculator,**

and **his homework.**

or

- He can never find his **textbooks, tapes, calculator,** and

homework.

// punct
23j

PUNCTUATING PARALLEL ELEMENTS

23j Join most paired elements without an intervening comma.

To show that two elements are meant to be parallel, omit a comma
after the first one.

DON'T:

x Last night's storm destroyed **our storage shed,** and **our**

carport.

> The comma implies that the only direct object of *destroyed*
> has already been given and that the main statement is over.
> By removing the comma the writer can show that the *x* and
> *y* elements are parallel objects.

DON'T:

$$\overset{\text{x}}{\overbrace{\qquad\qquad\qquad}}\qquad\qquad\overset{\text{y}}{\overbrace{\qquad\qquad}}$$

x Aspirin has been called **a blessing by some,** and **a dangerous**

drug by others.

> Aspirin has been called *x* and *y;* remove the comma to show
> that *x* and *y* are tightly related.

Pairing Independent Clauses

The no-comma rule above need not apply when the *x* element is an
independent clause (p. 213, 17c), as in *Not only did they adjust the
fan belt, but they also adjusted the brakes.* But in *either . . . or* constructions you should omit the comma to keep the *y* statement from
escaping the controlling effect of the parallelism.

DON'T:

$$\overset{\text{x}}{\overbrace{\qquad\qquad\qquad\qquad\qquad\qquad}}\qquad\overbrace{\qquad}$$

- Either **you are wrong about the guitar strings,** or **I have**

$$\overset{\text{y}}{\overbrace{\qquad\qquad\qquad\qquad}}$$

forgotten everything I knew.

**// punct
23k**

> Remove the comma and notice how the two statements then
> fit more tightly together.

**23k As a rule, use commas and a word like *and*
      to separate items in a series.**

- I used to sprinkle my writing with $\overset{\text{x}}{\textbf{commas,}}$ $\overset{\text{y}}{\textbf{semicolons,}}$ and

$\overset{\text{z}}{\textbf{dashes}}$ as though they were salt and pepper.

The normal way to present a **series** (three or more parallel items) is
to separate the items with commas, adding a coordinating conjunction
such as *and* or *or* before the last one.

Optional Final Comma

Many writers, especially journalists, omit the final comma in a series.
So can you if you are consistent about it throughout a given piece of
writing.

ACCEPTABLE:

- **Football, baseball** and **basketball** were his only passions.

x   y   z

Note, however, that the *x, y and z* formula may not always allow your meaning to come through clearly. Consider the following sentences, which are identical except for the comma or its absence after *swimsuit.*

ACCEPTABLE:

$\overbrace{}^{x}$ $\overbrace{}^{y}$ $\overbrace{}^{z}$

- For Christmas Alex got **a telescope, a swimsuit** and **a shirt that didn't fit.**

  What didn't fit—the shirt or the swimsuit and the shirt? A comma clears up the momentary confusion.

PREFERABLE:

- For Christmas Alex got a telescope, a swimsuit, and a shirt that didn't fit.

  Now there is no chance of misunderstanding. You can see why many good writers always use a final comma in a series.

---

231   If an item within a series contains a comma, use semicolons to show where each of the items ends.

Once you have begun a series, you may find yourself using commas for two quite different purposes: to separate the *x, y,* and *z* items and to punctuate *within* one or more of those items. If so, your reader may have trouble seeing where each item ends. To show the important breaks between the main parallel items, separate *x, y,* and *z* with semicolons:

- After dinner, they sat talking in their accustomed places, Jack and Fern at opposite ends of the long table; Mike, Dan, and Pat on the side nearest the living room; and the two youngest, Mark and Joanne, watching their older siblings from the opposite side through a maze of tumblers, coffee cups, jam jars, and half-empty serving bowls.

The semicolons separate three main items, two of which contain series of their own. If the sentence relied solely on commas, it would be difficult to follow. Note that items in a series separated by semicolons need not be independent clauses.

For more advice about arranging items in a series, see page 161, 13c.

// punct
231

24 Relations between Tenses

Every time you write a sentence, you are expressing a **tense,** or time of action, through your verb. For a review of verb forms showing not only their tenses but also their **voices** and **moods,** see Chapter 31.

Some tenses are obviously appropriate to certain functions—the present for statements of opinion, the past for storytelling, the future for prediction. But choice of tense becomes trickier when you need to combine two or more time frames within a sentence (*He said he would have been ready if the plane had not been late; She will have finished by the day we get home;* etc.). When revising your work, check to see that your combinations of tenses follow the advice given below.

24a Choose one governing tense for a piece of writing.

Stating Facts and Ideas

The normal way to state facts, ask questions, or offer your ideas about any general or current topic is to use the present tense:

- Water boils at 100° Celsius.
- Does the new divorce law protect the rights of children?

Note how the following passage establishes a present time frame, departing from it only to narrate events that occurred previously:

- The great debate **continues** between heredity and environment. Both sides have strong arguments, but I **am convinced** that technology **adjusts** our fate. My grandfather, for example,

PAST
was dead at forty from diabetes, a disease that my father
PRES PERF
has lived with for sixty years, thanks to this century's advances in medical research.

If you are stating ideas about the past, many of your verbs will be in the past tense. Even so, the present is appropriate for conveying your current reflections about past events:

PRES   PRES   PAST
- I **believe** we **can prove** that the Etruscans **had** much more
PRES
  influence on Roman civilization than most people **realize.**

Narrating Events

The usual tense for narrating events is the past:

PAST   PAST
- She **arrived** home in a fury, and she **was** still upset when the
PAST
  phone **rang.**

PAST
- The solution **was allowed** to stand for three minutes, after
PAST
  which 200 cc of nitrogen **were added.**

tense 24a

In this second example the past verbs are in the passive voice (p. 379, 31d).

Sometimes, to get a special effect of immediacy, you may even want to use the present for narration:

PRES   PRES
- When he **phones** her, she **tells** him to leave her alone.

But note that once you adopt this present-tense convention for storytelling, you have committed yourself to it throughout the piece of writing. Do not try to switch back to the more usual past.

DON'T:

PRES   PRES
x When he **phones** her, she **tells** him to leave her alone. But he
PAST   PAST PERF
acted as if he **hadn't understood** her point.

For consistency, the second sentence should read: *But he <u>acts</u> as if he <u>hasn't</u> understood. . . .*

24b Relate your other tenses to the governing tense.

Once you have established a controlling time frame, or **governing tense,** shift into other tenses as logic requires.

Present Time Frame

A present time frame, established by a present governing tense, allows you to use a variety of other tenses to indicate the times of actions or states. The following are ways of combining other tenses with the present:

tense
24b

- He **meditates** every day, and . . .

REST OF SENTENCE	TENSE
he **is meditating** right now.	present progressive (action ongoing in the present)
he **has meditated** five thousand times.	present perfect (past action completed thus far)
he **has been meditating** since dawn.	present perfect progressive (action begun in the past and continuing in the present)
he **meditated** for ten hours yesterday.	past (completed action)
he **was meditating** before I was born.	past progressive (action that was ongoing in a previous time)
he **had meditated** for years before hearing about the popularity of meditation.	past perfect (action completed before another past time)
he **had been meditating** for three hours before the interview.	past perfect progressive (ongoing action completed before another past time)

REST OF SENTENCE	TENSE
he **will meditate** tomorrow.	future (action to occur later)
he **will be meditating** for the rest of his life.	future progressive (ongoing action to occur later)
by next year he **will have meditated** for more hours than anyone ever has.	future perfect (action regarded as completed at a later time)
he **will have been meditating** for ten years by the time he is thirty.	future perfect progressive (ongoing action regarded as having begun before a later time)

Past Time Frame

When your time frame is in the past, choose other tenses according to the following patterns:

• There *were* rumors around school . . .

tense
24b

REST OF SENTENCE	TENSE
that the dean **had been** a sergeant in Vietnam.	past perfect (action completed in an earlier past time)
that the dean **had been lifting** weights all these years.	past perfect progressive (ongoing action that began earlier)
that the dean **would take** disciplinary matters into his own hands.	conditional (later action)

Hypothetical Condition

Certain sentences containing *if* clauses set forth hypothetical conditions. That is, they tell what would be true or would have been true in certain imagined circumstances. Note that such sentences differ in both form and meaning from sentences proposing likely conditions.

LIKELY CONDITION	HYPOTHETICAL CONDITION
I **will dance** if you **clear** a space on the floor.	I **would** dance if you **cleared** a space on the floor.
If she **studies** now, she **will pass.**	If she **studied** now, she **would pass.**
If I **marry** your sister, we **will be** brothers.	If I **married** your sister, we **would be** brothers.

The "likely condition" sentences anticipate that the condition may be met, but the "hypothetical condition" sentences are sheer speculation: what would happen if . . . ? These require use of the *subjunctive mood* (p. 381, 31e) in the *if* clause. And in the "consequence" clause they require a *conditional* form, either present or past:

CONDITIONAL FORMS		
Present	$\left.\begin{array}{l} would \\ could \end{array}\right\}$ + base verb	would go could go
Past	$\left.\begin{array}{l} would \\ could \end{array}\right\}$ + *have* + past participle	would have gone could have gone

tense 24b

Thus:

IF CLAUSE	CONSEQUENCE CLAUSE
PRESS SUBJN If you **worked** overtime,	PRES CONDL you **would have** more spending money.
PRES SUBJN If they **won** a million dollars,	PRES CONDL what **would** they **do** with the money?
PAST SUBJN If she **had concentrated,**	PAST CONDL she **could have written** a perfect translation.
PAST SUBJN If you **had been** old enough,	PAST CONDL **would** you **have married** Barbara?

The most common mistake in combining tenses is to use *would* in both parts of a conditional statement. Remember that *would* goes only in the consequence clause, not in the *if* clause.

DON'T:

x If they **would** try harder, they would succeed.

DO:

• If they **tried** harder, they would succeed.

DON'T:

x If they **would have** tried harder, they would have succeeded.

DO:

• If they **had tried** harder, they would have succeeded.

24c Learn how tenses differ between quotation and indirect discourse.

tense
24c

In the following chart, notice what happens to tenses when you shift from what was actually said (quotation or **direct discourse**) to a report of what was said (**indirect discourse**).

	QUOTATION	INDIRECT DISCOURSE
Present verb in quotation	"I **want** to join the Navy after graduation," he said.	He said that he **wanted** to join the Navy after graduation.
Past verb in quotation	"I **wanted** to join the Navy after my graduation," he revealed.	He revealed that he **had wanted** to join the Navy after his graduation.
Present perfect verb in quotation	He protested, "I **have** never **wanted** to join the Air Force."	He protested that he **had** never **wanted** to join the Air Force.

	QUOTATION	INDIRECT DISCOURSE
Past perfect verb in quotation	"Until then," he reminded us, "I **had** always **planned** to study photography."	He reminded us that until then he **had** always **planned** to study photography.
Future verb in quotation	"I **will want** to look into photographic training in the military," he said.	He said that he **would want** to look into photographic training in the military.

To summarize these changes of tense, indirect discourse:

<table>
<tr><td rowspan="2" style="background:black;color:white">tense
24c</td><td></td><td>QUOTATION</td><td>INDIRECT DISCOURSE</td></tr>
<tr><td>**Makes a present verb past**</td><td>want ⟶</td><td>wanted</td></tr>
<tr><td></td><td>**Makes a past or present perfect verb past perfect**</td><td>wanted
have wanted ⟶</td><td>had wanted</td></tr>
<tr><td></td><td>**Leaves a past perfect verb past perfect**</td><td>had wanted ⟶</td><td>had wanted</td></tr>
<tr><td></td><td>**Turns a future verb into *would* + a base (infinitive) form**</td><td>will want ⟶</td><td>would want</td></tr>
</table>

You can deduce other tense changes in indirect discourse from these basic ones: *will have wanted* becomes *would have wanted, has been wanting* becomes *had been wanting,* and so forth.

24d   Use the present tense to write about action within a plot or about an author's ideas within a work.

Discussing Actions within a Plot

Unlike a real event, a scene within a work of art does not happen once and for all. It is always ready to be experienced afresh by a new reader, viewer, or listener. Consequently, the time frame for discussing such a scene is the present. Though you should use the past tense to write about the historical creating of the artwork, you should use the present tense to convey what the work "says to us." This function is called the **"literary" present tense.**

HISTORICAL PAST:
- Shakespeare **was** probably familiar with the plays of Kyd and Marlowe when he **wrote** his great tragedies. He **expressed** his deepest feelings in those plays.

"LITERARY" PRESENT:
- Shakespeare **reveals** Hamlet's mind through soliloquy.
- Hamlet's unrelenting psychological dilemma **drives** him toward catastrophe.
- The Misfit, in Flannery O'Connor's story "A Good Man Is Hard to Find," **murders** an entire family.
- In the 1949 film version of *Oliver Twist,* Alec Guinness **plays** Fagin.

   If the verb in this last example were *played,* the sentence would be making a statement not about the movie but about an event in Alec Guinness's acting career.

tense
24d

Discussing Ideas within a Work

No matter how long ago a book or other publication was written, use the "literary" present tense to characterize the idea it expresses:

- In *The Republic* Plato **maintains** that artists **are** a menace to the ideal state.

- Thoreau **says** in *Walden* that we **can** find peace by staying exactly where we **are.**

   The present-tense verbs are appropriate because any book "speaks to" its readers in a continuing present time.

If, on the other hand, you want to refer to a noncontemporary author's ideas without reference to a particular work, use the past:

- Plato **believed** that artists **were** a menace to the ideal state.
- Thoreau **was convinced** that people **could** find peace by staying exactly where they **were.**

24e In discussing a plot, relate other tenses to the "literary" present.

Once you have established the "literary" present for action in a plot that is "happening right now" (24d), refer to earlier or later actions in that plot by using the past, future, and related tenses.

tense
24f

- When Hamlet's suspicions **were** confirmed by the ghost, he

   PAST

   PAST   PRES

   vowed revenge. But by Act Two he **fears** that his self-doubts

   PRES PERF   PRES

   have dulled his purpose. He **engages** a troupe of players to

                      PRES   FUTURE

   reenact the murder and **swears** that the play **will "catch** the conscience of the King."

   Notice how the writer has chosen a point of focus in Act Two of *Hamlet*. The use of the "literary" present for that time determines which tenses are appropriate for the other described actions.

24f Do not allow the past form of a quoted verb to influence your own choice of tense.

It is hard to keep to the "literary" present (24d) when you have just quoted a passage containing verbs in the past tense. The tendency is to allow your own verbs to slip into the past. Keep to the rule, however, and use the present tense for actions or states under immediate discussion:

- D. H. Lawrence **describes** Cecilia as "a big dark-complexioned, pug-faced young woman who very rarely **spoke.** . . ." When she **does speak,** however, her words **are** sharp enough to kill her aunt Pauline.

tense
24f

VI
PUNCTUATION

Punctuation

Marks of punctuation are essential for clear meaning in written prose. Beyond showing where pauses or stops would occur in speech, they indicate logical relations that would otherwise be hard for a reader to make out. For example, parentheses, brackets, dashes, and commas all signal a pause, but they suggest different relations between main and subordinate material. The only way to be sure that your punctuation marks are working with your meaning, not against it, is to learn the rules.

Part V above, "Usage," covers a good many punctuation rules for handling such grammatical features as independent clauses, modifying elements, and parallel constructions. This part repeats those rules (giving cross references to the fuller discussions), adds other rules, and shows how you can choose between punctuation marks that are closely related in function.

Note that the conventions of quoting are handled in Chapter 29. Apostrophes and hyphens are treated, respectively, in Chapters 32 and 34. To see how you should form and space the various punctuation marks, see Chapter 30.

25 Periods, Question Marks, Exclamation Points

PERIODS

25a Place a period at the end of a sentence making a statement, a polite command, or a mild exclamation.

STATEMENT:
- I think the Olympic Games have become too politicized.
- Art historians are showing new respect for nineteenth-century narrative painting.

POLITE COMMAND:
- Tell me why you think the Olympic Games have become too politicized.
- Consider the new respect that art historians are showing toward nineteenth-century narrative painting.

MILD EXCLAMATION:
- What a pity that the Olympic Games have become so politicized.
- How remarkable it is to see the art historians reversing their former scorn for nineteenth-century narrative painting.

   Exclamation points at the end of these two sentences would have made them more emphatic; see page 324, 25j.

25b   End an indirect question with a period.

- Ted asked me whether I was good at boardsailing.

An **indirect question,** instead of taking a question form, reports that a question is or was asked. Thus an indirect question is a **declarative sentence**–one that makes a statement. As such, it should be completed by a period, not a question mark.

25c   Consider a period optional after a courtesy question.

- Would you be kind enough to reply within thirty days.

or

- Would you be kind enough to reply within thirty days?

Some questions in business letters (Chapter 42) are really requests or mild commands. You can end such a sentence with either a period or a question mark. The period makes a more impersonal and routine effect. If you want to express actual courtesy toward a reader you know, keep to the question mark.

25d

25d   Repair an unacceptable sentence fragment [see discussion on p. 215, 17d].

DON'T:

- Professor Chavkin has earned a reputation as an innovative

FRAG

teacher. **Especially in his undergraduate courses.**

DO:

- Professor Chavkin has earned a reputation as an innovative teacher, especially in his undergraduate courses.

25e If a sentence ends with an abbreviation, use only one period.

- She made many sacrifices to complete her Ph.D.

QUESTION MARKS

25f Place a question mark after a direct question.

Most questions are complete sentences, but now and then you may want to add a question to a statement or insert a question within a statement. In every instance, put a question mark immediately after the question:

- Do you like to write?
- Many people are proud of their written work, but does anyone really like to write?
- "Can you imagine someone finding it easier to write," I asked, "than to call?"
- You and I—is it possible?—may yet learn to enjoy writing.

But if your sentence poses a question that is then modified by other language, place the question mark at the end:

How could he treat me like that, after all the consideration I showed him?

?
25g

25g To express doubt, use a question mark within parentheses.

- Saint Thomas Aquinas, 1225(?)–1274, considered faith more important than reason.

    If the dates here were in parentheses, the question mark would go inside brackets: *(1225[?]–1274)*.

Sarcastic Question Mark
No grammatical rule prevents you from getting a sarcastic effect from the "doubting" question mark. But if you are determined to be

sarcastic, quotation marks will do a better job of conveying your attitude.

AVOID:
- The president expects to make four nonpolitical (?) speeches in the month before the election.

PREFER:
- The president expects to make four "nonpolitical" speeches in the month before the election.

25h If a sentence asking a question contains another question at the end, use only one question mark.

- Are you the skeptic who asked, "Why write?"

25i After a question mark, omit a comma or a period.

- Now I know the answer to the question, "Why study?"
- "Where is my journal?" she asked.

EXCLAMATION POINTS

25j Use exclamation points sparingly to express intense feeling or a strong command.

- My wallet, my glasses, my notes—all gone!
- So this is the result of their so-called peace offensive!
- Call a doctor!

Note that frequent use of exclamation points dulls their effect, while making the writer appear too excitable. And though an exclamation point, like a question mark, can be inserted parenthetically to convey sarcasm (25g), the effect is usually weak.

AVOID:

x Warren thought that a black-and-white photocopy (!) of the Rembrandt painting would give him everything he needed to write his art history paper.

!
25j

26 Commas

This chapter brings together all the comma rules in three charts, showing (a) where you should use a comma or pair of commas, (b) where you should omit a comma, and (c) where you can consider a comma optional. Fuller discussions of most rules appear in other chapters; whenever you need more examples or background, consult the cross-referenced material.

26a Learn where you should include a comma or pair of commas.

INCLUDE A COMMA OR PAIR OF COMMAS WHEN YOU . . .

Join independent clauses (see p. 221, 18a):

- **Every blink is like fire, and tears well up constantly.**

The two clauses *Every blink is like fire* and *tears well up constantly* are **independent** because each of them could stand as a complete sentence. To avoid a **comma splice** or a **fused sentence,** you should join them either with a comma and a coordinating conjunction, as here, or with a semicolon: *Every blink is like fire; tears well up constantly.*

Begin with a subordinate clause (see p. 261, 20i):

SUB CLAUSE

- **Since you asked,** I will admit that I am exhausted.

Since you asked is a **clause** because it contains both a **subject** (*you*) and a **verb** (*asked*). It is a **subordinate clause** because it cannot stand alone as a complete sentence. Whenever you begin a sentence with such a clause, add a comma.

INCLUDE A COMMA OR PAIR OF COMMAS WHEN YOU . . .

Begin with a modifying phrase that is more than a few words long (see p. 261, 20i):

MOD PHRASE

● **In a spontaneous wave of enthusiasm,** the audience rose to its feet.

In a spontaneous wave of enthusiasm is a **phrase** because it forms a multiword unit without a subject-verb combination. Unless an opening phrase is very brief, follow it with a comma.

Use an interrupting element (see p. 263, 20l):

INT EL

● The deficit, **as a matter of fact,** has continued to grow.

An **interrupting element** forces a break in the main flow of a sentence. Set it off on both sides.

Include a nonrestrictive (nondefining) modifying element (see pp. 264–268, 20m–n):

NONR EL

● Women, **who have rarely been treated equally in the job market,** still tend to be relatively underpaid.

The sentence refers to all women. Thus the subordinate clause *who have rarely been treated equally in the job market* does not serve to define or restrict the class of women who are meant. Such a **nonrestrictive element** should always be set off from the rest of the sentence.

Include items in a series (see p. 305, 23k):

● **Modems, plotters, baud rates, and programming languages** danced continually in Wilbur's busy mind.

A **series,** or set of three or more parallel items, usually requires commas after each item but the last.

Present certain quotations (see pp. 357–358, 29l–m):

● **She said,** "I intend to be there early."

When you introduce a complete quoted sentence with a tag like *she said* or *he exclaimed,* follow it with a comma. If the tag appears later, surround it with commas: *"I intend,"* she said, *"to be there early."*

,
26a

INCLUDE A COMMA OR PAIR OF COMMAS WHEN YOU . . .

Present a place name with a more inclusive location:
- **Laramie, Wyoming,** celebrates its Jubilee Days every July.

When you add the name of a state, province, or country after a place name, set off the second name with commas on both sides.

Present an address or a month-first date:
- 13920 Tieton Drive, Yakima, WA 98908
- November 8, 1974, was their lucky day.

Note the commas both before and after *1974*.

Include a title or degree:
- Monica Wu, **Ph.D.,** holds office hours on Monday.

Note the commas both before and after *Ph.D.*

Include a number of more than four digits:
- 29,368,452

Set off every three digits, working from right to left.

26b   Learn where you should omit a comma.

OMIT A COMMA WHEN YOU . . .

Join a subject and verb (see p. 248, 19o):
- A **bird** in the hand **is** worth two in the bush.   no comma

Note that *in the hand* does not interrupt the main statement; it is a **restrictive element** (see below), showing which bird is meant. Thus a comma after *hand* would wrongly separate the subject and verb.

Join a verb and direct object (see p. 209, 17a):
- She **recognized** in a flash the **meaning** of her dream.   no comma

OMIT A COMMA WHEN YOU . . .

Since no comma sets off *in a flash* at the front end, a comma after *flash* would be inappropriate. The verb *recognized* must be allowed to hook up with its object *meaning* without a pause.

Join a verb and its complement (see p. 210, 17a):

● The laws against drug use
    v   **c**
  were not always so **strict** as
  they are today. no comma

A verb's **complement,** appearing in the **predicate,** identifies or modifies the subject—in this case, *laws.* Since there is no real interruption between *were* and *strict,* a comma after *always* would be wrong.

Join a subordinating conjunction and the rest of its subordinate clause (see pp. 213–215, 17c):

● One further reason for using the shopping mall is

        SUB CLAUSE

  that parking is ample there.
  SUB   no comma
  CONJ

That parking is ample there forms a **subordinate clause**—a subject-predicate combination that cannot stand alone. Since *that* is an essential part of the clause, a comma following it would be inappropriate.

Join a preposition and its object (see p. 625):

                  PREP
● My worries keep returning **to**
    OBJ OF PREP no comma

  inflation, unemployment,
  and natural disasters.

Even when the object of a preposition is lengthy, making you want to "catch a breath" just before it, you should resist the temptation to insert a comma. By omitting the comma, you honor the unity of the complete prepositional phrase. Note that a colon would also be unacceptable here (p. 237, 27g).

26b

OMIT A COMMA WHEN YOU . . .

Include a restrictive (defining) modifying element (see pp. 264–268, 20m–n):

no comma   RESTR EL

● A child **who likes to play with electrical outlets** must be carefully watched. no commas

The subordinate clause *who likes to play with electrical outlets* serves to identify which child is meant. Thus it is defining, or **restrictive.** If you wrongly added commas after *child* and *outlets,* making that element **nonrestrictive,** you would be drastically changing the meaning of the sentence: every single child, everywhere, likes to play with electrical outlets and therefore must be carefully watched.

Join a final modifier and the modified term (see p. 270, 20p):

● It was an intensely vivid,

FINAL MOD
compelling, **anxiety-producing**

MODIFIED TERM   no comma
account of the disaster.

No matter how many modifiers you string together, omit a comma between the final one and the modified term—in this case, *account.*

Join paired elements (see p. 304, 23j):

● The cause of the fire was either

x
a leak from the ancient gas

y
heater or **a short circuit.**
no comma

The formula here is *either x or y.* To cement the connection between the *x* and *y* items, join them without a comma.

Include a day-first date:

● They were married on **23 January 1989.**

Note that a comma would be required if the month came first: *January 23, 1989.*

Include a numeral after a name:

● Oswald Humbert **IV** lost all his money.
no commas

26b

26c   Learn where a comma is optional.

CONSIDER A COMMA OPTIONAL WHEN YOU . . .

Begin with a brief phrase (see p. 261, 20j):

- **After the storm,** the ground was strewn with leaves.
- **After the storm** the ground was strewn with leaves.

When in doubt, you cannot go wrong by supplying the comma.

Join independent clauses if the first one is brief (see p. 229, 18d):

- **He called collect,** but his uncle refused to accept the charges.
- **He called collect** but his uncle refused to accept the charges.

A comma and a coordinating conjunction are the surest means to join such clauses (p. 221, 18a), but if the first clause is brief, you can do without the comma.

Use *thus* or *hence* (see p. 262, 20k).

- **Hence,** there is no need for alarm.
- **Hence** there is no need for alarm.

Invert the normal order of sentence elements:

- **What she calls happiness,** I call slavery.
- **What she calls happiness** I call slavery.

What she calls happiness is an objective complement—a complement of the direct object *slavery*. It normally follows the direct object, as in *They appointed him <u>secretary</u>.*

Use one modifier to qualify the preceding one (see p. 270, 20q):

- It was a difficult, **but by no means impossible,** assignment.
- It was a difficult **but by no means impossible** as-signment

,
26c

CONSIDER A COMMA OPTIONAL WHEN YOU . . .

Note how the second modifier, beginning with *but,* answers the modifier before it. Commas are optional in such a case.

Follow a month with a year:
- **May, 1968,** was the time of the famous uprising.
- **May 1968** was the time of the famous uprising.

If you add the day, commas are required on both sides: *May 14, 1968, was the time. . . .* Note also that a comma before the year obliges you to add another comma after the year.

Use a four-digit number:
- 8,354
- 8354

---

27 Semicolons and Colons

SEMICOLON (Relates two statements)	COLON (Equates two items)
• We did not bully or threaten; we knew that justice was on our side. [The two parts of the sentence are logically connected; the second statement explains why no bullying or threatening was considered necessary.]	• We asked for just one thing: the return of our stolen land. [Everything following the colon serves to specify the *thing* preceding it. The colon means *namely*.]

SEMICOLONS

27a To keep two closely related statements within the same sentence, join them with a semicolon.

- My oldest sister is the boss in our family; what she says goes.
- The university conducts art history classes in Europe; the accessibility of great museums and monuments gives students a firsthand sense of the subject.
- Some of those painters influenced Cézanne; others were influenced by him.

The punctuation mark that comes nearest in function to the semicolon is the period. But whereas a period keeps two statements apart as separate sentences, a semicolon shows that two statements within one sentence are intimately related. When one statement is a consequence of another or contrasts sharply with it, you can bring out that tight connection by joining them with a semicolon instead of with a comma and a coordinating conjunction (p. 221, 18a).

Note that when a semicolon is used, the second statement often contains a sentence adverb or transitional phrase (p. 262, 20k) pointing out the logical relation between the two clauses:

- Misunderstanding is often the root of injustice; perfect under-
  SENT ADV
  standing, **however,** is impossible to attain.

- Some parents weigh every word they speak; others,
  TRANS
  PHRASE
  in contrast, do not think twice about their harsh language.

27b Make sure that a semicolon is followed by a complete statement.

;
27b

DO:
- I used to be afraid to talk to people; even asking the time of day was an ordeal. I always let my brother speak for me; he was everyone's buddy.

DON'T:

FRAG

x I used to be afraid to talk to people; **even to ask the time of day.**

FRAG

I always let my brother speak for me; **because he was everyone's buddy.**

An unacceptable sentence fragment (p. 215, 17d) is just as faulty when it follows a semicolon as when it stands alone.

27c Feel free to use a word like *and* or *but* after a semicolon.

There is nothing wrong with following a semicolon with a conjunction, so long as the second statement contains an independent clause (p. 213, 17c). Do so if you want to make explicit the logical connection between the statements coming before and after the semicolon:

CONJ
- All day long we loaded the van with our worldy goods; **but** when we were ready to leave the next morning, full of eagerness for the trip, we saw that the van had a flat tire.

  A comma after *goods* would also be appropriate, but the semicolon recommends itself because the second statement already contains two commas. Thus the semicolon helps to show the main separation in the sentence.

27d If an item within a series contains a comma, use semicolons to show where each of the items ends [see discussion on p. 306, 23l].

- Student dining halls include the Servery, which is located on the ground floor of the Student Union; the Cafeteria, temporarily relocated in Jim Thorpe Gymnasium; and the Rathskeller, now in the basement of Anne Bradstreet Hall.

COLONS

27e Use a colon to show an equivalence between items on either side.

A colon introduces a restatement, a formal list, or a quotation. Use a colon if you can plausibly insert *namely* after it:

- Lunch arrives: [*namely*] a tuna fish sandwich, a bowl of tomato soup, and a cup of tea.

- He wanted only one thing: [*namely*] silence.
- Samuel Johnson offered the following wise advice: [*namely*] "If you would have a faithful servant, and one that you like, serve yourself."

The *namely* test can help you avoid putting semicolons where colons belong and vice versa.

DON'T:

x The results of the poll were surprising; 7 percent in favor, 11 percent opposed, and 82 percent no opinion.

Namely would be appropriate here; therefore, the semicolon should be a colon.

x We slaved for years: we remained as poor as ever.

Namely is inappropriate, since the second clause makes a new point. The colon should be a semicolon.

27f   Make sure you have a complete statement before a colon.

Like a semicolon, a colon must be preceded by a complete statement.

DON'T:

FRAG
x **Occupations that interest me:** beekeeper, horse groomer, dog trainer, veterinarian.

DO:

COMPLETE STATEMENT
- **Occupations involving animals interest me:** beekeeper, horse groomer, dog trainer, veterinarian.

But remember that, unlike a semicolon, a colon need not be *followed* by a whole statement (p. 334, 27b).

27g Omit a colon if it would separate elements that belong together.

DON'T:

                                                    V   **D OBJ**

x Before buying my Saturn, I **tested: a Toyota Corolla, a Ford Escort, and a Nissan Sentra.**

> The colon separates a verb from its three-part direct object.

> Note that this practice would still be wrong if the direct object had any number of parts and extended for many lines.

                          V   **COMPL**

x Her favorite fruits **are: raspberries, strawberries, and nectarines.**

> The colon separates a verb from its three-part complement (p. 210, 17a).

x The exhibit contained works by many famous photographers,

    PREP   **OBJ OF PREP**

such as: Avedon, Adams, Weston, and Lange.

> The colon separates a preposition from its four-part object.

x The Renaissance naval adventurers set out **to: sack enemy**

                 COMPLETION OF INF PHRASES

cities, find precious metals, and claim colonial territory.

> The colon separates the infinitive marker *to* from the completion of three infinitive phrases (p. 626). Even if you had a long series of such phrases, the colon would be wrong.

In each of the four examples above, you need only drop the colon to make the sentence acceptable.

27h   Use a colon to separate hours and minutes, to end the salutation of a business letter, and to introduce a subtitle.

HOURS AND MINUTES:
- The train should arrive at 10:15 P.M.

SALUTATION:
- Dear Mr. Gorman:

SUBTITLE:
- *Virginia Woolf: A Biography*

:
27h

28 Dashes and Parentheses

Both dashes and parentheses, as well as commas, can be used to set off interrupting elements (p. 263, 201). The difference is that dashes call attention to the interrupting material, whereas parentheses suggest that it is truly subordinate in meaning.

Dashes	—	most emphatic	The monsoon season—with incessant driving rain and flooding—causes much hardship.
Commas	,	"neutral"	The monsoon season, with incessant driving rain and flooding, causes much hardship.
Parentheses	( )	least emphatic	The monsoon season (with incessant driving rain and flooding) causes much hardship.

DASHES

28a Use a dash or pair of dashes to set off and emphasize a striking insertion.

- Poets have been fascinated by Narcissus—**the most modern of mythological lovers.**

- Narcissus—**the most modern of mythological lovers**—fell in love with himself.

28b   If your sentence resumes after an interruption, use a second dash.

When you begin an interruption with one dash, you must end it with another.

DON'T:

x Narcissus looked into a lake—**so the story goes,** and fell in love with his own reflection.

DO:

- Narcissus looked into a lake—**so the story goes**—and fell in love with his own reflection.

DON'T:

x Somehow my aunt sensed the danger—**perhaps she realized that my uncle should have been home by then,** and she phoned me to come at once.

DO:

- Somehow may aunt sensed the danger—**perhaps she realized that my uncle should have been home by then**—and she phoned me to come at once.

28c   Make sure your sentence would be coherent if the part within dashes were omitted.

The elements of your sentence before and after the dashes must fit together grammatically.

DON'T:

x **Because** he paid no attention to her—**he was riveted to his cable sports channel day and night**—**so** she finally lost her temper.

Ask yourself if the sentence makes sense without the material between dashes: x *Because he paid no attention to her so she finally lost her temper.* Recognizing that this shortened sentence is grammatically askew, you can then correct the original.

DO:

- Because he paid no attention to her—**he was riveted to his cable sports channel day and night**—she finally lost her temper.

28d Note the other uses of the dash.

TO INTRODUCE AN EMPHATIC EXPLANATION:

- Narcissus was the most modern of mythological lovers—**he fell in love with himself.**

TO INTRODUCE A LIST ABRUPTLY:

- The new house has marvelous devices to let in light—**skylights in the dining room, living room walls that slide open, and a breakfast porch constructed like a greenhouse.**

TO MARK AN INTERRUPTION OF DIALOGUE:

- The man behind menaced us with his umbrella. "If you don't step aside, I'll—"

    "This is a line for people with tickets," I said. "We're not—"

    But our dispute was cut short by the usher, who was urging the line forward.

28d

If a character's speech "trails off" instead of being interrupted, an ellipsis (p. 259, 29o) is more suitable than a dash: *"We're not . . ."* Note that you should begin a new paragraph for each change of speaker.

TO ISOLATE AN INTRODUCTORY ELEMENT THAT IS NOT THE GRAMMATICAL SUBJECT:

APP
- **Depression, compulsion, phobia, hallucination**—these disorders often require quick and emphatic treatment.

In a sentence that makes a "false start" for rhetorical effect (p. 168, 13i), you want to give a signal that the opening element is an appositive (p. 268, 20n) rather than the subject of the verb. A dash serves the purpose.

28e Do not use more than one set of dashes in a sentence.

Dashes work best when used sparingly. Within a single sentence, one interruption marked by dashes should be the maximum.

DON'T:

x We cannot expect a tax reform bill—or indeed any major legislation—to be considered on its merits in an election year—a time when the voters' feelings—not the country's interests—are uppermost in the minds of lawmakers.

DO:

• We cannot expect a tax reform bill, or indeed any major legislation, to be considered on its merits in an election year—a time when the voters' feelings, not the country's interests, are uppermost in the minds of lawmakers.

28f Do not combine a dash with a comma or a period.

DON'T:

x After a grueling eight-hour drive,—it was snowing all the way—Judith arrived in Fargo.

x Edgar's beagles—he owned three of them.—kept the neighborhood cats on red alert.

In both sentences, the dashes should stand alone, without the adjacent punctuation.

PARENTHESES

28g Use parentheses to enclose and subordinate an incidental insertion.

Parentheses are appropriate for showing the incidental, lesser status of an illustration, explanation, or passing comment.

ILLUSTRATION:
- Some tropical reptiles **(the Galápagos tortoise, for example)** sleep in puddles of water to cool themselves.

EXPLANATION:
- A modem **(a device for connecting a computer terminal to a central source of data)** could easily be mistaken for an ordinary telephone.

PASSING COMMENT:
- The Ouse **(a rather pretty, harmless-looking river)** is known to literary people as the body of water in which Virginia Woolf drowned herself.

28h Note the other uses of parentheses.

TO RESTATE A NUMBER:
- The furniture will be repossessed in thirty **(30)** days.

TO ENCLOSE A DATE:
- The article on race and gender in literary study appears in *Feminist Studies* 9, no. 3 **(Fall 1983)**, pages 435–63.

TO ENCLOSE A CITATION:
- Guevara first began studying Marxism in Guatemala in 1954 **(Liss 256–57)**.

28i Learn when to supply end punctuation for a parenthetic sentence within another sentence.

If your whole sentence-within-a-sentence is a statement, do not end it with a period:

- Shyness **(mine was extreme)** can be overcome with time.

But if you are asking a question or making an exclamation, do supply the end punctuation:

- Today I am outspoken **(who would have predicted it?)** and sometimes even eloquent.
- To be able to give a talk without panic **(what a relief at last!)** is a great advantage in the business world.

Notice that the parenthetic sentence-within-a-sentence does not begin with a capital letter.

28j When placing a parenthetic sentence between complete sentences, punctuate it as a complete sentence.

A whole sentence within parentheses, if it is not part of another sentence, must begin with a capital letter and contain end punctuation of its own, *within* the close-parenthesis mark:

- Shyness can be a crippling affliction. **(The clinical literature is full of tragic cases.)** Yet some victims suddenly reach a point where they decide they have been bullied long enough.

28k Do not allow parentheses to affect other punctuation.

Remember these two rules:

1. No mark of punctuation comes just before an open-parenthesis mark.

2. The rest of the sentence must keep to its own punctuation, as if the parenthetic portion were not there.

Thus, to decide whether a close-parenthesis mark should be followed by a comma, mentally disregard the interruption:

- Shyness **(mine was extreme)** can be overcome with time.

  A comma after the close-parenthesis mark would make the following stripped-down sentence: x *Shyness, can be overcome with time.* Since that sentence would wrongly separate a subject (*Shyness*) from its verb (*can be overcome*), the comma must be omitted. (See p. 248, 19o.)

- My father was not as shy as I was **(otherwise he could not have succeeded in his work),** but he was soft-spoken and reserved.

  The stripped-down sentence correctly links two independent clauses with a comma and a coordinating conjunction (p. 221, 18a). Since the comma is appropriate without the parenthetic interruption, it is also appropriate with it. Note, however, that the comma belongs after the parenthesis, not before it.

28l Use brackets, not parentheses, to interrupt a quotation.

28l

Brackets (p. 362, 29r), not parentheses, are required when you want to insert information or commentary into quoted material.

DON'T:
x "Gwen (Torrence) should win this race," Karen said.

DO:
- "Gwen [Torrence] should win this race," Karen said.

29 Quoting

This chapter covers the details of managing quotation—introducing the words smoothly, showing just where they begin and end, and signaling where you have made an omission or inserted an explanatory word or phrase. But handling quoted material is more than a matter of following the right technical procedures. You want to quote only where the quoted language is important to your point, and you want to avoid letting quotations crowd out your own ideas. For advice on these larger matters, consult the segment on quotation as evidence (p. 45, 4h) and the advice about using quotation in a research paper (p. 472, 38b). And to learn how to give proper acknowledgment to quoted sources, see page 477, 38c.

29a Recognize the punctuation marks used with quotations.

The marks used in handling quotations are double and single quotation marks, the slash, the ellipsis, and brackets.

MARK	FORM	FUNCTION
double quotation marks (29d)	" "	to mark the beginning and end of a quotation
single quotation marks (29e)	' '	to mark a quotation within a quotation
slash (29f)	/	to mark a line break in a brief quotation of poetry
ellipsis (29o)	. . .	to mark an omission from a quotation
brackets (29r)	[ ]	to mark an explanatory insertion within a quotation

Note that these marks have other functions as well.

MARK	OTHER FUNCTION	EXAMPLE
quotation marks	to show distance from a dubious or offensive expression	Hitler's "final solution" destroyed six million Jews.
slash	to indicate alternatives	Try writing an invoice and/or a purchase order.
	to mean "per" in measurements	ft./sec. (feet per second)
	to indicate overlapping times	the Winter/Spring issue of the journal
ellipsis	to show that a statement contains further implications	And thus he came to feel that he had triumphed over the government. How little he understood about bureaucracy....
	to show that dialogue "trails off"	"What I am trying to tell you is ... is ..."
brackets	to insert material into a passage that is already within parentheses	(See, however, D. L. Rosenhan in *Science* 179 [1973]:250–58.)

66 99
29b

THE LOGIC OF QUOTATION

29b Avoid the unnecessary use of quotation marks.

Slang and Clichés

DON'T:

x After years of "working like a dog," Jim was finally able to "take it easy" last summer.

DO:

• After years of hard work, Jim was finally able to relax last summer.

When you have to apologize for your language by quarantining it within quotation marks, choose other language.

Widely Recognized Nicknames

DON'T:

x "Magic" Johnson dazzled professional basketball fans for more than a decade.

DO:

• Magic Johnson dazzled professional basketball fans for more than a decade.

or

• Earvin "Magic" Johnson dazzled professional basketball fans for more than a decade.

Only when you are adding the nickname to the rest of the name, as in the last example, should you put the nickname in quotation marks.

" "

29b

The Title of Your Paper

DON'T:

x "The New Head Trippers"

DO:

• The New Head Trippers

DON'T:

x " 'No Greater Love': Friendship in Owen's War Poems"

DO:

• "No Greater Love": Friendship in Owen's War Poems

When your title contains a quotation, indicate that fact with quotation marks. But your title itself, as it stands at the head of your paper, is not a quotation.

29c Do not shift between quotation and indirect discourse within a sentence.

Once you have begun to quote someone's speech or writing, do not suddenly move into indirect discourse—a report of what was spoken or written (p. 313, 24c). Similarly, do not leap from indirect discourse to quotation.

DON'T:

QUOTATION

x She said, **"I love science fiction movies,"** and **had I seen**

INDIRECT DISCOURSE

the one about the teenage Martians on a rampage?

DO:

QUOTATION

• She said, **"I love science fiction movies,"** and asked me,

QUOTATION

"Have you seen the one about the teenage Martians on a rampage?"

DON'T:

INDIRECT
DISCOURSE   QUOTATION

x My boss said **the key was gone** and **are you the one who took it?**

DO:

INDIRECT   INDIRECT
DISCOURSE   DISCOURSE

x My boss said **the key was gone** and asked **if I was the one who had taken it.**

INCORPORATING A QUOTATION

29d Use double quotation marks to set off quoted material that you have incorporated into your own prose.

If you are representing someone's speech or quoting a fairly brief passage of written work—no more than five typed lines of prose or no more than two or three lines of poetry—you should **incorporate** the quotation. That is, you should make it continuous with your own text instead of **indenting** it (p. 354, 29h). Be sure to enclose an incorporated quotation in quotation marks. In North American (as opposed to British) English, those marks should be double (" "):

- "Computers," as Bertini points out, "are unforgiving toward even the tiniest mistake in the instructions you give them."

29e Use single quotation marks for a quotation within a quotation.

If the passage you are incorporating already contains quotation marks, change them to single marks (' '):

- E. F. Carpenter, writing in *Contemporary Dramatists,* says of Butterfield: "The playwright knows where his best work originated. 'Everything that touches an audience,' he told me, 'comes from memories of the period when I was down and out.'"

Similarly, if a title you are quoting already contains quotation marks, change them to single marks:

- I refer to Joyce Molnar's recent article, "Norma Jean: Comic Self-Discovery in Bobbie Ann Mason's 'Shiloh.'"

Double Quotation within a Quotation

Try to avoid quoting a passage that already contains single quotation marks; the effect will be confusing. But if you find no alternative, change those single marks to double ones. Then check carefully to see that your *three* sets of marks are kept straight (" " " ' "):

- Orwell's friend Richard Rees informs us that "when Socialists told him that under Socialism there would be no such feeling of being at the mercy of unpredictable and irresponsible powers, he remarked: 'I notice people always say "*under* Socialism." They look forward to being on top—with all others underneath, being told what is good for them.'"

> Here the main quotation is from Rees. Since Rees quotes Orwell, Orwell's words appear within single marks. But when those words themselves contain a quotation, that phrase ("*under* Socialism") is set off with double marks.

Note that British practice is just the opposite of North American: single marks for the first quotation, double marks for a quotation appearing within it, and single marks again for the very rare third quotation.

29f When incorporating more than one line of poetry, use a slash to show where a line ends.

You can incorporate as many as three lines of poetry instead of indenting them (29h). But if your passage runs beyond a line ending, you should indicate that ending with a slash preceded and followed by a space:

- In a snowstorm, says the noted Japanese poet Bashō, "Even a horse / Is a spectacle."

29g Learn how to combine quotation marks with other marks of punctuation.

1. Always place commas and periods inside the close-quotation marks. You do not have to consider whether the comma or period is part of the quotation or whether the quotation is short or long. Just routinely put the comma or period first:

- Francis Bacon said, "To spend too much time in study is sloth."
- "To spend too much time in study is sloth," said Francis Bacon.

2. Always place colons and semicolons outside the close-quotation marks:

- "Sloth": that was Bacon's term for too much study.
- Francis Bacon called excessive study "sloth"; I call it inefficiency.

3. Place question marks, exclamation points, and dashes either inside or outside the close-quotation marks, depending on their function. If they are punctuating the quoted material itself, place them inside:

- "Do you think it will snow?" she asked.
- "Of course it will!" he replied.

But put the same marks *outside* the close-quotation marks if they are not part of the question or exclamation:

- Was Stephanie a sophomore when she said, "I am going to have a job lined up long before I graduate"?
- I have told you for the last time to stop calling me your "little sweetie"!

29g

4. When the quotation must end with a question mark or exclamation point and your own sentence calls for a closing period, drop the period:

- Grandpa listens to Dan Rather every evening and constantly shouts, "Horsefeathers!"

5. Otherwise, the end punctuation of the quotation makes way for your own punctuation. For example, if the quoted passage ends with a period but your own sentence does not stop there, drop the period and substitute your own punctuation, if any:

- "I wonder why they don't impeach newscasters," said Grandpa.

The quoted passage would normally end with a period, but the main sentence calls for a comma at that point.

6. When a quotation is accompanied by a footnote number, that number comes after all other punctuation except a dash that resumes your own part of the sentence:

- Bloomingdale's advertises women's skirts as "pencil-thin, get the point?"[6]
- Bloomingdale's advertises women's skirts as "pencil-thin, get the point?"[6]—but in fact the skirts come in all sizes.

7. When a quotation is incorporated into your text (without indention) and is followed by a parenthetic citation (p. 485, 39a; p. 534, 40a), the open-parenthesis mark comes after the final quotation mark but before a comma or period—even if the comma or period occurs in the quoted passage:

- John Keegan begins his book *The Face of Battle* by confessing, "I have not been in a battle; nor near one, nor heard one from afar, nor seen the aftermath" (15).

8. But if the incorporated quotation ends with a question mark or exclamation point, include it before the close-quotation mark and add your own punctuation after the close-parenthesis mark:

- He raises the question, "How would *I* behave in a battle?" (Keegan 18).

9. If you indent a quotation, setting it apart from your text, and if you then supply a parenthetic citation, place that citation after all punctuation:

- Gladly will I sell
  For profit,
  Dear merchants of the town,
  My hat laden with snow. (Bashō 60)

" "
29g

INDENTING A QUOTATION ("BLOCK QUOTATION")

29h Indent a longer quotation.

The Modern Language Association (MLA) recommends the following guidelines for indenting longer quotations:

PROSE	**POETRY**
Indent by ten spaces a passage of more than four lines.	Indent by ten spaces a passage of more than two or three lines; indent by fewer spaces if the lines are very long.

In the examples below, the numbers in color are keyed to rules given on page 355–356.

INDENTED PROSE:

Margot Slade points to the bond between siblings that

is like no other connection between human beings: ——— 1

——— 2

5 ——⌈—— Welcome to the sibling bond, that twilight

zone of relationships between brothers and

sisters, and any combination thereof, where

parents must walk but often fear to tread.

With good reason. As one well-seasoned

father puts it: "Under most circumstances,

it can be suicide to interfere."——————— 6

3, 4 ⎰

7——Siblings generally constitute an

exclusive state--exclusive, that is, of

parents. They are the keepers of each

other's secrets and the supporters of each

```
    ⎧   other's goals.  They can be friends in the
    ⎨
    ⎩   morning and enemies at night.│ (80)
                                   5
```
——— 2

```
Now let us see if this special relationship exists

between the famous pair of siblings under

consideration here.
```

The writer is quoting from Margot Slade's article, "Siblings: War and Peace." For proper citation form, see page 490, 39b (MLA style), and page 537, 40b (APA style).

INDENTED POETRY:

```
In "Crossing Brooklyn Ferry" Whitman calls out to his

fellow citizens of the future as well as the present: ── 1
                                                        ── 2
   5──⎧I am with you, you men and women of a generation,

        ⎪    or ever so many generations hence.

        ⎪Just as you feel when look on the river and
3, 4, 8 ⎨
        ⎪    sky, so I felt.

        ⎪Just as any of you is one of a living crowd, I was
        ⎩    one of a crowd.│ (323)
                            5
```
——— 2

```
By creating a bond with unborn Americans, Whitman

prophesies the coming greatness of his country.
```

1. In most cases, introduce the passage with a colon. (See page 359, 29n.)

2. Unless your instructor tells you otherwise, do not add extra space above and below the quotation.

3. Indent the whole passage ten spaces from your left margin, or somewhat less if the quoted lines of poetry are very long.

4. Double-space a quoted passage unless your instructor prefers single spacing.

5. Omit the quotation marks you would have used to surround an incorporated quotation.

6. Copy exactly any quotation marks you find in the quoted passage itself.

7. In indenting prose, indent all lines equally if the passage consists of one paragraph or less. When you are quoting more than one paragraph of prose, indent the first line of each full paragraph after the first one by an additional three spaces.

8. In indenting poetry, follow the spacing (beginnings and endings of lines) found in the original passage. If a line is too long to reproduce exactly as it appears in the source, continue on the next line, indenting three spaces.

29i When quoting dialogue, indent for a new paragraph with each change of speaker.

After you have completed a quotation of speech, you can comment on it without starting a new paragraph. You can also resume quoting the speaker's words after your own. But do indent for a new paragraph as soon as you get to someone else's speech.

" "
29j

"I can't understand," I said, "how you can win world-class distance races without having been coached in high school or college."

"Oh, but sir," he protested with a polite smile, "I have been running since I was a little child. In Kenya this is how we get from village to village."

"Yes, yes, but where did you get your training?" This man seemed to defy everything I knew about the making of a great runner.

"Oh, my *training*!" He threw his head back and laughed. "Mister reporter, *you* run every day, year after year, at 8,000 feet, carrying boxes and fuel and whatnot. Then please come back and tell me if you think you need some training!"

29j Learn how to punctuate a quoted speech that continues into a new paragraph.

In general, quotation marks come in pairs; for every mark that opens a quotation there must be another to close it. But there is one exception. To show that someone's quoted speech continues in a new paragraph, put quotation marks at the beginning of that paragraph, and keep doing so until the quotation ends:

> "I have two things to bring up with you," she said. "In the first place, which of us is going to be keeping the stereo? I'd like to have it, but it's no big deal to me.
>
> "Second, what about the dog? I'm the one who brought her home as a puppy, and I intend to keep her."

Note that in such a passage, no close-quotation marks are used until the full quotation is completed.

INTRODUCING A QUOTATION

29k If a quotation fits into your preceding phrase or clause, introduce it without punctuation.

The way to decide which punctuation, if any, to use in introducing a quotation is to read the quoted matter as part of your own sentence. Use introductory punctuation only if it would have been called for anyway, with or without the quotation marks:

- Macbeth expresses the depth of his despair when he characterizes life as "a tale told by an idiot."

  Since the quotation serves as an object of the writer's preposition *as,* a preceding comma would be wrong here (see p. 329, 26b). Note how smoothly the quoted passage completes the writer's sentence.

29l If a quotation does not fit into your preceding phrase or clause, introduce it with a comma or a colon.

- Reynolds comments, "A close look at Melville's fiction reveals that his literary development was even more closely tied to popular reform than was Hawthorne's."

- Baym's thesis rests on one central assumption: that "we never read American literature directly or freely, but always through the perspective allowed by theories."

In these examples, the quotations do not complete the writer's own statements—as would occur, for example, in *Baym's thesis rests on the assumption that "we never read...."* You can choose between a comma and a colon to introduce a quotation that stands apart from your own prose. The comma is more appropriate for tags such as *She said* and *He remarked* (29m). When the quotation is long enough to be indented (29h), you should prefer the more formal colon (29n).

- Gandhi, when asked what he thought of Western civilization, smiled and replied, "I think it would be a very good idea."

    A colon would be equally correct here, but it would mark a more formal pause.

- Surrounded by surging reporters and photographers, the accused dean tried to hold them all at bay with one repeated sentence: "I will have no statement to make before tomorrow."

    The colon is especially appropriate here because it matches *one repeated sentence* with the actual words of that sentence.

" "
29m

29m Follow an introductory tag like *He said* with a comma.

Even if you do not feel that a pause is called for, put a comma after an introductory clause such as *He said* or *She replied:*

- He said, "I'd like to comment on that."
- She replied, "Yes, you are always making comments, aren't you?"

If the tag follows or interrupts the quoted speech, it must still be set apart:

- "I'd like to comment on that," he said.
- "Yes," she replied, "you are always making comments, aren't you?"

29n As a rule, use a colon before an indented quotation.

Since an indented passage (p. 354, 29h) appears on the page as an interruption of your prose, you should usually introduce it with a colon, implying a formal stop.

- Here is Macbeth's gloomiest pronouncement about life:

> it is a tale
> Told by an idiot, full of sound and fury,
> Signifying nothing.

But if the passage begins with a fragment that completes your own sentence, omit the colon:

- Macbeth considers life to be

> a tale
> Told by an idiot, full of sound and fury,
> Signifying nothing.

A colon would be wrong here, since it would separate an infinitive (*to be*) from its complement (*a tale* ...). Note that a comma would be unacceptable for the same reason.

" "
29o

OMITTING OR INSERTING MATERIAL

29o Use an ellipsis mark to show that something has been omitted from a quotation.

If you want to omit unneeded words or sentences from a quoted passage, accuracy requires that you show where you are doing so.

WHOLE PASSAGE:
- As I have repeatedly stated, those claims, which irresponsible promoters of tax shelter schemes continue to represent as valid, have been disallowed every time they have come before the IRS.

PARTIAL QUOTATION:

- Gomez reports that "those claims ... have been disallowed every time they have come before the IRS."

29p   Distinguish between three kinds of ellipses.

Three Dots

If an omission is followed by material from the same sentence being quoted, type the ellipsis mark as three spaced periods preceded and followed by a space:

- She characterized her early years as "a bad joke ... hardly a childhood at all."

Four Dots

Use four dots—a normal period followed by three spaced dots—if you are omitting (1) the last part of the quoted sentence, (2) the beginning of the next sentence, (3) a complete sentence or more, or (4) one or two complete paragraphs:

- She wrote, "I am always bored. ... There is nothing here to keep me occupied."
- She described the apartment tower as seeming "ridiculous, improbable. ... I feel like a fairy princess who has been tucked away in the wrong castle by mistake."

If the sentence preceding your ellipsis ends with a question mark or exclamation point, keep that mark and add just three spaced dots:

- "Is Shaw," he asked, "really the equal of Shakespeare? ... That seems extremely dubious."
- The champion shouted, "I am the greatest! ... Nobody can mess up my pretty face."

A four-dot ellipsis is appropriate whenever your quotation skips material and then goes on to a new sentence, whether or not you are omitting material *within* a sentence. But note that you should always have grammatically complete statements on both sides of a four-dot ellipsis.

DON'T:

x She wrote, "I am always bored. . . . nothing here to keep me occupied."

Here the four-dot ellipsis is wrongly followed by a fragment.

Row of Dots

Mark the omission of a whole line or more of poetry by a complete line of spaced periods:

• Pope writes:

> First follow nature, and your judgment frame
> By her just standard, which is still the same;
>
> . . . .
>
> Life, force, and beauty must to all impart,
> At once the source, and end, and test of art.

Notice that the line of spaced periods is about the same length as the preceding line of poetry.

" "
29q

29q Avoid beginning a quotation with an ellipsis.

If you make a quoted clause or phrase fit in with your own sentence structure (p. 357, 29k), you should not use an ellipsis mark to show that you have left something out.

DON'T:

x The signers of the Declaration of Independence characterized George III as ". . . unfit to be the ruler of a free people."

DO:

• The signers of the Declaration of Independence characterized George III as "unfit to be the ruler of a free people."

29r Use brackets to insert your own words into a quotation.

To show that you are interrupting a quotation rather than quoting a parenthetical remark, be sure to enclose your interruption in brackets, not parentheses (p. 344, 28k):

- "I hope to be buried in Kansas City [her birthplace]," she said.

  Parentheses here would indicate that the woman who wanted to be buried in Kansas City was referring to another woman's birthplace. The brackets show that it is the writer, not the woman being quoted, who is supplying the extra information.

[sic]

The bracketed and usually italicized Latin word *sic* (meaning "thus") signifies that a peculiarity—for example, a misspelling—occurs in the quoted material:

- He wrote, "I am teaching these kids how to live outdoors [*sic*] without being afraid."

Do not abuse the legitimate function of *[sic]* by applying it sarcastically to claims that you find dubious.

DON'T:

x Are we supposed to believe the "humane" [*sic*] pretensions of the National Rifle Association?

  The quotation marks are already sarcastic enough without *[sic]* to redouble the effect. But why not eliminate both devices and let the language of the sentence do its own work?

DO:

- Are we supposed to believe the humane pretensions of the National Rifle Association?

30 Forming and Spacing Punctuation Marks

To see how punctuation marks are normally handled by typewriter or word processor, examine the typescript essays beginning on pages 68, 83, 500, and 545. In addition, note the following advice about forming marks and leaving or omitting spaces around them.

30a Learn the three ways of forming a dash.

Dashes come in three lengths, depending on their function.

1. A dash separating numbers is typed as a hyphen:

- pages 32-39

- October 8-14

- Social Security Number 203-64-7853

2. As a sign of a break in thought—its most usual function—a dash is typed as two hyphens with no space between:

- Try it--if you dare.

- They promise--but do not always come through with--
  overnight delivery.

3. Use four unspaced hyphens for a dash that stands in the place of an omitted word:

● He refused to disclose the name of Ms. ----

> This is the only kind of dash that is preceded by a space; see 30g.

30b   Learn how to form brackets.

If your typewriter lacks keys for brackets, you can

1. type slashes (/) and complete the sides with underlinings:
   $\overline{[}\ \overline{]}$

2. type slashes and add the horizontal lines later in ink:
   $[\ ]$

3. Leave blank spaces and later write the brackets entirely in ink:
   $[\ ]$

30c   Learn how to form the three kinds of ellipses.

1. An ellipsis (p. 359, 29o) is formed with three spaced dots if it signifies the omission of material within a quoted sentence. Note that a space is left before and after the whole ellipsis as well as after each dot:

● "The government," she said, "appears to be

  abandoning its . . . efforts to prevent nuclear

  proliferation."

2. A four-dot ellipsis, signifying the omission of quoted material that covers at least one mark of end punctuation, begins with that *unspaced* mark:

- "The government," she said, "appears to be abandoning its formerly urgent efforts to prevent nuclear proliferation. . . . There may be a terrible price to pay for this negligence."

3. Leave spaces between all the dots of an ellipsis that covers a whole row, signifying the omission of one or more lines of poetry:

- The river glideth at its own sweet will:

  . . . .

  And all that mighty heart is lying still!

30d Learn the two ways of spacing a slash.

1. When a slash separates two quoted lines of poetry that you are incorporating into your text (p. 351, 29f), leave a space before and after the slash:

- Shakespeare writes, "Shall I compare thee to a summer's day? / Thou art more lovely and more temperate."

p/
form
30d

2. But if your slash indicates alternatives or a span of time, leave no space before or after the slanted line:

- We are not dealing with an either/or situation here.
- The article will appear in the Winter/Spring issue of the journal.

30e Leave two spaces after a period, a question mark, an exclamation point, or a four-dot ellipsis.

• The Chinese leaders appear to be ready for a new dialogue with the United States. Should we let this opportunity slip away? Certainly not! Remember the words of the Foreign Minister: "If we do not take steps to ensure peace, we may find ourselves drifting into war. . . . Our two nations can work together without agreeing about everything."

30f Leave one space after a comma, a colon, a semicolon, a closing quotation mark, a closing parenthesis, or a closing bracket.

• Here is the real story, we believe, of last week's disturbance: it was not a riot but a legitimate demonstration. The city police chief thinks otherwise; but his description of the "riot" is grossly inaccurate. The chief (a foe of all progressive causes) erred in more than his spelling when he wrote of a "Comunist [sic] uprising."

p/
form
30g

30g Leave no space before or after a dash, a hyphen, or an apostrophe within a word.

• Wilbur--a first-rate judge of toothpaste flavors-- prefers Carter's Sparklefoam for its gum-tickling goodness.

30h When an apostrophe ends a word, leave no space before any following punctuation of the word.

- This ranch, the Johnsons', has been in the family for generations.

30i When a word is immediately followed by two punctuation marks, put them together without a space.

- Here is the true story of the "riot."
- When I heard the truth about the riot (as the police chief called it), I was outraged.
- The protest, which the police chief called the work of "Comunists" [sic], was actually organized by members of the business community.

30j Do not begin a line with any mark that belongs with the last word of the preceding line.

DON'T:

x Here is why Carol refuses to sign the petition
    : she objects to the dangerously vague language about
    waterfront development.

DO:

- Here is why Carol refuses to sign the petition:
    she objects to the dangerously vague language about
    waterfront development.

p/
form
30j

30k Do not divide an ellipsis between one line and the next.

DON'T:

x Carol objected to the petition because of "the . .

. language about waterfront development."

DO:

● Carol objected to the petition because of "the . . .

language about waterfront development."

For combining quotation marks with other punctuation marks, see page 351, 29g. For the spacing of periods within abbreviations, see page 434, 36k.

p/
form
30k

VII
CONVENTIONS

Conventions

In this section we consider rules affecting the form a word can take. These are small matters—if you get them right. If you do not, you will be handicapped in communicating your ideas. It is essential, then, to spell and hyphenate correctly and to be accurate in showing different forms of verbs, nouns, and pronouns. And it is useful, if less urgent, to know where such conventions as italics, abbreviations, and written-out numbers are considered appropriate in a piece of writing. Once the conventions have become second nature, both you and your reader can put them out of mind and concentrate on larger issues.

31 Verb Forms

31a Note how verbs change their form to show person and number in the present tense.

Within most **tenses,** or times of action, English verbs show no differences of form for person and number. That is, the verb remains the same whether its subject is the speaker, someone spoken to, or someone (or something) spoken about, and whether that subject is one person or thing or more than one. The past-tense forms of *move,* for example, look like this.

	SINGULAR	PLURAL
First Person	I moved	we moved
Second Person	you moved	you moved
Third Person	he, she, it moved	they moved

But in the most common tense, the present, the third-person singular verb shows **inflection**—that is, it changes its form without becoming a different word.

	SINGULAR	PLURAL
First Person	I move	we move
Second Person	you move	you move
Third Person	he, she, it **moves**	they move

The third-person singular form of a present-tense verb ends in *-s.* If the base form of the verb ends in *-ch, -s, -sh, -x,* or *-z,* the addition is *-es.*

BASE FORM	THIRD-PERSON SINGULAR PRESENT
lurch	he lurches
pass	she passes
wash	Harry washes
fix	Betty fixes
buzz	it buzzes

In some spoken dialects of English, this third-person *-s* or *-es* does not occur. Standard written English, however, requires that you observe it. You may have to check your final drafts to be sure that your *-s* or *-es* endings are in place.

DON'T:

x When Meg **get** a new idea, she always **say** something worth hearing.

DO:

• When Meg **gets** a new idea, she always **says** something worth hearing.

31b Learn the principal parts of regular and irregular verbs.

**verb
31b**

	BASE	PAST TENSE	PAST PARTICIPLE
Regular	bake	baked	baked
	adopt	adopted	adopted
	compute	computed	computed
Irregular	choose	chose	chosen
	eat	ate	eaten
	write	wrote	written

All verbs have three **principal parts** used in tense formation: the infinitive or base form (*bake, choose*), the past tense (*baked, chose*), and the past participle (*baked, chosen*). The past participle is used with forms of *have* and with auxiliaries (*could have, would have*, etc.) to form various other past tenses (*had baked, would have chosen*, etc.) **Regular verbs**—those that simply add *-d* or *-ed* to form both the past tense and the past participle—cause few problems of tense formation. But you must take greater care to see how the following **irregular verbs** are formed.

PRINCIPAL PARTS OF IRREGULAR VERBS		
BASE	**PAST TENSE**	**PAST PARTICIPLE**
awake	awaked, awoke	awaked, awoke, awoken
be	was, were	been
beat	beat	beaten, beat
become	became	become
begin	began	begun
bend	bent	bent
bite	bit	bit, bitten
bleed	bled	bled
blow	blew	blown
break	broke	broken
bring	brought	brought
build	built	built
burst	burst	burst
buy	bought	bought
catch	caught	caught
choose	chose	chosen
come	came	come
cost	cost	cost
cut	cut	cut
deal	dealt	dealt
dig	dug	dug

verb
31b

PRINCIPAL PARTS OF IRREGULAR VERBS		
BASE	**PAST TENSE**	**PAST PARTICIPLE**
dive	dived, dove	dived
do	did	done
draw	drew	drawn
dream	dreamed, dreamt	dreamed, dreamt
drink	drank	drunk
drive	drove	driven
eat	ate	eaten
fall	fell	fallen
feed	fed	fed
feel	felt	felt
fight	fought	fought
find	found	found
fit	fitted, fit	fitted, fit
fly	flew	flown
forget	forgot	forgotten, forgot
freeze	froze	frozen
get	got	gotten, got
give	gave	given
go	went	gone
grow	grew	grown
hang (an object)	hung	hung
hang (a person)	hanged	hanged
hear	heard	heard
hide	hid	hidden, hid
hit	hit	hit
hold	held	held
hurt	hurt	hurt
keep	kept	kept
kneel	knelt, kneeled	knelt, kneeled
knit	knit, knitted	knit, knitted
know	knew	known

**verb
31b**

PRINCIPAL PARTS OF IRREGULAR VERBS		
BASE	**PAST TENSE**	**PAST PARTICIPLE**
lay (put)	laid	laid
lead	led	led
lean	leaned, leant	leaned, leant
leave	left	left
lend	lent	lent
let	let	let
lie (recline)	lay	lain
light	lighted, lit	lighted, lit
lose	lost	lost
make	made	made
mean	meant	meant
meet	met	met
pay	paid	paid
prove	proved	proved, proven
put	put	put
quit	quit, quitted	quit, quitted
read	read	read
rid	rid, ridded	rid, ridded
ride	rode	ridden
ring	rang	rung
run	ran	run
say	said	said
see	saw	seen
sell	sold	sold
send	sent	sent
set	set	set
shake	shook	shaken
shine	shone, shined	shone, shined (transitive)
shoot	shot	shot
show	showed	showed, shown

verb 31b

PRINCIPAL PARTS OF IRREGULAR VERBS		
BASE	**PAST TENSE**	**PAST PARTICIPLE**
shrink	shrank	shrunk
shut	shut	shut
sing	sang, sung	sung
sink	sank	sunk
sit	sat	sat
sleep	slept	slept
slide	slid	slid
speak	spoke	spoken
speed	sped, speeded	sped, speeded
spend	spent	spent
spin	spun	spun
spring	sprang, sprung	sprung
stand	stood	stood
steal	stole	stolen
stick	stuck	stuck
sting	stung	stung
strike	struck	struck, stricken
swear	swore	sworn
swim	swam	swum
swing	swung	swung
take	took	taken
teach	taught	taught
tear	tore	torn
tell	told	told
think	thought	thought
throw	threw	thrown
wake	waked, woke	waked, woke, woken
wear	wore	worn
win	won	won
wring	wrung	wrung
write	wrote	written

verb
31b

Distinguishing between Past-Tense and Past-Participle Forms

It is not enough to know the correct forms for the past participles of irregular verbs. You must also remember that past participles can form tenses only when they are combined with other words (*have gone, would have paid*). Do not use an irregular past participle where the past tense is called for.

DON'T:

x She **begun** her singing lessons last Tuesday.

DO:

• She **began** her singing lessons last Tuesday.

DON'T:

x They **seen** him put on the wrong jacket.

DO:

• They **saw** him put on the wrong jacket.

DON'T:

x We **swum** across the pool.

DO:

• We **swam** across the pool.

Similarly, do not use the past-tense form of an irregular verb with an auxiliary.

verb
31c

DON'T:

x We **have** already **swam** across the pool.

DO:

• We **have** already **swum** across the pool.

31c Learn the tense forms in the active voice.

The various tenses are shown by changed forms of the base verb (*try—tried; go—went*) and through forms of *be* and *have* in combination with base (*try*) and participial (*trying*) forms (*will try, was trying, had tried, will have tried*). Here are all the active-voice forms—first, second, and third person, singular and plural—for a verb, *walk*, in eight commonly used tenses. (For passive forms, see 31d.)

TENSE FORMS: ACTIVE VOICE		
Present: I walk	he, she, it walks	we, you (sing./pl.), they walk
Present Progressive: I am walking	he, she, it is walking	we, you (sing./pl.), they are walking
Present Perfect: I have walked	he, she, it has walked	we, you (sing./pl.), they have walked
Past: I walked	he, she, it walked	we, you (sing./pl.), they walked
Past Progressive: I was walking	he, she, it was walking	we, you (sing./pl.), they were walking
Past Perfect: I had walked	he, she, it had walked	we, you (sing./pl.) they had walked
Future: I will walk	he, she, it will walk	we, you (sing./pl.), they will walk
Future Perfect: I will have walked	he, she, it will have walked	we, you (sing./pl.), they will have walked

In the future tense, *I* and *we* can be accompanied by *shall* instead of *will*. *Shall* is normal in questions about plans:

* **Shall** we go to the movies?

In addition, some writers still keep to the once common use of *shall* for all first-person statements (*I shall go to the movies*) and for taking a commanding tone (*You shall go the movies!*) But *will* is now usual in these functions. Keep to *will* unless you want to make an unusually formal effect.

31d   Learn the tense forms in the passive voice.

The **voice** of a verb shows whether its grammatical subject performs or receives the action it expresses. A verb is **active** when the subject performs the action (*Frankie shot Johnny*) but **passive** when the subject is acted upon by the verb (*Johnny was shot by Frankie*).

ACTIVE VOICE:
* The paramedics **took** the old man to the hospital.

  Note that the performers of the action (the paramedics) are also the grammatical subject.

PASSIVE VOICE:
* The old man *was taken* to the hospital by the paramedics.

  Note that the performers of the action (the paramedics) are not the grammatical subject of the passive verb *was taken*.

verb
31d

One peculiarity of the passive voice is that you need not mention the performer of action at all: *Johnny was shot; The old man was taken to the hospital.* This feature can help you to remember the difference between the passive voice and the past tense. In *The ambulance went to the hospital,* the verb is past but not passive.

Here are the passive-voice forms of one verb, *show,* in the same tenses we reviewed in the active voice (p. 378):

TENSE FORMS: PASSIVE VOICE

Present:

I	he, she, it	we, you (sing./pl.), they
am shown	is shown	are shown

Present Progressive:

I	he, she, it	we, you (sing./pl.), they
am being shown	is being shown	are being shown

Present Perfect:

I	he, she, it	we, you (sing./pl.), they
have been shown	has been shown	have been shown

Past:

I	he, she, it	we, you (sing./pl.), they
was shown	was shown	were shown

Past Progressive:

I	he, she, it	we, you (sing./pl.), they
was being shown	was being shown	were being shown

Past Perfect:

I	he, she, it	we, you (sing./pl.), they
had been shown	had been shown	had been shown

Future:

I	he, she, it	we, you (sing./pl.), they
will be shown	will be shown	will be shown

Future Perfect:

I	he, she, it	we, you (sing./pl.), they
will have been shown	will have been shown	will have been shown

**verb
31d**

For the use of *shall* as an alternative to *will,* see page 379, 31c.

For the stylistic uses and limitations of the passive voice, see page 144, 11e.

31e Learn the forms and uses of the indicative, imperative, and subjunctive moods.

Verbs show certain other changes of form to convey **mood,** or the manner of their action. Use the **indicative** mood for a statement (*Ann walks the dog*) or a question (*Does Ann walk the dog?*). To give directions (*Walk the dog*) or commands (*Watch out for the rabid dog!*), use the **imperative** mood.

For a variety of less common purposes, as follows, use the **subjunctive** mood.

1. Hypothetical conditions:

   * He is, as it **were,** a termite gnawing at the foundations of our business.

     As it were is a fixed expression indicating that the writer is using a figure of speech (p. 199, 16a) instead of making a literal statement.

   * If I **were** on the moon now, I would tidy up the junk that has been left there. [not *was*]
   * I wish I **were** in Haiti now. [not *was*]

2. *That* clauses expressing requirements or recommendations:

   * The IRS requires that everyone **submit** a return by April 15. [not *submits*]
   * It is important that all new students **be** tested immediately. [not *are*]

   verb 31e

3. Expressions of a wish in which *may* is understood:

   * long **live** the Queen [not *lives*]
   * **be** it known [not *is*]
   * so **be** it [not *is*]
   * **suffice** it to say [not *suffices*]

For nearly all verbs, the subjunctive differs from the indicative only in that the third-person singular verb loses its *-s* or *-es: come what may,* not *comes what may.* The verb *to be* uses *be* for "requirement" clauses (*I demand that she be here early*) and *were* for hypothetical conditions (*if he were an emperor*).

The following chart summarizes the contrast between the subjunctive and indicative moods. Subjunctive verbs are underscored. For further discussion of sentences proposing the imagined consequences of hypothetical conditions, see 311, 24b.

	SUBJUNCTIVE	**INDICATIVE**
	Hypothetical conditions with imagined consequences:	**Possibilities or probabilities with real consequences:**
Verb *to be*	● If I **were** a parent, I **would carry** life insurance.	● When I **am** a parent, I **will carry** life insurance.
Other verbs	● If he **married** your sister, you **would be** brothers.	● If he **marries** your sister, you **will be** brothers.
	***That* clauses expressing requirements or recommendations:**	**Actions that occur, have occurred, or will occur:**
Verb *to be*	● The government requires that tax returns **be** strictly accurate.	● My tax return **was** as accurate as I could make it.
Other verbs	● The art department insists that a lecturer **leave** all lights on during a slide show.	● Because my art lecturer **leaves** the lights on during every slide show, the class **stays** awake.

verb
31e

32 Plurals and Possessives

32a Do not confuse the plural and possessive forms of nouns.

SINGULAR	PLURAL	SINGULAR POSSESSIVE	PLURAL POSSESSIVE
temple	temples	temple's	temples'
pass	passes	pass's	passes'
squash	squashes	squash's	squashes'
annex	annexes	annex's	annexes'
Ford	Fords	Ford's	Fords'

In making a noun plural (*two temples; three Fords*), *do not* use an apostrophe. (For the only exception, see 32h.) In making a noun possessive (*the temple's roof; the Fords' debt to their grandfather*), *always* use an apostrophe.

DON'T:

x The two **priest's** made many **contribution's** to the parish.

DO:

• The two **priests** made many **contributions** to the parish.

DON'T:

x The **Kennedy's** have been stalked by tragedy.

DO:

• The **Kennedys** have been stalked by tragedy.

DON'T:

x In many **place's** the **oceans** depth is unknown.

DO:

• In many **places** the **ocean's** depth is unknown.

DON'T:

x The **clocks** hands stopped all across the city.

DO:

• The **clocks'** hands stopped all across the city.

PLURALS

32b Form the plural of most nouns by adding *-s* or *-es* to the singular, as in *computers.*

bat	bats
class	classes
house	houses
song	songs
summons	summonses
waltz	waltzes

plur
32c

32c To form the plural of a noun ending in a consonant plus *-y,* change the *-y* to *-i* and add *-es,* as in *securities.*

army	armies
candy	candies
duty	duties
penny	pennies
warranty	warranties

32d Note the different plural forms for nouns ending in *-o.*

Most nouns ending in a vowel plus *-o* become plural by adding *-s:*

patio	patios
studio	studios

Nouns ending in a consonant plus *-o* becomes plural by adding *-es:*

potato	potatoes
veto	vetoes

But some plurals disobey the rule:

piano	pianos
solo	solos
soprano	sopranos

And some words have alternative, equally correct forms:

zero	zeros/zeroes
cargo	cargos/cargoes

Where your dictionary lists two forms, always adopt the first, which is more commonly used.

32e To make a name plural, add *-s* or *-es* without an apostrophe, as in *the Smiths.*

Add *-s* to most names:

Smith	the Smiths
Perry	the Perrys
Helen	both Helens
Goodman	the Goodmans
Carolina	two Carolinas

plur
32e

When a name ends in *-ch, -s, -sh, -x,* or *-z,* add *-es.* The extra syllable that results should be pronounced:

Burch	the Burches
Jones	the Joneses
Weiss	the Weisses
Cash	the Cashes
Fox	the Foxes
Perez	the Perezes

32f Form the plural of a noun ending in *-ful* by adding *-s* to the end.

cupful	cupfuls
shovelful	shovelfuls
spoonful	spoonfuls

Beware of the "genteel" but incorrect *cupsful, shovelsful,* and so forth.

32g Follow common practice in forming the plural of a noun derived from another language.

plur
32g

A number of words taken from foreign languages, especially Greek and Latin, keep their foreign plural forms. But some foreign-based words have also acquired English plural forms. The rule for deciding which plural to use is this: look it up!

Even so, the dictionary cannot settle your doubts in every instance. It may not tell you, for example, that the plural of *appendix* is *appendixes* if you are referring to the organ but either *appendixes* or *appendices* if you mean supplementary sections at the ends of books. Similarly, your dictionary may not reveal that while an insect has *antennae,* television sets have *antennas.* The way to get such information is to note the practice of other speakers and writers.

When in doubt, prefer the English plural.

SINGULAR	PREFER	NOT
cherub	cherubs	cherubim
crocus	crocuses	croci
podium	podiums	podia
sanatorium	sanatoriums	sanatoria
stadium	stadiums	stadia

But note that certain foreign plurals are still preferred:

alumna	alumnae
alumnus	alumni
criterion	criteria
datum	data
phenomenon	phenomena
vertebra	vertebrae

Confusions between the singular and plural forms of these terms are common. Indeed, *data* as a singular is often seen in scientific publications. Many careful writers, however, while avoiding the rare *datum,* use *data* only when its sense is clearly plural: *these data,* not *this data.*

Note that Greek derivatives ending in *-is* regularly change to *-es* in the plural:

analysis	analyses
crisis	crises
parenthesis	parentheses
thesis	theses

**plur
32h**

32h   To form the plural of a word presented *as* a word, add -'s.

Add an apostrophe and an *-s* to show the plural of a word you are discussing as a word, not as the thing it signifies:

- The editor changed all the *he*'s in Chapter 4 to *she*'s.

  Note how the writer's meaning is made clearer by the italicizing of each isolated word but not of the *'s* that follows it.

32i **Add** *-s,* **without an apostrophe, to form the plural of most hyphenated nouns, capital letters, capitalized abbreviations without periods, written-out numbers, and figures.**

- two stand-ins
- three Bs
- four VCRs
- counting by fives and tens
- counting by 5s and 10s
- the 1980s

Use *-'s* whenever it is needed to avoid confusion.

DON'T:

x Bridget earned straight **As** on her report card.

  Here the plural of *A* looks confusingly like the preposition *as.*

DO:

- Bridget earned straight **A's** on her report card.

When the first part of a compound term is the key identifying noun, as in *sister-in-law* and *president-elect,* add the *-s* to that noun: *sisters-in-law, presidents-elect.*

32j **Add** *-'s* **to form the plural of an uncapitalized letter, an abbreviation ending in a period, or a lowercase abbreviation.**

- *a*'s, *b*'s, and *c*'s
- the two *i*'s in *iris*

- too many *etc.*'s in your paper
- a shortage of M.D.'s
- thousands of rpm's

POSSESSIVES

A possessive form implies either actual ownership (*my neighbor's willow, Alice's computer*) or some other close relation (*a stone's throw, the Governor's enemies*). Nouns and some pronouns form the possessive either by adding an apostrophe with or without an *-s* or by preceding the "possessing" element with *of: my husband's first wife, her parents' car, the wings of the canary*.

32k Avoid confusing possessive pronouns like *its* and *whose* with contractions like *it's* and *who's*.

Its vs. *It's*

Its is the possessive form of the pronoun *it:*

- The dog lost **its** collar.
- The college canceled **its** film series.

It's is a contraction meaning *it is* or *it has:*

- **It's** raining cats and dogs.
- **It's** never been canceled before.

**poss
32k**

   To avoid confusing *its* with *it's,* make sure that you mean *it is* or *it has* every time you write the word with an apostrophe. If, on the other hand, you intend to show possession (*its collar, its film series*), leave out the apostrophe.

Whose vs. *Who's*

Another commonly confused pair, *whose* and *who's,* follows the same principle. *Whose* is the possessive form of the pronoun *who* and never includes an apostrophe:

- This is the woman **whose** Porsche I bought.
- **Whose** porridge did you eat?

Who's is a contraction meaning *who is* or *who has:*

- I am the lucky person **who's** driving the Porsche.
- **Who's** been eating my porridge?

Other Possessive Pronouns

Note that certain other possessive pronouns ending in *-s* are already possessive in meaning and should never include apostrophes.

DON'T	DO
x his'	• his
x her's, hers'	• hers
x our's, ours'	• ours
x your's, yours'	• yours
x their's, theirs'	• theirs

32I Add *-'s* to form the possessive of a singular noun, as in *the computer's power.*

- farm's
- Bill's
- Hayakawa's

poss
32I

Follow the rule even if the singular noun ends with an *-s* sound:

- horse's
- bus's
- quiz's

- Les's
- Jones's
- Keats's

Exception for Certain Names

In names of more than one syllable, the *-s* after the apostrophe is optional when it might not be pronounced.

PRONOUNCED -*S*	UNPRONOUNCED -*S*
Dickens's	Dickens'
Berlioz's	Berlioz'
Demosthenes's	Demosthenes'

Whichever of these practices you follow, make sure you keep to it throughout a given piece of writing.

32m Watch for certain unusual singular possessives.

Where an added -*s* would make for three closely bunched -*s* sounds, use the apostrophe alone:

- Moses'
- Ulysses'
- Jesus'

Note also that in certain fixed expressions (*for ——— sake*), the possessive -*s* after a final -*s* sound is missing: *for goodness' sake, for conscience' sake, for righteousness' sake.* Some writers even drop the apostrophe from such phrases. But note the *'s* in *for heaven's sake.*

32n Make most plural nouns possessive by adding an apostrophe alone, as in *the elephants' stampede.*

poss
32o

- several **days'** work
- the **Americans'** views
- the **Stuarts'** reigns
- the **Beatles'** influence

32o If a plural noun does not end in -*s*, add -*'s* to form the possessive.

- the **children's** room
- those **deer's** habitat
- the **mice's** tracks
- the **alumni's** representative

32p In "joint ownership" possessives like *Simon and Garfunkel's music,* give the possessive form only to the final name.

When two or more words are "joint possessors," make only the last one possessive:

- Laurel and **Hardy's** comedies
- John, Paul, George, and **Ringo's** movie
- Sally and **Vic's** restaurant

But give the possessive form to each party if different things are "owned":

- **John's, Paul's, George's,** and **Ringo's** personal attorneys once met to see if the Beatles could be kept from splitting up.

32q In a phrase like *my father-in-law's car,* add *-'s* to the last of the hyphenated elements.

- the mayor-**elect's** assistant
- a Johnny-come-**lately's** arrogance

32r To avoid an awkward possessive, use the *of* construction.

poss
32r

DON'T:

x the **revised and expanded edition's** index

DO:

- the index **of the revised and expanded edition**

Wherever an *-'s* possessive sounds awkward, consider shifting to the *of* form. Suppose, for example, your "possessing" term or your "possessed" one is preceded by several modifiers. You can get rid of the bunched effect by resorting to *of.*

A possessive form following a word in quotation marks may sound all right but look awkward on the page. Again, prefer the *of* construction.

DON'T:

x **"La Bamba"'s** insistent rhythm

DO:

• the insistent rhythm **of "La Bamba"**

Watch, too, for an unnatural separation of the *-'s* from the word it belongs with.

DON'T:

x **the house on the corner's** roof

DO:

• the roof **of the house on the corner**

Finally, nouns for inanimate (nonliving) things often make awkward possessives.

DON'T:

x **the page's** bottom
x **social chaos's** outcome

DO:

• the bottom **of the page**
• the outcome **of social chaos**

poss
32s

32s   Notice which indefinite pronouns use *of* to form the possessive.

Some indefinite pronouns (p. 243, 19k) form the possessive in the same manner as nouns: *another's, nobody's, one's.* But others can be made possessive only with *of:*

	all	each	most	some
of	any	few	much	such
	both	many	several	

DON'T:

x I have two friends in Seattle. I can give you **each's** address.

DO:

• I have two friends in Seattle. I can give you the address **of each.**

32t   Learn the other uses of the apostrophe.

Contractions

Use an apostrophe to join two words in a contraction:

did not	didn't
have not	haven't
can not, cannot	can't
she will	she'll
we will	we'll
they are	they're
he is	he's
he has	he's
you have	you've

poss
32t

Beware of placing the apostrophe at the end of the first word instead of at the point where the omission occurs.

DON'T:

x He **did'nt** have a chance.

x They **have'nt** done a thing to deserve such punishment.

DO:

• He **didn't** have a chance.

• They **haven't** done a thing to deserve such punishment.

Omission of Digits

Use an apostrophe to mark the omission of one or more digits of a number, particularly of a year: *the summer of '88*. In dates expressing a span of time, however, drop the apostrophe: *1847-63*. And omit the apostrophe when you are shortening page numbers: *pp. 267-91*.

Certain Past-Tense and Passive Forms and Past Participles

Use an apostrophe to form the past tense or past participle of a verb derived from an abbreviation or a name:

- Martinez was **KO'd** in the twelfth round.
- They **Disney'd** the old amusement park beyond recognition.

"Possessives" Indicating Duration

- an **hour's** wait
- five **years'** worth of wasted effort

poss
32t

33 Spelling

If spelling causes you trouble, you can attack the problem on two fronts, memorizing the right spellings of single words and learning rules that apply to whole classes of words. We cover both strategies below.

If there is one key to better spelling, it is the habit of consulting a college dictionary whenever you are in doubt (p. 175, 14a). You need not pick up the dictionary until you have completed a draft, but you should check your final copy carefully for both habitual misspellings and typing errors.

For the role of hyphenation in spelling, see the following chapter. For the use of a spelling checker with a word processor, see page 584, 44c.

TROUBLESOME WORDS

33a   Keep a spelling list.

Keep an ongoing spelling list, including not only the words you have already misspelled in your essays but also words whose spelling in published sources looks odd to you. To begin that list, review the "words that look or sound alike" (pp. 398–399) and the "commonly misspelled words" (pp. 400–403) later in this chapter.

The most serious misspellings are not those that would eliminate you from the finals of a spelling contest but slips with ordinary words. If you regularly make such slips, you may not be able to cure them simply by noting the correct versions. You will need to jog your memory with a special reminder. Try a three-column spelling list, using the middle column to show how the real word differs from the misspelling.

MISSPELLING	REMEMBER	CORRECT SPELLING
x (seperate)	not like *desperate*	• separate
x (alot)	one word is not *a lot*	• a lot
x (hypocracy)	not like *democracy*	• hypocrisy
x (heighth)	get the *h* out of here!	• height
x (concieve)	*i* before *e* except after *c*	• conceive
x (wierd)	a *weird* exception to *i* before *e*	• weird
x (mispell)	don't *miss* this one!	• misspell
x (fiting)	doesn't sound like *fighting*	• fitting
x (beautyful)	*y* misspell it?	• beautiful
x goverment)	*govern* + *ment*	• government
x (complection)	*x* marks the spots	• complexion
x (enviroment)	*n* for *nature*	• environment

33b Note how spelling differs among English-speaking countries.

Many words that are correctly spelled in British English are considered wrong in American English. Canadian English resembles British in most but not all features. Study the following differences, which are typical.

sp
33b

AMERICAN	CANADIAN	BRITISH
center	centre	centre
flavor	flavour	flavour
pretense	pretence	pretence
realize	realize	realise
traveler	traveller	traveller

33c   Beware of words that look or sound alike.

Review the following list of easily confused words, all of which are
discussed in the Index of Usage beginning on page 585.

accept	cite	it's
except	sight	its
adapt	site	lead
adopt	coarse	led
advice	course	loose
advise	complement	lose
affect	compliment	moral
effect	council	morale
all ready	counsel	passed
already	desert	past
all together	dessert	personal
altogether	device	personnel
allusion	devise	precede
illusion	elicit	proceed
ante-	illicit	predominant
anti-	eminent	predominate
bare	imminent	prejudice
bear	every day	prejudiced
beside	everyday	principal
besides	every one	principle
breadth	everyone	prophecy
breath	fair	prophesy
breathe	fare	rain
buy	faze	rein
by	phase	reign
capital	foreword	some time
capitol	forward	sometime

sp
33c

stationary	to	who's
stationery	too	whose
than	two	your
then	weather	you're
their	whether	
there		
they're		

33d   Check the spelling of words with unusual pronunciation.

Words Having Silent Letters

- column
- mortgage

- sword
- Wednesday

Words Having Letters Unpronounced by Some Speakers

- environment
- government
- pumpkin

- recognize
- strength
- withdrawal

Words Frequently Mispronounced

1. Added or erroneous sound:

   - athlete   x (not athalete)
   - escape   x (not excape)
   - height   x (not heighth)
   - memento   x (not momento)
   - pejorative   x (not perjorative)
   - realtor   x (not realator)
   - wintry   x (not wintery)

sp
33d

2. Sound sometimes left unpronounced:

- arc̲tic
- can̲didate
- probab̲ly
- quant̲ity
- soph̲omore

- sur̲prise
- temper̲ament
- temper̲ature
- vet̲eran

3. Sounds sometimes wrongly reversed:

- jewelry   x (not jewl̲ery)
- modern   x (not modr̲en)
- nuclear   x (not nucul̲ar)
- perform   x (not pr̲eform)
- perspiration   x (not pr̲espiration)
- professor   x (not per̲fessor)

33e Review other commonly misspelled words.

A good way to begin your private spelling list (p. 396, 33a) is to look through the following commonly misspelled words, along with those already mentioned above, and pick out the ones that trouble you.

sp
33e

absence	aggressive	appreciation
accidentally	allege	aquatic
accommodate	all right	argument
acknowledgment	a lot	assassin
across	altogether	assassination
actually	always	assistance
address	analysis	assistant
adolescence	analyze	attendance
adolescent	anesthesia	
aggravate	annihilate	bachelor
aggravated	apparent	balloon
aggravating	appearance	beggar
aggression	appreciate	benefit

benefited
besiege
bigoted
bureau
bureaucracy
bureaucratic
burglar
bus

cafeteria
calendar
camouflage
category
ceiling
cemetery
changeable
commit
commitment
committee
competent
concomitant
conscience
conscious
consensus
consistency
consistent
consummate
control
controlled
controlling
controversy
convenience
convenient
coolly
corollary
correlate
correspondence
corroborate

counterfeit
criticism
criticize

decathlon
deceive
defendant
defense
definite
definitely
deity
dependent
desirable
despair
desperate
desperation
destroy
develop
development
diarrhea
dilapidated
dilemma
disastrous
discipline
dispensable
divide
divine
drunkenness
duly

ecstasy
eighth
emanate
embarrass
equip
equipment
equipped
evenness
exaggerate

exceed
excellence
excellent
exercise
exhilarate
existence
exorbitant
expel
extraordinary

fallacy
familiar
fascinate
fascist
February
fiend
fiery
finally
forehead
foresee
foreseeable
forfeit
forty
fourth
friend
fulfill
fulsome
futilely

gases
gauge
glamorous
glamour
grammar
grammatically
greenness
grievance
grievous
gruesome

sp
33e

guarantee
guard

handkerchief
harangue
harass
heroes
hindrance
hoping

idiosyncrasy
imagery
immediate
impel
inadvertent
incidentally
incredible
independence
independent
indestructible
indispensable
infinitely
innuendo
inoculate
interrupt
irrelevant
irreparable
irreparably
irreplaceable
irreplaceably
irresistible
irresistibly

jeopardy
judgment

knowledge
knowledgeably

laboratory
legitimate
leisure
length
library
license
loneliness
lying

maintenance
maneuver
manual
marriage
marshal
marshaled
marshaling
mathematics
medicine
mimic
mimicked
mischief
mischievous
missile
more so

naive
necessary
nickel
niece
noncommittal
noticeable
noticing

occasion
occur
occurred
occurrence
occurring
omission

omit
omitted
omitting
opportunity
optimist
optimistic

paid
pajamas
parallel
paralleled
paralysis
paralyze
parliament
pastime
perceive
perennial
perfectibility
perfectible
permanent
permissible
phony
physical
physician
picnic
picnicked
picnicking
playwright
pleasant
pleasurable
possess
possession
practically
practice
prairie
privilege
probably
pronunciation

sp
33e

propaganda
propagate
psychiatry
psychology
pursue
pursuit
putrefy

quizzes

rarefied
realize
receipt
receive
recipe
recognizable
recommend
refer
referred
referring
regretted
regretting
relevance
relevant
relieve
remembrance
reminisce
reminiscence
repellent
repentance
repetition
resistance
restaurant
rhythm
ridiculous
roommate

sacrilegious
said

schedule
secretary
seize
sergeant
sheriff
shining
shriek
siege
significance
similar
smooth
solely
soliloquy
sovereign
sovereignty
specimen
sponsor
stupefy
subtlety
subtly
succeed
success
succumb
suffrage
superintendent
supersede
suppress
surprise
symmetry
sympathize

tariff
tendency
terrific
than
therefore
thinness
thorough

threshold
through
traffic
trafficked
trafficking
tranquil
tranquillity
transcendent
transcendental
transfer
transferred
transferring
tried
tries
truly

unconscious
unmistakable
unmistakably
unnecessary
unshakable
unwieldy

vacillate
vacuum
vegetable
vengeance
venomous
vice
vilification
vilify
villain

wield
withhold
woeful
worldly
writing

yield

sp
33e

SPELLING RULES

33f Note how words change their spelling when certain suffixes are added to them.

A **suffix** is one or more letters that can be added at the end of a word to make a new word (*-ship, -ness,* etc.) or a new form of the same word (*-ed, -ing,* etc.). Since many spelling mistakes are caused by uncertainty over whether and how the root word changes when the suffix is tacked on, you should go over the following rules. (If a rule is hard to follow, you can get the point by studying the sample words that accompany it.)

1. **Beauty→Beautiful.** Change a final *-y* preceded by a consonant to *-i* when adding suffixes other than *-ing.*

easy	easily
happy	happier, happiest
hurry	hurries
imply	implies
ordinary	ordinarily
salty	saltier
tyranny	tyrannical
ugly	ugliness

2. **Hurry→Hurrying.** Do not drop the final *-y* of a word adding *-ing.*

embody	embodying
gratify	gratifying
study	studying

3. **Desire→Desirable.** When adding a suffix that begins with a vowel, usually drop a final *-e.*

drive	driving
future	futuristic
hope	hoping

impulse	impulsive
mate	mating
sincere	sincerity
suicide	suicidal

Exceptions: In words ending in *-ce* or *-ge,* retain the "s" or "j" pronunciation by keeping the *-e* before a suffix that begins with *a* or *o.*

notice	noticeable
peace	peaceable
courage	courageous
manage	manageable

And note two further exceptions:

| acre | acreage |
| mile | mileage |

4. **Advance→Advancement.** Usually keep the final *-e* of a word when adding a suffix that begins with a consonant.

precise	precisely
safe	safely
tame	tameness

Exceptions: Look out for a few words that drop the *-e* before adding a suffix beginning with a consonant.

argue	argument
judge	judgment (in American English)
nine	ninth
true	truly

5. **Beg→Begging.** In a one-syllable word having a final consonant that is preceded by a single vowel, double the consonant before adding a suffix beginning with a vowel.

sp
33f

chop	cho**pp**er
clip	cli**pp**ed
fun	fu**nn**ier
thin	thi**nn**est

6. In a word of more than one syllable having a final consonant that is preceded by a single vowel, follow these suffix rules.

   a. **Prefer→Preferring.** If the word is accented on its last syllable, double the consonant before adding a suffix that begins with a vowel.

begín	begi**nn**ing
contról	contro**ll**ed
detér	dete**rr**ent
occúr	occu**rr**ence
regrét	regre**tt**able

   b. **Differ→Difference.** If the accent does not fall on the last syllable, do not double the final consonant.

ópen	ope**n**er
shórten	shorte**n**ed
stámmer	stamme**r**ing
trável	trave**l**er (in American English)

   c. **Prefer→Preference.** If, when you add the suffix, the accent shifts to an earlier syllable, do not double the final consonant.

confér	co**n**ference
infér	i**n**ference
refér	ré**f**erence

33g Remember the old jingle for *ie/ei.*

i before *e*	(achieve, believe, friend, grieve)
except after *c*	(ceiling, deceive, receive)

or when sounded like *a*
as in *neighbor* and *weigh*   (freight, neighbor, vein, weigh)

Exceptions:

ancient	feisty	science
conscience	foreign	seize
efficient	leisure	weird

33h Overcome the confusion between *-cede, -ceed,* and *-sede.*

accede
concede
intercede   }   Several words end in *-cede.*
precede
recede
secede

exceed
proceed   }   Only three words end in *-ceed.*
succeed

supersede   This is the only word that ends in *-sede.*

34 Hyphenation

34a Observe the conventions for dividing words at line endings.

In a manuscript or typescript, where right-hand margins are normally uneven, you can avoid breaking words at line endings. Just finish each line with the last word you can complete. A word processing program (Chapter 44) will do this for you automatically unless you specify otherwise.

When you do choose to hyphenate, follow these conventions:

1. Divide words at syllable breaks as marked in your dictionary. Spaces or heavy dots between parts of a word indicate such breaks: *en•cy•clo•pe•di•a.*

2. Never divide a one-syllable word, even if you might manage to pronounce it as two syllables (*rhythm, schism*).

3. Do not leave one letter stranded at the end of a line (*o-ver, i-dea*), and do not leave a solitary letter for the beginning of the next line (*Ontari-o, seed-y*).

4. If possible, avoid hyphenating the last word on a page.

5. If a word is already hyphenated, divide it only at the fixed hyphen. Avoid x *self-con-scious, ex-pre-mier.*

6. You can anticipate what your dictionary will say about word division by remembering that:

    a. Double consonants are usually separated: *ar-rogant, sup-ply.*

    b. When a word has acquired a double consonant through the adding of a suffix, the second consonant belongs to the suffix: *bet-ting, fad-dish.*

c. When the root of a word with a suffix has a double consonant, the break follows both consonants: *stall-ing, kiss-able.*

34b In terms like *ex-student,* use a hyphen to separate the prefix from the root word.

A **prefix** is a letter or a group of letters that can be placed *before* a root word to make a new word. (Compare **suffix,** p. 404, 33f.) Dictionaries do not always agree with each other about hyphenation after a prefix, but the following guidelines will enable you to be consistent in your practice.

All-, Ex-, Self-

Words beginning with *all-, ex-,* and *self-,* when these are prefixes, are hyphenated after the prefix:

- all-powerful
- ex-minister
- self-motivated

Note that in words like *selfhood, selfish, selfless,* and *selfsame,* the accented syllable *self* is not a true prefix; no hyphen is called for.

Prefixes with Names

Prefixes before a name are always hyphenated:

hyph
34b

- pre-Whitman
- un-American
- anti-Russian

Words like Anti-Intellectual and Preempt

Prefixes ending with a vowel usually take a hyphen if that same vowel comes next or if a different following letter would make for an awkward or misleading combination:

- anti-intellectual
- semi-independent
- pro-organic
- co-worker

But prefixed terms that are very common are less likely to be misconstrued, and many double vowels remain unhyphenated:

- cooperate
- coordinate
- preempt
- reentry

Some dictionaries recommend a dieresis mark over the second vowel to show that it is separately pronounced: *reëntry*. In contemporary prose, however, you will not come across many instances of the dieresis.

Constructions like <u>Post-Heart Surgery</u>

When a prefix applies to two or more words, attach it to the first one with a hyphen:

- a **pre-**aurora borealis phenomenon
- the **anti-**status quo faction

Constructions like <u>Pre- and Postwar</u>

When a modifier contains compound prefixes, the first prefix usually stands alone with a hyphen, whether or not it would take a hyphen when joined directly to the root word.

hyph
34c

- There was quite a difference between **pre-** and postwar prices.
- **Pro-** and antifascist students battled openly in the streets of Rome.

34c Follow your dictionary in deciding whether to hyphenate words like *bull's-eye* and *skydive*.

Many compound words (formed from more than one word) are hyphenated in most dictionaries: *bull's-eye, secretary-treasurer, spring-cleaning, water-ski* (verb only), and so forth. Many others, however, are usually written as separate words (*fire fighter, head start, ice cream, oil spill,* etc.) or as single unhyphenated words (*earring, scofflaw, scoutmaster, skydive,* etc.). To make matters more confusing, practice is always in flux; as compound terms become more familiar, they tend to lose their hyphens. All you can do, then, is to be alert to the compound words you see in print and consult an up-to-date dictionary whenever you are in doubt.

34d Study the guidelines for hyphenating compound modifiers.

Compound modifiers (containing more than one word) such as *light-sensitive* and *secondhand* pose especially tricky problems of hyphenation. The rules (below) are hard to remember and are not always observed by otherwise careful writers. You will often have to call on your assessment of the case at hand. If an expression would be ambiguous (uncertain in meaning) without a hyphen, include it; but omit the hyphen if you see that your reader can get along without it.

Before Modified Term: a Well-Trained Philosopher

A compound modifier is usually hyphenated if it meets two conditions:

1. it comes before the term it modifies; and

2. its first element is itself a modifier.

These two conditions are met in the following examples:

> MOD
- a **short-tempered** umpire
> MOD
- some **deep-ocean** drilling
> MOD
- **nineteenth-century** art
> MOD
- an **out-of-work** barber

hyph
34d

In such phrases the hyphens sometimes prevent confusion. Consider what would happen, for example, if you wrote:

- a short tempered umpire
- some deep ocean drilling

Is the umpire short in stature but tempered in judgment? Is it the drilling rather than the ocean that is deep? When hyphens are added, a reader can see at once that *short* is part of the compound modifier *short-tempered* and that *deep* is part of the compound modifier *deep-ocean.* In such a case the hyphen tells us not to take the next word to be the modified term.

If the first word in a compound modifier is a noun, as in *school program administrator,* do not put a hyphen after it. A noun generally runs a low risk of being mistaken for a modifier of the next word. The following phrases are correct:

MOD
- the **ocean salinity** level

MOD
- a **barbecue sauce** cookbook

MOD
- a **mercury vapor** lamp

But do use a hyphen if the initial noun is followed by a modifier:

MOD
- a **picture-perfect** landing

MOD
- that **time-honored** principle

> Here the hyphens are needed to show that the initial noun does not stand alone; it is part of a compound modifier.

hyph
34d

Even when the first part of a compound modifier is itself a modifier, leave it unhyphenated if it forms a familiar pair with the following word and if there is no danger of confusion:

MOD
- the **Modern Language** Association

MOD
- an **electric typewriter** store

MOD
- the **happy birthday** card

After Modified Term: A Philosopher Well Trained in Logic

When a compound modifier *follows* the modified term, the hyphen usually disappears:

- A barber **out of work** resents people who cut their own hair.

Modifiers like Barely Suppressed

When a compound modifier contains an adverb in the *-ly* form, it does not have to be hyphenated in any position. There is no danger of ambiguity, since the adverb, clearly identifiable *as* an adverb, can only modify the next word:

- a **barely suppressed** gasp
- an **openly polygamous** chieftain
- a **hypocritically worded** apology

Modifiers like Fast-Developing

Adverbs lacking the *-ly* form do run the risk of ambiguity. Whether they come before or after the modified term, you should always hyphenate them:

- a **fast-developing** crisis
- a **close-cropped** head of hair
- The traffic was **slow-moving.**

hyph
34d

Modifiers with Fixed Hyphens

If you find that a modifier is hyphenated in the dictionary, keep it hyphenated wherever it occurs:

- She was an **even-tempered** instructor.
- She was **even-tempered.**

34e Study the guidelines for hyphenating numbers

Numbers Twenty-One to Ninety-Nine

Always hyphenate these numbers, even when they form part of a larger number:

- Two hundred **seventy-five** years ago, religious toleration was almost unknown.

Number as Part of a Modifier

If the number and the term it modifies work together as a modifier, place a hyphen after the number:

- A **twelve-yard** pool is hardly long enough for swimming.

Noun Formed from a Number

Hyphenate all such nouns:

- Two **eighty-year-olds** were sitting on the bench.
- Three **sixty-five-year-olds** were standing nearby.

Fractions

Hyphenate all fractions, regardless of whether or not they serve as modifiers.

hyph
34e

AS MODIFIER:
- The luggage compartment was **five-eighths** full.

NOT AS MODIFIER:
- **Five-eighths** of the space had already been taken.

  In the first sentence, *five-eighths* modifies the adjective *full*. In the second, *five-eighths* is the subject of the verb.

34f Use a hyphen to connect numbers expressing a range, as in *1993–99*.

- pages 37–49 [the pages 37 through and including 49]
- March 9–May 3 [from March 9 through May 3]
- 1861–65 [from 1861 through 1865]

35 Capitals

35a Capitalize the first letter of every sentence or intentional sentence fragment.

- **She** will need help when she moves.
- **Count** on me.
- **Will** you be able to come over on Sunday?
- **With** pleasure!

35b Learn when to capitalize within a quotation.

First Letter of the Quotation

Capitalize the first letter of a quotation if (1) it begins your own sentence, (2) it begins the sentence of a speaker or thinker whose words you are representing, (3) it is capitalized in the original and it doesn't help to complete a clause or phrase of your own, or (4) it is a customary capital beginning a line of poetry.

BEGINNING OF THE WRITER'S OWN SENTENCE:
- **"When** to stop" is the crucial lesson a dieter must learn.

BEGINNING OF A SPEAKER'S OR THINKER'S SENTENCE:
- Leslie told Mark, **"After** you dismantle the stereo, bring the truck around to the back."
- Mark thought, **"Let's** hope she saved the original packing boxes."

CAPITALIZED IN THE ORIGINAL:
- As Ben Jonson remarked, **"Talking** and eloquence are not the same: to speak, and to speak well, are two things."

Notice how the sentence from Ben Johnson stands apart from the language introducing it. But when a passage beginning with a capital letter does help to complete a clause or phrase of your own, change the capital to lowercase:

- Ben Johnson believed that "**talking** and eloquence are not the same: to speak, and to speak well, are two things."

    Here, *talking* is part of the quoter's subordinate clause (p. 213, 17c) already under way, *that talking and eloquence are not the same.*

INITIAL CAPITAL IN LINE OF POETRY:
- One would have thought, writes Spenser, that nature had imitated "**Art,** and that Art at nature did repine."

    Here, although the quotation helps to complete the quoter's own clause (*that nature had imitated art*), the capital *A* is retained because it begins a poetic line.

Significant Capital in the Quoted Passage

- Spenser fancies that "**Art** at nature did repine."

    Even though this *Art* is not the first word in the line of poetry, its capitalization seems to be important in the original passage and thus is retained.

35c Learn when to capitalize after a colon.

cap
35c

As a rule, leave the next letter after a colon uncapitalized.

UNCAPITALIZED:
- Home was never like this: **twenty-four** roommates and a day starting at 5:00 A.M.
- I finally understood how the Air Force makes a pilot of you: **after** the crowded barracks, every cadet yearns for the solitude of flight.

CAPITALS

Do use a capital letter, however, if (1) you are quoting a passage that begins with such a letter, (2) you want to make an especially formal effect, or (3) the element following your colon consists of more than one sentence.

CAPITALIZED:
- At Antony's death, Cleopatra speaks her unforgettable lament: "**And** there is nothing left remarkable / Beneath the visiting moon."
- The sign at the gate left no room for misunderstanding: **Trespassers** would be shot.
- Jacqueline was left with two nagging questions: **To** whom could she turn for help? And would anyone believe her story?

35d Capitalize the first word of a sentence in parentheses only if the parenthetic sentence stands between complete sentences.

CAPITALIZED:
- In the Air Force we learned to fly. (**We** also learned a good deal about life on the ground.) I would not have traded the experience for any other.

UNCAPITALIZED:
- Life in the Air Force (**the** Army and Navy never attracted me) was just what the doctor ordered for a lazy, smart-aleck eighteen-year-old.

35e Capitalize the first, the last, and all other important words in a title or subtitle.

If an article, a coordinating conjunction, or a preposition does not occur in the first or last position, leave it in lowercase:

- *On **the** Banks of Plum Creek*
- *The Power **and the** Glory*
- "On **a** Landscape **by** Li Ch'eng"

Do capitalize the first letter of a subtitle:

- *In Black and White:* **The** *Graphics of Charles Tomlinson*
- "Suburbia: **Of** Thee I Sing"

35f Capitalize both parts of most hyphenated terms in a title.

The Modern Language Association recommends that you capitalize both parts of a hyphenated term in a title:

- ***Fail-Safe***
- *Through the **Looking-Glass***
- ***Self-Consuming** Artifacts*

When an obviously minor element is included in a hyphenated term, however, leave it uncapitalized:

- "A Guide to Over-**the**-Counter Medications"

35g Capitalize the name of a person, place, business, or organization.

- Joyce Carol Oates
- Western Hemisphere
- New Canaan, Connecticut
- Lifeboat Associates
- Canadian Broadcasting Corporation
- Xerox Corporation

cap
35h

35h Capitalize an adjective derived from a name.

- Shakespearean
- Malthusian
- the French language
- Roman numerals

But note the use of lowercase in *roman type* and *french fries.*

35i Capitalize a word like *father* only if you are using it as a name or part of a name.

NAME OR PART OF NAME (CAPITALIZED):
- Everyone has seen posters of **Uncle** Sam.
- Oh, **Mother,** I miss you!

NOT PART OF NAME (UNCAPITALIZED):
- My **uncle** Sam bought me my first baseball mitt.
- I cabled my **mother** when I reached Athens.

35j Capitalize a rank or title only when it is joined to a name or when it stands for a specific person.

CAPITALIZED:
- **General** Norman Schwarzkopf
- The **Colonel** was promoted in 1983.

UNCAPITALIZED:
- Two **generals** and a **colonel** attended the parade.
- She was elected **mayor** in 1989.

---

cap
35k

35k Capitalize the name of a specific institution or its formal subdivision, but not of an unspecified institution.

When you are designating a particular school or museum, or one of its departments, use capitals:

- Museum of Modern Art
- University of Chicago
- the Department of Business Administration
- Franklin High School

Subsequent, shortened references to the institution or department are sometimes left uncapitalized:

- She retired from the **university** last year.

    But *University* would also be correct here.

Do not capitalize a name that identifies only the *type* of institution you have in mind:

- a strife-torn **museum**
- Every **university** must rely on contributions.
- She attends **high school** in the daytime and **ballet school** after dinner.

35l Capitalize a specific course of study but not a general branch of learning.

CAPITALIZED:
- **Physics** 1A
- **Computer Science** 142B

UNCAPITALIZED:
- He never learned the rudiments of **physics.**
- Her training in **computer science** won her a job as a programmer.

35m Capitalize a sacred name but not a secular word derived from it.

cap
35m

Whether or not you are a believer, use capitals for the names of deities, revered figures, and holy books:

- the **Bible**
- **God**
- the **Lord**
- **Allah**

- the **Virgin Mary**
- **Buddha**
- the **Gospels**
- the **Koran**

But do not capitalize a secular word derived from a sacred name:

- **biblical** tones
- a **godlike** grandeur
- her **scriptural** authority
- the **gospel** of getting ahead

The pronouns *he* and *him,* when referring to the Judeo-Christian deity, have traditionally been capitalized, but this practice is less common today. You can consider it optional.

35n Capitalize the name of a historical event, movement, or period.

- the **Civil War**
- the **Depression**
- the **Romantic** poets
- the **Bronze Age**
- the **Roaring Twenties**

Note that *the* is uncapitalized in these examples.

35o Capitalize a day of the week, a month, or a holiday but not a season or the numerical part of a date.

cap
35o

CAPITALIZED:
- next **Tuesday**
- **May** 1988
- **Christmas**
- **Passover**
- **Columbus Day**

UNCAPITALIZED:
- next **fall**
- a **winter** storm
- July **twenty-first**
- the **third** of August

35p Capitalize the name of a group or nationality but not of a looser grouping.

CAPITALIZED:

- **Moslem**
- **Hungarian**
- **Friends** of the **Earth**

UNCAPITALIZED:

- the **upper class**
- the **underprivileged**
- **environmentalists**

35q Capitalize a word like *south* only if you are using it as a place name.

CAPITALIZED:

- **Northwest** Passage
- **Southeast** Asia
- The **South** and the **Midwest** will be crucial in the election.

UNCAPITALIZED:

- **northwest** of here
- Go **west** for two miles and then turn **south.**

cap
35r

35r Reproduce a foreign word or title as you find it in the original language.

- *Märchen* [Ger.: fairy tale]
- *una cubana* [Sp.: a Cuban woman]
- *La terre* [title of a French novel: *The Earth*]

36 Italics, Abbreviations, Numbers

ITALICS

Ordinary typeface is known as **roman,** and the thin, slightly slanted typeface that contrasts with it is **italic**—as in *these three words*. In manuscript or typescript, "italics" are indicated by underlining, although with a word processor and an appropriate printer, you can make direct use of italics.

MANUSCRIPT:

● *The Great Gatsby*

TYPESCRIPT:

● The Great Gatsby

PRINT OR WORD PROCESSOR:

● *The Great Gatsby*

36a Learn which kinds of titles belong in italics.

ITALICS:

The Color Purple	[book]
Paradise Lost	[book-length poem]
Waiting for Godot	[play]

Dances with Wolves	[film]
New York Times	[newspaper]
Popular Mechanics	[magazine]
Abused Children	[pamphlet]
The Firebird	[long musical work]
Meet the Beatles	[record album]
Jazz Matinee	[radio series]
Northern Exposure	[television series]
Van Gogh's *Starry Night*	[painting]
Rodin's *Adam*	[sculpture]
Quicken 1.5	[computer software]

QUOTATION MARKS:

"Araby"	[short story]
"To Autumn"	[poem]
"Search for Columbus"	[article]
"Magic and Paraphysics"	[chapter of a book]
"Satin Doll"	[song]

Note the following special conditions:

1. In the name of a newspaper, include the place of publication in the italicized title:

    - She read it in the *Philadelphia Inquirer.*

    ital
    36a

    The article preceding the place name is usually not italicized (or capitalized).

2. The title of a poem, story, or chapter may also be the title of the whole volume in which that smaller unit is found. Use italics only when you mean to designate the whole volume:

    - "The Magic Barrel" [Bernard Malamud's short story]
    - *The Magic Barrel* [the book in which Malamud's story was eventually republished]

3. Some publications, especially newspapers, use italics sparingly or not at all. If you are writing for a specific publication, follow its style. If not, observe the rules given here.

4. Do not italicize or use quotation marks around sacred works and their divisions.

   DO:
   - The Talmud
   - the Vedas
   - the Book of the Dead
   - the Bible
   - the New Testament
   - Leviticus

5. When one title contains another title that would normally be italicized, make the embedded title roman. That is, you should not underline it.

   - She was reading *The Senses of* Walden to get ideas for her paper.

36b Italicize a foreign term that has not yet been adopted as a common English expression.

STILL "FOREIGN" (ITALICIZE):
- *la dolce vita*
- *sine qua non*
- *La Belle Époque*
- *Schadenfreude*

ital
36b

FAMILIAR IN ENGLISH (DO NOT ITALICIZE):
- ad hoc
- blitzkrieg
- cliché
- de facto
- guru
- junta
- status quo
- sushi

Latin Abbreviations

Latin abbreviations are often italicized, but the tendency is now to leave them in roman. For example, according to the general practice these may be left in roman:

| cf. | et al. | i.e. | viz. |
| e.g. | f., ff. | q.v. | vs. |

See pages 429–430, 36g, for the meanings of these and other abbreviations used in documentation.

Translating a Foreign Term

When translating into English, put the foreign term in italics and the English one in quotation marks:

- The Italian term for "the book" is *il libro;* the French term is *le livre.*

The Modern Language Association also allows a translation to be placed within single quotation marks without intervening punctuation:

- *ein wenig* 'a little'
- They called the Fiat 500 *Topolino* 'little mouse.'

36c Italicize the name of a ship, aircraft, or spacecraft.

- *Cristoforo Colombo*
- *Air Force One*
- *Voyager 2*

But do not italicize abbreviations such as *SS* or *HMS* preceding a ship's name:

- SS *Enterprise*

ital 36d

36d Use italics or quotation marks to show that you are treating a word *as* a word.

- When Frank and Edith visited the rebuilt neighborhoods of their youth, they understood the meaning of the word *gentrified.*

It would be equally correct to keep *gentrified* in roman type and enclose it in quotation marks: "gentrified."

36e To add emphasis to part of a quoted expression, italicize the key element.

If you want to emphasize one part of a quotation, put that part in italics. And to show that the italics are your own rather than the author's, follow the quotation with a parenthetical acknowledgment such as *emphasis added* or *emphasis mine:*

- The author writes mysteriously of a "*rival* system of waste management" (emphasis added).

36f Use italics sparingly to emphasize a key element in your own prose.

To distinguish one term from another or to lend a point rhetorical emphasis, you can italicize (underline) some of your own language:

No doubt she can explain where she was in the month of June. *But what about July?* This is the unresolved question.

Beware, however, of relying on emphatic italics to do the work that should be done by effective sentence structure and diction. Prose that is riddled with italics creates a frenzied effect.

DON'T:

x The hazard from *immediate radiation* is one issue—and a *very important* one. But the *long-term* effects from *improper waste storage* are *even more crucial,* and *practically nobody* within the industry seems to take it seriously.

This passage would inspire more confidence if it lacked italics altogether.

ABBREVIATIONS

36g Use abbreviations in parenthetic citations, notes, reference lists, and bibliographies.

For purposes of documentation (Chapters 39 and 40), you can use the following abbreviations.

ABBREVIATION	MEANING
anon.	anonymous
b.	born
bibliog.	bibliography
©	copyright
c. or ca.	about [with dates only]
cf.	compare [not *see*]
ch., chs.	chapter(s)
d.	died
diss.	dissertation
ed., eds.	editor(s), edition(s), edited by
e.g.	for example [not *that is*]
esp.	especially
et al.	and others [people only]
etc.	and so forth [not interchangeable with *et al.*)
f., ff.	and the following [page or pages]
ibid.	the same [title as the one mentioned in the previous note]
i.e.	that is [not *for example*]
introd.	introduction
l., ll.	line(s)
ms., mss.	manuscript(s)
n., nn.	note(s)
N.B.	mark well, take notice [*nota bene*]

ABBREVIATION	MEANING
n.d.	no date (in a book's imprint)
no., nos.	number(s)
p., pp.	page(s)
pl., pls.	plate(s)
pref.	preface
pt., pts.	part(s)
q.v.	see elsewhere in this text [literally *which see*]
rev.	revised, revision; review, reviewed by [beware of ambiguity between meanings; if necessary, write out instead of abbreviating]
rpt.	reprint
sc.	scene
sec., secs., sect., sects.	section(s)
ser.	series
st., sts.	stanza(s)
tr., trans.	translator, translation, translated by
v.	versus [legal citations]
viz.	namely
vol., vols.	volume(s)
vs.	versus [ordinary usage]

**abbr
36g**

Note that *passim,* meaning "throughout," and *sic,* meaning "thus," are not to be followed by a period; they are complete Latin words. For the function of *sic,* see page 362, 29r.

36h   Learn which abbreviations are allowable in your main text.

Allowed in Main Text

Some abbreviations are considered standard in any piece of writing, including the main body of an essay:

1. *Mr., Ms., Mrs., Dr., Messrs., Mme., Mlle., St.,* etc., when used before names. Some publications now refer to all women as *Ms.,* and this title has rapidly gained favor as a means of avoiding designation of marital status.

2. *Jr., Sr., Esq., M.D., D.D., D.D.S., M.A., Ph.D., LL.D.,* etc., when used after names: *Olivia Martinez, M.D.*

3. abbreviations of, and acronyms (words formed from the initial letters in multiword names) for, organizations that are widely known by the shorter name: CIA, FBI, ROTC, NOW, NAACP, EPA, IBM, and so on. Note that very familiar designations such as these are usually written without periods between the letters.

4. *B.C., A.D., A.M., P.M., mph.* These abbreviations should never be used apart from numbers (not x *I use the computer in the P.M.* but *I use the computer between 8 and 11 P.M.*). *B.C.* always follows the year, but *A.D.* usually precedes it: *252 B.C.,* but *A.D. 147.*

5. places commonly known by their abbreviations: *U.S., D.C.,* etc. One writes *in the U.S.,* not *in U.S.* Do not use *D.C.* alone as a place name: x She commutes into *D.C.* Prefer *Washington.*

**abbr
36h**

Inappropriate in Main Text

	DON'T	DO
1. titles	x the Rev., the Hon., Sen., Pres., Gen.	• the Reverend, the Honorable, Senator, President, General

	DON'T	DO
2. given names	x Geo., Eliz., Robt.	• George, Elizabeth, Robert
3. months, days of the week, and holidays	x Oct., Mon., Vets. Day	• October, Monday, Veterans Day
4. localities, cities, counties, states, provinces, and countries	x Pt. Reyes Natl. Seashore, Phila., Sta. Clara, N.M., Ont., N.Z.	• Point Reyes National Seashore, Philadelphia, Santa Clara, New Mexico, Ontario, New Zealand
5. roadways	x St., La., Ave., Blvd.	• Street, Lane, Avenue, Boulevard
6. courses of instruction	x Bot., PE	• Botany, Physical Education
7. units of measurement	x ft., kg, lbs., qt., hr., mos., yrs.	• feet, kilogram, pounds, quart, hour, months, years

Technical versus Nontechnical Prose

In general, you can do more abbreviating in technical than in nontechnical writing. See the following examples.

**abbr
36h**

TECHNICAL PROSE	OTHER PROSE
km	kilometer(s)
mg	milligram(s)
sq.	square

Even in general-interest prose, however, abbreviation of a much-used term can be a convenience. Give one full reference before relying on the abbreviation:

- Among its many services, the Harvard Student Agency (HSA) sponsors the *Let's Go* series of travel books for students. HSA also functions as a custodial agency, rents photographic equipment and linens, acts as an employment clearinghouse, and caters parties.

36i Be consistent in using either *A.M./P.M.* or *a.m./p.m.* to abbreviate the time of day.

Authorities disagree over A.M. and P.M. versus *a.m.* and *p.m.* Either form will do, but do not mix them.

DON'T:
x She was scheduled to arrive at 11 a.m., but we had to wait for her until 2 P.M.

DO:
- She was scheduled to arrive at 11 **a.m.,** but we had to wait for her until 2 **p.m.**

or
- She was scheduled to arrive at 11 A.M., but we had to wait for her until 2 P.M.

36j Learn which kinds of abbreviations can be written without periods.

abbr
36j

Good writers differ in their preference for periods or no periods within an abbreviation. Practice is shifting toward omission of periods. In general, you can feel safe in omitting periods from abbreviations written in capital letters, provided the abbreviation does not appear to spell out another word. Thus *USA* needs no periods but *U.S.* does, since otherwise it might be mistaken for a capitalization of the pronoun *us*. Other typical abbreviations without periods are the following:

- JFK
- USSR

- IOU
- NJ

Note that *N.J.,* with periods, is an option for abbreviating *New Jersey* but not for supplying a mail code before a ZIP number: *NJ 08540.*

But most abbreviations that end in a lowercase letter still require periods:

- Ont.
- Chi.

- Inc.
- i.e.

Note that there are commonly recognized exceptions such as *mph* and *rpm.* Also, abbreviations for metric measures are usually written without periods: *ml, kg,* etc.

36k   Leave single spaces between the initials of a name, but close up all other abbreviations and acronyms, including postal abbreviations for states.

SPACED:
- W. H. Auden
- E. F. Hutton

- B. B. King
- A. J. C. Ingram

UNSPACED:
- e.g.
- A.M. (or a.m.)

- Ph.D.
- CIA

**abbr
36k**

POSTAL ABBREVIATIONS FOR STATES

Alabama	AL	Montana	MT
Alaska	AK	Nebraska	NE
Arizona	AZ	Nevada	NV
Arkansas	AR	New Hampshire	NH
California	CA	New Jersey	NJ
Colorado	CO	New Mexico	NM
Connecticut	CT	New York	NY
Delaware	DE	North Carolina	NC
District of	DC	North Dakota	ND
Columbia		Ohio	OH
Florida	FL	Oklahoma	OK
Georgia	GA	Oregon	OR
Hawaii	HI	Pennsylvania	PA
Idaho	ID	Rhode Island	RI
Illinois	IL	South Carolina	SC
Indiana	IN	South Dakota	SD
Iowa	IA	Tennessee	TN
Kansas	KS	Texas	TX
Kentucky	KY	Utah	UT
Louisiana	LA	Vermont	VT
Maine	ME	Virginia	VA
Maryland	MD	Washington	WA
Massachusetts	MA	West Virginia	WV
Michigan	MI	Wisconsin	WI
Minnesota	MN	Wyoming	WY
Mississippi	MS		
Missouri	MO		

abbr
36k

NUMBERS AND FIGURES

36l Know which circumstances call for written-out numbers.

Technical versus Nontechnical Prose

In scientific and technical prose, figures (*67*) are preferred to written-out numbers (*sixty-seven*), though very large multiples such as *million, billion,* and *trillion* are written out. Newspapers customarily spell out only numbers *one* through *nine* and such round numbers as *two hundred* and *five million.* In your nontechnical writing, prefer written-out numbers for the whole numbers *one* through *ninety-nine* and for any of those numbers followed by *hundred, billion,* and so on.

TECHNICAL PROSE	NONTECHNICAL PROSE
3/4	three-quarters
4	four
93	ninety-three
202	202
1500 (or 1,500)	fifteen hundred
10,000	ten thousand
38 million	thirty-eight million
101 million	101 million
54 billion	forty-four billion
205 billion	205 billion

num
36l

Special Uses for Written-Out Numbers

1. In nontechnical prose, write out a concise number between one thousand and ten thousand that you can express in hundreds: not *1600* but *sixteen hundred.* This rule does not apply to dates, however.

2. Write out round (approximate) numbers that are even hundred thousands:

- Over six hundred thousand refugees arrived here last year.

3. Always write out a number that begins a sentence.

   - *Eighty-four* students scored above grade level.

     But if the number would not ordinarily be written out, you would usually do better to recast the sentence.

   - The results were less encouraging for *213* other takers of the test.

     It would have been awkward to begin the sentence with *Two hundred thirteen*

4. Write out a whole hour, unmodified by minutes, if it appears before *o'clock, noon,* or *midnight: one o'clock, twelve noon, twelve midnight.* Do not write *twelve-thirty o'clock* or *12:30 o'clock.*

Special Uses for Figures

1. Use figures with abbreviated units of measure:

   - 7 lbs
   - 11 g
   - 88 mm

2. If you have several numbers bunched together, use figures regardless of the amounts.

   - Harvey skipped his birthday celebrations at ages 21, 35, and 40.

3. When two or more related amounts call for different styles of representation, use figures for all of them:

   - The injured people included 101 women and 9 children.

num
36l

4. Use figures for all of the following:

   a. apartment numbers, house and building numbers, and ZIP codes:

   - Apt. 17C, 544 Lowell Ave., Palo Alto, CA 94301.

   b. tables of statistics.

   c. numbers containing decimal points: *7.456, $5.58, 52.1 percent.*

   d. dates (except in extremely formal communications such as wedding announcements): *October 25, 1989; 25 October 1989.*

   e. times, when they precede A.M. or P.M. (*a.m.* or *p.m.*): *8 A.M., 6 P.M., 2:47 P.M.*

   f. page numbers: *p. 47, pp. 341–53.*

   g. volumes (*vol. 2*), books of the Bible (*2 Corinthians*), and acts, scenes, and lines of plays (*Macbeth I.iii.89–104*).

36m   Use Roman numerals only where convention requires them.

In general, **Roman numerals** (*XI, LVIII*) have been falling into disuse as **Arabic numerals** (*11, 58*) have taken over their function. But note the following exceptions.

num
36m

1. In some citation styles, upper- and lowercase Roman numerals are still used in combination with Arabic numerals to show sets of numbers in combination. Thus *Hamlet III.ii.47* refers to line 47 in the second scene of the play's third act.

2. Use Roman numerals for the main divisions of a formal outline (p. 31, 3d).

3. Use lowercase Roman numerals to cite pages at the beginning of a book that are so numbered:

- (Preface v)
- (Introduction xvi-xviii)

4. Use Roman numerals as you find them in the names of monarchs, popes, same-named sons in the third generation, ships, and so forth:

- Louis XIV
- Pope John XXIII
- James J. Pendergast III
- *Queen Elizabeth II*

The following list reminds you how to form Roman numerals.

1 I	10 X	50 L	200 CC
2 II	11 XI	60 LX	400 CD
3 III	15 XV	70 LXX	499 CDXCIX
4 IV	19 XIX	80 LXXX	500 D
5 V	20 XX	90 XC	900 CM
6 VI	21 XXI	99 XCIX	999 CMXCIX
7 VII	29 XXIX	100 C	1000 M
8 VIII	30 XXX	110 CX	1500 MD
9 IX	40 XL	199 CXCIX	3000 MMM

36n Distinguish between the uses of cardinal and ordinal numbers

Numbers like *one, two,* and *three (1, 2, 3)* are called **cardinal numbers;** those like *first, second,* and *third (1st, 2d, 3d;* note the shortened spelling) are called **ordinal numbers.** The choice between cardinal and ordinal numbers is usually automatic, but there are several differences between spoken and written convention:

num.
36n

SPEECH	WRITING
Louis the Fourteenth	Louis XIV
July seventh, 1989	July 7, 1989 *or* 7 July 1989
But: July seventh [no year]	July 7th *or* July seventh

Note that the rules of choice between written-out numbers and figures are the same for cardinal as for ordinal numbers (36l).

Terms like *Firstly*

The word *firstly* is now rarely seen; *first* can serve as an adverb as well as an adjective.

ADJECTIVE:
• The *first* item on the agenda is the budget.

ADVERB:
• There are several items on the agenda. *First, . . .*

When you begin a list with *first,* you have the option of continuing either with *second, third,* or with *secondly, thirdly.* For consistency of effect, drop all the *-ly* forms:

• Let me say, *first,* that the crisis has passed. *Second,* I want to thank all of our employees for their extraordinary sacrifices. And *third, . . .*

But as soon as you write *secondly,* you have committed yourself to *thirdly, fourthly,* and so on.

Finally, beware of mixing cardinal and ordinal forms.

DON'T:

num
36n

x *One,* a career as a writer presents financial hardship. *Second,* I am not sure I have enough emotional stamina to face rejection. *Third, . . .*

For consistency, change *One* to *First.*

VIII
RESEARCH
PAPERS

Research Papers

When assigned a research paper, some students set aside what they know about writing essays and concentrate instead on showing how much library reading they have done. The result may be a paper crammed with references but lacking purpose and interest. Remember that a research paper is above all an essay-one that happens to be based in part on library materials. You should regard this section, then, not as a self-sufficient unit but as a supplement to Chapters 1–6, which you can review as necessary for advice about discovering a topic, forming a thesis, organizing and developing ideas, and revising to engage and sustain your reader's interest.

Keep in mind, however, that a research paper, because it involves library work, will require more time and planning than a regular essay. When undertaking such a paper, start early and develop a schedule that includes sufficient time for each step in the process:

STEPS IN WRITING A RESEARCH PAPER	STUDY THESE SECTIONS	REVIEW AS NEEDED
Tour your campus library.	37a	
Select a trial topic.	37b	1
Gather sources.	37c–f	
Take notes.	37g	
Develop a trial thesis and outline.	38a	2–3
Write the first draft.	38b	4
Revise the paper.	38c	5a–g
Prepare formal documentation.	38d, 39–40	
Type and proofread the final copy.	39c, 40c	5h

In making your plans, allow room for the detours and setbacks that are a normal part of writing any essay (p. 3, 1a). And be prepared whenever necessary to double back and rethink an earlier phase of your work.

37 Conducting Research

37a Get acquainted with the parts of your library.

Perhaps your college library strikes you as mysterious or even vaguely threatening. If so, bear in mind that you do not have to understand the whole system—just the basic procedures for retrieving the books and articles you need to complete your project. The best way to get acquainted with any library is to spend some time exploring it. Take an hour or two to find out what resources your campus library offers, where they are located, and how you can use them efficiently. Your instructor may schedule a library tour or orientation session for your entire class. If not, ask about the library's own tours and information packets.

Above all, do not hesitate to ask a *reference librarian* for help. Some students feel uneasy about doing so, but librarians are there for that very purpose. They can recommend appropriate sources; show you how to use the library's catalogs, indexes, and computer terminals; and even help you narrow the focus of your topic. Most college librarians are not only trained professionals but also avid readers and researchers who enjoy tracking down information and exploring new subjects.

No two libraries are exactly alike, but nearly all of them include several features that you should know about before you begin your research:

1. *Stacks.* These are the shelves on which most books and bound periodicals are stored. In a typical college library, the stacks are open—that is, directly accessible to researchers. If your library has closed stacks, you will have to request books at the circulation desk.

2. *Circulation Desk.* You can check out books here. If a book you need is listed in the library's catalog but not found in the stacks, a clerk at the circulation desk can tell you whether the book is out to another borrower or missing. If a book is checked out, you can "put a hold" on it—that is, indicate that you want to be notified as soon as the book has been returned. Since you may have to wait as long as two weeks for some items, it is important to begin your research early. You may also discover that a book is "on reserve," or available only for short-term use. If so, ask a clerk for the location of the *reserve desk,* where you can find a copy of the book.

3. *Catalog.* Near the circulation desk you will find a *card catalog* that lists all the library's holdings by author, title, and subject. In many libraries, this traditional catalog has been supplemented or replaced by an *on-line catalog*—that is, a continually updated computer file that you can consult by using terminals near the circulation desk and, in many cases, at various other locations throughout the building. Whatever its form, the catalog will play a key role in your research, for it gives you the call numbers you need to locate books in the stacks.

4. *Reference Area.* In this part of the library you will find sets of encyclopedias, periodical indexes, dictionaries, bibliographies, and similar research tools. You cannot check out reference volumes, but you can consult them long enough to get the names of promising-looking books and articles that you *will* be able to find in the stacks. The reference area may also house computer terminals from which you can consult electronic indexes and other reference items. The librarians who work in this area can help you learn which sources are best suited for your research topic.

5. *Periodical Area.* In this part of the library you will find magazines, journals, and newspapers that are too recent to have been bound as books or stored on microfilm (see below). If you conduct research on a current topic, you are certain to find yourself visiting this area for up-to-date information.

6. *Microfilm Area.* Most older newspapers and some periodicals are kept on *microfilm,* which can be read only with a microfilm reader. Ask a clerk to show you how the machine works.

Thus your research is likely to take you back and forth between various parts of the library:

search
37a

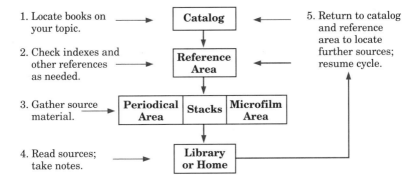

1. Locate books on your topic. → **Catalog** ← 5. Return to catalog and reference area to locate further sources; resume cycle.

2. Check indexes and other references as needed. → **Reference Area** ←

3. Gather source material. → **Periodical Area** | **Stacks** | **Microfilm Area**

4. Read sources; take notes. → **Library or Home**

At some point, obviously, this cycle has to be interrupted; the first draft beckons. But even as you write successive drafts, you may find yourself dipping back into library sources to check new leads and follow up ideas that now look more fruitful than they did at first.

37b Use a trial topic to narrow the focus of your research.

The sooner you settle on a topic for your research paper, the better. In fact, you should have a **trial topic** (p. 15, 1h) in mind *before* you start searching for library materials. You can use one or more of the techniques described in Chapter 1 to arrive at a tentative research question that interests you and seems worth pursuing in the library. Doing so will give your search direction and purpose; instead of reading aimlessly about a broad subject area (p. 4, 1b) like "sign language" or "the Persian Gulf War," you can look for information that bears directly on a particular topic. Thus, within the broad subject area "contemporary film," you might consider exploring one of the following questions:

search
37b

How has the colorization of classic films affected their popularity among contemporary audiences?

To what extent have films about the war in Vietnam shaped public perceptions of the war?

What do Woody Allen's films tell us about contemporary urban life?

How have Westerns changed during the past twenty years?

Why does the Frankenstein story remain a classic subject for filmmakers?

How have developments in computer technology affected film-making during the past decade?

Once you start researching a particular question, you may find that it leads quickly to a dead end or is still too broad for a paper of the assigned length. Be prepared, then, to modify or even abandon your initial plans. Preliminary research on the last "film" question just given, for example, might lead to a much narrower topic: the effects of computer technology on recent animated films. And that topic might be further limited to a comparison of computer animation techniques in two particular films—*Who Framed Roger Rabbit?* and Disney's *Beauty and the Beast.*

Once you have a definite trial topic in mind, make sure that it meets the same five tests you would apply to any essay topic (see p. 15, 1h). Be especially careful to consider whether or not you are likely to have enough supporting evidence to work with—in this case, library materials. Your instructor may require that you use various types of sources—books, periodicals, journals—or that you draw evidence from a minimum number of different sources. If you choose a topic of current controversy, you may find little information outside recent magazines and newspapers. If, on the other hand, you pursue a question that can be answered quickly by looking up specific factual information, you may find that a single book covers the topic thoroughly and leaves little room for further research.

It is best, then, to start with a topic that is narrow enough for a paper of the assigned length but complex enough to assure a sufficient range of material in published sources. Remember that the topic itself need not be strikingly original. What matters, finally, is that you develop a convincing and interesting point *about* your topic. Library research is a means to that end, not an end in itself.

search
37b

37c   Learn the most efficient ways to search for books.

Subject Catalog

Once you have a topic in mind, you should check your library's hold-ings in the general subject area under which that topic falls. You can do so by consulting the *subject catalog,* which is arranged not by authors or titles of books but by fields of knowledge, problems, move-ments, schools of thought, and so forth. Once you locate several appro-priate-looking works, you can copy down their call numbers and get the books from the stacks. If you find just one recent book that includes a **bibliography**—a list of consulted works—you may dis-cover that you already have the names of all the further books and articles you will need.

Guide to Subject Headings

But how do you know which headings your subject catalog uses to classify entries about your topic? You can try your luck, sampling alternative phrases, or you can take a more systematic approach. Your subject catalog follows the headings listed in a reference work called *Library of Congress Subject Headings (LCSH).* If you look up a plausible-sounding phrase in this book, you will not only learn whether it is a subject heading, you will also be directed to other phrases that do serve as headings.

The *LCSH* is useful not only as a guide to your library's subject catalog but also as a tool for narrowing the focus of your research. Suppose, for example, you wanted to write a paper about recycling but had not yet settled on a specific aspect of the subject. By con-sulting the *LCSH* entry on "Recycling" (see next page), you would find a list of subheadings, one of which might lead you toward a fruitful research topic.

search
37c

Observe that:

1. The entry gives the call number of a key work on the subject. You would find relevant material in the stacks near TD794.5.

2. Special instructions explain what types of works are and are not included under this heading.

Recycling (Waste, etc.)
1 ——————— *[TD794.5]*
2 ——————— Here are entered works on the processing of waste
paper, cans, bottles, etc. Works on reclaiming and
reusing equipment, parts, structures, etc. are entered
under Salvage (Waste, etc.)
3 ——————— UF Conversion of waste products
Recovery of natural resources
Recovery of waste materials
Resource recovery
Waste recycling
Waste reuse
4 ——————— BT Conservation of natural resources
Pollution control industry
Refuse and refuse disposal
5 ——————— RT Energy conservation
Salvage (Waste, etc.)
Waste products
6 ——————— SA *subdivision* Recycling *under subjects,*
e.g. Waste paper–Recycling; Glass
waste–Recycling
7 ——————— NT Agricultural wastes–Recycling
Animal waste–Recycling
Copper–Recycling
Deposit-refund systems
Fish-culture–Water-supply–Recycling
Metals–Recycling
Organic wastes–Recycling
Pavements, Asphalt–Recycling
Pavements, Concrete–Recycling
Recycling industry
Resource recovery facilities
Scrap metals–Recycling
Waste products as road materials
Water reuse

**search
37c**

3. *UF* ("used for") indicates headings that will *not* be used elsewhere in the *LCSH*. Thus, there would be no point in searching
for further information under "Waste reuse."

4. *BT* ("broader topics") sends you to topics that put the subject
"Recycling" in a wider perspective.

5. *RT* ("related topics") sends you to other headings that may be useful.

6. *SA* ("see also") tells you to check for the subdivision "Recycling" under the names of specific recyclable products.

7. *NT* ("narrower topics") gives other, more specific headings that you can look up in the *LCSH*. If you wanted to focus your research topic, this list would be especially helpful.

Author-Title Catalog

If you know that your paper will deal with a certain author or public figure, you can bypass a subject search and go directly to the *author-title catalog,* which lists works alphabetically by both author and title. (In many libraries, subject cards are interfiled within the author-title catalog.)

Thus the student doing research for a paper on Thomas Jefferson's career as an architect (p. 500–525, 39c) looked in her library's catalog under "Jefferson, Thomas" and found, first, a number of works written *by* Jefferson. Following these, she found books *about* Jefferson, including several biographies, one of which was specifically relevant to her topic: Jack McLaughlin's *Jefferson and Monticello: The Biography of a Builder.* Note that this book could also be found in the catalog under its title or under the author's last name.

The most useful piece of information in any catalog entry is the *call number,* which tells where the book or bound journal is shelved. But you can also get several other kinds of information from a card, as did the student doing research for a paper on bats (pp. 545–553, 40c). The cards for one of the books he used are shown on the next page. Notice the following:

1. The author's name.

2. The call number, showing where the book is located in the stacks.

3. The title of the book, the author's name as it appears on the title page, the name of a coauthor, the place of publication, the publisher, the date of the copyright. If you planned to use the

search
37c

book, you would want to get all this information recorded on a bibliography card (p. 464, 37g).

4. Physical features of the book. It contains 247 pages, is illustrated, and is 22 centimeters in height.

5. Notes on the content of the book. *The Lives of Bats* includes an index and a nine-page bibliography—that is, a list of other related material—that could be useful in locating additional sources.

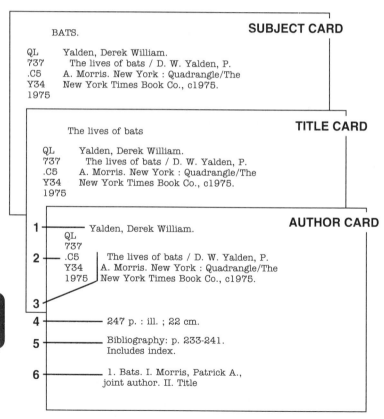

6. A list of all the headings under which this book is filed in the library's catalogs: the subject, the joint author, the title of the book. By going to "Bats" in the subject catalog, you might find several items of related interest.

Once in a while you may come across a reference to an apparently indispensable book or periodical that is not listed in your library's catalog. You can probably borrow the material through *interlibrary loan.* Check with a reference librarian for information.

On-Line Catalog

Most card catalogs are now being supplemented or replaced by *on-line* (computer) *catalogs* that serve the same function, but with greater efficiency and ease of use. A writer of a research paper on Chinese-American business relations, for example, guided by the *Library of Congress Subject Headings* (p. 447 above), used a library terminal to run a subject search on "China—Economic conditions—1976– ." This is what came up on the screen.

Your search for the Subject: CHINA ECONOMIC CONDITIONS 1976 –
retrieved multiple records.

Title List
    1. China trade: a guide to doing business with the People's Re
    2. China's economy in global perspective /A. Doak Barnett
    3. China takes off: technology transfer and modernization/E.E.
    4. The second economy of rural China /Anita Chan and Jonathan
    5. China's allocation of authority and responsibility in ener
    6. China's economic development: growth and structural change /
    7. Mainland China: why still backward? /by Cheng Chu-Yuan
    8. China among the nations of the Pacific /edited by Harrison
    9. China and Southeast Asia: contemporary politics and economi
10. China, economic structure in international perspective.
11. China in transition: papers /Kenneth Lieberthal . . . [et al.

search
37c

By requesting further information about item 3, the student was shown the equivalent of a catalog card for a book that eventually proved useful to him.

Call #:	HC430.T4.B381 1986 Chinese Stdy. Main Stack. Business/SS
Author:	Bauer, E. E.
Title:	China takes off : technology transfer and modernization / E.E. Bauer ; introduction by Michel Oksenberg. Seattle : University of Washington Press. © 1986. xvi. 227 p. : ill. ; 25 cm.
Notes:	Includes bibliographical references
Subjects:	Technology transfer-China. China-Economic conditions-1976–

For more information about on-line searching, see pages 455–457.

37d   Learn how to find recent articles.

If you have chosen a topic of current interest—the spread and control of a new disease, say, or the changing American family structure—you will want the latest available information. Newspaper articles are best for following events as they occur. Magazine articles, such as those in *Newsweek* or *The Atlantic,* give you a general perspective that may be just right for the audience and level you have in mind. And in journals—specialized periodicals such as the *New England Journal of Medicine* or *Shakespeare Quarterly*—you can find detailed knowledge not yet available in books.

search
37d

Indexes and Abstracts

The most efficient way to find recent articles is to consult indexes and abstracts, which are shelved in your library's reference area. *Indexes* are books, usually with a new volume each year, containing alphabetically ordered references to articles on a particular subject.

And *abstracts* are summaries of articles, allowing you to tell whether or not a particular article is worth tracking down.

1. *To Newspapers.* Use the *New York Times Index* (1913–   ) for up-to-date news and commentary having national or international importance. For coverage of other national newspapers, try *Newspaper Index* (1972–   ). And for international coverage, consult the *Index to the* [London] *Times* (1906–   ).

2. *To Magazines.* The best index to general-interest magazines is the *Reader's Guide to Periodical Literature* (1900–   ). Indeed, this index is so useful that for a typical research paper many students begin with it instead of the library's catalog. Browsing through the headings in the *Reader's Guide* may even help you narrow the focus of your research. If you draw a blank from the *Guide,* your topic may be too broad, too narrow, too specialized, or too outdated to be worth pursuing.

A sample entry from the *Reader's Guide* is printed below. The student who wrote the paper on Thomas Jefferson's architecture (pp. 500–525, 39c) located a potentially useful article (c) by consulting this entry.

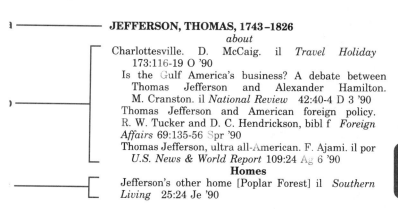

JEFFERSON, THOMAS, 1743–1826
about
Charlottesville. D. McCaig. il *Travel Holiday* 173:116-19 O '90
Is the Gulf America's business? A debate between Thomas Jefferson and Alexander Hamilton. M. Cranston. il *National Review* 42:40-4 D 3 '90
Thomas Jefferson and American foreign policy. R. W. Tucker and D. C. Hendrickson, bibl f *Foreign Affairs* 69:135-56 Spr '90
Thomas Jefferson, ultra all-American. F. Ajami. il por *U.S. News & World Report* 109:24 Ag 6 '90
Homes
Jefferson's other home [Poplar Forest] il *Southern Living* 25:24 Je '90

search
37d

a. A subject entry from the *Guide's* alphabetic listings.

b. Four articles published *about* Jefferson during the year.

c. One article published about Jefferson's homes. The article is illustrated (*il*) and appears in the June (*Je*) 1990 issue of *Southern Living,* volume 25, page 24.

3. *To Journals.* While the *Reader's Guide* gives you good access to such popular magazines as *Time* and *Business Week,* it does not cover journals such as *Science* and *Modern Language Quarterly,* which you may want to consult if you need more specialized information. For articles in such fields as archaeology, history, literature, art, music, and philosophy, use the *Humanities Index* (1974–). If you are working in anthropology, economics, environmental sciences, geography, political science, psychology, or sociology, try the *Social Sciences Index* (1974–). Note that these two indexes list articles published since 1973. For earlier years, consult the *International Index* (1907–1965) and the *Social Sciences and Humanities Index* (1965–1974).

If your research paper has a general-interest focus, you will probably find more than enough material by using some of the sources just named. But if you need technical information within a single discipline, you may want to consult one of the following:

Abstracts in Anthropology (1970–)
Applied Science and Technology Index (1913–)
Art Index (1947–)
Astronomy and Astrophysics Abstracts (1969–)
Biography Index (1947–)
Biological Abstracts (1926–)
Business Periodicals Index (1958–)
Chemical Abstracts (1907–)
Current Index to Journals in Education (1969–)
Education Index (1929–)
Engineering Index (1920–)
Environment Abstracts (1971–)
Film Literature Index (1973–)
Historical Abstracts (1955–)
MLA International Bibliography (1921–)
Music Index (1949–)
Philosopher's Index (1967–)

search
37d

Physics Abstracts (1895–)
Psychological Abstracts (1927–)
Religious and Theological Abstracts (1958–)
Sociological Abstracts (1977–)
Women's Studies Abstracts (1972–)

Electronic Databases

Many printed indexes, abstracts, and other reference materials are now available in the alternative form of *databases*—that is, computer files that can be scanned instantly. Such *on-line searching* can save time, unearth very recent references, and ferret out specific topics that are not listed as subject headings in the index itself. Suppose, for example, you are interested in the connection between child abuse and alcoholism. Instead of asking for all entries within each of those large subjects, you can tell the computer to display only those items whose titles refer to *both* problems.

To gain access to some electronic databases, you may have to pay a fee and ask a technician to connect you to a national computer network. Increasingly, however, libraries have been purchasing CD-ROM (compact disk—read-only memory) databases that you can consult without charge from a library workstation. With very little practice, you can learn to make thorough, efficient, and up-to-date searches for articles, statistics, and other useful sources, eliminating the tedium of having to hunt through multiple printed volumes. Note, however, that in many instances the CD-ROM coverage begins in a later year than in the printed version.

To find out which databases your library owns, ask a reference librarian. Some of the most useful sources that might be available are listed below.

search
37d

GENERAL DATABASES:
Academic Index. Bibliographic references to 390 scholarly and general-interest periodicals in the humanities, social sciences, and general sciences. Covers journals for latest three to four years; *New York Times* for latest six months.

CIS Statistical Masterfile. Combines three printed indexes: *Ameri-*

can Statistics Index, Statistical Reference Index, and *Index to International Statistics.* Covers early 1970s– .

General Periodicals Index. An index to over 1100 popular and scholarly publications in the humanities, sciences, social sciences, business, education, and current events. Coverage begins in 1980; updated monthly. Because of its comprehensiveness, this database is useful for nearly any general-interest research project. Here is a sample entry found by the student researching Thomas Jefferson's work as an architect (pp. 500–525):

1 ——————— **JEFFERSON, THOMAS**
–Design and construction

Reroofing a landmark. (pavilions at
2 ——————— University Virginia) by Darl Rastorfer il
v177 Architectural Record Feb '89 p124(4)
3 ——————— LIBRARY SUBSCRIBES TO JOURNAL

1. The heading and subheading under which the student conducted her search.

2. The bibliographic information needed to track down the source. Notice the parenthetic notation about the content of the article.

3. An indication that the student's library carries *Architectural Record.*

National Newspaper Index. Covers *New York Times, Wall Street Journal, Christian Science Monitor, Washington Post,* and *Los Angeles Times.* Covers latest four years.

search
37d

SPECIALIZED DATABASES:

Applied Science and Technology Index. Indexes 335 journals in chemistry, engineering, computer science, physics, etc. 1983– .

Art Index. Indexes over 200 periodicals, yearbooks, and museum publications in art, art history, architecture, graphic art, design, photography, etc. 1984– .

Census Data. Statistical data from the U.S. Bureau of the Census.

Current Contents. Specialized databases issued under this general title cover engineering, life sciences, medicine, and various other fields.

MLA International Bibliography. Indexes articles in literature, language, and folklore published in all modern languages in over 3000 journals. 1981–   .

PsycLIT. The CD-ROM version of *Psychological Abstracts.* Gives citations and abstracts for articles in psychology and related fields. 1974–   .

Science Citation Index. Covers over 3300 worldwide science and technical journals. 1986–   .

Social Sciences Index. Indexes articles from over 353 journals in area studies, political science, geography, sociology, psychology, etc. 1983–   .

Sociofile. The CD-ROM version of *Sociological Abstracts.* For journals, 1974–   . For dissertations, 1986–   .

37e   Consult background sources as necessary.

The steps we have already covered should be enough to give you all the information you need for a typical research paper. Sometimes, however, you may want an out-of-the-way bit of knowledge or a broad introduction to the field you are going to treat. You will find such information in reference works—books that survey a field and tell you how to find materials within that field. Such books are so numerous that you may need to consult an even more general book that lists reference works and explains their scope. Try especially *Guide to Reference Books,* by Eugene P. Sheehy, which can lead you to the most appropriate bibliographies and indexes.

search
37e

   For most college research papers, however, you will probably need no more than one survey of your field and one guide to sources. Here is a representative list of titles to consult:

ART:
Encyclopedia of World Art (1959–83)

BUSINESS AND ECONOMICS:
Dictionary of Economics and Business, ed. Erwin E. Nemmers
(1978)

DRAMA:
McGraw-Hill Encyclopedia of World Drama (1984)
How to Locate Reviews of Plays and Films, by Gordon Samples
(1976)

EDUCATION:
A Dictionary of Education, by Derek Rowntree (1982)

FILM:
The World Encyclopedia of the Film (1972)

FOLKLORE AND MYTHOLOGY:
*Funk & Wagnalls Standard Dictionary of Folklore, Mythology, and
Legend* (1972)

Motif-Index of Folk-Literature, by Stith Thompson (1955–58)

HISTORY:
An Encyclopedia of World History, ed. William L. Langer (1972)

LITERATURE:
A Handbook to Literature, by C. Hugh Holman (1986)

Literary Research Guide, by James L. Harner (1989)

**search
37e**

MUSIC:
The New Oxford Companion to Music (1983)

PHILOSOPHY:
The Encyclopedia of Philosophy, ed. Paul Edwards (1972–   )

PSYCHOLOGY:
Encyclopedia of Psychology, ed. Raymond J. Corsini (1984)

RELIGION:
A Reader's Guide to the Great Religions, ed. Charles J. Adams (1977)

SCIENCE AND TECHNOLOGY:
McGraw-Hill Encyclopedia of Science and Technology (1987)

SOCIAL AND POLITICAL SCIENCE:
International Encyclopedia of the Social Sciences, ed. David L. Sills (1977–79)

WOMEN'S STUDIES:
Handbook of International Data on Women (1976)

When you need to draw on a particular fact—the population of a country, an event in someone's life, the origin of an important term, the source of a quotation—you can go to one of the following sources:

GENERAL ENCYCLOPEDIAS:
Encyclopaedia Britannica (1986)
Encyclopedia Americana (revised annually)

COMPILATIONS OF FACTS:
The World Almanac and Book of Facts (1990)

ATLASES:
National Geographic Atlas of the World (1981)
The Times Atlas of the World (1985)

DICTIONARIES (See p. 175 for college dictionaries.):
A Comprehensive Etymological Dictionary of the English Language, by Ernest Klein (1979)
The Oxford English Dictionary (1989)

search
37e

BIOGRAPHY:
Who's Who in the World (1976–   )
The McGraw-Hill Encyclopedia of World Biography (1973)

QUOTATIONS:
Familiar Quotations, by John Bartlett, ed. Justin Kaplan (1992)
The Oxford Dictionary of Quotations (1980)

37f   Consider using field research.

You need not limit your research to the library. **Field research—** gathering firsthand information through surveys, interviews, and other means of direct observation—can add immediacy and authenticity to many research projects. Suppose, for example, you are writing about changing attitudes toward alcohol consumption among college students. While you would naturally want to base your findings primarily on reliable published sources, a survey of dormitory residents or members of another campus group might give you up-to-date information to supplement your primary evidence. If you plan to use such an informal survey, keep it simple. Ask a few clearly worded questions, perhaps multiple-choice items, that respondents can complete quickly on a one-page survey form. For a more elaborate or specialized survey, seek advice from your instructor before proceeding.

Interviews can be especially useful when you are working on a topic of local interest. If, for example, you are writing a paper about the plight of the homeless in your community, an interview with the director of a nearby food bank or shelter would supply current, firsthand information that you could not find in the library. But interviews need not be limited to local issues. On your campus you will find professors willing to share their expertise on a range of topics. One student, writing a paper about acid rain, narrowed her focus and gathered information by interviewing a political science professor. She had learned from a course lecture that her instructor knew a great deal about disputes between the United States and Canada over the environmental damage caused by acid rain. The same student later talked with a biology professor, who supplied

search
37f

useful details about the toxic effects of acid rain on plant and animal life.

GUIDELINES FOR CONDUCTING INTERVIEWS

- Make an appointment for the interview well in advance; clearly explain the nature and purpose of the interview, and let the person know how much time you will need.
- Go to the interview well prepared; have in hand a series of *written* questions you want to ask.
- Take accurate notes during the interview, asking the person to repeat or clarify key points (take an extra pen or pencil for backup).
- Ask permission of the person you are interviewing *before* you use a tape recorder.
- Keep the interview brief; avoid straying from the point.
- Ask the person for advice about further sources that bear on your topic.
- Offer to send the person a copy of your finished paper.

37g Take full and careful notes from your reading.

A typical library book will be available to you for only a few days or weeks, and magazine and journal articles may be limited to use within the library itself. Thus you will need an efficient system for deciding which sources to use and an accurate, orderly way of taking notes from those sources.

Evaluating Sources

**search
37g**

To avoid wasting time reading irrelevant material, you should evaluate the potential usefulness of each book and article before you begin taking notes. Be aware, first of all, of any guidelines your instructor has established for the number and types of sources to be used in your paper. There is little point in poring over a dozen articles from popular magazines if you have been asked to rely mainly on books and scholarly journals. And even if your instructor sets no specific guidelines, try to draw sources from a variety of publications. If you rely too heavily on a single book or article, your paper will lack the breadth and perspective that readers look for in research writing.

Besides choosing varied sources, you should also select books and articles that are appropriate, current, and reliable.

1. *Is the source appropriate?* A source that is closely related to your research question will be far more useful than one that approaches it in a roundabout way. To see if a book bears directly on your topic, check the table of contents, the index, and the preface to get an idea of the scope and nature of the book. Rule out books that contain only passing references to your topic. For an article, read the first few paragraphs and check headings in the text to see if the piece contains useful material. Finally, check both books and articles for their level of specialization. If you are writing a paper on, say, the benefits of a high-fiber diet, an article in a general-interest magazine will be more appropriate and accessible than one in a technical publication read primarily by professional dietitians.

2. *Is the source current?* Recent sources usually contain more up-to-date information than older ones. If you are exploring a topic of contemporary controversy—say, methods of controlling illegal-drug abuse—you will want to have the latest available information. For other topics the date of publication is less important. If, for example, you are researching a historical subject or analyzing a classic political or literary text, you might well find vital material in a book twenty years old. Generally, though, look first at more recent books and articles about your topic.

3. *Is the source reliable?* You will want to base your research paper on sources that are accurate and trustworthy. If you have doubts about the reliability of a particular magazine, journal, or book, ask your instructor or a reference librarian for an opinion as to its general reputation. You can also rely to an extent on your own judgment. Skim the book or article to see if its approach seems fair and balanced. If the author's tone strikes you as shrill or if the treatment of the subject looks obviously biased, be wary of using the source.

search
37g

A more systematic approach to evaluating the reliability of a book is to check expert opinion. You can consult *Book Review Digest* (1905–) to learn what some of the book's original reviewers had to say about it. Or you can check the author's credentials in a biographical reference work (ask a librarian to recommend an appropriate volume). Evaluating a book's reliability is especially important if you plan to make it a dominant source in your paper. Simply by drawing from a variety of books and articles, you can limit the risk of basing your findings on a single unreliable source.

Using Notecards

The notes you take from your reading will serve two purposes: to keep an accurate list of the works you have consulted and to record key information from your sources. You may choose to jot down sources and ideas on sheets of paper, but most researchers soon discover that notecards are easier to organize and rearrange as an essay takes shape.

To compile a *bibliography,* or list of works consulted, one card per entry is ideal; *content* notes, on the other hand, may run through many cards. To avoid confusion, use $3'' \times 5''$ bibliography cards to identify your sources and larger (usually $4'' \times 6''$) content cards for quotations, summaries, paraphrases, and miscellaneous comments. Or, if you prefer, use cards of different colors.

Observe the sample cards that follow. Note that once you prepare a separate bibliography card, you can give the briefest of references on a content card: *Peterson, p. 395.*

ORIGINAL SOURCE:

Although Jefferson was the recognized architect of Monticello, the importance of that achievement, and of his architectural work generally, both from a professional and an artistic standpoint, went comparatively unnoticed until the second decade of this century. For a century or more, practicing architects in this country worked in a tradition of classical design, especially in public buildings, without realizing Jefferson's seminal role. [from *The Jefferson Image in the American Mind,* by Merrill D. Peterson, published in New York by Oxford University Press, 1960]

search
37g

BIBLIOGRAPHY CARD:

E 332
P. 4

Peterson, Merrill D. <u>The Jefferson Image in
the American Mind</u>. New York: Oxford
U P, 1960.

(See pp. 395-98 for discussion of J's 20th - c.
reputation as an architect.)

Notice that the card includes the book's call number—useful for relo-
cating a source if you need to consult it again. The bibliographic
information should come not from the book's cover but from its title
and copyright pages: the author's name, the title of the book, the
city of publication, the name of the publisher ("UP" is a standard
abbreviation for "University Press"), and the year of publication. The
parenthetical note reminds the researcher of key information contained in the source.

CONTENT CARD—QUOTATION:

The card at the top of the next page quotes directly from the source
(p. 463). Brackets indicate the insertion of a word not found in the
quoted passage, and ellipsis dots signal an omission. A brief notation
(*Peterson, p. 395*) links this card to the bibliography card and supplies
a page number. Another notation reminds the researcher of the type
of information recorded on the card.

   In writing a quotation card, take care to record the exact words
of the source, including any oddities of spelling or punctuation. If, for
instance, the original text omits a comma that you would have included, you can place a bracketed [*sic*], meaning *this is the way I*

search
37g

Peterson, p. 395   J's 20ᵗʰ-c. reputation

The "importance of ... his [Jefferson's]
architectural work ... went comparatively
unnoticed until the second decade of
this century."

found it, at the questionable spot. Doing so will remind you not to
improve the quotation if you use it in your paper.

CONTENT CARD—SUMMARY:

Peterson, p. 395   J's 20ᵗʰ-c. reputation

Until the 1920's, J's work as an architect was
relatively unknown. Before then, American
architects designed buildings in the classical
style without being aware of J's importance
in developing that style.

A **summary** concisely presents the key idea of a passage, omitting any examples and descriptive detail. The summary on the above notecard, for example, is less than half as long as the original source (p. 463). When writing a summary, you should use your own language, though some repetition of the author's terms may be inevitable. If you do borrow phrasing from the source, put it in quotation marks. And remember that whenever you summarize someone else's ideas—even if you express those ideas in your own words—you must acknowledge the source (see p. 477, 38c).

CONTENT CARD—PARAPHRASE:

> Peterson, p. 395   J's 20th–c. reputation
>
> J has long been known as the designer of Monticello, but the significance of this work and of his other architecture was not widely known until the 1920s. Before then, his artistic and professional contributions to the field were relatively unnoticed. American architects were unaware of J's influence on classical style, even though they used that style for public buildings.

A **paraphrase** is a running restatement of the original passage using the researcher's own words. An ample paraphrase may be nearly as long as the original passage (compare the above notecard, for instance, with the source on page 463). Since a paraphrase is closer to the original wording than a summary, you must be especially careful not to repeat the author's words without using quotation marks; doing so could lead to accidental **plagiarism** (p. 477, 38c), or the presentation of someone else's words (or ideas) as your own.

search 37g

Whether you are quoting, summarizing, or paraphrasing, remember these additional guidelines for writing content cards:

1. Use ink. Penciled notecards smudge when pressed against each other.

2. Do not put information from more than one source on a given card, and avoid writing on the reverse side of a card.

3. Supply page references for all quotations, paraphrases, and summaries. If you copy a passage that runs from one page to another, mark on your notecard where the first page ends: *"Bats eat millions of mosquitoes and help / pollinate local fruit trees."* If you do finally use only a portion of the excerpt in your paper, you will want to know where it ended in the original.

4. Use a portion of any given card (a) to record your evaluation of the source, (b) to remind yourself of possibilities for further study, or (c) to make your own comments on the material. Be sure, however, to indicate (with a slash, parentheses, or initials) which remarks are yours and which come from the source. Remember, too, that you can use separate cards to jot down your own ideas whenever they occur to you.

5. Leave some space in the margin of each card for an indexing symbol, so that you can later sort items efficiently. If you do use any symbols or abbreviations, keep them consistent throughout your notecards.

Photocopying Sources

Instead of handwriting your notes, you may want to photocopy important pages directly from your source material, either in the library or at a copy center. If you do use this method, make sure to gather all the bibliographic information you will need. You can write that information on your first photocopied sheet or make copies of the title and copyright pages. To avoid confusion, keep the material from each source stapled or clipped together.

search
37g

With photocopied pages in hand, you can highlight or underline key passages, using different colors of ink to identify various types of material. You can also make marginal annotations (p. 11, 1e) indicating the usefulness of a source or reminding yourself to check other relevant passages. Keep in mind, however, that photocopying has its drawbacks. For one thing, you may find it difficult to sort and organize highlighted passages, especially if you have accumulated a large stack of material. For another, photocopying postpones the inevitable work of selecting, paraphrasing, and summarizing evidence for use in your paper. If you do that work early, as you take notes in the library, you will have more time later to concentrate on planning, organizing, and drafting the paper itself.

38 Writing from Sources

38a Use your notes and trial topic to plan your paper.

Discovering a Thesis

In the process of conducting research—locating and evaluating sources, taking notes, reacting to the ideas of others—you are almost certain to narrow the focus of your trial topic. You may find, for example, that your original idea is too broad or complex to meet the terms of the assignment, or you may come across a more engaging line of thought that gradually pushes aside the idea you started with. In any case, by the time you have finished your initial research, you will probably be ready to move from a topic to a **trial thesis** (p. 19, 2a). The sooner you do so, the better; a thesis, however tentative, can give your note taking even more direction than a specific topic can. Once you know the point you plan to make, you can weigh and sift the available evidence with that point firmly in mind.

If you have not settled on a thesis by the time you finish your initial note taking, you can follow the steps outlined in Chapter 2 as a means of doing so. All the advice given there about limiting a thesis, giving it definite purpose and content, and turning it into a full **thesis statement** (p. 25, 2e) applies as much to a research paper as it does to any other essay. There is, however, one additional strategy you may want to use to develop a thesis for your research paper: reviewing and sorting your notes.

Make sure to set aside enough time to undertake a complete and careful survey of all the material you have on hand. Reread your notecards with pen in hand, jotting down any ideas or patterns that occur to you as you read. Check to see if your source material falls into several categories, one of which might mesh with a tentative thesis you have in mind. Or look for a significant disagreement among your sources. In reading about Thomas Jefferson's career as an architect, for example, you might find that some experts emphasize his practical innovations, while others stress his aesthetic achievements. Such a contrast could help you define your own position on the matter.

Spreading groups of notecards on a large table or even on the floor can sometimes help you notice a pattern you had not seen before. Suppose, for example, you were researching the destruction of South American rain forests. In arranging and rearranging your notecards, you might find that many of them address an issue that arouses your interest: efforts to replant areas that have already been logged. Sorting and reviewing your source material could thus lead to a thesis about, say, the success or failure of governmental attempts at reforestation.

Finally, whatever thesis you decide to pursue, it should satisfy two requirements. First, it should be an idea that grows out of your own thinking about the topic. And second, you should be able to support it with the available evidence. Once you arrive at a carefully considered thesis, check your source material. If it looks skimpy, consider shifting your focus or returning to the library for additional information. With a definite thesis in mind, you may be able to find that information quickly and efficiently.

Organizing Your Ideas

In planning the organization of your research paper, follow the same principles that you would for any essay (see Chapter 3). Keep in mind, however, that a research paper, because of its length or complexity, will require more planning than, say, a brief essay based mainly on personal experience. Try, nevertheless, to avoid developing an overly rigid outline that prevents you from taking detours and exploring unexpected lines of thought as you write a first draft. Think of your initial outline as a flexible guide—a rough working plan, not a final blueprint.

source 38a

Just as sorting your notecards can help you narrow your thesis, it can also help you determine the structure of your paper. Try arranging the cards that bear directly on your topic into several groups, each of which might become a subtopic within your paper or a stage in your argument. If you were writing, for example, on governmental efforts to replant trees in logged rain forests, your notecards might fall into a chronological sequence: (1) efforts during the 1980s, (2) current efforts, (3) plans for future reforestation. Or you might discover an entirely different arrangement: (1) opponents of reforestation, (2) supporters of reforestation, (3) compromise between the two groups, (4) results of the compromise.

One especially helpful way of organizing a research paper—or any longer essay—is to think in terms of **paragraph blocks,** closely related groups of paragraphs that address significant subtopics within an essay. The advantage of this strategy is simple: it allows you to work with one manageable section of your paper at a time. Thus a student writing about the development of a new landfill site in his hometown planned a five-part structure for his paper. His first few paragraphs (Part I) would introduce three major problems in developing the new site. The next three sections (Parts II–IV) would discuss in detail the potential solution to each problem. Within each of these sections, he would include as many paragraphs as needed to make his point. Finally, he would end the paper (Part V) by evaluating the proposed solutions. The scheme gave the student writer a definite structure—a clear sense of where he was going—yet allowed him to remain flexible while drafting each section, or paragraph block, within his essay.

While a flexible outline may be useful for composing your paper, sometime before submitting the final copy you may be asked to construct a **formal outline** showing main and subordinate points in your argument. If so, review the advice on pages 31–33, 3d. Note especially the distinction between a *sentence outline* and a *topic outline.* You will find an example of the first type on page 32, the second on page 501.

38b   Use sources pointedly as you draft your paper.

source
38b

However definite your thesis or thorough your outline may be, facing down the blank page can be intimidating. If you find yourself reluctant to start a draft, review the advice in the box on page 35. Note especially the recommendation that you delay writing your introductory paragraph, which can be a particularly big obstacle. Especially for a longer paper, it makes sense to draft the opening *after* you have gotten other sections of the paper under control.

You might also want to review all of Chapter 4 for additional advice about writing a first draft—maintaining an appropriate voice, stance, and tone (4b–e) and supporting your thesis with sound and reasonable evidence (4f–l). Here is some additional advice about drafting that applies especially to research writing:

ADVICE FOR DRAFTING A RESEARCH PAPER

- If your paper is going to be long, start by writing a brief summary to give yourself an overview of the paper; show the summary to your instructor or a classmate for comments.

- As you write, rely primarily on your own language; do not let your sources overpower your voice or point of view.

- Divide the project into manageable sections, and draft one of them at a time; start with a section that will be relatively easy to write.

- Review your thesis frequently, making sure that each section of the paper stays within the control of that thesis.

- Keep track of your sources as you write by inserting informal parenthetical references in the draft (*Heaberlin, p. 27*); supply formal documentation later.

Using Quotations

Before you draft your essay, it may be useful to review Chapter 29, which gives detailed advice about the mechanics of using quotations. And later, as you revise and polish your research paper, you will want to keep the handbook open to that chapter, consulting it frequently for advice about how to combine quoted passages with your own language. Following standard procedures for integrating quoted material helps readers concentrate on your ideas; when you stray from those procedures, you distract readers and thus undermine the effectiveness of your presentation.

Handling quoted material, of course, is more than a matter of knowing where to put punctuation marks. In almost any essay, a passage of quoted speech or an example borrowed from a text can serve as fresh and compelling evidence (p. 45, 4h). But in a research paper, such language is crucial for establishing the authenticity and authority of your argument.

Remember, however, that quotations work best when you use them sparingly. Some writers, anxious to reach a minimum word limit, look to quotation not just for support but also for padding. They typically start a paragraph with an introductory sentence and follow it with one or more long, unanalyzed quotations, thus accumulating words but not ideas. In such a paper the writer's language becomes a bare rack on which to hang an assortment of quoted examples that lack point and purpose. The writer's own ideas get lost in a patchwork of sources.

To avoid this effect, you should write your research paper in your own language, carefully summarizing and paraphrasing source material (see below) rather than quoting extensively. This does not mean, of course, that you should avoid direct quotation altogether. When the language of your source is especially concise or memorable or when it explains a complex idea clearly, a lengthy quotation may be the right choice. But in general, integrating brief excerpts—words, phrases, an occasional sentence—into your own prose is a more effective way to use quotation. To see how two student writers make judicious use of quoted material, review the sample research papers beginning on pages 500 and 545.

When you do use quotations, make sure to *introduce* them rather than simply dropping them into your prose. A skillfully handled introductory phrase can tie the quoted material to your own writing and help show how that material supports your point. Such phrases should usually give the author's name, especially when you are quoting a source for the first time.

QUOTATION NOT INTRODUCED:

x Many working couples now question the wisdom of directing so much of their time and energy into advancing their careers. "Some families in the 1990s are scaling back, striking a balance between work and play, between making a living and making a life" (Gravitt 78).

source 38b

QUOTATION INTRODUCED:

• Many working couples now question the wisdom of directing so much of their time and energy into advancing their careers.

According to sociologist Ellen Gravitt, "Some families in the 1990s are scaling back, striking a balance between work and play, between making a living and making a life" (78).

If the purpose of a quotation is not immediately apparent, you may also want to provide a brief discussion to establish its relevance. In the following passage, for example, the quotation is ineffectively linked to the sentence before it.

QUOTATION INTRODUCED TOO ABRUPTLY:

x The elegies that W. H. Auden wrote in 1939 depart from tradition. In writing about W. B. Yeats and Sigmund Freud, Auden "emphasizes that they performed extraordinary deeds despite their ordinary imperfections" (Mendelson 366).

Here, in a revised version, the purpose of the quotation becomes immediately clar:

QUOTATION EFFECTIVELY INTRODUCED:

• The elegies that W. H. Auden wrote in 1939 depart from tradition. **Whereas traditional elegists treat the honored person as a flawless hero, Auden makes his subjects seem fully human. Thus in elegizing Yeats and Freud,** Auden "emphasizes that they performed extraordinary deeds despite their ordinary imperfections" (Mendelson 366).

When using quotations—as well as summaries and paraphrases—you should avoid monotonously repeating the same introductory word: *Chavkin says, One psychologist says, Brennan says, Another expert says. . . .* Using a variety of words and structures can reduce tedium and let readers know the approach your source is taking. In selecting a particular verb, for example, you can indicate whether the quoted author is reporting a fact, making a comment, adopting an attitude, or arguing for or against a given position.

**source
38b**

VERBS FOR INTRODUCING SOURCES		
adds	defends	points out
agrees	defines	proposes

VERBS FOR INTRODUCING SOURCES		
analyzes	describes	refutes
argues	disagrees	remarks
asks	emphasizes	says
believes	evaluates	shows
claims	explains	stresses
comments	illustrates	summarizes
compares	maintains	tells
concedes	mentions	thinks
concludes	notes	warns
contrasts	observes	writes

Again, remember to consult Chapter 29 whenever you have a technical question about introducing a quotation smoothly into your text.

Using Paraphrase and Summary

If you have carefully *summarized* or *paraphrased* source material in your notes (p. 461, 37g), you should be able to use those notes directly in drafting your research paper. Keep in mind, however, that many of the cautions about using quotations also apply to paraphrase and summary. It is not enough to follow a long passage of paraphrase with a single parenthetic reference to the source. Just as you would in quoting, you must indicate clearly where a summary or paraphrase begins and ends. Otherwise, readers will be hard-pressed to distinguish your own ideas from those you have borrowed. (See 38c below for specific information about avoiding plagiarism.)

To learn how to integrate summary and paraphrase into your prose, read the source given below and study its use in the passages that follow.

source 38b

ORIGINAL SOURCE:
Alcohol, in excess, is by far the most devastating of drugs—wrecking families and friendships, impairing health, filling jails, hospitals, and morgues. . . . The invoice for damages does not lie entirely on that se-

verely afflicted minority we call alcoholics. Much of it is from other heavy and even moderate drinkers—there being so many more of them—who are not yet, but could become, alcoholics. (The point where heavy drinking merges into alcohol dependence is blurry.) Ten percent of drinkers in the United States drink heavily—they account for half of all alcohol consumed.

—BOYD GIBBONS, "Alcohol: The Legal Drug"

Notice in the following example how the writer uses summary to make a point. The idea borrowed from Gibbons's article is clearly introduced and acknowledged:

SUMMARY (boldfaced):
From first-hand experience, from reading, or from the media, most Americans are now aware of the harmful consequences of alcohol addiction, both for the alcoholic and for those whose lives are directly affected by his or her behavior. **But, according to one recent article, excessive drinking that falls short of alcoholism also takes a heavy toll on the lives of many Americans and on the society at large (Gibbons 21).** That toll is especially evident. . . .

And here is a paraphrase that draws more heavily on the original source. Notice, however, that the writer carefully avoids using Gibbons's wording (except for one quoted phrase) and indicates exactly where the borrowing begins and ends.

PARAPHRASE (boldfaced):
From first-hand experience, from reading, or from the media, most Americans are now aware of the harmful consequences of alcohol addiction, both for the alcoholic and for those whose lives are directly affected by his or her behavior. **According to Boyd Gibbons, however, damage from alcohol abuse is not caused solely by "that severely afflicted minority we call alcoholics" (21). Gibbons explains that heavy and moderate drinkers, whose numbers far exceed those of alcoholics, contribute to the stress this drug places on personal relationships and on the nation's criminal justice and health care systems (21).** That effect has been especially obvious. . . .

source
38b

Notice that paraphrase and summary allow a writer to use a source without repeating its language. The source material thus supports, rather than dominates, the discussion. Note also that indirect borrowing can be combined comfortably with an occasional quotation. In the example just given, the paraphrase includes an apt phrase from the original source—*that severely afflicted minority we call alcoholics.*

38c Identify and acknowledge all borrowed material.

Once you have a full draft of your research paper in hand, you can turn to the work of revision. Remember that such a paper needs the same careful attention to large-scale and editorial revision as any essay does. You should allow ample time for rethinking and polishing, working your way through the Checklist for Revision on the inside front cover of this book. And if you need fundamental advice about the process of improving an essay, review Chapter 5.

Ideally, you will be able to get detailed comments on your draft from a peer editor before you revise it. If that is not possible, find a friend or classmate who is willing to read the paper and give you an impression of its strengths and weaknesses. Anything you can do to get an outside perspective on your work will help. You may even be able to approximate that perspective yourself by setting the draft aside for a few days and then coming back to it with a fresh outlook.

As you revise your research paper, take special care to check for fairness and accuracy in your use of source material. If you have taken careful notes and used them wisely while drafting the paper, you will already have done much of the necessary work. But however scrupulous you may have been, you should take the time to double-check your references. Compare all quoted passages with your notes or, better, with the original sources, and review each paraphrase and summary to make sure that it does not rely improperly on another writer's language.

Avoiding Plagiarism

You must acknowledge your indebtedness to a source whenever you

- quote a passage verbatim
- summarize a passage

source
38c

- paraphrase a passage
- include facts or figures that are not common knowledge
- borrow someone else's idea or opinion

Failure to provide documentation in any one of these cases will result in **plagiarism**—the serious ethical violation of presenting other people's words or ideas as your own. Plagiarism tempts some student writers who feel too rushed or insecure to arrive at their own conclusions. Yet systematic dishonesty is only part of the problem. For every student who buys a term paper or copies a whole article without acknowledgment, there are dozens who indulge in "little" ethical lapses through thoughtlessness, haste, or a momentary sense of opportunity. Though nearly all of their work is original, they, too, are plagiarists—just as someone who robs a bank of $2.39 is a bank robber.

Unlike the robber, however, some plagiarists fail to realize what they have done wrong. Students who once copied encyclopedia articles for school assignments may never have learned the necessity of using quotation marks and citing sources. Others may think that by using *summary* or *paraphrase* they have turned an idea into public property. Some acknowledge the source of their idea but fail to indicate that they have borrowed words as well as thoughts, and others plagiarize by relying on faulty notes (p. 461, 37g) that fail to distinguish adequately between personal observations and borrowed ideas. And finally, some students blunder into plagiarism by failing to distinguish between fact and opinion. They may think, for example, that a famous critic's opinion about a piece of literature is authoritative and belongs in the realm of common facts—and so they paraphrase it without acknowledgment. All these errors are understandable, but none of them constitutes a good excuse for plagiarism.

**source
38c**

Learning What to Acknowledge

Consider the following source and four ways that a student might be tempted to use it.

ORIGINAL SOURCE:

Because women's wages often continue to reflect the fiction that men earn the family wage, single mothers rarely earn enough to support themselves and their children adequately. And because work is still organized around the assumption that mothers stay home with children, even though few mothers can afford to do so, child-care facilities in the United States remain woefully inadequate.

—ELAINE TYLER MAY, "Myths and Realities of the American Family"

VERSION A:

Since women's wages often continue to reflect the mistaken notion that men are the main wage earners in the family, single mothers rarely make enough to support themselves and their children very well. Also, because work is still based on the assumption that mothers stay home with children, facilities for child care remain woefully inadequate in the United States.

Comment: Clearly plagiarism. The writer tries to paraphrase the original, changing several words, dropping one phrase entirely, and interweaving new language into the source. But the borrowing is far too extensive. The basic sentence structure and much of the wording belong to May, not to the writer. Even if May were acknowledged as the source, the writer would still be guilty of plagiarism, having used phrases verbatim without supplying the necessary quotation marks.

VERSION B:

As Elaine Tyler May points out, "women's wages often continue to reflect the fiction that men earn the family wage" (588). Thus many single mothers cannot support themselves and their children adequately.

source
38c

```
Furthermore, since work is based on the assumption that

mothers stay home with children, facilities for day

care in this country are still "woefully inadequate"

(May 589).
```

Comment: Still plagiarism. The two citations of May serve as a kind of alibi for the improper use of other unacknowledged phrases: *support themselves and their children adequately, the assumption that mothers stay home with children.*

VERSION C:
```
By and large, our economy still operates on the

mistaken notion that men are the main breadwinners in

the family. Thus, women continue to earn lower wages

than men. This means, in effect, that many single

mothers cannot earn a decent living. Furthermore,

adequate day care is not available in the United States

because of the mistaken assumption that mothers remain

at home with their children.
```

Comment: Still plagiarism. The paraphrase is now adequate; the writer uses new wording and sentence structure. But unless May is acknowledged as the source of the ideas, the writer has plagiarized. Even though it is widely known that women earn less than men and that many single mothers live in poverty, May uses this common knowledge to make a particular point. The writer borrows that point without acknowledgment.

source 38c

VERSION D:
```
Women today still earn less than men--so much less

that many single mothers and their children live near

or below the poverty line. Elaine Tyler May argues
```

```
that this situation stems in part from "the fiction

that men earn the family wage" (588).  May further

suggests that the American workplace still operates on

the assumption that mothers with children stay home to

care for them (589).

     This assumption, in my opinion, does not have the

force it once did.  More and more businesses today

offer in-house day-care facilities. . . .
```

Comment: No plagiarism. The opening sentence is influenced by the common knowledge cited in May's passage, but the writer has not tried to pass off May's conclusion as original work. The one direct quotation is properly acknowledged, as is the brief paraphrase later in the passage. At the end of the passage, the writer starts to develop an opinion contrary to May's.

There *is* room for disagreement about what to acknowledge; but precisely because this is so, you ought to make your documentation relatively ample. Ask yourself, in doubtful cases, whether the point you are borrowing is an opinion or a fact. Opinions, by definition, are debatable (for example, the idea that the American workplace is "still organized around the assumption that mothers stay home with children"). If you borrow an opinion, document it.

As for facts, do not bother to document those that could be found in any commonly used source—for example, the fact that the Persian Gulf War occurred in 1991. But give references for less accessible facts, such as the number of oil wells set afire in Kuwait during the war. The harder it would be for readers to come across a fact through their own efforts, the more surely you need to document it.

source
38c

If you are quoting, paraphrasing, or making an **allusion** to statements or literary passages that are not generally familiar, cite the source. A phrase from Lincoln's Gettysburg Address could get by without a citation, but a remark made in a presidential news conference could not.

DO NOT DOCUMENT	DOCUMENT
the population of China	the Chinese balance of payments in 1992
the existence of a disease syndrome called AIDS	a possible connection between AIDS and the virus that carries cat leukemia
the fact that Dickens visited America	the supposed effect of Dickens's American visit on his subsequently written novels
the fact that huge sums are wagered illegally on professional football games	an alleged "fix" of a certain football game
a line from a nursery rhyme	a line from a poem by Yeats

38d Choose an appropriate style of documentation for your final copy.

In your reading you will encounter many documentation styles, but every version will belong to one of two general schemes. In *parenthetic citation form,* citations within parentheses in the main text are keyed to a list of "Works Cited" or "References" appearing at the end of the paper, article, chapter, or book. In *footnote/endnote form,* raised numbers in the main text—usually at the ends of sentences—are keyed to notes appearing either at the foot of the page **(footnotes)** or at the end of the whole text **(endnotes).** Both forms allow for **supplemental notes** (p. 489, 39a) that make comments or mention further references.

**source
38d**

PARENTHETIC CITATION FORM	FOOTNOTE/ENDNOTE FORM
No note numbers are used (except for supplemental notes).	Raised numbers appear in text.
No notes are used to cite works.	Notes appearing at foot of page or at end of text give citations corresponding to note numbers in text.

PARENTHETIC CITATION FORM	FOOTNOTE/ENDNOTE FORM
All references are made through parenthetic citations within text.	Parenthetic citations within text are used only for "subsequent references" to frequently cited works.
Supplemental notes, if any, appear after main text but before reference list.	Supplemental notes, if any, are integrated into footnotes or endnotes.
A reference list, identifying only works cited or consulted, appears at the end. The listed works match the parenthetic citations in the text.	A bibliography, identifying both works cited and works consulted, may appear after all the notes.

Until recently, parenthetic citation form has generally prevailed in the physical and social sciences and footnote/endnote form in the humanities. Parenthetic citation form is now gaining ground in the humanities as well. But if your instructor prefers footnote/endnote form, you should know how it works; see page 526, 39d.

Most research papers for composition courses are now written in parenthetic citation form, following the style of either the Modern Language Association or the American Psychological Association. We present the essential features of both styles in the next two chapters—**MLA style** in Chapter 39 and **APA style** in Chapter 40.

If you are writing a research paper for a course in a particular discipline—for example, biology, history, or mathematics—check with your instructor for the recommended style of citation. If you plan to publish a paper, look at a relevant journal and adopt its conventions. You can also consult one of the following style manuals if it corresponds to your subject matter.

source 38d

BIOLOGY:
CBE Style Manual: A Guide for Authors, Editors, and Publishers in the Biological Sciences (1983)

BUSINESS:
Report Writing for Businesses, by Raymond V. Lesikar (1986)

CHEMISTRY:
Handbook for Authors of Papers in American Chemical Society Publications (1978)

EDUCATION:
NEA Style Manual for Writers and Editors (1974)

GEOLOGY:
Guide to Authors: A Guide for the Preparation of Geological Maps and Reports, by Robert G. Blackadar et al. (1980)

HISTORY:
Historical Journals: A Handbook for Writers and Reviewers, by Dale R. Steiner (1981)

JOURNALISM:
The UPI Stylebook: A Handbook for Writers and Editors (1977)

LAW:
A Uniform System of Citation, ed. Harvard Law Review Association (1986)

LIBRARY SCIENCE:
A Style Manual for Citing Microform and Nonprint Media, by Eugene B. Fleisher (1978)

LINGUISTICS:
LSA Bulletin, Dec. issue, annually

MATHEMATICS:
A Manual for Authors of Mathematical Papers, ed. American Mathematical Society (1984)

source
38d

MEDICINE:
American Medical Association Manual of Style, by Cheryl Iverson et al. (1989)

PHYSICS:
Style Manual for Guidance in the Preparation of Papers, ed. Publication Board, American Institute of Physics (1978)

39 Using MLA Documentation

If your instructor asks you to follow the style of documentation recommended by the Modern Language Association (**MLA style**), you will find the information you need in this chapter. For a complete student research paper using MLA style, see pages 500–525 below. And if you need further detail, consult Joseph Gibaldi and Walter S. Achtert, *MLA Handbook for Writers of Research Papers* (3d ed., 1988).

MLA style includes two basic features:

1. Parenthetic citations *within* the text of the paper (39a)

2. An alphabetical list of works cited on a separate page at the *end* of the paper (39b)

You may also include **supplemental notes** to give information that is inappropriate for the main text of your paper. For the form and placement of such notes, see page 489 below.

39a Include MLA parenthetic citations within the text of your paper.

The parenthetic citations in your paper should give readers the minimum information they need to find (1) the correct item in the list of works cited at the end of your paper and (2) the part of the work from which you have borrowed material—usually a specific page. MLA citations rely on authors' *names* and, if necessary for clarity, the *titles* of their works.

As a general rule, place a citation at the end of the sentence in which you quote, summarize, paraphrase, or otherwise use a source.

Consult the student research paper on pages 500–525 for specific examples of how to place and punctuate citations.

Form of Citations

If you mention the author's name in your text, you should include only a page number in the parenthetic citation:

```
According to Kristina Orfali, Swedish family law

prohibits "all forms of corporal punishment, including

spankings" (430).
```

But if your text does not mention the author, you will need to include the author's last name in the citation:

```
One expert on Swedish family life points out that "all

forms of corporal punishment, including spankings," are

prohibited by law (Orfali 430).
```

Notice that the period comes after the citation. For an indented quotation (p. 354, 29h), place the end punctuation before the open-parenthesis mark.

The following sample MLA citations cover a variety of circumstances you may encounter in documenting sources.

A WORK BY TWO OR THREE AUTHORS:

```
The Dominion of Canada "embodied principles which

Edmund Burke and Benjamin Franklin had vainly

recommended" for the American colonies a hundred years

earlier (Palmer and Colton 547-48).

The visit of Henry II to Ireland in 1171 signaled the

beginning of English domination of the Irish (McCrum,

Cran, and MacNeil 165).
```

**MLA
39a**

Note that in both examples, the authors' names would be excluded from the citation if they were given in the text.

A WORK BY MORE THAN THREE AUTHORS:

The architectural committee recommended that the

building's staircase be restored rather than replaced

(Brunson et al. 27).

The Latin abbreviation *et al.* ("and others") indicates that Brunson has more than two coauthors.

A MULTIVOLUME WORK:

In 1892, Shaw began his battle against government

censorship of the theater (Holroyd 2:224).

Note that the volume number comes first and is followed by a colon and the page number.

AN ANONYMOUS WORK:

The word "Saint" is disregarded in the alphabetizing of

saints' names (Chicago Manual 18.103).

If a work lists no author, use its title in your parenthetic citation. To save space, you may shorten the title, but make sure that any shortened title begins with the first important word in the full title; otherwise, readers will have trouble locating the source in your list of works cited. Thus the *Chicago Manual of Style* becomes *Chicago Manual.* Note that an item number, rather than a page number, is used for a reference work in which all entries are consecutively numbered.

**MLA
39a**

A WORK BY A CORPORATE AUTHOR:

The American Society of Hospital Pharmacists considers

methicillin "particularly useful" in treating hospital-

acquired infections (89).

"Corporate" names are usually too long to be inserted into a parenthetic citation without distracting the reader. Make an effort to get the name into the main part of your sentence. The above source would appear in the list of works cited under the name of its corporate author: American Society of Hospital Pharmacists.

TWO OR MORE WORKS BY THE SAME AUTHOR:

As his wife irons the tablecloth, Mick slips "a fat

slab of breaded eggplant into a pan of spitting oil"

(Brennan, <u>Wild Desire</u> 41).

The title of the work is included in the citation when two or more works by the same author appear in the list of works cited (see p. 492, item 2).

AN INDIRECT SOURCE:

Writing in <u>Temps Modernes</u> in 1957, Woroszylski

expressed surprise at "how much political nonsense we

allowed ourselves to be talked into" (qtd. in Liehm and

Liehm 116).

If you have no access to the original text, use *qtd. in* to show that your source for the quotation is another work.

A CLASSIC VERSE PLAY OR POEM:

"I prithee, daughter," begs Lear, "do not make me mad"

(II.iv.212).

Cite acts, scenes, and lines instead of pages. The capital and lowercase Roman numerals here help to distinguish the act and scene from the line number; however, *2.4.212* would also be acceptable.

AN ENTIRE WORK:

Marilynn Olson provides an excellent overview of

Raskin's fiction.

> If you are referring to a whole work and if the author's name appears in your sentence, you need not supply any other information.

MORE THAN ONE WORK IN A CITATION:

Interest in the war poets shows no sign of flagging

(Crawford; Giddings; Hynes).

> But if your parenthetic citation becomes too cumbersome, consider replacing it with a supplemental note (see below).

Supplemental Notes

If you are following MLA parenthetic citation form, you will not be routinely using footnotes or endnotes to cite your sources. But on a rare occasion you may want to include **supplemental notes** to give information not appropriate for your main text. You can use such notes to add interesting but nonessential details:

> [1] According to Jalby, the peasants of Languedoc
> dressed lightly on the whole, but on feastdays,
> regardless of the heat, they wore their best winter
> clothes <u>over</u> their best summer ones to demonstrate
> their sense of luxury (194).

MLA
39a

Or you can use supplemental notes to supply more references than you could gracefully fit into one set of parentheses:

> [2] See also E. R. Dodds, <u>The Greeks and the</u>
> <u>Irrational</u> (Berkeley: U of California P, 1951) 145-62;

```
Richard Stillwell, "The Siting of Classical Greek
Temples," Journal of the Society of Architectural
Historians 13 (1954): 5; and Robert Scranton, "Group
Design in Greek Architecture," Art Bulletin 31 (1949):
251.
```

If the sources given in this note appeared in the list of works cited, the note could be briefer:

```
   2 See also Dodds 145-62; Stillwell 5; Scranton
251.
```

To add a supplemental note, put a raised number at the appropriate point in your main text and place the note either at the bottom of the page or on a separate page just before your "Works Cited" list. See page 520, 39c, for an example.

39b   At the end of your paper, include an MLA list of works cited.

Each parenthetical citation (39a) in your text must refer to an entry in the "Works Cited" list at the end of the paper. Order this list alphabetically by authors' last names or, when no author appears, by the first significant word of the title (omitting *A, An,* and *The*). If the author is an institution—for example, the Canadian Broadcasting Corporation—list the item by the first word in the corporate name (in this case *Canadian*).

MLA
39b

If you are citing more than one work by a given author, follow the alphabetical order of that author's *titles* (see p. 492, item 2, below for an example). And if a cited author is the coauthor of another work in your list, put the single-author work first. For a sample MLA "Works Cited" list, see pages 522–525.

The directory below gives typical kinds of entries that might appear in your "Works Cited" list. Locate the appropriate numbered item in the directory; then look up that item in the list that follows.

DIRECTORY OF ENTRIES: MLA LIST OF WORKS CITED

Books

1. A book by a single author
2. Two or more books by the same author
3. A book by two or three authors
4. A book by more than three authors
5. A book by a corporate author
6. An anonymous book
7. A book's preface, foreword, introduction, or afterword
8. The edited work of an author
9. An edited book or anthology
10. A work in an anthology
11. Two or more works in the same anthology
12. A book edited by two or three people
13. A book edited by more than three people
14. A translation
15. A republished book
16. A multivolume work

Articles

17. An article in a journal paginated by volume
18. An article in a journal paginated by issue
19. An article in a monthly magazine
20. An article in a weekly magazine
21. A review
22. An unsigned magazine article
23. A signed newspaper article
24. An unsigned newspaper article
25. An unsigned editorial

Other Written Works

26. An encyclopedia entry
27. A pamphlet or manual
28. A dissertation
29. A government publication
30. A published letter
31. An unpublished letter

Nonwritten Works

32. A theatrical performance
33. A film
34. A radio or television program
35. A recording
36. A lecture
37. An interview
38. Computer software

MLA 39b

Books

1. A BOOK BY A SINGLE AUTHOR:

Kendall, Elizabeth. <u>The Runaway Bride: Hollywood</u>

  <u>Romantic Comedy of the 1930s</u>. New York: Knopf,

  1990.

> Notice that each main division within the entry (author's name, title, and publication information) is followed by a period. In general, shorten the name of the publisher, usually to a single word. Thus *Alfred A. Knopf* becomes *Knopf, McGraw-Hill* becomes *McGraw,* and so forth.

2. TWO OR MORE BOOKS BY THE SAME AUTHOR:

Brennan, Karen. <u>Here on Earth</u>. Middletown: Wesleyan

  UP, 1988.

---. <u>Wild Desire</u>. Amherst: U of Massachusetts P,

  1991.

> *U* and *P* stand for *University* and *Press.*

3. A BOOK BY TWO OR THREE AUTHORS:

Liehm, Mira, and Antonin J. Liehm. <u>The Most Important</u>

  <u>Art: Soviet and Eastern European Film after 1945</u>.

  Berkeley: U of California P, 1977.

Alred, Gerald J., Walter E. Oliu, and Charles Brusaw.

  <u>The Professional Writer: A Guide for Advanced</u>

  <u>Technical Writing</u>. New York: St. Martin's, 1992.

**MLA
39b**

4. A BOOK BY MORE THAN THREE AUTHORS:

Lauer, Janice M., et al. <u>Four Worlds of Writing</u>. 2nd

  ed. New York: Harper, 1985.

5. A BOOK BY A CORPORATE AUTHOR:

American Society of Hospital Pharmacists. Consumer

    Drug Digest. New York: Facts on File, 1982.

6. AN ANONYMOUS BOOK:

Chicago Manual of Style. 13th ed. Chicago: U of

    Chicago P, 1982.

7. A BOOK'S PREFACE, FORWARD, INTRODUCTION, OR AFTERWORD:

Auden, W. H. Preface. Collected Shorter Poems: 1927-

    1957. By Auden. New York: Random, 1966.

Eliot, T. S. Introduction. Nightwood. By Djuna

    Barnes. New York: New Directions, 1961.

> Note that in the first example, the same person wrote
> the preface and the book. In the second example, the
> introduction is by a separate author.

8. THE EDITED WORK OF AN AUTHOR:

Plato. The Collected Dialogues of Plato: Including

    the Letters. Ed. Edith Hamilton and Huntington

    Cairns. Princeton: Princeton UP, 1961.

9. AN EDITED BOOK OR ANTHOLOGY:

DiYanni, Robert, ed. Literature: Reading Fiction,

    Poetry, Drama, and the Essay. 2nd ed. New York:

    McGraw, 1990.

> The abbreviation *ed.* following the name means *editor.*
> Later in the entry, *2nd ed.* indicates that the book is
> in its second edition.

MLA 39b

10. A WORK IN AN ANTHOLOGY:

Dillard, Annie. "Living Like Weasels." Literature:

    Reading Fiction, Poetry, Drama, and the Essay.

```
2nd ed.  Ed. Robert DiYanni.  New York: McGraw,

1990.  1568-73.
```

The title of Dillard's work—an essay—goes in quotation marks. The numbers at the end (*1568–73*) indicate the pages on which her essay appears.

11. TWO OR MORE WORKS IN THE SAME ANTHOLOGY:

```
DiYanni, Robert, ed.  Literature: Reading Fiction,

    Poetry, Drama, and the Essay.  2nd ed.  New York:

McGraw, 1990.
```

Supply an entry for the whole anthology (as above). Then include a separate entry for each selection you cite from the anthology, as follows:

```
Baldwin, James.  "Notes of a Native Son."  DiYanni

    1620-33.

Dillard, Annie.  "Living Like Weasels."  DiYanni 1568-

    73.
```

The cross reference at the end gives (a) the last name of the editor, sending readers to full bibliographic information elsewhere in the list, and (b) the page numbers of the selection.

12. A BOOK EDITED BY TWO OR THREE PEOPLE:

```
White, George Abbott, and Charles Newman, eds.

    Literature in Revolution.  New York: Holt, 1972.
```

13. A BOOK EDITED BY MORE THAN THREE PEOPLE:

```
Kermode, Frank, et al., eds.  The Oxford Anthology of

    English Literature. 2 vols.  New York: Oxford UP,

    1973.
```

14. A TRANSLATION:

Soseki, Natsume. The Miner. Trans. Jay Rubin.

Stanford: Stanford UP, 1988.

15. A REPUBLISHED BOOK:

Conroy, Frank. Stop-time. 1967. New York: Penguin,

1977.

16. A MULTIVOLUME WORK:

Kermode, Frank, et al. The Oxford Anthology of

English Literature. Vol. 1. New York: Oxford

UP, 1973. 2 vols.

> Follow the above format when you cite only one volume (in this case the first) of a multivolume work. If you cite two or more volumes, use the format given in item 13 above. When the volume you are citing has its own title, use the format given below. Note that the inclusive dates of publication appear at the end of the entry for a work published over several years.

Holroyd, Michael. The Pursuit of Power. New York:

Random, 1989. Vol. 2. of Bernard Shaw. 3 vols.

1988-91.

Articles

17. AN ARTICLE IN A JOURNAL PAGINATED BY VOLUME:

Cooper, Arnold M. "Psychoanalysis at One Hundred:

Beginnings of Maturity." Journal of the American

Psychoanalytic Association 32 (1984): 245-67.

MLA 39b

> Use this form for professional journals in which page numbering continues through an entire annual volume instead of starting with page 1 for each new issue.

Supply the volume number (*32* in this example), the year (*1984*), and the page numbers of the article (*245–67*).

18. AN ARTICLE IN A JOURNAL PAGINATED BY ISSUE:

Leach, Laurie. "'The Difficult Business of Intimacy':

Friendship and Writing in Virginia Woolf's The

Waves." South Central Review 7.2 (1990): 53-66.

If the journal starts each issue with page 1, supply the volume and issue numbers (in this case volume *7*, number *2*).

19. AN ARTICLE IN A MONTHLY MAGAZINE:

Renfro, William. "Washington: Green Pastures."

Atlantic Feb. 1992: 24-26.

Abbreviate the names of the months except *May, June,* and *July*.

20. AN ARTICLE IN A WEEKLY MAGAZINE:

Auchincloss, Kenneth. "Limits of Democracy."

Newsweek 27 Jan. 1992: 28-30.

21. A REVIEW:

Singer, Brett. "Husbands at Bay." Rev. of Only

Children, by Rafael Yglesias. New York Times

Book Review 17 July 1988: 19.

22. AN UNSIGNED MAGAZINE ARTICLE:

"Mozartiana." New Yorker 24 June 1991: 23-24.

23. A SIGNED NEWSPAPER ARTICLE:

Nevius, C. W. "When Choices Were Simpler." San

Francisco Chronicle 20 Feb. 1991, five-star ed.:

D1.

After the date, specify the edition, if one is indicated, and supply both the section and the page number(s).

24. AN UNSIGNED NEWSPAPER ARTICLE:

"For Lasting Peace: Tougher Terms." New York Times 20

Feb. 1991, national ed,: A14.

25. AN UNSIGNED EDITORIAL:

"Head Start Plan Only a Half-Ounce of Prevention."

Editorial. Austin American-Statesman 25 Jan.

1992: A20.

Other Written Works

26. AN ENCYCLOPEDIA ENTRY:

L[ustig], L[awrence] K. "Alluvial Fans."

Encyclopaedia Britannica: Macropaedia. 1985.

> The author's initials appear at the end of the encyclope-
> dia entry; they are identified elsewhere. Note that vol-
> ume and page numbers are unnecessary when items
> appear in alphabetical order. But since the *Britannica*
> from 1974 onward has three sets of contents, the note
> should indicate which one is intended—in this case the
> *Macropaedia.*

27. A PAMPHLET OR MANUAL:

Wiggins, Robert R., and Steve Brecher, with William P.

Steinberg. Suitcase User's Guide. Sunnyvale:

Software Supply, 1987.

28. A DISSERTATION:

Boudin, Henry Morton. "The Ripple Effect in Classroom

Management." Diss. U of Michigan, 1970.

**MLA
39b**

29. A GOVERNMENT PUBLICATION:

United States. Internal Revenue Service. Your

Federal Income Tax. Washington: GPO, 1991.

30. A PUBLISHED LETTER:

McFann, Winfried S. Letter. <u>Popular Photography</u> Aug.

1988: 8.

31. AN UNPUBLISHED LETTER:

Graff, Gerald. Letter to the author. 18 Jan. 1993.

Nonwritten Works

32. A THEATRICAL PERFORMANCE:

<u>Six Degrees of Separation</u>. By John Guare. Dir. Jerry

Zaks. With Stockard Channing, Courtney B. Vance,

and John Cunningham. Vivian Beaumont Theatre,

New York. 20 Feb. 1991.

33. FILM:

<u>The Hard Way</u>. Dir. John Badham. With Michael J. Fox

and James Woods. Universal, 1991.

34. A RADIO OR TELEVISION PROGRAM:

<u>Knocking on Armageddon's Door</u>. Prod. and dir. Torv

Carlsen and John R. Magnus. PBS. 19 July 1988.

35. A RECORDING:

Beethoven, Ludwig van. Symphony no. 8 in F, op. 93.

Cond. Pierre Monteux. Vienna Philharmonic Orch.

Decca, STS 15238, 1964.

MLA 39b

> MLA requires that names of musical works be under-
> lined except when (as here) the work is identified by
> its form, number, and key rather than by a title.

36. A LECTURE:

Hirsch, E. D., Jr. "Frontiers of Critical Theory."

    Wyoming Conference on Freshman and Sophomore

    English, U of Wyoming. Laramie, 9 July 1979.

37. AN INTERVIEW:

Collier, Peter, and David Horowitz. Personal

    interview. 5 Jan. 1991.

38. COMPUTER SOFTWARE:

Word. Release 5.0. Computer software. Microsoft,

    1991. Macintosh.

39c   Note the features of a research paper using MLA documentation style.

Lovell White wrote the research paper on the following pages for her first-year composition course. White's instructor supplied a list of fifty well-known historical figures and asked for an essay of about 1500 words analyzing some contribution made by one of those figures. Since White had done some preliminary reading about Thomas Jefferson in her history course, she decided to explore his work in more detail, focusing on either his theories of education or his architectural achievement. She quickly settled on architecture after discovering that her campus library had ample material on the topic.

    Note these features of White's finished paper:

1. Title page (p. 500). For an essay without a separate title page, see page 83.

2. Topic outline (p. 501). If your instructor prefers a sentence outline, see the model on page 32.

3. Text of the paper (pp. 502–519).

4. Supplemental notes (p. 520).

5. List of works cited (pp. 522–525).

MLA
39c

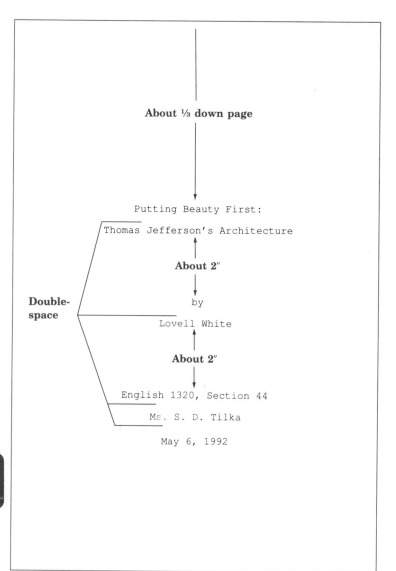

About ⅓ down page

Putting Beauty First:

Thomas Jefferson's Architecture

About 2″

Double-space

by

Lovell White

About 2″

English 1320, Section 44

Ms. S. D. Tilka

May 6, 1992

**Use lowercase Roman numerals
to number outline pages (*i, ii, iii*, etc.).**   i

Thesis: Although Thomas Jefferson was committed to
practicality as well as beauty in his architectural
designs, he consistently placed aesthetic
considerations first.   **The writer uses
                                                a topic outline
                                                (p. 32).**

                        Outline

   I. Introduction: Jefferson as architect

       A. A lifelong passion

       B. Putting beauty first

  II. Jefferson's aesthetic ideal

       A. The study of architecture

           1. Learning from books

           2. Travels in Europe

       B. An innate sense of the beautiful

       C. Rejecting the merely functional

       D. A love of natural beauty

 III. Balancing theory and practice

       A. Beauty vs. utility

           1. No inherent conflict

           2. The dome of Monticello

           3. The Virginia capitol building

       B. Beauty vs. cost

       C. Beauty vs. simplicity

  IV. Conclusion: shaping a national architecture

**MLA
39c**

Putting Beauty First:

Thomas Jefferson's Architecture

Thomas Jefferson was, among other things, author of the Declaration of Independence, Secretary of State under Washington, foreign ambassador to France, governor of Virginia, and the third president of the United States. But according to Jane Margolies, architecture, not politics, was his lifelong passion.[1] Among the many fruits of that passion are Jefferson's widely admired plans for the University of Virginia and for his home, Monticello, whose design and construction occupied him off and on for forty years (Bottorff 17). Fiske Kimball, a leading expert on Jefferson's architectural influence, calls him "the father of our national architecture" (89).

Jefferson the architect had a heart for beauty and a mind for practicality. The Marquis de Chastellux, after visiting Monticello, said, "Mr. Jefferson is the first American who has consulted the Fine Arts to know how he should shelter himself from the weather" (qtd. in Iovine). Indeed, in all of his work Jefferson blended the practical considerations of "shelter" with a sense of what is

MLA
39c

1. *Format.* On standard 8½″ × 11″ paper, the writer's last name and a page number should appear one-half inch from the top of each page. All other margins—bottom and sides—should be one inch. Note the use of double spacing throughout the paper.

2. *Title.* The title of the paper forecasts its thesis: Jefferson's preference for aesthetics over practicality.

3. *Introduction.* White's introduction is two paragraphs long. The first paragraph announces her topic—Jefferson as architect. The second narrows the focus of the paper, discussing the balance of practical and aesthetic considerations in Jefferson's work.

4. *Common knowledge.* Since the information in White's opening sentence is common knowledge, no documentation is necessary.

5. *Supplemental note.* A raised number sends readers to a supplemental note (p. 489, 39a) located on a separate page following the main text.

6. *Indirect source.* By including the phrase *qtd. in,* White indicates that the borrowed words are "quoted in" a work by Iovine, not taken directly from a source by the Marquis de Chastellux. Note also that since Iovine's article is only one page long, a page reference is not needed in the parenthetic citation.

White 2

artful and aesthetically pleasing. Writing about
the great demand for new housing in America, he
acknowledged the practical importance of
architecture but insisted on the need "to introduce
taste into an art which shows so much" (<u>Writings</u>
660). Jefferson's architectural standards,
according to William Bottorff, included not just
beauty but also functionalism, economy, simplicity,
and fidelity to tradition (98). Of all these
qualities, though, Jefferson was most firmly
committed to beauty; when he had to choose between
the practical and the aesthetically pleasing, he
consistently favored the latter.

This aesthetic preference may have derived in
part from Jefferson's scholarly inclinations. His
personal library included an extensive collection of
architectural classics,[2] which were his greatest
tutors, and he added to his knowledge during his
travels in Europe (Nichols 164). While in Paris for
political purposes, Jefferson "studied as many
buildings as his duties would allow" (Smith 599).
And although Parisian architecture interested him
most, he "was not content to study those [buildings]

MLA
39c

7. *Two sources by the same author.* Since the paper includes quotations from two different volumes by Jefferson (*Writings* and *Notes on the State of Virginia*), White includes a title in her parenthetic citation, indicating which work she is quoting.

8. *Thesis.* White states her thesis, placing it prominently at the end of the two-paragraph introduction.

9. *Paragraph based on several sources.* This paragraph draws from three different sources. Since naming each author in the text would be cumbersome, White gives their names in the parenthetic citations.

10. *Use of brackets.* In order to clarify the quotation from Bruce, White inserts the word *buildings* in brackets (p. 362, 29r). Here is the original material as White recorded it on a quotation card:

Bruce, p. 42   J's travels

J "was not content to study those [buildings] in Paris alone, but travelled through England, Holland, Italy, and Southern France on a tour of inspection."

in Paris alone, but travelled through England, Holland, Italy, and Southern France on a tour of inspection" (Bruce 42).

Because he learned architecture by studying books and the outside features of buildings, Jefferson tended not to consider the practical uses of structures until he had assessed their aesthetic value. He wrote of humanity's "innate sense" of the beautiful, and he saw architecture as a subject that appealed to that sense through the imagination (Writings 1336). According to Bottorff, Jefferson "loved to talk . . . of the 'sublime,' by which he sometimes simply meant the 'beautiful'" (88). It is not surprising, then, that he perceived architecture above all as an expression of beauty and secondarily as a practical craft.

For Jefferson, if the first condition--beauty-- was not met, mere practicality was inadequate. Thus he criticized the architecture of the old capitol building in Richmond, Virginia, for its lack of symmetry and called the state's Hospital and College "rude, mis-shapen piles" (Notes 153). And even though it was a functional, useful building, he drew

11

12

11. *Use of ellipsis.* An ellipsis (p. 359, 29o) indicates where White omits material from the quotation. Note also the use of single quotation marks (p. 350, 29e) to indicate words quoted in Bottorff's book.

> **ORIGINAL PASSAGE:**
> He loved to talk in terms of the eighteenth-century notion of the "sublime," by which he sometimes simply meant the "beautiful."

12. *Title incuded in a parenthetic citation.* White quotes a book by Jefferson, using a title to distinguish it from another book by Jefferson in her list of works cited. To avoid an overly long parenthetic citation, she shortens the title. Thus *Notes on the State of Virginia* becomes *Notes*. If White had included both Jefferson's name and the title of his book in her text, a page number alone would have sufficed in the parenthetic citation.

MLA 39c

White 4

new sketches for remodeling the Governor's Palace at Williamsburg simply because he considered the building aesthetically unattractive (Bottorff 97).

Jefferson's preference for beauty over function may also have stemmed from his love of nature. He wrote fondly, for example, of the site he chose for Monticello: "where has nature spread so rich a mantle under the eye?" (qtd. in McLaughlin 35). Jack McLaughlin, author of a book about Monticello, explains that Jefferson's choice alone shows a preference for aesthetics over practicality. In building his home on a mountain, he "defied conventional wisdom" and thus "forfeited the economic benefits and practical conveniences of a riverside location" (34). He did so, clearly, for the sake of a spectacular view. "How sublime," he writes, "to look down into the workhouse of nature . . . all fabricated at our feet!" (qtd. in McLaughlin 35).

Jefferson, of course, may not have seen his choice as one between two irreconcilable opposites. According to biographer Dumas Malone, he "perceived no conflict between utility and beauty" (45), and

MLA 39c

13

14

15

13. *Paragraph based on information from a single source.* White indicates exactly where she found the borrowed material, supplying three page references, two for McLaughlin's quotations of Jefferson (*qtd. in*) and one for McLaughlin himself. Notice that one quotation from Jefferson ends with a question mark, the other with an exclamation point. In each case, the terminal punctuation comes *before* the close-quotation mark, while an added period follows the parenthetic citation. In all other cases, the period *after* the citation suffices by itself to end a sentence.

14. *Quotation integrated without punctuation.* Because she integrates the quotation from Malone into her own sentence structure, White incudes no comma or colon between the word *he* and the quoted phrase *perceived no conflict . . .* (see p. 357, 29k).

15. *Placement of a parenthetic citation.* Since White borrows from Malone only in the first clause of her sentence, her parenthetic citation immediately follows that clause. Note that the comma comes after, not before, the parentheses. As a general rule, parenthetic citations go at the ends of sentences, where they are less distracting to readers.

MLA
39c

very often, his plans reflect a remarkable harmony
between the two. In designing Monticello, for
example, Jefferson added practical features that
ensured a degree of privacy for occupants--a rarity
in an eighteenth-century home with servants
(McLaughlin 255). He also designed the
"dependencies" (service areas such as the kitchen,
smokehouse, and stable) for easy access to the
mansion without allowing them to disrupt the
building's aesthetic beauty (Smith 600). According
to architectural historian Leland Roth, Jefferson
built the dependencies partially underground to
"preserve the view" from the main house (73).

While he saw no inherent conflict between
beauty and function, Jefferson often put much energy
into achieving a harmonious effect. His method of
design, writes McLaughlin, was to start with "an
impractical but aesthetically satisfying
architectural motif" and then to alter it, making
"the space as comfortable and livable as possible"
(36). The dome atop Monticello is a good example.
As McLaughlin explains, this "outstanding
architectural feature" met Jefferson's high

MLA
39c

16

17

18

19

16. *Use of summary.* White summarizes a point from McLaughlin.

   ORIGINAL PASSAGE:
   Another modern convenience Jefferson designed into his house was privacy. In the eighteenth century, domestic privacy was rare. Houses were invariably overcrowded—particularly the bedrooms—and floor plans made most rooms public spaces. In the South, house servants were ubiquitous.

17. *Summary and quotation combined in one sentence.* White integrates a brief quoted phrase into her summary of Roth. Here is her notecard, showing both summary and direct quotation:

   Roth, p. 13   *Monticello*

   Unlike earlier American architects, I de-emphasized auxiliary bldgs. He "pushed the dependencies [service bldgs.] at Monticello into the earth so as to preserve the view."

   ---

18. *Summary and quotation combined within a paragraph.* In this paragraph, based on information from a single key source, White blends summary and quotation. Even though all borrowed material comes from the same page of McLaughlin's book, White gives three separate parenthetic citations. A single citation at the end of the paragraph would not have been adequate to give readers the location of all borrowed ideas and quotations.

**MLA
39c**

19. *Page numbers alone in parenthetic citations.* Since McLaughlin's name is given in the text itself, each parenthetic citation includes only a page number.

aesthetic expectations, but it served little
practical purpose (36). Despite Jefferson's
attempts to make the dome room functional, it
remained "useless as lived-in space" and eventually
became "an elegant, expensive attic storeroom" (36).

Not all of Jefferson's adaptations, however,
resulted in unnecessary storage space. When invited
to submit a design for the capitol building at
Richmond, Virginia, he used as his model a Roman
temple, the Maison Carrée at Nîmes in southern
France (Roth 74). Jefferson described his plan in a
letter to James Madison: "It will be superior in
beauty to any thing in America and not inferior to
any thing in the world" (qtd. in Bottorff 98). In
order to achieve "superior beauty," Jefferson had to
create rooms and spatial arrangements that would fit
the templelike shape of the structure. Says
Bottorff, "In all this he succeeded marvelously,"
making the building both functional and beautiful
(23).

In Jefferson's mind, aesthetics took priority
not just over function but over cost as well. Of
his work on the University of Virginia, Malone

20

21

22

**MLA
39c**

20. *Transitions between paragraphs.* Here and elsewhere in the paper, White uses explicit transitions to link her paragraphs.

21. *Colon used to introduce a quotation.* Here a colon emphatically introduces a key sentence from Jefferson's letter (see p. 357, 291).

22. *Comma used to introduce a quotation.* White introduces this quotation with an introductory tag (*Says Bottorff*) followed by a comma (see p. 357, 291).

MLA
39c

White 7

writes: "Until the end of his days, Jefferson was
accused of setting his sights too high, and he was
charged more than once with underestimating costs"
(385). Having envisioned a complex of buildings
"original and unique" (qtd. in Guinness and Sadler
149), he seemed unconcerned with budgetary
constraints. According to Malone, many Virginia
legislators thought that Jefferson's plans were
extravagant and thus hesitated to fund campus
construction (385). Guinness and Sadler note:

> Jefferson insisted that his University
> could not have been built more
> economically than it was, and here the
> practical side of his nature comes face to
> face with the visionary. [A comparable
> set of buildings] could of course have
> been built for less, but at the cost of
> beauty. (150)

And that was clearly a cost Jefferson was unwilling
to pay.

Simplicity, too, lost out to beauty when
Jefferson was forced to decide between the two.
This became evident when, as president, he took an

23

24

25

26

23. *Citing a source by two authors.* White includes both names in her parenthetic citation. If a work has more than three authors, MLA requires inclusion of the first name only, followed by the abbreviation *et al.,* meaning "and others."

24. *Indented quotation.* For a passage of more than four lines of prose, White uses an indented quotation (p. 354, 29h). Notice the double spacing before, after, and within the quotation. Since the ten-space indention alone suffices to indicate quoted material, no quotation marks appear at the beginning and end of the passage.

25. *Bracketed material within an indented quotation.* For the sake of clarity, White replaces a phrase from Guinness and Sadler with a bracketed phrase of her own.

26. *Parenthetic citation for an indented quotation.* The period at the end of an indented quotation comes before, not after, the parenthetic citation.

MLA
39c

active role in the building of the nation's capitol.
Paul Norton explains that Jefferson wanted panel
skylights in the dome of the Hall of
Representatives, while the architect in charge,
Benjamin Latrobe, argued for a simpler lighting
scheme to avoid the leakage, condensation, and other
difficulties that the skylights would cause (220).
In a letter to Jefferson, Latrobe insisted, "nothing
in the field of good taste . . . can be beautiful
which appears useless or unmeaning" (qtd. in Norton
222). But in the end, Jefferson would not waver.
The practical architect had to capitulate to the
visionary one, and the skylights were installed.

    Of all the architectural standards Jefferson
set forth, beauty is the only one to which he
consistently, even adamantly, adhered. Although
this commitment sometimes went against common sense
and budgetary demands, it enabled Jefferson to bring
style and elegance to the new country's edifices.
Bottorff concludes that Jefferson's "architectural
contributions to American culture are outweighed
only by his political ones" (97). And while his
work is largely classical in style, he was, as Smith

MLA
39c

27. *Indirect source with an ellipsis.* Again, White uses an indirect source, quoting Latrobe's words as they appear in a work by Norton. An ellipsis indicates White's omission from the quoted material.

> **ORIGINAL MATERIAL (NORTON QUOTING LATROBE):**
> "The question would be as to its [a cupola's] real or apparent utility in the place in which it appeared," he continued, "for nothing in the field of good taste, which ought never to be at warfare with good sense, can be beautiful which appears useless or unmeaning."

28. *Conclusion.* In the final paragraph, White reinforces her main point and then looks beyond the thesis, offering a broader perspective on Jefferson's achievement as an architect (see p. 134, 10k).

MLA
39c

White 9

points out, "no copyist" (599). On the contrary,

Jefferson used classical designs in a visionary way,

combining book learning with firsthand observation

to become his country's "first great native-born

architect" (Nichols 163).

29. *Ending the paper.* White saves a clinching statement for her final sentence (p. 133, 10i). The quotation from Nichols summarizes Jefferson's standing as an architect and echoes Fiske's assessment, quoted at the end of the first paragraph.

Notes

30

31

¹ Jefferson also had a passion for horticulture. According to Dumas Malone, "Gardening supplemented architecture as an interest, and, like it, was one of the most absorbing and abiding of his life" (45). At Monticello Jefferson planted a three-tiered vegetable garden and, at one point, had 384 fruit trees (48).

32

² For a list of the architectural books in Jefferson's collection, see Kimball 90-101. Kimball also reprints many of Jefferson's surviving architectural drawings. For additional drawings and photographs, see Guinness and Sadler.

MLA
39c

30. *Format.* Supplemental notes go on a separate page following the last page of text. White follows recommended MLA form, centering the heading and double-spacing within and between the notes.

31. *Adding a further comment.* The first supplemental note offers a related point that would disrupt White's argument if placed in the main text. Notice that any source mentioned in the notes should be included in the list of works cited.

32. *Adding bibliographic information.* A second supplemental note gives bibliographic information about Jefferson's architectural books and drawings.

Works Cited

Adams, William Howard, ed. Jefferson and the Arts: An   **34**
    Extended View. Washington: National Gallery of
    Art, 1976.

Bottorff, William. Thomas Jefferson. Boston: Twayne,
    1979.

Bruce, Philip Alexander. History of the University of
    Virginia, 1819-1991. New York: Macmillan, 1920.

Guinness, Desmond, and Julius Trousdale Sadler, Jr.
    Mr. Jefferson: Architect. New York: Viking, 1973.

Iovine, Julie V. "Thomas Jefferson at Home."
    Connoisseur June 1987: 26.

Jefferson, Thomas. Notes on the State of Virginia.   **35**
    Ed. William Peden. Chapel Hill: U of North
    Carolina P, 1955.

---. Writings. Ed. Merrill D. Peterson. New York:
    Library of America, 1984.

Kimball, Fiske. Thomas Jefferson: Architect. 1916.   **36**
    New York: Da Capo, 1968.

Malone, Dumas. The Sage of Monticello. Boston: **37**
    Little, 1981. Vol. 6 of Jefferson and His Time.
    6 vols. 1948-81.

33. *Format.* The alphabetized list of works cited begins on a separate page. See page 490, 39b, for information about ordering works within the list. The centered heading starts two inches from the top of the page. Notice the double spacing within and between entries.

34. *Form of entries.* Sample MLA entries for various types of works appear on pages 492–499. The comments on this page point out special circumstances in White's list of works cited.

35. *Two works by one author.* Two works by Jefferson (a collection and a single volume) appear under his name, not under the names of the editors. These entries are alphabetized by title. Three unspaced hyphens replace Jefferson's name in the second entry.

36. *A republished book.* The original date of publication (1916) goes after the title, the date of republication (1968) at the end.

37. *A multivolume work.* White uses only one volume of Malone's six-volume work. Information about that volume comes first and is followed by information about the entire work: its title, the total number of volumes, and the range of years during which it appeared. If White were using more than one volume, she would cite only the entire work, using the citation form given in item 13, page 494. Notice that the final entry in White's list is also a multivolume work, whose three volumes appeared in the same year, 1981.

MLA
39c

White 12

Margolies, Jane. "Our Architect President." House
    Beautiful June 1990: 144.
McLaughlin, Jack. Jefferson and Monticello: The
    Biography of a Builder. New York: Holt, 1988.
Nichols, Frederick D. "Jefferson: The Making of an
    Architect." Adams 159-85.
Norton, Paul F. "Thomas Jefferson and the Planning of
    the National Capitol." Adams 187-232.
Roth, Leland M. A Concise History of Architecture.
    New York: Harper, 1979.
Smith, G. E. Kidder. The South and Midwest. Garden
    City: Anchor-Doubleday, 1981. Vol. 2 of The
    Architecture of the United States. 3 vols.

38

38. *Two selections from an anthology.* The essays by Nichols and Norton appear in an anthology. Note that for each essay, White supplies a cross reference to the anthology itself, which has its own entry earlier in the list of works cited. If White were using only one essay from the anthology, she would combine all bibliographic information (for the essay and the anthology) in a single entry. For further information and sample entries, see pages 493–494, items 10 and 11.

**MLA
39c**

39d Note the features of "alternative MLA" footnote/endnote style.

If your instructor prefers the "alternative MLA" style of citation, you will use either **footnotes** or **endnotes** instead of parenthetic citations and a reference list. A footnote appears at the bottom of the page on which its corresponding number appears within the text. Endnotes, by contrast, appear in a sequence at the end of the paper. If you include any supplemental notes (p. 489, 39a), integrate them with your other footnotes or endnotes.

Wherever you decide to put your notes, you should follow these rules for handling the note numbers within your text:

1. Number all the notes consecutively (1, 2, 3, . . .).

2. Elevate the note numbers slightly, as here.[8]

3. Place the numbers after, not before, the quotations or other information being cited: not x As Rosenhan says,[11] "the evidence is simply not compelling," but As Rosenhan says, "the evidence is simply not compelling."[11]

4. Place the numbers after all punctuation except a dash; even parentheses, colons, and semicolons should precede note numbers.

Endnotes versus Footnotes

Type endnotes on a new page after your main text, but before a bibliography if you are supplying one. Here is the standard form for endnotes.

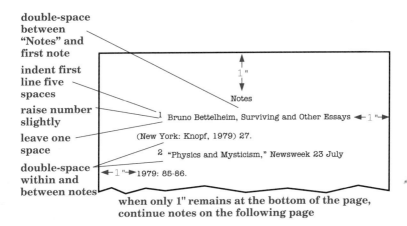

double-space between "Notes" and first note

indent first line five spaces

raise number slightly

leave one space

double-space within and between notes

1 "

Notes

¹ Bruno Bettelheim, Surviving and Other Essays ◄─ 1 "─►

(New York: Knopf, 1979) 27.

² "Physics and Mysticism," Newsweek 23 July

◄─ 1 "─► 1979: 85-86.

when only 1" remains at the bottom of the page, continue notes on the following page

Handle footnotes just like endnotes except for these differences:

1. On each page where you will have notes, stop your main text high enough to leave room for the notes.

2. Quadruple-space between the end of the text and the first note on a page.

3. Single-space within the notes, but double-space between them.

4. If you have to carry a note over to the next page, type a solid line a full line below the last line of text on that new page, quadruple-space, and continue the note. Then add any new notes.

**MLA
39d**

Thus, footnotes at the bottom of a page look like this.

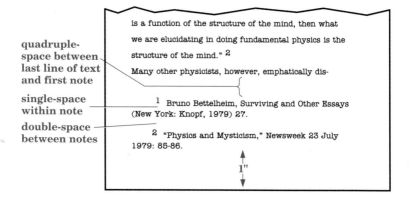

quadruple-space between last line of text and first note

single-space within note

double-space between notes

is a function of the structure of the mind, then what we are elucidating in doing fundamental physics is the structure of the mind." [2]

Many other physicists, however, emphatically dis-

   [1] Bruno Bettelheim, Surviving and Other Essays (New York: Knopf, 1979) 27.

   [2] "Physics and Mysticism," Newsweek 23 July 1979: 85-86.

1"

And here is a footnote carried over from a preceding page.

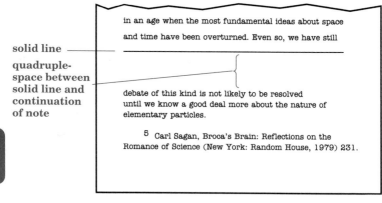

solid line

quadruple-space between solid line and continuation of note

in an age when the most fundamental ideas about space and time have been overturned. Even so, we have still

debate of this kind is not likely to be resolved until we know a good deal more about the nature of elementary particles.

   [5] Carl Sagan, Broca's Brain: Reflections on the Romance of Science (New York: Random House, 1979) 231.

MLA
39d

First Notes

To see how notes differ from entries in a list of works cited, compare the following sample notes with the corresponding entries on pages 492–499. Notes 1–17 include references to specific parts of the book or article cited.

1 Elizabeth Kendall, The Runaway Bride: Hollywood Romantic Comedy of the 1930s (New York: Knopf, 1990) 107.

2 Mira Liehm and Antonin J. Liehm, The Most Important Art: Soviet and Eastern European Film after 1945 (Berkeley: U of California P, 1977) 234–45.

3 American Society of Hospital Pharmacists, Consumer Drug Digest (New York: Facts on File, 1982) 107.

4 Chicago Manual of Style, 13th ed. (Chicago: U of Chicago P, 1982) 18.103.

5 T. S. Eliot, introduction, Nightwood, by Djuna Barnes (New York: New Directions, 1961) xiii.

6 Plato, The Collected Dialogues of Plato: Including the Letters, ed. Edith Hamilton and Huntington Cairns (Princeton: Princeton UP, 1961) 327.

MLA 39d

7 Annie Dillard, "Living Like Weasels." Literature: Reading Fiction, Poetry, Drama, and the Essay, ed. Robert DiYanni, 2nd ed. (New York: McGraw, 1990) 1571.

[8] Frank Kermode et al., eds., The Oxford Anthology of English Literature, 2 vols. (New York: Oxford UP, 1973) 1:209-11.

[9] Natsume Soseki, The Miner, trans. Jay Rubin (Stanford: Stanford UP, 1988) 99-103.

[10] Frank Conroy, Stop-time (1967; New York: Penguin, 1977) 8.

[11] Arnold M. Cooper, "Psychoanalysis at One Hundred: Beginnings of Maturity," Journal of the American Psychoanalytic Association 32 (1984): 250.

[12] Laurie Leach, "'The Difficult Business of Intimacy': Friendship and Writing in Virginia Woolf's The Waves," South Central Review 7.2 (1990): 57-58.

[13] William Renfro, "Washington: Green Pastures," Atlantic Feb. 1992: 24.

[14] Brett Singer, "Husbands at Bay," rev. of Only Children, by Rafael Yglesias, New York Times Book Review 17 July 1988: 19.

[15] "Mozartiana," New Yorker 24 June 1991: 24.

[16] C. W. Nevius, "When Choices Were Simpler," San Francisco Chronicle 20 Feb. 1991, five-star ed.: D1.

[17] "For Lasting Peace: Tougher Terms," New York Times 20 Feb. 1991, national ed.: A14.

[18] L[awrence] K. L[ustig], "Alluvial Fans," Encyclopaedia Britannica, 1985, Macropaedia.

19 Robert R. Wiggins and Steve Brecher, with William P. Steinberg, Suitcase User's Guide (Sunnyvale: Software Supply, 1987).

20 Henry Morton Boudin, "The Ripple Effect in Classroom Management," diss., U of Michigan, 1970, 78-93.

21 United States, Internal Revenue Service, Your Federal Income Tax (Washington: GPO, 1991).

22 Winfried S. McFann, letter, Popular Photography Aug. 1988: 8.

23 Gerald Graff, letter to the author, 18 Jan. 1993.

24 John Guare, Six Degrees of Separation, dir. Jerry Zaks, with Stockard Channing, Courtney B. Vance, and John Cunningham, Vivian Beaumont Theatre, New York, 20 Feb. 1991.

25 The Hard Way, dir. John Badham, with Michael J. Fox and James Woods, Universal, 1991.

26 Knocking on Armageddon's Door, prod. and dir. Torv Carlsen and John R. Magnus, PBS, 19 July 1988.

27 Ludwig van Beethoven, Symphony no. 8 in F, op. 93, cond. Pierre Monteux, Vienna Philharmonic Orch., Decca, STS 15238, 1964.

28 E. D. Hirsch, Jr., "Frontiers of Critical Theory," Wyoming Conference on Freshman and Sophomore English, U of Wyoming, Laramie, 9 July 1979.

MLA
39d

^{29} Peter Collier and David Horowitz, personal interview, 5 Jan. 1991.

^{30} <u>Word</u>, release 5.0, computer software, Microsoft, 1991, Macintosh.

Subsequent References

After you have provided one full endnote or footnote, you can be brief in citing the same work again:

^{31} Kendall 197.

If you refer to more than one work by the same author, add a shortened title:

^{32} Michaels, <u>Men's Club</u> 45.

^{33} Michaels, <u>I Would Have Saved Them</u> 89-91.

If you cite the same work a third time, do not use the obsolete abbreviations *ibid.* or *op. cit.;* repeat the identifying information given in your first shortened reference. If the title of the whole work is cumbersome, abbreviate it.

FIRST NOTE:

^{34} <u>The McGraw-Hill Encyclopedia of World Biography</u>, 12 vols. (New York: McGraw, 1973) 6:563; hereafter cited as <u>MEWB</u>.

SUBSEQUENT NOTE:

^{35} <u>MEWB</u> 8:354.

If the same work comes up repeatedly in your notes, provide one full reference and then shift to parenthetic citations.

FIRST NOTE:
   36 William Shakespeare, <u>The Merchant of Venice</u>,

ed. Louis B. Wright and Virginia LaMar (New York:

Washington Square, 1957) II.iii.43.

SUBSEQUENT PARENTHETIC REFERENCE:
Portia tells Nerissa that she will do anything "ere I

will be married to a sponge" (I.ii.90-91).

Bibliography

A **bibliography** is a list of works that you have consulted or that you recommend to your readers for further reference. Research papers, dissertations, and scholarly books that do not follow a parenthetic citation style of documentation (39a–c, 40a–c) typically contain bibliographies at the end. If you are supplying endnotes or footnotes, you can decide whether or not to include a bibliography by asking whether your notes have given a sufficient idea of your sources.

For bibliographical form, follow the conventions specified for an MLA reference list of "Works Cited" (p. 490). In practice, the only differences between a bibliography and a reference list are that (a) parenthetic citations are not keyed directly to a bibliography, and (b) a bibliography may include some works that were consulted but are not actually cited in the text.

**MLA
39d**

40 Using APA Documentation

The documentation style recommended by the American Psychological Association (**APA style**) is used widely in the social sciences. But as the sample paper on p. 545 illustrates, the style is also well suited for general-interest research projects. If your instructor asks you to follow APA style, you will find the information you need in this chapter. If you need further detail, consult the *Publication Manual of the American Psychological Association* (3rd ed., 1983).

APA style includes two basic features:

1. Parenthetic citations *within* the text of the paper (see 40a below)

2. An alphabetic reference list on a separate page at the *end* of the paper (see 40b below)

APA generally discourages the use of supplemental notes to give information beyond what is included in the main text of your paper. If, for some reason, you do want to use such notes, follow the guidelines on p. 489, 39a.

40a Include APA parenthetic citations within the text of your paper.

APA parenthetic citations should give readers the minimum information needed to find (1) the correct item in the reference list at the end of your paper and, if appropriate, (2) the part of the work from which you have borrowed material—often a specific page. APA citations rely on authors' *names* and *dates* of publication.

Use the following guidelines for incorporating parenthetic citations into your paper, and consult the student research paper on pages 545–553 for further examples of how to place and punctuate citations.

Form of Citations

If you include the author's name in your text, give the date of publication immediately after the name, and place a page reference at the end of the borrowed material:

```
According to Kristina Orfali (1991), Swedish family law
prohibits "all forms of corporal punishment, including
spankings" (p. 430).
```

But if your text does not mention the author, you will need to include the author's last name, the date, and the page reference at the end of the borrowed material:

```
One expert on Swedish family life points out that "all
forms of corporal punishment, including spankings," are
prohibited by law (Orfali, 1991, p. 430).
```

When referring to the whole work rather than to a specific part of the work, omit the page reference.

The following sample APA citations cover a variety of circumstances you may encounter in documenting sources.

A WORK BY TWO AUTHORS:

```
According to Palmer and Colton (1965), the Dominion of
Canada "embodied principles which Edmund Burke and
Benjamin Franklin had vainly recommended" for the
American colonies a hundred years earlier (pp. 547-
548).
```

APA
40a

The Dominion of Canada "embodied principles which
Edmund Burke and Benjamin Franklin had vainly
recommended" for the American colonies a hundred years
earlier (Palmer & Colton, 1965, pp. 547-548).

When you mention the two authors in the text, join their names
with *and,* but when the names appear in a parenthetic citation,
use an ampersand (*&*).

A WORK BY THREE TO FIVE AUTHORS:

The visit of Henry II to Ireland in 1171 signaled the
beginning of English domination of the Irish (McCrum,
Cran, & MacNeil, 1986, p. 165).

The first time you mention a work by three to five authors, give
all names, either in the text or in the parenthetic citation. If you
mention the same work later in your paper, supply only the first
name followed by the abbreviation *et al. (and others)*: (*McCrum
et al., 1986, p. 275*).

A WORK BY SIX OR MORE AUTHORS:

The architectural committee recommended that the
building's staircase be restored rather than replaced
(Brunson et al., 1992, p. 27).

If a work has six or more authors, give only the name of the
first one followed by the abbreviation *et al.,* even when citing
the work for the first time.

AN ANONYMOUS WORK:

The term <u>gutter</u> refers to the "two inner margins (back
margins) of facing pages of a book" (<u>Chicago Manual</u>,
1982, p. 660).

**APA
40a**

If a work lists no author, refer to it by the full title in the text itself or, as above, by a shortened title in the parenthetic citation.

A WORK BY A CORPORATE AUTHOR:

The American Society of Hospital Pharmacists (1982) considers methicillin "particularly useful" in treating hospital-acquired infections (p. 89).

Since "corporate" names are often long, try to avoid placing them in a parenthetic citation.

AN INDIRECT SOURCE:

According to Nietzsche, Greek tragedy arose "out of the spirit of music" (cited in Merquior, p. 83).

TWO OR MORE WORKS BY THE SAME AUTHOR:

Karsh (1987b) has proposed rival explanations.

Even though your reference list may contain more than one work by the same author, the date alone suffices to show which one you mean. But if you cite two or more works by the same author published in the same year, use a date plus a letter (as above) to distinguish one work from the other(s).

MORE THAN ONE WORK IN A CITATION:

Interest in the war poets shows no sign of flagging (Crawford, 1988; Giddings, 1988; Hynes, 1990).

APA
40b

40b Include an APA reference list at the end of your paper.

Each parenthetic citation (40a) in your text must refer to an entry in the reference list at the end of the paper. Order this list alphabetically by authors' last names or, when no author appears, by the first significant word of the title (omitting *A, An,* and *The*). If the author is an institution – for example, the Canadian Broadcasting Corporation—list the item by the first word in the corporate name (in this case *Canadian*).

If you are citing more than one work by a given author, follow the order of that author's dates of publication (see p. 538, item 2, below for an example and further details). And if a cited author is coauthor of another work in your list, put the single-author work first. For a sample APA reference list, see page 553.

The directory below gives typical kinds of entries that might appear in your APA reference list. Locate the appropriate numbered item in the directory; then look up that item in the list that follows.

DIRECTORY OF ENTRIES: APA REFERENCE LIST

Books

1. A book by a single author
2. Two or more books by the same author
3. A book by two or more authors
4. A book by a corporate author
5. An anonymous book
6. An edited book or anthology
7. A work in an anthology
8. A book edited by two or more people
9. A translation
10. A republished book

APA 40b

Articles

11. An article in a journal paginated by volume
12. An article in a journal paginated by issue
13. An article in a monthly or weekly magazine
14. An article in a newspaper
15. A review
16. An unsigned article

Other Written Works

17. An encyclopedia entry
18. A pamphlet or manual
19. A dissertation
20. A government publication
21. A published letter
22. An unpublished letter

Nonwritten Works

23. A film
24. A radio or television program
25. A lecture
26. An interview
27. Computer software

Books

1. A BOOK BY A SINGLE AUTHOR:

Kendall, E. (1990). The runaway bride: Hollywood

romantic comedy of the 1930s. New York: Alfred A.

Knopf.

> Notice that APA entries give the author's initial(s) and that only the first word of the title and subtitle are capitalized (also capitalize proper nouns). Observe also that one space, not two, follows a period and that subsequent lines of each entry are indented three spaces.

2. TWO OR MORE BOOKS BY THE SAME AUTHOR:

Brennan, K. (1988). Here on earth. Middletown:

Wesleyan University Press.

Brennan, K. (1991). Wild desire. Amherst: University

of Massachusetts Press.

> Two works by the same author are ordered by date of publication. If two works show the same author(s) and date, follow the alphabetical order of the titles and add lowercase letters to the dates:
>
> Olson, D., & Laird, E. (1993a). *Astronomy* . . .
> Olson, D., & Laird, E. (1993b). *Botany* . . .

3. A BOOK BY TWO OR MORE AUTHORS:

Alred, G. J., Oliu, W. E., & Brusaw, C. (1992). The

professional writer: A guide for advanced technical

writing. New York: St. Martin's.

> Include all authors, regardless of the number.

**APA
40b**

4. A BOOK BY A CORPORATE AUTHOR:

American Society of Hospital Pharmacists. (1982).

Consumer drug digest. New York: Facts on File.

5. AN ANONYMOUS BOOK:

Chicago manual of style. (1982). (13th ed.). Chicago:

   University of Chicago Press.

6. AN EDITED BOOK OR ANTHOLOGY:

DiYanni, R. (Ed.). (1987). Literature: Reading

   fiction, poetry, drama, and the essay (2nd ed.).

   New York: McGraw-Hill, 1990.

> The abbreviation *Ed.* following the name means *editor.*
> Later in the entry, *2nd ed.* indicates that the book is in
> its second edition.

7. A WORK IN AN ANTHOLOGY:

Dillard, A. (1990). Living like weasels. In R. DiYanni

   (Ed.), Literature: Reading fiction, poetry, drama,

   and the essay (2nd ed.) (pp. 1568–1573). New York:

   McGraw-Hill, 1990.

> Note that the title of the selection is not placed in quota-
> tion marks.

8. A BOOK EDITED BY TWO OR MORE PEOPLE:

White, G. A., & Newman, C. (Eds.). (1972). Literature

   in revolution. New York: Holt.

> Include all editors, regardless of number.

**APA
40b**

9. A TRANSLATION:

Soseki, N. (1988). The miner. (J. Rubin, Trans.).

   Stanford: Stanford University Press.

10. A REPUBLISHED BOOK:

Conroy, F. (1977). Stop-time. New York: Penguin.

   (Original work published 1967).

Articles

11. AN ARTICLE IN A JOURNAL PAGINATED BY VOLUME:

Cooper, A. M. (1984). Psychoanalysis at one hundred:

Beginnings of maturity. Journal of the American

Psychoanalytic Association, 32, 245-267.

> Use this form for professional journals in which page
> numbering continues through an entire annual volume
> instead of starting with page 1 for each new issue. Under-
> line the volume number (*32* in this example) and the
> name of the journal, but notice that the title of the article
> is not placed in quotation marks.

12. AN ARTICLE IN A JOURNAL PAGINATED BY ISSUE:

Leach, L. (1990). "The difficult business of

initimacy": Friendship and writing in Virginia

Woolf's The waves. South Central Review, 7(2), 53-

66.

> If the journal starts each issue with page 1, supply the
> volume and issue numbers (in this case volume 7, number
> *2*). Notice that the quoted phrase included within the title
> of the article is placed in quotation marks and that the
> title of Woolf's novel is underlined.

13. AN ARTICLE IN A MONTHLY OR WEEKLY MAGAZINE:

Auchincloss, K. (1992, January 27). Limits of

democracy. Newsweek, pp. 28-30.

APA
40b

14. AN ARTICLE IN A NEWSPAPER:

Nevius, C. W. (1991, February 20). When choices were

simpler. San Francisco Chronicle, sec. D, p. 1.

15. A REVIEW:

Singer, B. (1988, July 17). Husbands at bay. [Review

of Only children, by R. Yglesias]. New York Times

Book Review, p. 19.

16. AN UNSIGNED ARTICLE:

Mozartiana. (1991, June 24). New Yorker, pp. 23–24.

Other Written Works

17. AN ENCYCLOPEDIA ENTRY:

L[ustig], L. K. (1985). Alluvial fans. Encyclopaedia

Britannica: Macropaedia.

> Note that volume and page numbers are unnecessary
> when items appear in alphabetic order. But since the
> *Britannica* from 1974 onward has three sets of contents,
> the note should indicate which one is intended—in this
> case the *Macropaedia.*

18. A PAMPHLET OR MANUAL:

Wiggins, R. R., & Brecher, S., with Steinberg, W. P.

(1987). Suitcase user's guide. Sunnyvale, CA:

Software Supply.

19. A DISSERTATION:

Boudin, H. M. (1970). The ripple effect in classroom

management. Unpublished doctoral dissertation,

University of Michigan, Ann Arbor.

**APA
40b**

20. A GOVERNMENT PUBLICATION:

Internal Revenue Service. (1991). Your federal income

tax. Washington, DC: U.S. Government Printing

Office.

21. A PUBLISHED LETTER:

McFann, W. (1988, August). [Letter to the editor].

  Popular Photography, p. 8.

22. AN UNPUBLISHED LETTER:

Graff, G. (1993, January 18). [Letter to the author].

Nonwritten Works

23. A FILM:

Badham, J. (Director). (1991). The hard way.

  Universal.

24. A RADIO OR TELEVISION PROGRAM:

Carlsen, T., & Magnus, J. R. (Producer & Director).

  (1988, July 19). Knocking on Armageddon's door.

  PBS.

25. A LECTURE:

Hirsch, E. D., Jr. (1979, July). Frontiers of critical

  theory. Paper presented at the Wyoming Conference

  on Freshman and Sophomore English, University of

  Wyoming, Laramie.

26. AN INTERVIEW:

Collier, P., & Horowitz, D. (1991, January 5).

  [Interview with the author].

**APA
40b**

27. COMPUTER SOFTWARE:

Word. (1991). [Computer program]. Microsoft,

  Macintosh, Version 5.0.

40c   Note the features of a research paper using APA documentation style.

Chad Campbell wrote the research paper on the following pages for his first-year composition course. The assignment called for an essay of about 1200 words on a topic of general interest. Because he lived in an area known for its many species of bats and because he was intrigued by the animals, Campbell decided to study the widespread perception that bats are dangerous and mysterious. He eventually wrote a paper to undercut that perception, showing the various ways that bats benefit people.

Campbell was not asked to submit a formal outline (p. 31, 3d). If your instructor requires one, see the examples on pages 32 and 501. Here is the scratch outline Campbell followed in drafting his paper:

1. Introduction/thesis—bats benefit people

2. Myths and folklore about bats

3. Unfounded fears about bats—2 ¶s

4. Benefit #1—insect control

5. Benefit #2—pollination and seed dispersal

6. Benefit #3—medical research

7. Despite benefits, humans continue to destroy bats

8. Conclusion—call for new attitudes, preservation of bats

APA
40c

And the Answer

1

> A "short title" (the first 2 or 3 words from the title of the paper) and a page number appear on each page.

And the Answer Is . . . BATS!

Chad A. Campbell

> The title of the paper, the author's name, and other identifying information appear on the title page.

English 1320, Section 46

Professor Carolyn Pate

16 November 1992

> For an example of a paper without a separate title page, see p. 83.

APA
40c

And the Answer

2

And the Answer Is . . . BATS!

The title of the paper is centered above the first line of text.

What creatures can "fly with their fingers, see with their ears (as well as their eyes), sleep hanging upside-down, and walk or crawl using their thumbs" (Cohn, 1987, p. 14)? What is the only mammal that can truly fly? The answer? Bats. Bats make up one-fourth of all the mammal species on earth, yet these nocturnal animals remain mysterious and frightening to most of us. Only a few wild animals have ever faced more persecution from humans than bats, and the public's ignorance and fear have overshadowed the positive impact bats have on our lives.

Parenthetic citations keyed to the reference list (p. 553).

Thesis: Bats benefit people.

This and next two paragraphs explain myths and fears surrounding bats.

A lack of knowledge about bats has stirred the imagination of people around the world. The Kanarese, a society in India, believe bats were once birds. According to legend, the bats went to the temples to pray to be made like humans. They received the teeth, hair, and faces of people but remained birdlike. Ever since, ashamed to fly with other birds, bats fly only at night and remain in the temples during the day (Allen, 1939, p. 14).

APA 40c

And the Answer

3

Bats also play a role in many superstitions. In witchcraft, a bat's blood, heart, and hair are used to make mischief and cure ills. Even literature associates bats with the unknown. In Shakespeare's Macbeth, for example, the witches give their potion a spice of mystery by adding the wool of bat (Yalden & Morris, 1975, p. 175). Such folklore, myths, and superstitions have combined to give most of us an extremely negative impression of bats.

Citation of a source by two authors.

For years people have been warned by horror stories and vampire movies of the strange and mysterious behavior of bats. In virtually every case, these warnings are entirely false. The story, for instance, that bats will become tangled in human hair probably dates back to a time when houses had no ceilings. A baby bat might fall from the rafters and land in someone's hair, clutching out of desperation. While a very young bat might behave this way, "adults are normally not likely to land on humans and it is actually quite difficult to get one to become tangled in hair even when it is given every assistance" (Yalden & Morris, 1975, p. 185).

APA 40c

And the Answer

4

Another myth is that bats spread rabies. According to Merlin Tuttle (1988), a leading expert in the field, bats contract rabies no more frequently than other animals do, and when they do, they are rarely aggressive (p. 18). In four decades, only ten Americans are known to have died from diseases caused by bats. "More people die annually from dog attacks, falling coconuts or food poisoning contracted at church picnics" (Tuttle, 1984, p. 81). One writer claims that in Pennsylvania "rabid cows outnumbered rabid bats" (Givens, 1990, p. 63).

Separate dates distinguish two sources by Tuttle cited within this paragraph.

Myths have hidden an important fact: bats benefit people. First of all, they eat mosquitoes and other insects that destroy crops (Wood & Rink, inside front cover). In fact, bats are "the primary nocturnal predator of bugs" (Givens, 1990, p. 63). According to Tuttle (1988), the numbers are staggering. One mouse-eared bat--a type found throughout North America--can eat 600 mosquitoes in an hour (p. 13); at Bracken Cave, in central Texas, between one-fourth and one-half million pounds of

The first benefit of bats explained.

APA
40c

And the Answer

5

insects are devoured each night by twenty million
Mexican free-tailed bats (p. 14); and at Chautauqua
summer resort in New York, pesticides have not been
used for fifty years because the resort encourages
"bats to live there as an alternative to chemical
forms of mosquito control, and they report great
success" (p. 39).

Bats also play a vital role for many plant
species used by humans, especially in tropical
areas. A good example is the balsa tree, whose wood
is used widely for canoes, model airplanes, and
fishing lures. Various animals feed on nectar from
this tree, which grows in Mexico, Central America,
and parts of South America, but bats are the only
ones who "brush up against pollen-bearing and
-receiving organs within the flower to pollinate it"
(Cohn, 1987, pp. 16-17). Other tropical fruits--
figs, bananas, and mangoes--depend on bats for
pollination and seed dispersal. Bats pick the fruit
and carry it away to eat. Because of this action,
seeds fall in places where the plant had not grown
before. Bats also play a role in pollinating plants

**Page numbers
alone identify
three sub-
sequent
references to
Tuttle (1988).**

**The second
benefit of bats
explained.**

APA
40c

outside the tropics--several species of flowers in
the American Southwest, for instance (Méeuse &
Morris, 1984, p. 83). And for some parts of the
world, bat pollination carries important economic
benefits. Each year, for example, Southeast Asia
receives $120 million from the export of the durian
tree, which bats pollinate and disperse (Givens,
1990, p. 63).

**The third
benefit of bats
explained.**

One of the least widely known benefits of bats
is their use in medical research. According to
Tuttle (1984), they are

**Ellipsis
indicates
material
omitted from a
quotation.**

> extremely valuable to science. Research on
> bats . . . has contributed to development of
> navigational aids for the blind, to development

**APA block
quotation
(more than 40
words)
indented 5
spaces.**

> of artificial insemination and birth-control
> methods, to production of vaccines, to testing
> of drugs, and to studies of disease resistance,
> speech pathology, and aging. (p. 81)

**APA
40c**

Thanks to studies of the bat's sonar, some blind
people now use a device that allows them to detect
objects. The sound is emitted in front of the
person's head and received behind the ears with

And the Answer

7

detectors acting like the bat's sonar (Yalden &
Morris, 1975, pp. 175-176). And the study of
hibernation in bats has helped in surgical
procedures that require lowered body temperature
(p. 175).

Despite all the positive studies and
statistics, fear and lack of public knowledge are
causing bats to decrease in numbers. According to
Tuttle (1988), humans are responsible for the
rapid decline of a colony of free-tailed bats in
Eagle Creek Cave, Arizona. This colony housed 30
million free-tailed bats in 1963; six years later
only 30 thousand bats were found. This enormous
decline means that an estimated 350,000 pounds of
insects now remain uneaten in the area every day
(p. 50). In the United States, six species of bats
are endangered. "Millions have been burned,
poisoned, or dynamited" (p. 50). They are also
killed inadvertently by people exploring caves:
"Thousands of bats die every year because people
awaken them" from sleep or hibernation (Wood & Rink,
p. 11).

**Decline of bat
population
explained.**

APA
40c

And the Answer

8

Before the future of bats can be secure, the

Conclusion: effort needed to halt the decline. attitudes of Americans must change. We will have to overcome our unfounded fears and, like other nations, take steps to protect these animals. As nature writer Ted Williams (1984) explains, today "[a]lmost without exception other peoples of the world admire bats. Bats receive legal protection at the national level throughout Europe and the Soviet Union" (p. 16). Williams warns that a "passenger pigeon effect" may take place. "Bat numbers may decline below a point of no return--a point, perhaps, where a colony fails to heat the cave top sufficiently for young to survive" (p. 19). If bats do cease to exist in the United States, the ecological balance will shift, and we will lose the many benefits now derived from these fascinating and misunderstood creatures.

APA 40c

References   9

Allen, G. M. (1939). <u>Bats</u>. Cambridge: Harvard
    University Press.

Cohn, J. P. (1987, November–December). Applauding
    the beleaguered bat. <u>Americas</u>, pp. 14–17.

Givens, K. T. (1990, October–November). Going batty.
    <u>Modern maturity</u>, pp. 63, 66.

Méeuse, B., & Morris, S. (1984). <u>The sex life of
    flowers</u>. New York: Facts on File.

Tuttle, M. D. (1984, January). Harmless, highly
    beneficial, bats still get a bum rap.
    <u>Smithsonian</u>, pp. 74–81.

Tuttle, M. D. (1988). <u>America's neighborhood bats</u>.
    Austin: University of Texas Press.

Williams, T. (1984, September). On behalf of bats.
    <u>Audubon</u>, pp. 16–19.

Wood, L., & Rink, D. (1989). <u>Bats</u>. San Diego:
    Wildlife Federation.

Yalden, D. W., & Morris, P. A. (1975). <u>The lives of
    bats</u>. New York: Demeter.

APA-style reference list: works listed alphabetically by authors' last names.

Entry begins at left margin.

Subsequent lines indented 3 spaces.

Two sources by same author arranged by date of publication.

APA
40c

IX
APPLIED
WRITING

Applied Writing

Most of the skills you have developed for the writing of essays will serve you well in answering examination questions. At the same time, it is vital to understand the ways in which the in-class situation limits your options and calls for a more direct and emphatic style of writing (Chapter 41). And to operate successfully beyond the classroom, you must familiarize yourself with some new conventions. Chapter 42 gives standard forms for writing business letters and memorandums. By following these forms, you can make an impression of competence and confidence as you apply for a job, order merchandise, state a claim, request information, or communicate with colleagues. The same chapter tells you how to prepare an increasingly common form of business correspondence, the facsimile transmission. And Chapter 43 gives you a model for your résumé—a summary of your background that will show your accomplishments to best advantage in the eyes of potential employers.

41 Examination Answers and In-Class Essays

41a Be prepared for the special conditions of an examination.

Here are ten points of advice for improved examination taking, the first of which you can put into operation weeks before the exam.

1. *Try to anticipate questions.* Listen and take notes throughout the term. Attend especially to topics and theories that keep coming up week after week, so that you arrive at the exam with ideas that tie together the assigned material.

2. *Read through all instructions and questions before beginning any answer.* Determine whether you must answer all the questions. If you have a choice, decide which questions you can answer best. Responding to more than the required number may take time from your strong area, and the grader will usually be under no obligation to count "extra credit" answers.

3. *Gauge your available time.* Translate the point value of a question into a time value. A 30-point question in a 50-minute, 100-point exam should not take much more of your time than 15 minutes (30 percent of 50). If you find yourself running over, stop and leave some blank space while you get something written on *all* other questions.

4. *Note the key instruction in each question.* Always pause and study the wording of each question. Be aware that most questions begin with a key word that tells you what to do: *compare, contrast, discuss, analyze, classify, list, define, explain, summarize, describe,*

justify, outline. Let that word guide the writing of your answer. If you are asked to *describe* how lasers are used to unblock obstructed arteries, do not waste time *explaining* possible causes of the obstruction. And do not be tempted into writing prepared answers to questions that were not asked. If you are to contrast *X* with *Y,* be sure you are not setting out to give 90 percent of your emphasis to *X.* If you are to state the relationship between *A* and *B,* do not throw in *C* for good measure. And if the question tells you to analyze the content and style of a quoted passage, do not suppose that a double effort on content alone will gain you full credit. Break the question into its parts, and attend to all of them.

5. *Plan your answer.* For longer answers, draw up a scratch outline (p. 30, 3c), and check the outline against the question to make sure it covers the required ground.

6. *Begin with a clear statement of your thesis in the opening paragraph.* Avoid merely restating the question. Use your first paragraph to announce your main point and to establish the structure of everything that will follow. Do not fear that your strategy will be made too obvious. There is no such thing as being too obvious about your thesis in an examination answer. The danger, on the contrary, is that a harried grader will miss it.

7. *Highlight your main points.* Remember that your grader will be reading rapidly and will appreciate signals that make the structure of your answer clear. Consider enumerating key points, either with actual numbers (*1, 2, 3*) or with words (*First, Second, Third*); you can even underline the most essential statements to ensure that they will come to the grader's notice.

8. *Support your generalizations with specific references.* Most essay questions are broad enough to allow for a variety of "right" answers. Give your grader evidence that you have done the reading and have thought about it carefully. Your own ideas, backed by examples drawn from the assigned reading, will be much more impressive than unsupported statements taken directly from lectures and textbooks.

9. *Keep to the point.* In an examination answer you have no time for digressions—passages that stray from the case being made. You should not, for example, try to befriend your grader with humorous asides or pleas for sympathy.

10. *Read through your completed answer.* Try to leave time to go

exam 41a

over your answer. Read it as if you were the grader, and try to catch inconsistencies, incoherent sentences, illegible scribbles, and unfulfilled predictions about what follows. Do not hesitate to cross out whole paragraphs if necessary or to send your grader, through an inserted arrow and a boldly printed note, to an extra page in the back of the blue book.

Sample Answers

For a further idea of the way examination answers typically go straight to the point and reveal their structure, read the following answers, the first written for a political science exam, the second for a history final.

Question:
Survey and discuss Thurgood Marshall's career as a jurist.

Answer:

The answer begins with a thesis and a preview of the points that follow. ⟶ Thurgood Marshall was an accomplished jurist at every stage in his career. From legal counsel for the National Association for the Advancement of Colored People (NAACP), through high-level appointments as a federal judge and prosecutor, to Supreme Court Justice, Marshall fought to open the doors of education and political participation for African Americans.

Marshall began his career as an attorney for the NAACP. After he graduated from Howard University Law School, one of his first achievements was to help desegregate the all-white law school that had earlier rejected his application on the basis of color. Marshall later became the NAACP's national counsel, helped found the organization's Legal Defense and Education Fund, and campaigned for further desegregation across the South. He argued and won crucial cases before the U.S. Supreme Court, including *Brown v. the Board of Education of Topeka* (1954), which made racial segregation in public schools illegal.

Marshall's career moved into its second phase when President Kennedy appointed him, in 1961, to the U.S.

exam 41a

Court of Appeals. As appellate district judge, Marshall continued to target policies which denied civil rights. He attacked the loyalty oath required of New York teachers and fought to protect the rights of immigrants and the criminally accused. Marshall also pushed heavily for the Voting Rights Act of 1965, which further opened the polls to every American.

In 1965, Marshall was appointed by President Johnson to serve as Solicitor General, the nation's chief prosecutor. In this capacity, Marshall argued nineteen cases before the Supreme Court and won fourteen, thus achieving one of his primary objectives: to see the Court expand its definition of equality.

Two years later, in 1967, Marshall advanced to the final stage of his career when Johnson named him to a seat on the U.S. Supreme Court. He began his tenure as a part of the Warren Court's liberal majority, voting consistently to oppose the death penalty and to uphold civil liberties, the rights of the accused, affirmative action, and abortion rights. His battle for civil rights grew increasingly difficult, however, with each of the twenty-four years he served as a justice. In the last decade of his career, Marshall found himself voting frequently as a dissenter at odds with the growing conservative trend of the Court.

Marshall's achievements as NAACP lawyer, appellate judge, Solicitor General, and, finally, his country's first African American Supreme Court justice firmly establish his reputation as an important twentieth-century jurist.

Question:
What were the Acts of Trade and Navigation and what resulted from them?

Answer:
The Acts of Trade and Navigation were a series of measures issued by the British Crown between 1651 and 1673, aimed at controlling trade in the American colonies. The acts were intended to reinforce British control over trade, but they were difficult to enforce and, for the most part, served only to antagonize and further alienate the colonists.

Each paragraph in the body of the answer discusses one stage of Marshall's career. Underlined main sentences highlight key information.

A brief concluding paragraph indicates that the terms of the question have been met.

Opening paragraph defines the acts and clearly spells out their results.

exam 41a

Second paragraph explains *mercantilism,* **a key concept for understanding the acts.**	$\longrightarrow$ By restricting the colonists' growing trade with other nations, the British hoped to retain for themselves the benefits of British mercantilism in the colonies. <u>Mercantilism</u> was an economic system, common at the time, under which colonies provided both a source of cheap raw materials for the mother country and a guaranteed market for buying back finished products made from those materials.
Third paragraph briefly explains each act. Here and elsewhere, underlining highlights key material.	$\longrightarrow$ <u>The first act</u>, in 1651, stated that only English-built or owned ships could be used to transport goods between the colonies and anywhere else. <u>The second act</u>, in 1660, stated that certain colonial products, such as sugar, rice, tobacco, and indigo, would be "enumerated," or required to be sent only to England. <u>The third act</u>, in 1663, required that all goods imported to the colonies from other countries be shipped through England, where a special import tax would be added. And the <u>fourth act</u>, in 1673, stated that colonists could not make or sell anything that would compete with finished British products.
Fourth paragraph discusses the results of the acts.	$\longrightarrow$ <u>The acts were very difficult for the British to enforce from a distance</u>. For one thing, smugglers found it easy to bring goods into and out of the colonies along the lengthy American coastline. For another, colonial merchants, who had grown accustomed to trading freely, often used bribery to circumvent British trade laws.
Final paragraph discusses long-term consequences of the acts.	$\longrightarrow$ British efforts to enforce the Acts of Trade and Navigation were largely unsuccessful. In the long term, <u>the acts served to undermine British power in the colonies</u>. Efforts at enforcement added to the growing colonial animosity toward the mother country and eventually helped to bring about the American Revolution.

41b Modify your composing method to suit the conditions of an in-class essay.

Nearly all the advice in this book applies to the writing of in-class as well as at-home essays. But an in-class essay resembles an examination (41a) in requiring you to make the "first draft" fully adequate. As in an exam, you must carefully gauge your available time, be

in-class 41b

absolutely sure you are meeting the terms of the question, and fore-shorten your planning and revision.

If you are given an hour to produce an essay, take about ten minutes for planning, and try to finish in time to read through the whole essay and make emergency corrections. The key period is the beginning: you must not start writing until you have a clear idea of your thesis. If you search for ideas as you go along, your essay will probably seem rambling or even self-contradictory.

To guide your writing, make a scratch outline (p. 30, 3c) indicating the anticipated order of your points. Steer clear of elaborate or highly unusual structures that could turn out to be unworkable. Get your thesis into the first or second paragraph, and then concentrate on backing it with important points of evidence.

Your instructor will make allowances for the time constraint when judging your essay. Remember as you write, however, that it *is* an essay—one that should show such virtues as clear statement, coherent paragraph development, and variety of sentence structure. Do not, then, write like someone who has crammed for a test and who must now hastily spill out page after page of sheer information. The length of your in-class essay will be less crucial than the way it hangs together as a purposeful structure controlled by a thesis.

In your remaining time, check first to see that you have adequately developed your thesis, and insert any needed additions as neatly as you can (see p. 558, point 10). Then check for legibility and correctness of usage, punctuation, spelling, and diction, making needed changes as you go. Your instructor will not object to a marked-up manuscript if it remains reasonably easy to read.

in-class
41b

42 Business Writing

42a Learn the standard features of the business letter.

Customary Elements

Examine the business letter on page 569. There you see:

1. *The heading.* It contains your address and the date of writing. Notice the absence of end punctuation.

2. *The inside address.* Place this address high (or low) enough so that the body of the letter will appear centered on the page. Include the name of the addressee, that person's title or office, the name of the company or institution, and the full address:

```
Joan Lacey, M.D.              Mr. Kenneth Herbert
Pioneer Medical Group         Director of Personnel
45 Arrow Avenue               Cordial Fruit Cooperative
Omaha, NE 68104               636 Plumeria Boulevard
                              Honolulu, HI 96815
```

3. *The salutation.* This formal greeting appears two lines lower than the inside address:

```
Dear Dr. Lacey:              Dear Ms. Diaz:

Dear Mr. Herbert:            Dear Reverend Melville:
```

Ms. is now the preferred form for addressing a woman who has no title such as *Dr.* or *Professor.* Use *Miss* or *Mrs.* only if your correspondent has put that title before her own typed name in a letter to you: *(Mrs.) Estelle Kohut.* And unless you see otherwise, you should assume that a woman wishes to be known by her own first name, not her husband's.

563

When writing to an institution or a business, you can avoid the possibly offensive *Dear Sir* or *Sirs* by choosing a neutral salutation:

```
Dear Personnel Manager:     Dear Editor:

Dear Sir or Madam:          Dear Macy's:

Dear Bursar:                To Whom It May Concern:
```

Note that business salutations end with a colon. Only if the addressee happens to be a friend should you strike a more informal note: *Dear Estelle, Dear Andy, . . .*

4. *The body.* Use the body of your letter to explain the situation and to make your request or response in a straightforward, concise way. You can write briefer paragraphs than you would use in an essay. Prefer middle-level diction, avoiding both slang and legalese: not x *You really put one over on me* or x *The undersigned was heretofore not apprised of the circumstances cited hereabove* but *I was not aware of the problem.*

Single-space the paragraphs of your letter, but leave a double space between one paragraph and the next.

5. *The complimentary close.* Type the complimentary close two lines below the last line of the body. The most common formulas are the following:

```
Sincerely,                  Yours sincerely,

Sincerely yours,            Very truly yours,

Yours truly,                Cordially,
```

Of these tags, *Cordially* is the only one that hints at actual feeling.

6. *Your typed name.* Leave four lines between the complimentary close and your typed name as you intend to sign it. If you have a professional title or role that is relevant to the purpose of the letter, add it directly below your name:

```
Nicole Pinsky               Jackson Marley
Assistant Manager           Lecturer
```

**bus
42a**

In general, such titles are appropriate when you use letterhead stationery.

7. *Your signature.* Always use blue or black ink. Match your signature and your typed name; a briefer signature is a sign of impatience.

8. *Special notations.* Lowest on the page, always flush left, come notations to indicate the following circumstances if they are applicable:

NOTATION	MEANING
cc: A. Pitts F. Adler	"Carbon copies" (probably photocopies) are being simultaneously sent to interested parties Pitts and Adler.
encl.	The mailing contains an enclosure (always mentioned in the body of the letter).
att.	A document has been attached to the letter.
BR/clc	The writer (initials *BR*) has used the services of a typist (initials *clc*).

Alternative Formats

There are three common ways of arranging the elements of a business letter on the page. You can choose any of the three, but they make somewhat different impressions:

1. *Block format.* Use this arrangement for extreme impersonality. Begin every element at the left margin. See page 568 for an example.

2. *Modified block format.* For this widely used middle style, begin every element at the left margin except the heading, the complimentary close, the typed name, and the signature. Align these elements near the center of the page. See the sample letters on pages 569 and 570.

3. *Indented format.* If you want your business letter to have some of the flavor of a personal letter, use this format. Follow the conventions of the modified block format, with one exception: indent the first line of each paragraph. See page 571 for an example.

bus 42a

Form of Envelope

Make the address on your envelope identical to the inside address. In the upper left corner, type your address as it appears in the heading:

```
Kevin Oppenheimer
2264 N. Cruger Avenue
Milwaukee, WI 53211

                    Mr. Robert F. Stone
                    Customer Relations
                    Kaiser Appliances, Inc.
                    834 La Salle Street
                    Chicago, IL 60632
```

42b Recognize the main purposes of the business letter.

Asking for Information

Make your inquiry brief, and limit your request to information that can be sent in an available brochure or a brief reply. Be specific, so that there can be no doubt about which facts you need.

Stating a Claim

Take a courteous but firm tone, setting forth the facts so fully and clearly that your reader will be able to act on your letter without having to ask for more information. If you are complaining about a purchase, supply the date of purchase, the model and serial number, and a brief description. If you have been mistakenly billed twice for the same service or product, state what that service or product is, the date of your payment, and the check number if you paid by check. If possible, enclose a photocopy of the canceled check (both sides). In a second paragraph, calmly and fairly state what adjustment you think you are entitled to. (See page 569 for a sample claim letter.)

bus
42b

Ordering Merchandise

Begin by stating which items you are ordering, using both product names and stock or page numbers. Tell how many units of each item you are ordering, the price per item, and the total price. If you want to receive the shipment at a different address, say so. Mention that you are enclosing payment, ask to be billed, or provide a credit card name and number and expiration date. (See page 568 for an example of a letter ordering merchandise.)

Making an Application

Tailor your letter to the particular job, grant, or program of study you are applying for. Name the opening precisely. If you are asking to be considered for a job, explain how you heard about it. If a person in authority recommended that you apply, say who it was. Tell how you can be reached, and express your willingness to be interviewed.

When applying for a job, include your **résumé** (Chapter 43) and mention that you have included it. Emphasize those elements in the résumé that qualify you for *this* position. Avoid boasting and false modesty alike. The idea to get across is that the facts of your record make such a strong case for your application that no special pleading is necessary.

The letters on pages 570 and 571 illustrate how an applicant can state qualifications in different ways for different opportunities. Both letters pertain to the résumé appearing on page 576. Notice how each letter brings out "job-related" elements in the writer's background.

bus
42b

SAMPLE LETTERS

[BLOCK FORMAT]

```
36 Hawthorne Hall
University of the North
Bridgewater, CT 06413
April 16, 1993
```

```
MacWAREHOUSE, Inc.
P.O. Box 3031
Lakewood, NJ 08701
```

Dear MacWAREHOUSE:

Please send me, at the address above, the following software items as described in your insert in the March 1993 issue of <u>Macworld</u> magazine:

1 MacEKG 2.0	UT10285	$99.00
1 Dynodex 2.0	BUS0101	$75.00

I enclose a check for $177 to cover these items plus your standard $3 shipping charge. Thank you.

Sincerely yours,

Lily Marks

Lily Marks

[MODIFIED BLOCK FORMAT]

2264 N. Cruger Avenue
Milwaukee, WI 53211 —— **1. heading**
February 22, 1993

Mr. Robert F. Stone
Customer Relations
Kaiser Appliances, Inc. ————————————— **2. inside address**
834 La Salle Street
Chicago, IL 60632

Dear Mr. Stone: ——————————————— **3. salutation**

The Kitchen-Aid dishwasher I purchased in your
store on February 14 was installed yesterday.
Unfortunately, the installation was complete before
the plumber and I noticed a large chip on the edge
of the white front panel. Since the panel was
still in its carton when the plumber arrived, it
was probably defective upon delivery. The serial
number of the dishwasher is T53278004; I enclose a
copy of the bill, already paid.   **4. body**

In my phone conversation with you yesterday, I
agreed to put this complaint in writing. I would
like you to send a representative here to replace
the damaged panel. To fix a time, please call me
at home after 5:30 P.M. at (414) 565-9776.

Thank you for your prompt attention to this matter.

Sincerely, —— **5. complimentary close**

Kevin Oppenheimer —— **7. signature**

Kevin Oppenheimer ———— **6. typed name**

KO/sms ————————————— **8. special notations**
encl.

bus
40

[MODIFIED BLOCK FORMAT]

137-20 Crescent Street
Flushing, NY 11367
August 17, 1992

F 1384
New York Times
New York, NY 10018

Dear Personnel Manager:

I am applying for the position of "Accounting Aide to CPA firm," which was advertised in yesterday's Times. I have completed my second year at Queens College as an Accounting major and plan to take a year off to supplement my education with relevant work.

From my enclosed résumé, you can see that I have been working in the business offices of Gristede's Food Stores, where I have assisted the bookkeeper in auditing procedures, including applications to computerized systems. My work requires strong mathematics skills and some familiarity with the Lotus 1-2-3 and Excel spreadsheets.

As a prospective accountant, I am especially interested in spending next year with a CPA firm. I can send you the names of references both at Queens College and at Gristede's and would be grateful for the chance to be interviewed. Please write to me at the above address or call me at (718) 317-1964 after 5:30 P.M.

Sincerely yours,

Janet Madden

Janet Madden

enc.

bus
40

[INDENTED FORMAT]

137-20 Crescent Street
Flushing, NY 11367
August 17, 1993

Ms. Charlotte DeVico
Rock of Ages Health Related
 Facility
7481 Parsons Boulevard
Flushing, NY 11367

Dear Ms. DeVico:

Mr. Gene Connelly of the Flushing YMCA has suggested I write to you about working as a recreation assistant or bookkeeper in your facility beginning this fall. I am an Accounting major with a minor in Communications, and I plan to take a year off from school to supplement my education with relevant work.

From my enclosed résumé you can see that, in addition to a business background, I have experience in working with people. At the Flushing "Y" I have helped stage the annual talent show, held informal "chat" sessions, and presented films. I enjoy this work and find the elderly full of ideas and a willingness to make themselves happy.

Mr. Connelly has offered to write you about my work at the "Y," and I can also send you the name of my supervisor at Gristede's. I would be grateful for the chance to be interviewed. Please write to me at the above address or call me at (212) 975-1122 between 9:00 A.M. and 4:30 P.M.

Sincerely yours,

Janet Madden

Janet Madden

encl.

bus
40

42c Learn the standard features of a business memorandum.

Business memorandums (*memos,* for short) are used within an office or organization to communicate information, record decisions, make recommendations, and announce policies. Like a business letter, a memo should be brief, straightforward, and purposeful. If you cloud your message with lengthy explanations or needless details, readers are likely to lose patience and miss the point. Thus you should state your purpose immediately, using subheadings or numbers if necessary to highlight important points.

The example given below shows the features of a typical business memo.

March 6, 1993

Memorandum

To: Student Senators

From: Mary Ellen O'Meara
          Senate President

Subject: Computer Equipment for Flowers Hall

Thanks to a $10,000 grant from the Alumni Association, the college plans to add new computer equipment to the word processing lab in Flowers Hall. The lab director has asked us to make recommendations on the following questions:

1. Should the lab purchase more Macintosh hardware, or should it add IBM computers as well?

2. Should the money be used exclusively for computers, or should some of it go for new printers?

Please be prepared to discuss these issues at our regular meeting next Thursday. If you need information about the available equipment before the meeting, see the brochures and price lists on file in the Student Senate office.

42d Learn the standard features of a facsimile transmission.

A facsimile transmission, commonly known as a fax, is a document sent over phone lines from a sending "fax machine" to a receiving one. In the business world, faxes have become a standard means of communicating without the delay required by regular or even express mail.

A letter sent by fax can be identical to one sent by mail, but you should begin the letter on the second page of your transmission. The first page should consist of a cover sheet. For example:

Goldman and Delmer Publishers, Inc.
16 Park Plaza
Boston, MA 02116
TEL: (617) 482-2397
FAX: (617) 482-9211

FAX TRANSMITTAL SHEET

ATTN: Elizabeth Nahem

COMPANY: Stock Responses, Inc.

FAX NUMBER: (510) 525-9742

FROM: Adela Herndon

DATE: 2/4/93   **TIME:** 1:30 E.T.

RE: Photographs for an upcoming publication

We are transmitting 3 page(s), including cover sheet. If there are any problems with this transmission, please call us immediately at (617) 482-2397. Thank you.

---

43 Résumés

43a   **Recognize the standard features of a résumé.**

Your résumé is a brief (usually one-page) record of your career and qualifications. Along with your letter of application (p. 566, 42b), it can land you a job interview. To that end it should be clear, easy on the eye, and totally favorable in emphasis. Have your résumé typed by a professional if your typewriter or word processor cannot create a polished, near-printed look. Divide your résumé into the following sections:

1. *Personal information.* Provide only what is necessary: name, current address, permanent address, phone numbers.

2. *Career objective.* Include a statement of your career goals. Avoid being so specific that you exclude reasonable opportunities or so broad as to be uninformative. Cite two goals if necessary, and mention any geographic limitations.

3. *Education.* Begin with the college you currently attend or have attended most recently, and work backward to high school. (If you have already graduated from college, omit high school.) Give dates of attendance, degrees attained, major and minor areas of study, and memberships in special societies. Briefly explain any outstanding projects or courses. Include your grade point average only if it happens to be high.

4. *Work experience.* Begin with your current or most recent employment, and list all relevant jobs since high school. Try not to leave suspicious-looking gaps of time. Give the name and address of each employer, the dates of employment, and a brief description of your duties. Include part-time or volunteer work that may be relevant.

5. *Special skills, activities, and honors.* Include special competencies that make you a desirable candidate, such as proficiency in a foreign language, ability to operate equipment, or skill in unusual

procedures or techniques. Mention any honors, travel, or community service.

6. *References.* Supply the address of your college placement office, which will send out your dossier (dáhss-ee-ay) upon request. The dossier is a complete file of your credentials, including all letters of recommendation and transcripts. You may wish to give the names, positions, and addresses of three people you can trust to write strong letters in your behalf. Be sure you have their permission, however.

Further advice:

1. *Keep the format clear and the text concise.* Single-space within each section, and double-space between sections. Try to keep your résumé to one page; do not exceed two pages.

2. *Do not mention the salary you want.* You will be considered for more openings if you stay flexible on this point.

3. *Update your résumé periodically.* Do not hesitate to ask for new letters of recommendation.

43b Tailor your résumé to a particular job opening.

To give yourself an advantage in competing for a particular job, consider revising your résumé with that job in mind. Doing so will allow you to stress elements of your background and goals that suit the position you are aiming for. Remember especially that you can mention relevant skills learned on a job that otherwise seems unrelated to the kind of work you now want to do. Suppose, for example, you are applying for a part-time position as an assistant in a day-care facility. Even if you have no formal training or experience, you may be able to highlight information that does show your interest and your preparation for the job—say, the fact that you did baby-sitting in high school or that you took a course in children's literature the preceding semester.

You can also divide your work experience into separate categories depending on the type of job you are seeking. If, for example, you are applying for both teaching positions and technical writing positions, consider drafting two résumés—one that gives prominence to your teaching experience and another to your skills as a writer.

résumé
43b

JANET MADDEN

Current Address: Permanent Address:
  137-20 Crescent Street   28 Pasteur Drive
  Flushing, NY 11367   Glen Cove, NY 11542
  (718) 317—1964   (516) 676—0620

CAREER   Position as accountant or assistant
OBJECTIVE: accountant in an accounting firm.
                (Temporary position as a recreation
                assistant or bookkeeper in a
                recreational facility.)

EDUCATION: Queens College (CUNY)
                B.A. expected June 1996
                Majoring in Accounting
                Minoring in Communications

                Pratt High School, Glen Cove,
                New York
                Received Regents Diploma, June 1991

EXPERIENCE:

Summers: Assistant bookkeeper, Gristede
1993   Brothers Food Stores, Bronx, New
                York

1992   Dramatics Counselor, Robin Hill Day
                Camp, Glen Cove, New York

1991   Volunteer, Flushing YMCA. Worked
                with elderly. Assistant director,
                annual "Y" talent show.

SKILLS: Type 65 wpm.
                Use Lotus 1-2-3 and Excel spread-
                sheets.

REFERENCES: Placement Office
                Queens College
                Flushing, NY 11367

résumé
43

X
TOOLS

Tools

Have you made the leap from typing (or handwriting) to word processing? Sooner or later, you almost certainly will. Chapter 44 offers some orientation to this important aid to composing. In Chapter 45, we present an alphabetical listing of troublesome expressions that make for confusion of meaning and / or spelling. One way to discover where you have been misconstruing the language is simply to check each item in that Index of Usage. Finally, Chapter 46, the Glossary of Terms, explains all the concepts that appear in boldface type throughout this book. You can use the Glossary of Terms to "brush up on grammar" as well as for spot consultation.

44 Writing with a Word Processor

Like it or not, you already live in a society that depends heavily on electronic information storage and retrieval. As a college-educated person, you will inevitably have to become familiar with computers in your work. As a college writer, meanwhile, you probably have access to word processing facilities on your campus. At many colleges and universities, a writing center or computer center houses a bank of *microcomputers* (such as Macintoshes or IBM PCs) or terminals connected to a *mainframe computer* that serves many functions on a time-sharing basis. Even if your instructor doesn't require that you make use of a word processor, you should take advantage of scheduled demonstrations and get acquainted with this remarkable aid to composition.

44a Learn the functions of a word processor

ESSENTIAL TERMINOLOGY	
Hardware	the computer equipment itself, including the central processing unit, the keyboard, the monitor, the disk drives, and the printer
Software	a program, stored on a disk, that allows the computer to do a certain kind of work, such as word processing
Cursor	a blinking mark on the screen that shows "where you are" in your docu-

ESSENTIAL TERMINOLOGY	
	ment. By moving the cursor with keystrokes or a "mouse" (pointing device), you can make changes at different points in the text.
Disk	a storage device containing a program and/or space for filing your documents. A *floppy disk* is a plastic record that you insert into the computer's *disk drive.* A *hard disk,* with vastly greater capacity, serves the function of many floppies.
Document	one essay, chapter, chart, letter, etc., that you create and display on the monitor screen
Edit	a mode that allows you to insert, delete, and move letters, words, or blocks of text in a document you are composing or revising on the screen
File	a document that you have saved under a specific name, so that you can retrieve it for further editing or printing
Save	an instruction that the computer make a record (on a floppy disk or a hard disk) of the document you are working with at the time
Backup	a second copy of your file
Formatting	your instructions about margins, tabs, typeface and typesize, italics, etc.
Hard copy	a printed version of what you have created on the screen

Think of a word processor as an electronic chalkboard on which you can scribble, erase, and move text from one spot to another until you are satisfied. Then—presto!—with a keystroke or two, you can get unsmudged "hard copy" of your work from an adjacent printer.

Since you will never have to retype a page, a paragraph, or even a line that is already in final form, word processing will save you much time and trouble. (With "word wrap"—the computer's knack of going automatically to the next line and readjusting all the prior spaces in an altered paragraph—every change will leave the whole text looking like new.) Thus, by making small and large changes so painless, the word processor will dissolve much of your reluctance to revise. Once you have effortlessly moved a whole block of paragraphs from one section of an essay to another in half a minute, you will wonder how you ever got along without one of these superb machines.

Many writers, especially older ones, concede the marvels of a word processor but feel most comfortable when writing on a legal pad or marking up a crudely typewritten draft. You will quickly find, however, that you needn't make a final choice of medium. You can start in any way that feels right to you and take a break from composing by transcribing your text onto the computer screen for further editing. Then you can quickly get back to hard copy again by ordering a "draft mode" printout at any moment. But you will always need to have your text back on the screen when you are tidying it for a final, flawless-looking version to be handed in.

With a word processing program you can also *format* your essay at the outset, determining what it will look like on the page, including margins, space between lines, tabs, paragraph indents, type size and typeface, and a "header" or "footer"—for example, the placement of your name and the page number in the upper-right corner of each page. When you pare down a draft or add material to it, the program will continually repaginate for you. And a feature-rich program can do the same for footnotes or endnotes (p. 526, 39d), liberating you from any fuss over renumbering or trying to squeeze extra notes onto a crowded page. If you like, you can even command that the right margin of your document be *justified* (aligned, as on this page) instead of "ragged." But since right-justified margins make for oddly spaced words, you may want to ask if your instructor prefers ragged ones.

ADVICE FOR WORD PROCESSING

- "Save" your work frequently as you create a document so that an unexpected power failure cannot erase what you have written.

ADVICE FOR WORD PROCESSING (*Continued*)

- Make a backup copy (usually on a floppy disk) of all important documents; if you lose or botch one copy, you can easily switch to
  another.

- Take care of your disks; protect them from dust, moisture, and
  extreme heat, and keep them away from sources of magnetism
  (such as telephone receivers and electronic equipment) that can
  scramble stored files.

- When you need a hard copy of your work to edit with pen or pencil, save time by printing in "draft mode."

- When printing a final copy, always use the best available printing
  mode. Do not submit an essay with type that looks uneven or
  faded.

- Print your essay in a clean, ordinary-looking style of type. Fancy
  or unusual typefaces tend to distract, rather than impress, most
  readers. Keep to one typeface (with italics and boldface as needed)
  throughout your document.

- If you print on "continuous feed" computer paper, remove the side
  strips and separate the sheets before submitting your essay.

44b Note the unique ways in which a word processor can aid your composing.

Combined with adequate software, any computer can help you as a
writer in more specific ways than we have mentioned thus far:

1. *Freewriting* (p. 13, 1g). To keep yourself from pausing to edit
when you are freewriting, turn down the brightness with the control
knob on your monitor. Turn it back up again when the prescribed
time for freewriting has elapsed. You may also want to use the computer's alarm function as a stopwatch.

2. *Outlining* (pp. 30–33, 3c–d). If your word processing program
allows you to place "windows" on the screen beside your developing
draft, fill one window with your outline. Consult the outline as you
proceed from paragraph to paragraph. When you see that your essay

must deviate from the outline, stop to revise the entire rest of the outline, double-checking it for coherence.

3. *Linking paragraphs* (p. 99, 7i). If your program can highlight the first and last sentences of every paragraph, make use of this feature. (If not, you can still "select" those sentences and make a document out of them.) Check to see that the connections between last and next (paragraph-opening) sentences are clear, and revise if necessary to make effective use of these naturally strong positions.

4. *Word mastery* (p. 178, 14b). Put your draft papers through a "search all" command for the words that you have previously tended to misuse. With each questionable instance highlighted, you can check to see if you now have the problem under control.

5. *Saving redundant typing.* Instead of tapping out the full title of a work you are discussing at length, use a brief symbol for it—say, *pam* for *A Portrait of the Artist as a Young Man.* As you approach your final draft, instruct the word processor to find all instances of your use of a particular symbol and replace that symbol with the full title.

6. *Accurate quotation* (p. 464, 37g). If you are taking notes from a book or article when the word processor is handy, and you want to record a long quotation, take the trouble to store that passage as a document, first carefully checking for accuracy of wording, punctuation, and citation. Without retyping, you can transfer the quotation (or any part of it) directly into your first draft, reusing it any number of times until you have arrived at your final copy. This procedure will not only save labor but also ensure that you won't introduce errors while retranscribing the passage several times.

44c Take advantage of available accessories.

Some complex word processing programs contain built-in features that you can call on for special kinds of help. In other cases, such aids are separate from but compatible with the main program; to make use of them, you simply insert another disk and "open" them. Find out which features are available to you. They may include:

1. *Aids to invention.* Some programs include tutorial aids such as reporters' questions (p. 16, 1h), designed to stimulate your initial thinking. By responding to the questions and then performing further

operations on your answers, you can speed your search for an appropriate topic and thesis.

2. *Aids to organization.* To assist you in outlining, some programs allow you to make an outline of your existing draft by "selecting" a key sentence in each paragraph. Alternatively, you can make the outline and then flesh it out by writing paragraphs around its sentences. When your word processing program is in "outline mode," you can handily rearrange the order of points or assign different levels of subordination (indention) to different ideas.

3. *Thesaurus.* With an on-line thesaurus, you can pause and search for just the word you have been groping for. Be aware, however, that a thesaurus works only for expressions with which you are already familiar (p. 178, 14b).

4. *Spelling checker.* You can request that the checker search your whole document for possible misspellings. Unfortunately, being "suspicious" of every term not included in its resident dictionary, it will query some names and other correctly typed words that it doesn't recognize; you can simply bypass those queries. The spelling checker will also overlook "invisible" mistakes such as *to* for *too, it's* for *its,* or *cod* for *cog.* But it will alert you to all other typos and some other errors that may be more chronic with you. Thus you can use the spelling checker to add items to your ongoing list of expressions you habitually misspell (p. 396, 33a).

5. *Style checker.* Some programs can search your document for telltale flaws of usage and punctuation and locate sentences and paragraphs that may be skimpy or wordy. Like other electronic accessories, a style checker cannot discriminate between a mistake and a shrewdly chosen special effect. It is up to you, then, to approve or veto each suggestion that comes up on the screen. But if your instructor has already identified a typical problem in your work—an overreliance, say, on prepositional phrases or on the passive voice—the style checker may be able to flag relevant instances.

6. *Access to databases.* If your terminal is connected to a mainframe or if your microcomputer is accompanied by a *modem*—a telephone that transmits electronic data—you may be able to search databases such as your library's catalog (p. 451, 37c) or an index of articles in a certain field (p. 455, 37d). Thus you can get a start on library research before you even enter the building.

45 An Index of Usage

The Index of Usage does not dwell on differences between dialect expressions, slang, and informal usage. It simply labels *colloquial* any terms that are inadvisable for use in college essays. If you need further advice about the appropriateness of a word or expression, consult a dictionary.

a, an Use *a* before words that start with consonant sounds (*a* computer, *a* unicorn, *a* hotel); use *an* before words that start with vowel sounds (*an* umpire, *an* ex-student, *an* hour).

accept, except The first means *receive,* the second *exclude* or *excluding.*

A.D. Should precede the date: A.D. *1185.* It is redundant to write x *In the year* A.D. *1185,* since A.D. already says "in the year of our Lord" (Latin *anno domini*).

adapt, adopt To *adapt* is to *change for a purpose;* to *adopt* is to *take possession. She adapted her plan to the new circumstances; They adopted the baby.*

adverse, averse *Adverse* indicates that something is *unfavorable* or *antagonistic: The medicine caused an adverse reaction. Averse,* which is usually followed by *to,* means *having a strong feeling of opposition: He is averse to taking medicine.*

advice, advise The first is a noun, the second a verb: *He advised us that he had no need of further advice.*

affect, effect As a verb, *affect* means to *influence: Rain affected the final score. Affect* may also be used as a noun meaning *feeling* or *emotion.* The verb *effect* means to *bring about* or *cause: She effected a stunning reversal.* When *effect* is a noun, it means *result: The effect of the treatment was slight.*

ain't Colloquial for *is not, are not.*

all, all of Use either *all* or *all of* with separable items: either *All the skillets were sold* or *All of the skillets were sold.* When there are no items to be counted, use *all* without *of*: *All her enthusiasm vanished; He was a hermit all his life.*

all that Colloquial in sentences like x *I didn't like her all that much.* How much is *that much*? Try *I didn't like her very much* or, more straightforwardly, *I disliked her.*

allusion, illusion, delusion An *allusion* is a *glancing reference: an allusion to Shakespeare.* An *illusion* is a *deceptive impression: Shakespeare created the illusion of enormous battlefields.* A *delusion* is a *mistaken belief,* usually with pathological implications: *He suffered from the delusion that he was Shakespeare.*

alot A mistake for *a lot.*

already, all ready The first means *by this or that time,* the second *all prepared. It was already apparent that they were all ready for the trip.*

alright A mistake for *all right.*

also Do not use as a coordinating conjunction: x *She owned two cars, also a stereo.* Try *Along with her two cars, she also owned a stereo.* Here *also* serves its proper function as an adverb.

alternate, alternative (adjective) *Alternate* means *by turns: on alternate Fridays. Alternative* means *substitutive: Our alternative plan might work if this one fails.*

altogether, all together The first means *entirely,* the second *everyone assembled: I was altogether delighted that we were all together at last.*

A.M., P.M. These abbreviations, which most writers now capitalize, should not be used as nouns: x *at six in the A.M.* And do not accompany *A.M.* or *P.M.* with *o'clock,* which is already implied. Write *six A.M.* or *six o'clock* but not x *six A.M. o'clock.*

among, between *Among* is vaguer and more collective than *between,* which draws attention to each of the items:

- They hoped to find one good person *among* the fifty applicants.
- Agreement was reached *between* management and the union.

Many careful writers also reserve *between* for sentences in which only two items are involved. See also *between.*

amount, number For undivided quantities, use *amount of: a small amount of food.* For countable items, use *number of: a small number of meals.* The common error is to use *amount* for *number,* as in x *The amount of people in the hall was extraordinary.*

angry See *mad.*

ante-, anti- The first prefix means *before,* the second *against: In the antebellum period, there was much antiwar sentiment.*

anybody, any body; nobody, no body; somebody, some body The first member of each pair is an indefinite pronoun: *Anybody can see....* The others are adjective-noun pairs: *Any body can be dissected.*

anyplace Colloquial for *anywhere.*

anyway, any way, anyways *Anyway* is an adverb: *I am busy on that day, anyway. Any way* is an adjective-noun pair: *I can't find any way to break the date. Anyways* is colloquial.

anywheres Colloquial for *anywhere.*

apt, liable, likely Close in meaning. But some writers reserve *liable* to mean *exposed* or *responsible* in an undesirable sense: *liable to be misunderstood; liable for damages. Likely* means *probably destined: She is likely to succeed. Apt* is best used to indicate habitual disposition: *When you tell those slouchers to work faster, they are apt to complain.*

around If you mean *about,* it is better to write *about: about five months,* not x *around five months.*

as (conjunction, preposition) In the sense of *because,* the subordinating conjunction *as* is often ambiguous: x *As she said it, I obeyed.* Does *as* here mean *because* or *while?* Use one or the other of those terms. And do not use *as* to mean *whether* or *that:* x *I cannot say as I do.*

as, like Both *as* and *like* can be prepositions: *as a rule; like a rolling stone.* But when you want a conjunction that will introduce a subordinate clause, always prefer *as* to *like*: not x *Like the forecaster warned, it rained all day*, but *As the forecaster warned.* . . .

as far as . . . Be sure to complete this formula with *is / are concerned*. Do not write x *As far as money, I have no complaints.* Try *As far as money is concerned, I have no complaints,* or *As for money, I have no complaints,* or, better, *I have no complaints about money.*

as good as, as much as Colloquial when used for *practically*: x *He as good as promised me the job.*

author (verb) Widely used, but also widely condemned as substandard: *He authors historical novels.* Prefer *writes*, and keep *author* as a noun.

averse See *adverse, averse.*

back of Colloquial for *behind*, as in x *You can find it back of the stove.* Prefer *behind* to both *back of* and *in back of.*

bad Do not use as an adverb meaning *badly* or *severely*, as in x *It hurt him bad.*

bare, bear *Bare* is an adjective meaning *naked* and a verb meaning to *expose*: *She bared the secret about her bare cupboard.* To *bear* is to carry or endure: *Her guilt was hard to bear until she laid it bare.*

because See *reason is because.*

before, ago When referring to the past from a present perspective, use *ago*: *I told you to get ready two hours ago, and you still aren't even dressed.* When focusing on a past time and referring to an even more distant past, use *before*: *She had told him to get ready two hours before, but he still wasn't even dressed.*

being as, being that Colloquial for *because* or *since*, as in x *Being as I was late, I entered through the side door.*

beside, besides The first means *at the side of*, the second *in addition*: *Besides, she was beside the car when it happened.*

between Requires at least two items (see *among*). Do not write either x *Hamlet's conflict is between his own mind* or x *The poems were written between 1983–84.* In the second sentence *1983–84* is one item, a period of time. Try *The poems were written between 1983 and 1984.* *Between* always requires a following *and,* not *or.* Avoid x *The choice is between anarchy or civilization.*

between each, between every Because *between* implies at least two items, it should not be joined to singular adjectives like *each* and *every:* x *He took a rest between each inning.* Try *He rested after every inning* or *He rested between innings.*

between you and I A "genteel" mistake for *between you and me.* As twin objects of the preposition *between,* both pronouns must be objective in case.

bias, biased The first is a noun meaning *prejudice,* the second an adjective meaning *prejudiced.* Do not write x *Some people are bias.*

bored Should be followed by *with* or *by,* not *of.* Avoid x *He was bored of skiing.*

breadth, breath, breathe *Breadth* means *width;* the noun *breath* means *respiration;* the verb *breathe* means *to take breath.*

bring, take These words describe the same action but from different standpoints. You *bring* something *to* a location but *take* something *away* from it. Thus you can write *He took some flowers from the garden,* but you shouldn't write x *He took his mother some flowers.*

broke (adjective) Colloquial in the sense of *having no money* and as the past participle of *break:* x *The faucet was broke.* Prefer *broken* here.

burst, bursted; bust, busted *Burst* is an irregular verb meaning *to break open suddenly.* The correct past-tense form is *burst,* not *bursted.* *Bust* and *busted* are colloquial for *burst.*

but that, but what These are awkward equivalents of *that* in clauses following an expression of doubt: x *I do not doubt but that you intend to remain loyal.*

buy, by If you write x *I want to by it,* you have confused the verb *buy* with the preposition *by.*

can, may Both are now acceptable to indicate permission. *May* has a more polite and formal air: *May I leave?*

can not, cannot Unless you want to underline *not,* always prefer *cannot,* which makes the negative meaning immediately clear.

can't hardly, couldn't hardly Double negatives. Use *can hardly* and *could hardly.*

capital, capitol *Capital* means either *governmental city* or *funds;* a *capitol* is a *statehouse.*

cause is due to Redundant. Write *The cause was poverty,* not x *The cause was due to poverty.*

censor, censure (noun) A *censor* is an official who judges whether a publication or performance will be allowed. *Censure* is vehement criticism. *The censor heaped censure on the play.*

center around Since a center is a point, *center around* is imprecise. *Center on* or *center upon* would be better. *The investigation centered on tax evasion.*

character Often redundant. x *He was of a studious character* means, and should be written, *He was studious.*

chord, cord The first means *tones,* the second *rope.*

cite, sight, site To *cite* is to *mention.* A *sight* is a *view.* A *site* is a *locale.*

class (verb) *Classify* is preferable. Avoid x *She classed the documents under three headings.*

climactic, climatic The first means *of a climax,* the second *of a climate.*

coarse, course The first means *rough,* the second *direction* or *academic offering.*

commence Usually pompous for *begin, start.*

compare, contrast *Compare* means either *make a comparison* or *liken.* To compare something *with* something else is to make a comparison between them; the comparison may show either a resemblance or a difference. To compare something *to* something else is to assert a likeness between them.

To *contrast* is to emphasize *differences: She contrasted the gentle Athenians with the warlike Spartans.* As a verb, *contrast* should be followed by *with.*

complement, compliment As a noun, *complement* means *accompaniment: The salad was a perfect complement to the main course.* As a verb, *complement* means to *accompany: The salad complemented the main course. Compliment* means *praise: They complimented her on the outstanding meal; She received a compliment.*

concur in, concur with You *concur in* an action or decision: *He concurred in her seeking a new career.* But you *concur with* a person or group: *He concurred with her in her decision.*

conscience, conscious *Conscience* (a noun) has to do with responsiveness to ideas of right and wrong: *Al's conscience told him not to take the money. Conscious* (an adjective) describes mental awareness in general: *Jane was fully conscious after the accident.*

consensus Avoid this noun unless you mean something very close to unanimity. And beware of the redundant x *consensus of opinion* and x *general consensus. Opinion* and *general* are already contained in the meaning of *consensus.*

contemptible, contemptuous Very different. *Contemptible* means *deserving contempt. Contemptuous* means *feeling or showing contempt. They felt contemptuous of such a contemptible performance.*

continual, continuous *Continual* means *recurring at intervals. Continuous* means *uninterrupted.* A river flows *continuously* but may overflow its banks *continually* through the years.

convey Do not follow with a *that* clause: x *They conveyed that they were happy.* Choose a noun as object: *They conveyed the impression that they were happy.*

convince, persuade Often treated as synonyms, but you can preserve a valuable distinction by keeping *convince* for *win agreement* and *persuade* for *move to action.* If I *convince* you that I am right, I may *persuade* you to join my cause. Avoid x *He convinced his father to lend him the car.*

could of Always a mistake for *could have.*

council, counsel The first means *committee,* the second *advice* or *attorney: Her counsel sought counsel from the city council.*

criteria Always plural: *these criteria.* The singular is *criterion.*

data Opinion is divided over the number of *data,* which is technically the plural form of *datum.* The safe course is to continue treating *data* as plural: *The data have recently become available.* Even so, the singular *data* is by now very commonly seen.

delusion See *allusion, illusion, delusion.*

depend Do not omit *on* or *upon,* as in x *It depends whether the rain stops in time.* And avoid *it depends* without a following reason: x *It all depends* is incomplete.

desert, dessert *Desert* means *barren area* or to *abandon;* a *dessert* is the last course in a meal.

device, devise The first is a noun meaning *instrument;* the second is a verb meaning to *fashion.*

differ from, differ with To *differ from* people is to be *unlike* them; to *differ with* them is to *express disagreement with* them: *The Sioux differed from their neighbors in their religious practices; they differed with their neighbors over hunting rights.*

different from, different than Some readers regard *different than* as an error wherever it occurs. But most readers would not object to *different than* when it helps to save words. *The outcome was different than I expected* is more concise than *The outcome was different from what I expected.*

disinterested, uninterested Many writers use both to mean *not interested,* but in doing so they lose the unique meaning of *disinterested* as *impartial: What we need here is a disinterested observer.* Reserve *disinterested* for such uses. Avoid x *She was completely disinterested in dancing.*

due to Do not use adverbially, as in x *Due to her absence, the team lost the game.* In such a sentence use *because of* or *owing to,* and save *due to* for sentences like *The loss was due to her absence.*

dying, dyeing The first means *expiring,* the second *coloring.*

effect See *affect.*

e.g., i.e. Often confused. The abbreviation *e.g.* means *for example;* it can be used only when you are *not* citing all the relevant items. The abbreviation *i.e.* means *that is;* it can be used only when you are giving the *equivalent* of the preceding term. In the main text of an essay or paper, it is best to write out *for example* and *that is.*

Once you have written *e.g.,* do not add *etc.,* as in x *See, e.g., Chapters 4, 7, 11, etc.* The idea of unlisted further examples is already present in *e.g.*

elicit, illicit The first means *draw forth,* the second *unlawful.* Don't write x *His business dealings were elicit.*

eminent, imminent The first means *prominent,* the second *about to happen: The arrival of the eminent diplomat was imminent.*

enhance Does not mean *increase,* as in x *I want to enhance my bank account.* It means *increase the value or attractiveness of,* as in *He enhanced his good reputation by performing further generous acts.* In order to be enhanced, something must be already valued.

Note that the quality, not the person, gets enhanced. Avoid x *She was enhanced by receiving favorable reviews.*

especially, specially, special *Especially* means *outstandingly; an especially interesting idea. Specially* means *for a particular purpose, specifically: This racket was specially chosen by the champion.*

Watch for meaningless uses of *special:* x *There were two special reasons why I came here.* This would make sense only if there had been many reasons, only two of which were special ones. Just delete *special.*

et al. Means *and other people,* not *and other things.* It belongs in citations, not in your main text.

etc. Means *and other things,* not *and other people. Et al.* serves that rival meaning. In formal prose, use a substitute expression such as *and so forth.*

Do not use *etc.* after *for example* or *such as:* x *America is composed of many ethnic groups, such as Germans, Poles, Italians, etc.*

eventhough A mistake for *even though.*

everyday, every day The first means *normal,* the second *each day.*

everyone, every one *Everyone* means *everybody; every one* means *each one* of specified items.

everywheres A mistake for *everywhere.*

exceeding(ly), excessive(ly) *Exceeding* means *very much; excessive* means *too much.* It is not shameful to be *exceedingly rich,* but to be *excessively rich* is a demerit.

except Do not use as a conjunction, as in x *She told him to leave, except he preferred to stay.* Keep *except* as a preposition meaning *excluding: He remembered everything except his toothbrush.* See also *accept, except.*

expect Colloquial in the sense of *suppose, believe:* x *I expect it will snow tomorrow.*

fair, fare *Fair* means *just* or *pretty;* a *fare* is what you pay on the bus.

farther, further Many careful writers save *farther* for actual distances: *We drove three miles farther.* In all other cases, use *further: We gave the problem further thought.*

faze, phase To *faze* is to *daunt;* a *phase* is a *period.*

feel, feeling Many careful writers prefer to keep *feel* a verb, saving *feeling* for the noun. Thus they object to x *She had a feel for trigonometry.*

few, little *Few* refers to things or persons that can be counted; *little* refers to things that can be measured or estimated but not itemized. *Few people were on hand, and there was little enthusiasm for the speaker.*

fewer, less *Fewer* refers to numbers, *less* to amounts: *fewer members; less revenue.* Beware of advertising jargon: x *This drink contains less calories.* Since the calories are countable, only *fewer* would be correct here. Note that *fewer in number* is redundant.

figure Colloquial as a synonym of *think, suppose,* or *believe:* x *They figured she would be too frightened to complain.*

flaunt, flout Widely confused. To *flaunt* is to *display arrogantly: They flaunted their superior wisdom.* To *flout* is to *defy contemptuously: They flouted every rule of proper behavior.* The common error is to use *flout* for *flaunt:* x *The pitcher flouted his unbeaten record.*

flunk Colloquial for *fail,* as in x *He flunked Biology 23.*

fortuitous Means *by chance,* whether or not an advantage is implied. Do not allow *fortuitous* to mean simply *favorable, auspicious,* or *lucky;* x *How fortuitous it was that fate drew us together!*

forward, foreword The first means *ahead;* the second is a *preface.*

fulsome Does not mean *abundant;* it means *offensively insincere.* Thus it would be wrong to write: x *I love the fulsome scents of early spring.*

fun Colloquial as an adjective, as in x *a fun party.*

get Colloquial in such expressions as *get it together, get with it, get back at, have got to, gets to me,* and *get going.*

good, well *You look good tonight* means that you are attractive. *You look well tonight* means that you do not look sick.

guess Colloquial as a synonym of *suppose:* x *I guess I should give up trying.*

had better Do not shorten to *better,* as in x *You better pay attention.*

half a Do not precede with a redundant *a,* as in x *He was there for a half a day.*

hanged, hung The usual past participle of *hang* is *hung,* but many careful writers still use *hanged* when referring to capital punishment: *He was hanged for his heinous crimes; his lifeless body hung from the noose.*

hard, hardly Both can be adverbs. Fear of using *hard* as an adverb can lead to ambiguity: x *She was hardly pressed for time.* This could mean either *She was rushed* or, more probably, *She was scarcely* *rushed.* There is nothing wrong with writing *She was hard-pressed for time.* Note the hyphen, however.

hopefully Many readers accept this word in the sense of *it is hoped,* but others feel strongly that *hopefully* can mean only *in a hopeful manner.* Keep to this latter meaning if you want to give no offense. Write *He prayed hopefully* but not x *Hopefully, his pains will subside.*

how Avoid in the sense of *that,* as in x *I told her how I wouldn't stand for her sarcasm any more.*

hung See *hanged, hung.*

i.e. Means *that is;* see *e.g.*

ignorant, stupid Often confused. To be *ignorant* of something is simply not to know it: *Newton was ignorant of relativity.* An *ignorant* person is one who has been taught very little. A *stupid* person is mentally unable to learn: *The main cause of his ignorance was his stupidity.*

illicit See *elicit, illicit.*

illusion See *allusion, illusion, delusion.*

imminent See *eminent, imminent.*

implicit, explicit *Implicit* can be ambiguous, for it means both *implied* (left unstated) and *not giving cause for investigation.* Consider, e.g., x *My trust in her was implicit.* Was the trust left unstated, beyond question, or both? Try *My trust in her was left implicit* or *My trust in her was absolute.*

Explicit is the opposite of *implicit* in the sense of *implied: In his will he spelled out the explicit provisions that had previously been left implicit.*

imply, infer Widely confused. To *imply* is to *leave an implication;* to *infer* is to *take an implication. She implied that she was ready to leave the company, but the boss inferred that she was bluffing.* The common error is to use *infer* for *imply.*

in back of See *back of.*

in case Can usually be improved to *if: If* [not *In case*] *you do not like*

this model, we will refund your money. Save *in case* for *in the event:*
This sprinkler is provided in case of fire.

in regards to A mistake for *in regard to.*

in terms of, along the lines of, in connection with Vague and
wordy. Instead of writing x *In terms of prowess, Tarzan was uncon-*
querable, just write *Tarzan was unconquerable.* Similarly, x *He was*
pursuing his studies along the lines of sociology should be simply *He*
was studying sociology.

include Do not use loosely to mean *are,* as in x *The Marx Brothers*
included Groucho, Harpo, Chico, and Zeppo. Use *were* in this instance. Only when at least one member is omitted should you use
include: The Marx Brothers included Harpo and Zeppo.

individual (noun) Often pompous for *person:* x *He was a kind-*
hearted individual. Use *individual* where you want to draw attention
to the single person as contrasted with the collectivity, as in *Our laws*
respect the individual.

inside Widely regarded as colloquial; can always be shortened to
inside. Write *inside the car,* not x *inside of the car.*

inspite of A mistake for *in spite of.*

irregardless A mistake for *regardless.*

is because See *reason is because.*

is when, is where Often involved in faulty predication: x *A war is*
when opposing countries take up arms; x *Massage is where you lie on*
a table and. . . . Match *when* only with times, *where* only with places:
When she was ready, she went where she pleased. Most predication
problems can be solved by changing the verb: *A war occurs when.* . . .

it's, its The first means *it is,* the second *belonging to it.*

just because . . . doesn't mean Though common in speech, this
construction is indefensible in writing: x *Just because you passed the*
written test doesn't mean you know how to drive. A subordinate clause
cannot serve as the subject of a verb. Try *The fact that you passed*
the written test doesn't mean you know how to drive.

kind of, sort of, type of When used at all, these expressions should be followed by the singular: *this kind of woman.* But *such a woman* is preferable.

Sort of and *kind of* are awkward in the sense of *somewhat,* and they are sometimes followed by an unnecessary *a*: x *He was an odd sort of a king.* Do not use *sort of* or *kind of* unless your sentence needs the expression to make sense: *This kind of bike has been on the market for only three months.*

lay See *lie, lay.*

lead, led *Led* is the past tense of the verb *lead.* Avoid x *He lead her astray for years.*

leave, let Have different senses in clauses like *leave him alone* and *let him alone.* The first means *get out of his presence;* the second means *don't bother him* (even if you remain in his presence). Don't write x *leave him go in peace.*

level (noun) Overworked in the vague, colorless sense illustrated by x *at the public level;* x *on the wholesale level.* Use only when the idea of degree or ranking is present: *He was a competent amateur, but when he turned professional he found himself beyond his level.*

lie, lay If you mean *repose,* use the intransitive *lie: lie down.* The transitive *lay* means, among other things, *set* or *put: lay it here.*

All forms of these verbs are troublesome. The following sentences use three common tenses correctly:

PRESENT	PAST	PRESENT PERFECT
I lie in bed.	I lay in bed.	I have lain in bed.
I lay down my cards.	I laid down my cards.	I have laid down my cards

like See *as, like.*

likely Weak as an unmodified adverb: x *He likely had no idea what he was saying.* Some readers would also object to x *Very likely, he had no idea what he was saying.* Try *probably,* and reserve *likely* for adjectival uses: a *likely story.* See also *apt, liable, likely.*

likewise An adverb, not a conjunction. You can write *Likewise, Myrtle failed the quiz,* but not x *Jan failed the quiz, likewise Myrtle.*

usage
45

literally Means *precisely as stated, without a figurative sense.* If you write x *I literally died laughing,* you must be writing from beyond the grave. Do not use *literally* to mean *definitely* or *almost.* It is properly used in a sentence like *The poet writes literally about flowers, but her real subject is forgiveness.*

loose, lose *Loose* is usually an adjective meaning *slack* or *free: The door hinge was loose. Lose* means *mislay.* Avoid x *I loose my notes whenever I desperately need them.*

lot, lots Colloquial in the sense of *many:* x *I could give you lots of reasons.* A *lot* (note the spelling) and *lots* make colloquial modifiers, too: *She pleases me lots.* Try *very much.*

mad, angry *Mad* means *insane.* It is colloquial in the sense of *angry:* x *They were mad at me.*

majority Do not use unless you mean to contrast it with *minority: The majority of the caucus voted to disband the club.* In x *the majority of the time,* the term is out of place because *time* does not contain members that could be counted as a majority and a minority.

many, much *Many* refers to countable items, *much* to a total amount that cannot be divided into items (see *amount, number*): *Many problems make for much difficulty.* Do not write x *There were too much people in the line.*

may be, maybe *May be* is a verb phrase: *Todd may be hungry. Maybe* is an adverb meaning *perhaps: Maybe Todd is hungry.*

media Increasingly used as a singular term, but many good writers disapprove. Since *media* is the plural of *medium,* you would do well to keep it plural. Don't write x *The media is to blame.*

mislead, misled *Misled* is the past participle of *mislead.* Avoid x *He mislead her several times.*

moral, morale (nouns) *Moral* means *lesson: the moral of the story. Morale* means *mental condition* or *spirit: Lee's morale improved after he won the lottery.*

moreso A mistake for *more so.*

most Colloquial as an adverb meaning *almost:* x *We were most dead by the time we got there;* x *Most all the cows had found their way home.*

muchly A mistake for *much.*

myself Do not use this intensive pronoun merely as a substitute for *I* or *me:* x *My friends and myself are all old-timers now;* x *She gave the book to Steve and myself.* Save *myself* for emphatic or reflexive uses: *I myself intend to do it; I have forgiven myself.*

nauseated, nauseous The first means *experiencing nausea;* the second means *causing nausea: I felt nauseated when I heard his nauseous remarks.*

no place Colloquial for *nowhere.*

not too, not that Colloquial when used to mean *not very:* x *She was not too sure about that;* x *They are not that interested in sailing.*

nothing like, nowhere near Do not use in place of *not nearly,* as in x *I am nothing like* [or *nowhere near*] *as spry as I used to be.*

nowheres A mistake for *nowhere.*

number See *amount, number.*

off of Should be either *off* or *from: She jumped off the bridge* or *She jumped from the bridge.* Avoid x *She jumped off of the bridge.*

oftentimes Colloquial for *often.*

old-fashion Colloquial for *old-fashioned.*

on, upon *On* and *upon* mean the same thing, but you should save *upon* for formal effects: *She swore upon her word of honor.*

on account of Never preferable to *because of.*

only Do not use as a conjunction: x *He tries to be good, only his friends lead him astray.* Keep *only* as an adjective or adverb: *That is his only problem; He only needs some better advice.*

ourself Should be *ourselves.*

outside of Should be *outside.* And in figurative uses you should prefer *except for*: not x *outside of these reasons* but *except for these reasons*.

passed, past Do not mistake the adjective, noun, or preposition *past* for the verb *passed,* as in x *They past the test.* The following sentences are correct: *We passed the tennis courts; The past has passed us by; Past the tunnel lies the railroad station.*

personal, personnel The first means *individual,* the second *employees*.

phase See *faze, phase.*

phenomena Not a singular word, but the plural of *phenomenon.*

plus Not a coordinating conjunction or a sentence adverb: x *He was sleepy, plus he hadn't studied.* Keep *plus* as a preposition with numbers: *Two plus two is four.* When no number is involved, avoid *plus*: not x *Her challenging work plus her long vacations made her happy* but *Along with her vacations, her challenging work made her happy.*

poorly Colloquial in the sense of *ill* or *sick.* x *I feel poorly today.* Keep as an adverb: *I performed poorly in the exam.*

precede, proceed To *precede* is to *go ahead of;* to *proceed* is to *go forward. In the preceding announcement, we were instructed to proceed with caution.*

predominant, predominate The first is an adjective, the second a verb. *The Yankees were the predominant team; they predominated for years.*

prejudice, prejudiced The first is a noun meaning *bias;* the second is an adjective meaning *biased.* Do not write x *They were prejudice.*

principal, principle *Principal* is usually an adjective meaning *foremost; principle* is a noun meaning *rule. The principal reason for her success is that she keeps to her principles.* As a noun, *principal* usually refers to the head of a school. Do not write x *He had to go to the principle's office.*

prophecy, prophesy The first is a noun meaning *prediction,* the second a verb meaning to *make predictions.* Write *She prophesied his downfall,* not x *She prophecied his downfall.*

quote (noun) Often considered colloquial when used to mean *quotation,* as in x *this quote,* or when written in the plural to mean *quotation marks,* as in x *She put quotes around it.* In formal writing, take the trouble to use the full terms *quotation* and *quotation marks.*

rain, rein, reign *Rain* is precipitation; to *rein* is to *restrain;* to *reign* is to *rule.*

raise, rise (verbs) *Raise* takes an object: *Raise your arm. Rise* does not: *Rise and shine.*

real Colloquial as an adverb, as in x *I am real committed.* Prefer *really.*

reason is because A classic predication error. You can write either *She stayed home because of her health* or *The reason was her health,* but it is redundant to write x *The reason she stayed home was because of her health.*

reckon Colloquial for *suppose, think:* x *I reckon I can handle that.* Use in the sense of *count* or *consider: She is reckoned an indispensable member of the board.*

relation, relationship These overlap in meaning, and some writers use *relationship* in all contexts. But *relation* is preferable when you mean an abstract connection: *the relation of wages to prices.* Save *relationship* for mutuality: *the president's relationship with the press.*

relevant Requires a following prepositional phrase. Avoid x *The course was extremely relevant.* To what? Try *The course was extremely relevant to the issues of the hour.* Note, incidentally, that *revelant* is not a word.

respectfully, respectively *Respectfully* means *with respect: He treated her respectfully. Respectively* means *in the order given: They studied Paz and Galdós, who are, respectively, a Mexican poet and a Spanish novelist.*

reticent Does not mean *reluctant,* as in x *They were reticent to comply.* It means *disposed to be silent,* as in *Reticent people sometimes become talkative late at night.*

set, sit With few exceptions, *set* takes an object: *set the table. Sit* almost never takes an object: *sit down.* Avoid x *She set there sleeping and x I want to sit these weary bones to rest.*

should of A mistake for *should have.*

sight See *cite, sight, site.*

similar Means *resembling,* not *same.* Avoid x *Ted died in 1979, and Alice suffered a similar fate two years later.* Try *the same fate.*
     Do not use *similar* as an adverb meaning *like:* x *This steak smells similar to the one I ate yesterday.* Try *like the one.*

since An indispensable word, but watch for ambiguity: x *Since she left, he has been doing all the housework.* Here *since* could mean either *because* or *ever since.* Prefer one of these terms.

site See *cite, sight, site.*

some Do not use as an adverb meaning *somewhat,* as in x *He worried some about his health.* Try *He was somewhat worried about his health.*

someplace Colloquial for *somewhere.*

something Avoid as an adverb meaning *somewhat,* as in x *He is something over six feet tall.*

sometime, some time, sometimes *Sometime* is an adverb meaning *at an unspecified time; some time* is an adjective-noun pair meaning *a span of time. Sometime I must tell you how I spent some time in prison. Sometimes* means *at times.* Write *Sometimes I get lonely,* not x *Sometime I get lonely.*

somewheres A mistake for *somewhere.*

sort of See *kind of.*

special, specially See *especially.*

stationary, stationery The first means *still,* the second *paper.*

suppose to A mistake for *supposed to,* as in x *We are suppose to watch our manners.*

sure Colloquial as an adverb: x *She sure likes muffins.* Since *surely* would sound stuffy here, try *certainly.*

sure and Should be *sure to:* not x *Be sure and call me* but *Be sure to call me.*

than, then *Than* is for comparison; *then* means *at that time.* Avoid x *It was later then she thought.*

That Beware of using *that* as an unexplained demonstrative adjective: x *He didn't have that much to say. All that much to say* would not improve matters. Just write *He didn't have much to say.*

that, which In restrictive clauses (p. 264, 20m), most careful writers prefer *that* to *which: Alberta is the province that fascinates me.* Use *that* wherever the clause serves to narrow or identify the term it refers to. Compare: *Alberta, which fascinates me, is my favorite province.*

their, there, they're *Their* is a possessive pronoun: *We saw their car. There* is an adverb indicating place (*Put the book there*) or an expletive (*There are fifty states*). And *they're* is a contraction for *they are: They're late.*

theirself, theirselves Mistakes for *themselves.*

those kind, type, etc. Should be *that kind, type,* etc. But prefer *such,* which is more concise: *such people.*

thusly A mistake for *thus.*

till, until, til, 'til, 'till *Till* and *until* are interchangeable. The other three forms are inappropriate.

to, too, two *To* means *toward; too* means *also; two* is the number. *Too* is weak when used as a sentence adverb: x *It was dark and cold; too, the rain was heavy.* Try *moreover* or *furthermore.*

Avoid *too* as a synonym of *very:* x *It was too kind of them to come.* Just drop *too* here.

try and Should be *try to:* not x *Try and do better* but *Try to do better.*

type Colloquial in place of *type of:* x *You are a headstrong type person.* But *type of* is itself objectionably wordy; try *You are headstrong.*

unique Since it means *one of a kind, unique* cannot be modified. Avoid x *most unique* and x *very unique.*

use to In an affirmative past construction, be sure to write *used to*, not *use to:* x *They use to think so;* x *They are not use to the cold.* In addition, certain past negative constructions with *use* always sound awkward: x *Didn't she use to take the bus?* Try *She used to take the bus, didn't she?*

wait for, wait on *Wait for* means *to await: She is waiting for an answer. Wait on* means *to serve: He is waiting on customers.* Avoid the colloquial use of *wait on* to mean *await:* x *We were waiting on a diagnosis from the doctor.*

ways Avoid in the sense of *distance:* x *It was only a short ways.* The right form is *way.*

weather, whether *Weather* is the state of the atmosphere; *whether* means *if.*

where Do not use in place of *whereby*, as in x *T'ai chi is an exercise regimen where one slowly activates every muscle group. Whereby,* the right word here, means *by means of which.* Save *where* for actual places: *That storefront studio is where we study t'ai chi.*

where . . . at Redundant and colloquial, as in x *She had no idea where he was at.* Always delete the *at.*

who's, whose *Who's* means *who is; whose* means *of whom. Who's the person whose coat was left behind?*

-wise Avoid *-wise* in the sense of *with respect to:* x *taxwise, agriculturewise, conflict resolutionwise.* Such terms do save space, but many readers find them ugly. Look for concise alternatives: not x *the situation taxwise* but *the tax situation;* not x *America's superiority agriculturewise* but *America's superiority in agriculture.*

would like for Colloquial in sentences like x *They would like for me to quit.* Try *They would like me to quit.*

would of A mistake for *would have.*

your, you're The first is a possessive pronoun, the second a contraction of *you are.* Do not write x *Your certain to succeed* or x *Watch you're step!*

46 A Glossary of Terms

The Glossary of Terms offers definitions of terms appearing in headings and in **boldface** elsewhere in this book. Within the Glossary itself, words appearing in black boldface have separate entries that you can consult as necessary. The abbreviation *cf.* means "compare"— that is, note the difference between the term being defined and another. And *e.g.* means "for example."

abbreviation (p. 429) A shortened word, with the addition of a period to indicate the omission (*Dr.*).

absolute phrase (p. 259) A **phrase** that, instead of modifying a particular word, acts like an **adverb** to the rest of the sentence in which it appears:

> ABS PHRASE
> • **All struggle over,** the troops laid down their arms.

Absolute phrases are not considered mistakes of usage. Cf. **dangling modifier.**

abstract language (p. 189) Words that make no appeal to the senses: *agree, aspect, comprehensible, enthusiasm, virtuously,* etc. Cf. **concrete language.**

active voice See **voice.**

***ad hominem* reasoning** (p. 52) A **fallacy** whereby someone tries to discredit a position by attacking the person, party, or interest that supports that position.

additive phrase (p. 237) An expression beginning with a term like *accompanied by* or *as well as.* It is not strictly a part of a subject, and thus it should not affect the number of a verb.

adjectival clause See **clause.**

adjective (p. 251) A **modifier** of a **noun, pronoun,** or other **noun-like element**—e.g., *strong* in *a strong contender.* Most adjectives can be compared: *strong, stronger, strongest.* See **degree.** See also **interrogative adjective.**

adverb (p. 251) A word modifying either a **verb,** an **adjective,** another adverb, a **preposition,** an **infinitive,** a **participle,** a **phrase,** a **clause,** or a whole **sentence:** *now, clearly, moreover,* etc. Any one-word modifier that is not an adjective or an **article** is sure to be an adverb.

adverbial clause See **clause.**

agreement See **pronoun agreement, subject-verb agreement.**

allusion (p. 481) A passing reference to a work or idea, either by directly mentioning it or by borrowing its well-known language. Thus, someone who writes *She took arms against a sea of troubles* is alluding to, but not mentioning, Hamlet's most famous speech. The sentence *He did it with Shakespearean flair* alludes directly to Shakespeare. Quotation through allusion differs from **plagiarism** in that readers are expected to notice the reference.

"alternative MLA" style (p. 526) A documentation style, formerly preferred by the Modern Language Association, that makes use of **endnotes** or **footnotes** rather than **parenthetic citations.** Cf. **APA style, MLA style.**

analogy (p. 121) An extended likeness purporting to show that the rule or principle behind one thing also holds for a different thing being discussed.

analysis (p. 9) In a narrow sense, the breaking of something into its parts or functions and showing how those smaller units go to make up the whole. More broadly, analysis is the type of writing that explains some idea, phenomenon, or procedure. The primary purpose Of analysis is to make the reader understand. Cf. **description, narration,** and **argument.**

antecedent (p. 283) The word for which a **pronoun** stands:

- ANT   PRO
  Jane was here yesterday, but today **she** is at school.

anticipatory pattern (p. 298) A structure, such as *both x and y* or *not x but y*, that gives an early signal of the way it will be completed.

APA style (p. 534) The **parenthetic citation** documentation style of the American Psychological Association. Cf. **MLA style, "alternative MLA" style.**

aphorism (p. 162) A memorably concise sentence conveying a very general assertion: *If wishes were horses, beggars would ride.* Many aphorisms show **balance** in their structure.

appositive (p. 268) A word or group of words whose only function is to identify or restate a neighboring **noun, pronoun,** or **nounlike element:**

   APP
- Mike **the butcher** is quite a clown.

Arabic numeral (p. 438) A figure such as *3, 47,* or *106,* as opposed to a **Roman numeral** such as *III, XLVII,* or *CVI.*

argument (p. 9) The type of writing in which a writer tries to convince the reader that a certain position on an issue is well-founded. Cf. **description, analysis, narration.**

article An indicator or determiner immediately preceding a **noun** or **modifier.** Articles themselves may be considered modifiers, along with **adjectives** and **adverbs.** The *definite article* is *the;* the *indefinite articles* are *a* and *an.*

attributive noun (p. 182) A **noun** serving as an **adjective:** *beach* in *beach shoes,* or *Massachusetts* in *the Massachusetts way of doing things.*

auxiliary A **verb** form, usually lacking **inflection,** that combines with other verbs to express possibility, likelihood, necessity, obligation, etc.: *She can succeed; He could become jealous.* The commonly recognized auxiliaries are *can, could, dare, do, may, might, must, need, ought, should,* and *would. Is, have,* and their related forms act like auxiliaries in the formation of **tenses:** *He is coming; They have gone.*

baited opener (p. 127) An introductory **paragraph** that, by presenting its early sentences "out of context," teases its reader into taking further interest.

balance (p. 162) The effect created when a whole sentence is controlled by the matching of grammatically like elements, as in *He taught us the intricate ways of the city; we taught him the simple ways of nature.* A balanced sentence typically repeats a grammatical pattern and certain words in order to highlight important differences.

bandwagon appeal (p. 53) The **fallacy** of urging readers to agree with a position simply because many other people do.

base form of verb (p. 372) An **infinitive** without *to: see, think,* etc. Base forms appear with **auxiliaries** (*should see*) and in the formation of present and future **tenses** (*I see, I will see*).

begging the question (p. 50) The **fallacy** of treating a debatable idea as if it had already been proved. If, in a paper favoring national health insurance, you assert that only the greedy medical lobby could oppose such an obviously needed program, you are begging the question by assuming the rightness of your position instead of establishing it with **evidence.** Also called *circular reasoning.*

bibliography (p. 533) A list of consulted works presented at the end of a book, article, or **essay.**

block quotation See **indented quotation.**

bound element (p. 152) A modifying word, **phrase,** or subordinate **clause** that, because it is **restrictive,** is not set off by commas. Cf. **free element.**

brackets (p. 362) Punctuation marks used to insert an explanatory word or phrase into a sentence, as in *"I voted for [Dianne] Feinstein,"* *she said.* Also called *square brackets.*

brainstorming (p. 14) The process of entertaining many suggestions for a topic without regard for links between them.

cardinal number (p. 439) A number like *four (4)* or *twenty-seven (27),* as opoosed to an **ordinal number** like *fourth (4th)* or *twenty-seventh (27th).*

case (p. 272) The **inflection**al form of **nouns** and **pronouns** indicating whether they designate actors (*subjective case: I, we, they*), receivers of action (*objective case: me, us, them*), or "possessors" of the thing or quality modified (*possessive case: his Toyota, their indecision, Geraldine's influence*). *Personal pronouns* also have "second possessive" forms: *mine, theirs,* etc. Cf. **double possessive.**

choppiness (p. 164) The undesirable effect produced by a sequence of brief sentences lacking pauses marked by punctuation.

circular reasoning See **begging the question.**

circumlocution (p. 192) Roundabout expression, or one such expression—e.g., x *when all is said and done* in place of *finally.*

clause (p. 212) A cluster of words containing a **subject** and a **predicate.** All clauses are either *subordinate* (dependent) or *independent.* (An independent clause is sometimes called a *main clause.*)

A subordinate clause cannot stand alone: x *When he was hiding in the closet.* An independent clause, which is considered grammatically complete, can stand alone: *He was hiding in the closet.*

There are three kinds of subordinate clauses:

1. A *relative* clause serves the function of an **adjective:**

   REL CLAUSE
   • Marty, **who was extremely frightened,** did not want to make a sound.

   The relative clause modifies the **noun** *Marty.*

2. An *adverbial* clause serves the function of an **adverb:**

                                                         ADV CLAUSE
   • Marty held his breath for forty seconds **when he was hiding in the closet.**

   The adverbial clause modifies the **verb** *held.*

3. And a *noun* clause serves the function of a **noun:**

                          NOUN CLAUSE
   • **That an intruder might slip through his bedroom window** had never occurred to him.

   The noun clause serves as the **subject** of the **verb** *had occurred.*

cliché (p. 196) A trite, stereotyped, overused expression: *an open-and-shut case; a miss is as good as a mile.* Most clichés contain **figurative language** that has lost it vividness: *a heart of gold; bring the house down,* etc.

clustering (p. 14) Generating ideas by writing a word or phrase on a sheet of paper and then mapping out "clusters" of information triggered by the original concept.

collective noun (p. 239) A **noun** that, though singular in form, designates a group of members: *band, family,* etc.

comma splice (p. 223) A sentence in which two independent clauses are joined by a comma alone, without the necessary coordinating conjunction: x *It is raining today, I left my umbrella home.* Cf. **fused sentence.**

common gender (p. 185) The intended sexual neutrality of **pronouns** used to indicate an indefinite party. Traditionally, indefinite (*one*) and masculine personal pronouns (*he*) were used, but the masculine ones are now widely regarded as **sexist language.**

comparative degree See **degree.**

complement (p. 210) Usually, an element in a **predicate** that identifies or describes the **subject.** A single-word complement is either a *predicate noun* or a *predicate adjective:*

       PRED NOUN
- He is a **musician.**

       PRED ADJ
- His skill is **unbelievable.**

   In addition, a **direct object** can have a complement, known as an *objective complement:*

               OBJ
       D OBJ   COMPL
- They consider the **location desirable.**

Infinitives, too, can have complements:

               COMPL
      INF   OF INF
- They beg him **to be** more **cooperative.**

compound, adj. (p. 275) Consisting of more than one word, as in a compound verb (*They <u>whistled</u> and <u>sang</u>*), a compound noun (*ice cream*), a compound preposition (*in spite of*), a compound subject (*<u>He</u> and <u>she</u> were there*), or a compound modifier (*far-gone*).

concession (p. 53) The granting of an opposing point, usually to show that it does not overturn one's own **thesis.**

conciseness (p. 191) Economy of expression. Not to be confused with simplicity; conciseness enables a maximum of meaning to be communicated in a minimum of words.

concrete language (p. 189) Words describing a thing or quality appealing to the senses: *purple, car, buzz, dusty,* etc. Cf. **abstract language.**

conjunction (p. 214) An un**inflected** word that connects other words, **phrases,** or **clauses:** *and, although,* etc.

A *coordinating* conjunction—*and, but, for, nor, or, so, yet*—joins grammatically similar elements without turning one into a **modifier** of the other. *You are sad, <u>but</u> I am cheerful.*

A *subordinating* conjunction joins grammatically dissimilar elements, turning one of them into a modifier and specifying its logical relation to the other—e.g., *<u>Although</u> you are sad, I am cheerful; I understand <u>that</u> you like jazz.*

Correlative conjunctions are matched pairs with a coordinating or a disjunctive purpose: *either/or, neither/nor,* etc.

Cf. **preposition.**

connotation (p. 183) An association that a word calls up, as opposed to its **denotation,** or dictionary meaning. Thus, the word *exile* denotes enforced separation from one's home or country, but it connotes loneliness, homesickness, and any number of other, more private, thoughts and images.

continuity (p. 92) The felt linkage between sentences or whole paragraphs, achieved in part by keeping related sentences together and in part by using **transitions** and **signal words** to indicate how sentences tie in with the ones they follow.

contraction (p. 394) The condensing of two words to one, with an apostrophe added to replace the omitted letter or letters: *isn't, don't,* etc. Contractions are used primarily in speech and informal writing.

coordinating conjunction See **conjunction.**

coordination (p. 221) The giving of equal grammatical value to two or more parts of a sentence. Those parts are usually joined by a *coordinating conjunction: He tried, but he failed; The lifeguard reached for her megaphone and her whistle.* Cf. **subordination.**

correlative conjunction See **conjunction.**

cumulative sentence (p. 170) A sentence that continues to develop after its main idea has been stated, adding **clauses** or **phrases** that modify or explain that assertion: *She crumpled the letter in her fist, trembling with rage, wondering whether she should answer the accusations or simply say good riddance to the whole affair.* Cf. **suspended sentence.**

dangling modifier (p. 253) The **modifier** of a term that has been wrongly omitted from the sentence:

> DANGL MOD
> x **Not wishing to be bothered,** the telephone was left off the hook.

> The person who did not wish to be bothered goes unmentioned and is thus absurdly replaced by the telephone.

Cf. **misplaced modifier.**

dead metaphor (p. 204) A **metaphor** that has become so common that it usually does not call to mind an **image:** *a devil of a time, rock-bottom prices,* etc. When overworked, a dead metaphor becomes a **cliché.**

declarative sentence (p. 322) A sentence that presents a statement rather than a question or an **exclamation:** *Lambs are woolly.*

deduction (p. 47) The type of **reasoning** that applies general principles to specific instances, often in the form of a **syllogism.** Cf. **induction.**

degree (p. 251) The form of an **adjective** or **adverb** showing its quality, quantity, or intensity. The ordinary, uncompared form of an adjective or adverb is its *positive* degree: *quick, quickly.* The *comparative* degree is intermediate, indicating that the modified term surpasses at least one other member of its group: *quicker, more quickly.* And an adjective or adverb in the *superlative* degree indicates that the modified term surpasses all other members of its group: *quickest, most quickly.*

demonstrative adjective (p. 95) A *demonstrative pronoun* form serving as a **modifier,** e.g., *those* in *those laws.*

demonstrative pronoun See **pronoun.**

denotation (p. 175) The primary, "dictionary," meanings of a word. Cf. **connotation.**

dependent clause See **clause.**

description (p. 9) The type of writing in which a writer tries to acquaint the reader with a place, object, character, or group. Cf. **argument, analysis, narration.**

dialogue (p. 356) The direct representation of speech between two or more persons. Cf. **indirect discourse.**

diction (p. 180) The choice of words. Diction is commonly divided into three levels: formal (*deranged*), middle (*crazy*), and slang (*nuts*).

digression (p. 91) A temporary change of topic within a sentence, paragraph, or whole discourse. In an **essay,** an *apparent digression*—one that later turns out to have been pertinent after all—may sometimes serve a good purpose. In general, however, digressions are to be avoided.

direct discourse (p. 313) The use of quotation, as opposed to summary, of a speaker's or writer's words. Cf. **indirect discourse.**

direct object (p. 209) A word naming the item directly acted upon by a **subject** through the activity of a **verb:**

 S   V   D OBJ
 • **She hit** the **jackpot.**

Cf. **indirect object.**

direct paragraph (p. 101) A **paragraph** in which the **main sen-**

tence comes at or near the beginning and the remaining sentences support it, sometimes after a **limiting sentence** or two.

disjunctive subject (p. 240) A **subject** containing elements that are alternative to one another, as in *Either you or I must back down.*

double negative (p. 260) The nonstandard practice of conveying the same negative meaning twice: x *They don't want no potatoes.*

double possessive (p. 281) A possessive form using both *of* and *-'s: an idea of Linda's.* Double possessives do not constitute faulty usage.

either-or reasoning (p. 52) The depicting of one's own position as the better of an artificially limited and "loaded" pair of alternatives— e.g., x *If we do not raise taxes this year, a worldwide depression is inevitable.*

ellipsis (p. 360) The three or four spaced dots used to indicate material omitted from a quotation: *"about the . . . story."* A whole row of dots indicates omission of much more material, usually verse.

endnote (p. 526) A note placed in a consecutive series with others at the end of an **essay,** article, chapter, or book.

essay (p. 2) A fairly brief (usually between two and twenty typed pages) piece of nonfiction that tries to make a point in an interesting way.

euphemism (p. 195) A vague or "nice" expression inadvisedly used in place of a more direct one: e.g., *rehabilitation facility* for *prison,* or *disincentive* for *threat.*

evidence (p. 42) Examples, facts, reasons, and testimony used to support a **thesis.** One statement can be used as evidence for another only if there is a high likelihood that readers will accept it as true.

exclamation (p. 324) An extremely emphatic statement or outburst: *Get out of here! What a scandal!* Cf. **interjection.**

expletive The word *it* or *there* when used only to postpone a **subject** coming after the verb:

    EXPL   V   S
- **There** are many reasons to doubt his story.

exposition See **analysis.**

extended figure of speech (p. 204) A **figurative** image (metaphorical comparison) that is sustained for an extra sentence or more so that further implications can be drawn from it.

fad word (p. 181) A term that becomes temporarily popular in everyday speech: x *Fashionwise, Ron is a with-it person.* Prefer conventional diction: *Ron wears fashionable clothes.*

fallacy (p. 49) A formal error or illegitimate shortcut in reasoning. See *ad hominem* **reasoning, bandwagon appeal, begging the question, either-or reasoning, faulty generalization, non sequitur, oversimplification,** and *post hoc* **reasoning.**

"false start" (p. 169) A device whereby a sentence appears to present its grammatical **subject** first but then breaks off and begins again, thus turning the opening element into an **appositive:** *Elephants, gorillas, pandas—the list of endangered species grows longer every year.* A "false start" can be a good means of seizing a reader's attention. Cf. **mixed construction.**

faulty generalization (p. 49) The **fallacy** of drawing a general conclusion from insufficient **evidence**—e.g., concluding from one year's drought that the world's climate has entered a long period of change.

faulty predication See **predication.**

field research (p. 460) Gathering firsthand information using surveys, interviews, and other methods of direct observation.

figurative language (p. 199) Language that heightens expressiveness by suggesting an imaginative, not a **literal,** comparison to the thing described—e.g., *a man so emaciated that he looked more like an x-ray than a person.* See **metaphor, simile.** Cf. **literal language.**

footnote (p. 526) A note at the bottom of a page. Cf. **endnote.**

formal outline See **outline.**

fragment See **sentence fragment.**

free element (p. 151) A **modifying** word, **phrase,** or subordinate

clause that deserves to be set off by commas. Most but not all free elements are **nonrestrictive;** some **restrictive modifiers** at the beginnings of sentences can be treated as free—that is, followed by a comma. Cf. **bound element.**

freewriting (p. 13) The practice of writing continuously for a fixed period without concern for logic or correctness. In *focused freewriting* the writer begins with a specific **topic.**

funnel opener (p. 124) An introductory **paragraph** beginning with a broad assertion and gradually narrowing to a specific **topic.**

fused sentence (p. 223) A **sentence** in which two independent **clauses** are joined without either a comma or a coordinating **conjunction:** x *He is a dapper newscaster I love his slightly Canadian accent.* Cf. **comma splice.**

gender (p. 283) The grammatical concept of sexual classification determining the forms of masculine (*he*), feminine (*she*), and neuter (*it*) personal pronouns and the feminine forms of certain nouns (*actress*). Cf. **common gender, sexist language.**

gerund (p. 211) A form derived from a **verb** but functioning as a **noun**—e.g., *Skiing* in *Skiing is dangerous.* Gerunds take exactly the same form as **participles,** and they are capable of having **subjects** (usually possessive in **case**) as well as **objects:**

     S OF GER   GER   OBJ GER
- **Elizabeth's winning** the **pentathlon** was unexpected.

Cf. **participle.**

governing pronoun (p. 39) The prevailing **pronoun** in a piece of writing, helping to establish the writer's point of view.

governing tense (p. 308) The prevailing verb **tense** in a piece of writing, establishing a time frame for reported events.

hyperbole (p. 205) **Figurative language** that works by overstatement, as in *I will love you until the sun grows cold.*

idiom (p. 179) A fixed expression whose meaning cannot be deduced from its elements—for example, *come around,* meaning *agree or acquiesce after initial resistance.*

image (p. 199) An expression that appeals to the senses. More narrowly, an example of **figurative language.** In both senses, the use of images is called *imagery.*

imperative mood See **mood.**

implied subject (p. 213) A **subject** not actually present in a **clause** but nevertheless understood: *[You] Watch out!* The customary implied subject, as here, is *you.*

implied thesis (p. 22) A central point or impression that is implied rather than explicitly stated in an essay. Implied theses are most often used in essays of **narration** or **description.**

incorporated quotation (p. 350) A quotation placed within quotation marks and not set off from the writer's own prose. Cf. **indented quotation.**

indefinite pronoun See **pronoun.**

indented quotation (p. 354) A quoted passage set apart from the writer's own language. Prose quotations of more than four typed lines and verse quotations of more than two or three lines are customarily indented, without quotation marks. Also known as a *block quotation.* Cf. **incorporated quotation.**

indention (p. 354) The setting of the first word of a line to the right of the left margin, as in a new paragraph (5 spaces) or an **indented quotation** (usually 10 spaces).

independent clause See **clause.**

index (p. 452) A book, usually with a new volume each year, containing alphabetically ordered references to articles (and sometimes books) in a given field. Also, an alphabetical list of subjects and the page numbers where they are treated in a nonfiction book, as on pages 639–672 below.

indicative mood See **mood.**

indirect discourse (p. 313) Reporting what was said, as opposed to directly quoting it. Not *She said, "I am tired,"* but *She said she was tired.* Also called *indirect statement.* Cf. **direct discourse, indirect question.**

indirect object (p. 273) A word designating the person or thing for whom or which, or to whom or which, the action of a **verb** is performed. An indirect object never appears without a **direct object** occurring in the same clause:

         IND OBJ   D OBJ
- She sent **Fernando** a discouraging **letter**.

indirect question (p. 322) The reporting of a question without use of the question form—not *She asked, "Where should I turn?"* but *She asked where she should turn.* Cf. **indirect discourse.**

induction (p. 47) The type of **reasoning** that draws a general principle from a number of specific instances. Cf. **deduction.**

infinitive (p. 211) The **base form of a verb,** usually but not always preceded by *to: to win; to prove; prove.*

inflection (p. 371) A change in the ending or whole form of a word to show a change in function without creating a new word. Thus *he* can be inflected to *his, George* to *George's, go* to *went,* etc.

intensifier (p. 193) A "fortifying" expression like *absolutely, definitely,* or *very.* Habitual use of intensifiers weakens the force of assertion.

intensive pronoun See **pronoun.**

intentional sentence fragment See **sentence fragment.**

interjection A word that stands apart from other constructions in order to command attention or show strong feeling: *aha, hey, wow,* etc. Cf. **exclamation.**

interrogative adjective An interrogative **pronoun** form that combines with a **noun** to introduce a question—e.g., *Whose* in *Whose socks are these?*

interrogative pronoun See **pronoun.**

interrupting element (p. 263) A word or group of words that interrupts the main flow of a sentence:

        INT EL
- You, **I regret to say,** are not the one.

Interrupting elements (also called *parenthetical elements*) should be set off at both ends by punctuation, usually by commas.

intransitive verb (p. 210) A **verb** expressing an action or state without connection to a **direct object** or a **complement**—e.g., *complained* in *They complained.* Cf. **linking verb, transitive verb.**

introductory tag (p. 358) A **clause,** such as *He said* or *Agnes asked,* introducing a quotation. A tag may also interrupt or follow a quotation.

inverted syntax (p. 169) The reversal of the expected order among sentence elements, usually for rhetorical effect: *After many bitter hours came the dawn.*

irony (p. 40) The saying of one thing in order to convey a different or even opposite meaning: *Brutus is an honorable man* [he really isn't]. Cf. **sarcasm.**

irregular verb (p. 373) A **verb** that forms its past **tense** and its past **participle** in some way other than simply adding *-d* or *-ed: go* (*went, gone*), *swim* (*swam, swum*), etc.

italics (p. 424) Thin, slanting letters, *like these.* In handwritten or typewritten work, italics are indicated by underlining. Cf. **roman type.**

jargon (p. 187) Technical language used in inappropriate, nontechnical contexts—e.g., *upwardly mobile* for *ambitious, positive reinforcement* for *praise, paranoid* for *upset.*

leading idea (p. 89) The "point" of a **paragraph,** to which all other ideas in that paragraph should relate. Cf. **main sentence.**

limiting sentence (p. 101) A sentence that addresses a possible limitation, or contrary consideration, to the **leading idea** of a paragraph.

linking verb (p. 210) A **verb** connecting its **subject** to an identifying or modifying **complement.** Typical linking verbs are *be, seem, appear, become, feel, sense, grow, taste, look, sound:*

      S   LV   COMPL
- They **were** Mormons.

```
   S      LV    COMPL
```
• She **became** calmer.

Cf. **intransitive verb, transitive verb.**

literal language (p. 199) Words that factually represent what they describe, without poetic embellishment. Cf. **figurative language.**

"literary" present tense (p. 315) The present-**tense** form of a verb when it is used to express the ongoing action or meaning of an artwork or other text: *Willie Loman tries to hide from reality; The play addresses some of our deepest anxieties.*

main clause See **clause.**

main sentence (p. 89) The sentence in a paragraph that conveys its **leading idea.** Often called *topic sentence.*

metaphor (p. 201) An implied comparison whereby the thing at hand is figuratively asserted to be something else: *His fists were a hurricane of ceaseless assault.* Cf. **simile.**

misplaced modifier (p. 255) A **modifier** whose modified term is present in the sentence but not immediately identifiable as such:

```
MISPLACED MOD                          MODIFIED TERM?
```
x **Laughing** so hard, Nancy was offended by **Ellen's** frivolity in a time of crisis.

Compare:

• Laughing so hard, Ellen offended Nancy by her frivolity in a time of crisis.

Cf. **dangling modifier.**

mixed construction (p. 231) The use of two clashing structures within a sentence, as in *Even a friendly interviewer, it is hard to keep from being nervous.*

mixed metaphor (p. 203) A **metaphor** whose elements clash in their implications: x *Let's back off for a closer look;* x *He is a straight arrow who shoots from the hip.*

MLA style (p. 485) The **parenthetic citation** style of documentation now favored by the Modern Language Association. Cf. **APA style, "alternative MLA" style.**

modifier (p. 250) A word, **phrase,** or **clause** that limits or describes another element:

> MOD
> - the **gentle** soul

> MOD   MOD
> - **When leaving,** turn out the lights **on the porch.**

> MOD
> - **Before you explain,** I have something to tell you.

mood (p. 371) The manner or attitude that a speaker or writer intends a **verb** to convey, as shown in certain changes of form. Ordinary statements and questions are cast in the *indicative* mood: *Is he ill? He is.* The *imperative* mood is for commands: *Stop! Get out of the way!* And the *subjunctive* mood is used for certain formulas (*as it were*), unlikely or impossible conditions (*had she gone*), *that* clauses expressing requirements or recommendations (*They ask that she comply*), and *lest* clauses (*lest he forget*).

narration (p. 9) The type of writing in which a writer recounts something that has happened. Cf. **analysis, argument, description.**

non sequitur (p. 51) The **fallacy** in which an implied logical connection between two statements is not apparent.

nonrestrictive element (pp. 264–268) A **modifier,** often a **phrase** or a **clause,** that does not serve to identify ("restrict") the modified term and is therefore set off by punctuation, usually commas:

> NONR EL
> - That woman, **whom I met only yesterday,** already understands my problems.

Cf. **restrictive element.**

noun (p. 212) A word like *Jack, Pennsylvania, house,* or *assessment,* usually denoting a person, place, thing, or idea. A noun can undergo **inflection** for both plural and possessive forms (*houses, house's, houses'*), and it can serve a variety of sentence functions (subject, direct object, etc.).

noun clause See **clause.**

noun phrase See **phrase.**

nounlike element (p. 212) A word or group of words having the same function as a **noun** or **pronoun,** but not the same features of **inflection**—e.g., *what you mean* in *He knows what you mean.* Also called *nominal* or *substantive.*

number (p. 234) In grammar, the distinction between *singular* and *plural* form. The distinction applies to **verbs** (she *drives,* they *drive*), **nouns** (*boat, boats*), and personal **pronouns** (*I, we*).

numeral (p. 438) A number expressed as a figure (*6, 19*) or a group of letters (*VI, XIX*) instead of being written out.

object (p. 209) A **noun, pronoun,** or **nounlike element** representing a receiver of an action or relation. See **direct object, indirect object,** and **object of preposition.** In addition, **infinitives, participles,** and **gerunds** can take objects:

OBJ OF INF
- to chair the **convention**

OBJ OF PART
- Chairing the **convention** impartially, she allowed no disorder.

OBJ OF GER
- Chairing a turbulent **convention** is a thankless task.

object of preposition (p. 275) A **noun, pronoun,** or **nounlike element** following a **preposition** and completing the prepositional **phrase**—e.g., *November* in *throughout November,* or *siesta* in *during a long siesta.*

objective case See **case.**

objective complement See **complement.**

ordinal number (p. 439) A number like *fourth (4th)* or *twenty-seventh (27th),* as opposed to a **cardinal number** like *four (4)* or *twenty-seven (27).*

outline (p. 30) A schematic plan showing the organization of a piece of writing. A *scratch outline* merely lists points to be made, whereas a *formal outline* shows, through indention and more than one set of numbers, that some points are subordinate to others. A further distinction is made between the *topic outline,* whose headings are concise **phrases,** and the *sentence outline,* which calls for complete sentences.

oversimplification (p. 50) The **fallacy** of treating a complex point or issue as if it were simple.

paragraph (p. 88) A unit of prose, usually consisting of several sentences, marked by **indention** of the first line (or sometimes by an extra blank line). A well-wrought paragraph of **analysis** or **argument** is expected to provide support for one **leading idea.**

paragraph block (p. 471) A group of paragraphs addressing the same part of a **topic,** with strong continuity from one paragraph to the next.

parallelism (p. 293) The structure or the effect that results from matching two or more parts of a sentence—e.g., the words *Utica, Albany,* and *Rye* in the sentence *He went to Utica, Albany, and Rye,* or the three equally weighted **clauses** that begin this sentence: *That he wanted to leave, that permission was denied, and that he then tried to escape—these facts only became known after months of official secrecy.* Cf. **balance, coordination.**

paraphrase (p. 466) Sentence-by-sentence restatement, in different words, of the meaning of a passage. Cf. **summary.**

parenthetic citation (pp. 485 and 534) A reference to a work, given not in a **footnote** or **endnote** but in parentheses within a main text—e.g., (*Meyers 241–75*).

parenthetical element See **interrupting element.**

part of speech (p. 177) Any of the major classes into which words are customarily divided, depending on their dictionary meaning and their syntactic functions in sentences. Since many words belong to more than one part of speech, you must analyze the sentence at hand to see which part of speech a given word is occupying. The commonly recognized parts of speech are the following:

Verb	try, adopts, were allowing
Noun	Cynthia, paper, Manitoba
Pronoun	She, himself, each other, nothing, these, who

Preposition	to, among, according to
Conjunction	and, yet, because, although, if
Adjective	wide, lazier, more fortunate
Adverb	agreeably, seldom, ahead, together, however
Interjection	oh, ouch, gosh
Article	a, an, the
Expletive	it [is], there [were]

participle (p. 211) An **adjectival** form derived from a **verb**—e.g., *Showing* in *Showing fear, he began to sweat.* Participles can be present (*showing*) or past (*having shown*) and active or passive (*having been shown*). Like other **verbals,** they can have **objects** (*fear* in the sentence above), but unlike other verbals, they do not have **subjects.** Cf. **gerund.**

passive voice See **voice.**

past participle See **participle.**

peer editor (p. 55) A student writer who comments on another student writer's drafts, making suggestions for revision.

person (p. 234) In grammar, a characteristic of **pronouns** and **verbs** indicating whether someone is speaking (*first* person; *I go, we go*), being spoken to (*second* person; *you go*), or being spoken about (*third* person: *he, she, it goes; they go*).

personal pronoun See **pronoun.**

phrase (p. 215) A cluster of words functioning as a single **part of speech** and lacking a **subject-predicate** combination. Cf. **clause.**

   A **noun** and its **modifiers** are sometimes called a *noun phrase (the faulty billiard balls),* and a **verb** form consisting of more than one word is sometimes called a *verb phrase (had been trying).* But the types of phrases most commonly recognized are *prepositional, infinitive, participial, gerund,* and **absolute.**

   A *prepositional phrase* consists of a **preposition** and its **object,** along with any **modifiers** of those words:

                                                   OBJ
   PREP   MOD   MOD   MOD   PREP
 • **among her numerous painful regrets**
                    PREP PHRASE

An *infinitive phrase* consists of an **infinitive** and its **object** and/or **modifiers:**

OBJ
S INF   INF   MOD   MOD   MOD   INF

• They asked **John to hit the almost invisible target.**

INF PHRASE

A **participial phrase** consists of a **participle** and its **object** and/or **modifiers:**

OBJ
MOD   PART   MOD   MOD   PART

• **Quickly reaching the correct decision,** he rang the bell.

PART PHRASE

A *gerund phrase* consists of a **gerund** and its **object** and/or **modifiers,** and it may also include a *subject of the gerund:*

S GER   GER   OBJ GER   MOD

• **Their sending Matthew away** was a bad mistake.

GER PHRASE

An **absolute phrase** (see entry) may contain an **infinitive** or a **participle,** but it always modifies an entire statement.

pivoting paragraph (p. 104) A paragraph that begins with one or more **limiting sentences** but then makes a sharp turn to its **main sentence,** which may or may not be followed by **supporting sentences.**

plagiarism (p. 477) The taking of others' thoughts or words without due acknowledgment. Cf. **allusion.**

positive degree See **degree.**

possessive case See case.

post hoc **reasoning** (p. 51) A **fallacy** whereby the fact that one event followed another is wrongly taken to prove that the first event caused the later one.

predicate (p. 210) In a **clause,** the **verb** plus all the words belonging with it:

PRED

• He **had a serious heart attack.**

Cf. **subject.**

predicate adjective See **complement.**

predicate noun See **complement.**

predication (p. 233) The selection of a **predicate** for a given **subject.** The problem of *faulty predication* appears when subjects and predicates are mismatched in meaning: x *The purpose of the film wants to change your beliefs.* **Mixed construction** is a more radical form of faulty predication.

prefix (p. 409) One or more letters that can be attached before the root or base form of a word to make a new word: *pre-, with-,* etc., forming *prearranged, withstand,* etc. Cf. **suffix.**

preposition (p. 179) A function word that introduces a prepositional **phrase**—e.g., *to* in *to the lighthouse.* Other common prepositions include:

about	below	from	since
above	beneath	in	through
across	beside	into	till
after	between	like	under
against	beyond	near	until
along	by	of	up
at	during	off	with
before	except	on	without
behind	for	out	

A preposition consisting of more than one word is **compound:** *along with, apart from,* etc. See also **object of preposition.** Cf. **conjunction.**

present participle See **participle.**

principal parts (p. 373) The **base** or simple **infinitive** form of a **verb,** its past-**tense** form, and its past **participle:** *walk, walked, walked; grow, grew, grown.*

pronoun (p. 272) One of a small class of words mostly used in place of **nouns** for a variety of purposes:

1. A *demonstrative* pronoun (*this, that, these, those*) singles out what it refers to: *This is what we want.*

2. An *indefinite* pronoun (*anybody, each, whoever,* etc.) leaves unspecified the person or things it refers to: *Anyone can see that you are right.*

3. An *intensive* pronoun (*myself, yourself, itself, ourselves,* etc.) emphasizes a preceding noun or pronoun: *She herself is a vegetarian.*

4. An *interrogative* pronoun (*who, whom, whose, which, what*) introduces a question: *Who will win the election?*

5. A *personal* pronoun (*I, you, he, she, it, we, they*) stands for one or more persons or things and is used in the tense formation of verbs: *They are willing to compromise.* Personal pronouns also have objective (*him, them*) and possessive (*his, their*) forms: *We asked her to recognize our rights.*

6. A *reciprocal* pronoun (*each other, each other's, one another, one another's*) expresses mutual relation: *We recognized each other's differences of outlook.*

7. A *reflexive* pronoun (*myself, yourself, itself, ourselves,* etc.) differs from an intensive pronoun in serving as a **direct** or **indirect object.** The reflexive pronoun shows that the **subject** of the **clause** is the same person or thing acted upon by the **verb:** *He hurt himself on the track.*

8. A *relative* pronoun (*who, whom, that, which*) introduces a relative or adjectival clause: *My uncle, who lives next door, slept through the earthquake.* Some grammarians also recognize an "indefinite relative pronoun" (one lacking an antecedent): *She knows what you mean.* See also **relative clause.**

pronoun agreement (p. 283) The correspondence of a **pronoun** to its **antecedent,** which ought to share its **gender, number,** and **person.** Thus, in the sentence *When they saw Bill, they gave him a cool welcome,* the pronoun *him* properly agrees with the masculine, singular, third-person antecedent *Bill.* Cf. **pronoun reference, subject-verb agreement.**

pronoun reference (p. 287) The connection in a sentence between a **pronoun** and its **antecedent** whereby the antecedent is explicitly present and the pronoun's relation to it is clear. That is, no other word could be mistaken for the antecedent. Pronoun reference is faulty in a sentence like x *She smelled the cooking shrimp, which made her sick.* What made her sick, the shrimp or smelling them cooking? Cf. **pronoun agreement.**

punctuation marks (Chapters 25–30) Marks used to bring out the meaning of written **sentences.** They are as follows:

. period	( ) parentheses
? question mark	[ ] brackets
! exclamation point	. . . ellipsis
, comma	' apostrophe
; semicolon	- hyphen
: colon	" " quotation marks
— dash	/ slash

purpose (p. 9) The goal or aim of a piece of writing. Essays are sometimes divided into four types, according to purpose. See **analysis, argument, description, narration.**

racist language (p. 184) **Diction** that can give offense by using a derogatory name for an ethnic group or by perpetuating a demeaning stereotype: *greaser, dumb Pole,* etc.

reasoning (p. 47) Basing a logical conclusion on a set of established facts or premises. See **deduction, induction.**

reciprocal pronoun See **pronoun.**

redundancy (p. 191) The defect of unnecessarily conveying the same meaning more than once. Also, an expression that does so—e.g., *retreat back, ascend up.*

reference See **pronoun reference.**

reference list (pp. 490 and 537) A list of "Works Cited" or "References," supplied at the end of an **essay,** paper, article, or book, and showing where and when the cited or consulted materials appeared. The **parenthetic citations** within the text refer to items in the reference list.

reflexive pronoun See **pronoun.**

refutation (p. 53) The disproving of a point. By definition, all refutations are successful.

regular verb (p. 373) A **verb** that forms both its past **tense** and its past **participle** by adding *-d: hike (hiked, hiked),* etc. Cf. **irregular verb.**

relative clause (p. 214) A subordinate **clause** that functions like an adjective:

> REL CLAUSE
> • This is the tomb **that we visited.**

See also **clause.**

relative pronoun See pronoun.

restrictive element (p. 265) A **modifier,** often a phrase or clause, that "restricts" (establishes the identity of) the modified term. Unless it comes first in the sentence, a restrictive element is not set off by commas:

> RESTR EL
> • The woman **whom I met** has disappeared.
> RESTR EL
> • The man **in the black suit** is following you.
> RESTR EL
> • **On long ocean voyages,** seasickness is common.

(Because it is brief, the initial restrictive element in the last example could also appear without a comma; see p. 260.) Cf. **nonrestrictive element.**

résumé (p. 574) A brief record of a person's career and qualifications, typically used in a job application.

rhetoric (p. xvii) The strategic placement of ideas and choice of language, as in *Her rhetoric was effective* or *His ideas were sound, but his rhetoric was addressed to the wrong audience.* Note that *rhetoric* need not mean deception or manipulation.

rhetorical question (p. 168) A question posed for effect, without expectation of a reply: *Who can foretell the distant future?*

Roman numeral (p. 438) A figure such as *III, XLVII,* or *CVI,* as opposed to an **Arabic numeral** such as *3, 47,* or *106.*

roman type (p. 424) Plain letters, like these. Cf. **italics.**

run-on sentence See **fused sentence.**

sarcasm (p. 41) Abusive ridicule of a person, group, or idea, as in *What pretty phrases these killers speak!* Cf. **irony.**

scratch outline See **outline.**

sentence (p. 209) A grammatically complete unit of expression, usually containing at least one independent **clause,** beginning with a capital letter and ending with a period, question mark, or exclamation point. See also **sentence fragment.**

sentence adverb (p. 226) An **adverb** that serves to indicate a logical connection between the modified **clause** or whole **sentence** and a previous statement—e.g., *therefore* in *She took the job; therefore, she had to find child care.* Also called *conjunctive adverb.*

sentence fragment (p. 215) A set of words punctuated as a **sentence** but either lacking a **subject-verb** combination (x *A day ago.*) or introduced by a subordinating **conjunction** (x <u>*When*</u> *they last saw her.*).

In general, sentence fragments are regarded as blunders. But an *intentional sentence fragment*—one whose context shows that it is a shortened sentence rather than a dislocated piece of a neighboring sentence—can sometimes be effective:

INT FRAG

- How much longer can we resist? **As long as necessary!**

sentence outline See **outline.**

series (p. 161) A set of more than two **parallel** items within a sentence:

SERIES

- They were upset about **pollution, unemployment, and poverty.**

sexist language (p. 184) Expressions that can give offense by implying that one sex (almost always male) is superior or of primary importance or that the other sex is restricted to certain traditional roles: *lady doctor; a man-sized job; Every American pursues his own happiness,* etc.

signal words (p. 95) Words and phrases that promote paragraph **continuity** by indicating that something already mentioned is still under discussion. Repeated terms, **pronouns,** and **demonstrative adjectives** often function as signal words. Cf. **transition.**

simile (p. 201) An explicit or open comparison, whereby the object at hand is **figuratively** asserted to be like something else: *His eyes that morning were like an elephant's.* Cf. **metaphor.** Both similes and metaphors are called *metaphorical* or **figurative language.** See also **analogy, image.**

slash (p. 341) The punctuation mark /. A slash is used to separate alternatives (*either / or*) and to indicate line endings in **incorporated quotation** of verse. Sometimes called *virgule.*

split infinitive (p. 257) An **infinitive** interrupted by at least one **adverb:** *to firmly stand.* Some readers consider every split infinitive an error; others object only to conspicuously awkward ones such as x *Jane wanted to thoroughly and finally settle the matter.*

squinting modifier (p. 256) A **modifier** awkwardly trapped between sentence elements, either of which might be regarded as the modified term:

> SQ MOD
> x Why he collapsed **altogether** puzzles me.

Did he collapse altogether, or is the writer altogether puzzled?

stance (p. 39) The posture a writer adopts toward an audience, establishing a consistent point of view. This book recognizes two stances, *forthright* and *ironic.* A forthright stance implies that the writer's statements are to be taken "straight"; an ironic stance implies that the reader is to "read between the lines" and uncover a different or even opposite meaning.

subject (p. 212) The part of a **clause** about which something is **predicated:**

> SUBJ
> • **Ernest** shot the tiger.

The subject alone is called the *simple subject.* With its **modifiers** included it is called the *complete subject*—e.g., *The only thing to do* in *The only thing to do is compromise.*

Not only **verbs** but also **infinitives, gerunds,** and **absolute phrases** can have "subjects":

S OF INF   INF
- They wanted **Alexander** to be king.

S OF GER   GER
- **Alexander's** refusing upset them.

S OF ABS
PHRASE
- **The conference having ended,** the diplomats went home.

ABS PHRASE

subject area (p. 4) A wide range of related concerns within which the **topic** of an essay or paper may be found. Cf. **thesis, topic.**

subject-verb agreement (p. 234) The correspondence of a **verb** with its **subject** in **number** and **person.** In *I stumble,* e.g., the verb *stumble* "agrees with" the subject *I*; both are singular and first-person in form. Cf. **pronoun agreement.**

subjective case See **case.**

subjunctive mood See **mood.**

subordinate clause See **clause.**

subordinated outline See **outline.**

subordinating conjunction See **conjunction.**

subordination (p. 148) In general, the giving of minor emphasis to minor elements or ideas. In syntax, subordination entails making one element grammatically dependent on another, so that the subordinate element becomes a **modifier** of the other element, limiting or explaining it. Thus, in *They were relieved when it was over,* the subordinate **clause** *when it was over* limits the time to which the **verb** *were relieved* applies.

suffix (p. 404) One or more letters that can be added at the end of a word's root or base to make a new word or form: *-ed, -ing, -ship, -ness,* etc., as in *walked, singing, membership, weakness.* Cf. **prefix.**

summary (p. 466) A concise recapitulation of a passage. Cf. **paraphrase.**

supplemental note (p. 489) A **footnote** or **endnote** used to make added comments or to suggest further sources of information.

supporting sentence (p. 101) A **sentence** that restates, elaborates, or provides **evidence** or context for some aspect of a paragraph's **leading idea.**

suspended comparison (p. 300) A comparison proposing two possible relations between the compared items, in which the second item is stated only at the end of the construction: *Taco Bell is as good as, if not better than, Pizza Hut.*

suspended paragraph (p. 106) A paragraph that builds, without a decisive shift of direction, toward a **main sentence** at or near the end. Cf. **direct paragraph, pivoting paragraph.**

suspended sentence (p. 171) A **sentence** that significantly delays completing the statement of its idea while **clauses** and/or **phrases** intervene. *The important thing is not to study all night before the exam, not to try reading the instructor's mind, nor to butter up the TA, but to keep up with the assignments throughout the term.* Also called *periodic sentence.*

suspended verb (p. 299) A construction in which one subject governs two forms of the same delayed **verb:** *She can, and assuredly will, comply with the law.* Note how the verb *can comply* is "suspended" by the intervening element.

syllogism (p. 47) A chain of deduction from premises to a conclusion:

Premise:	All massive die-offs of fish in Lake Erie are caused by pollution.
Premise:	Last year there was a massive die-off of fish in Lake Erie.
Conclusion:	Last year's massive die-off of fish in Lake Erie was caused by pollution.

tense (p. 371) The time a **verb** expresses: present (*see*), future (*will see*), etc.

thesis (p. 6) The point, or one central idea, of an essay, paper, article, book, etc. Cf. **subject area, topic.**

thesis question (p. 20) The central question a writer plans to answer in an essay. Posing such a question can help the writer formulate a **trial thesis.**

thesis statement (p. 25) A one-sentence statement of the **thesis,** or central idea, of an essay or paper. In this book, a thesis statement is considered to be full only if it is complex enough to guide the essay's organization.

tone (p. 41) The quality of feeling that is conveyed in a piece of writing. Words like *factual, sober, fanciful, urgent, tongue-in-cheek, restrained, stern, pleading,* and *exuberant* may begin to suggest the range of tones found in **essays.** Cf. **stance, voice.**

topic (p. 4) The specific subject of an essay or paper; the ground to be covered or the question to be answered. Cf. **subject area, thesis.**

topic outline See **outline.**

topic sentence Replaced in this book by the term **main sentence,** since the key sentence in a paragraph is the one stating the **leading idea,** not the one announcing a "topic."

transition (p. 95) A word or phrase, such as *therefore, of course,* or *on the other hand,* that contributes to **continuity,** indicating how one statement relates to the one before it. Cf. **signal word.**

transitional phrase (p. 227) A **phrase** having the same function as a **sentence adverb,** modifying a whole **clause** or **sentence** while showing its logical connection to a previous statement:

TRANS PHRASE
- She says she simply can't bear to be late; **in other words,** she expects the rest of us to show up on time.

transitive verb (p. 209) A **verb** transmitting an action to a **direct object:**

TR V
- They **cast** the dice.

Cf. **intransitive verb, linking verb.**

tree diagram (p. 33) An aid to organization that displays graphically the relation between main and subordinate points in an essay.

trial thesis (p. 19) A possible **thesis,** or central idea, considered before a final thesis has been chosen.

trial topic (p. 15) A tentative **topic** that requires further evaluation before being judged suitable for an essay.

understatement (p. 205) Language used to convey the importance of something by appearing to take it lightly, often creating **irony:** *Living near the edge of a runway for jumbo jets is not altogether relaxing.*

verb (p. 209) A word or words like *goes, saw,* or *was leaving,* serving to convey the action performed by a **subject,** to express the state of that subject, or to connect the subject to a **complement.**

verb phrase See **phrase.**

verbal (p. 211) A form derived from, but different in function from, a **verb.** Verbals are either **infinitives, participles,** or **gerunds.** When mistakenly used as verbs, they cause **sentence fragments:**

> VERBAL
> x George **going** to the movies tonight.

voice (p. 37) The form of a **verb** indicating whether the **subject** performs the action (*active* voice: *we strike*) or receives the action (*passive* voice: *we are struck*). Also, the "self" projected by a given piece of writing (p. 23). In the latter sense, this book recognizes two voices, *personal* and *impersonal.*

weaseling thesis (p. 23) A **thesis** that fails to take any definite stand: x *People can be found who oppose gun control;* x *Abortion is quite a controversial topic.*

PERMISSIONS ACKNOWLEDGMENTS

INDEX

Note: Main entries in **boldface** are defined in the Glossary of Terms (pp. 606–636). Page numbers in *italics* indicate the main discussion of a topic; go to those pages first.